NOW YOU HAVE PURCHASED MILITARY AIRCRAFT MARKINGS WHY NOT EXPAND YOUR KNOWLEDGE WITH THE 'TAHS' RANGE OF SPECIALIST BOOKS FOR THE ENTHUSIAST, HISTORIAN OR SPOTTER?

AIRBAND RADIOS
We specialise in top quality airband radios. Usually available from stock are the YUPITERU range of radios, ie the VT125-11, VT-225, MVT7000 and the MVT-7100.

AIRLINES '96
The 14th edition available late March is the established spotters favourite for coverage of the world's airline fleet listing. Every airline in the world where aircraft from light twin to wide bodies are operated. 170 countries, 1,700 airlines, over 25,000 registrations. Each aircraft is listed with registration, type, c/n, p/i, and where applicable line and fleet number and name. Available as Comb Bound (ie metal lay flat binding at just £9.95 or in a loose leaf binder at £13.95.

AIRPORT MOVEMENTS
is a monthly magazine published and distributed by THE AVIATION HOBBY SHOP, AIRPORT MOVEMENTS gives airport movements on a regular basis for the following airports: Heathrow, Gatwick, Stanstead, Luton, Birmingham, Shannon, Bournemouth, Bristol, Cardiff, East Midlands, Jersey, Northolt, Southampton, Southend as well as foreign airport reports on a space available basis. Average monthly page content is around 28. AIRPORT MOVEMENTS is available around the 15th to the 20th of the month from a number of different outlets in the South of England, the Midlands and the Manchester area at a price of 75p per copy. However, should you wish to have a regular standing order for this publication to be dispatched hot from the press we will be more than happy to place your name on our regular mailing list. To have your own copy of AIRPORT MOVEMENTS sent to you each month costs £1 per copy and this includes first-class mail delivery in the UK. You can subscribe for three, six or 12 months. To recieve a free sample copy of our choice send a stamped 9in x 6in envelope.

TURBO PROP AIRLINER PRODUCTION LIST
Now available the second edition of Turbo Prop Airliners Production List gives full production and service histories of EVERY WESTERN - BUILT TURBOPROP AIRLINER to enter service since 1948. Each aircraft is listed by manufacturer and type in construction number sequence. Each individual entry then lists line number (where applicable), sub-type, and first flight date where known. The entry then goes on to list every registration carried by the airframe, owners and delivery dates, leases, crash or withdrawal from service dates and any other relevant information. There is a complete cross reference of registration to c/n for every type covered. This publication is available in two formats:- Soft-back in card covers with sewn binding at £10.95 or in a loose-leaf binder at £13.95.

WORLD AIRLINE FLEET NEWS
Published monthly, World Airline Fleet News is dedicated to the ever changin and exciting world of airlines and airliners-reporting new airlines, new and used airliner transactions, livery changes and much more. Unrivalled photographic coverage on a worldwide basis is complimented by the generous use of colour. Each issue contains approximately 50 illustrations with around 30 in colour. World Airline Fleet News is produced on quality gloss art paper for the best photographic reproduction. Sample issue £3.25.

MILITARY AIRCRAFT SERIALS OF EUROPE
The eagerly awaited third edition of MILITARY AIRCRAFT SERIALS OF EUROPE is now available. MILITARY AIRCRAFT SERIALS OF EUROPE covers thirty five European countries. Each county is listed in alphabetical order, with in most cases a brief synopsis of their serial systems and units. Each countries aircraft are then covered in details by typs, each line showing serial number, sub-type, unit allocation and date last noted as such. Where known or applicable fates are also shown, including write-off dates etc. COUNTRIES COVERED INCLUDE:- Albania, Austria, Belguim, Bosnia, Bulgaria, Croatia, Cyprus, Czech Republic, Denmark, Estonia, Finland, France, Germany, Greece, hungary, Iceland, Ireland, Italy, Latvia, Lithuania, Malta, NATO/Luxembourg, The Netherlands, Norway, Poland, Portugal, Romania, Slovak Republic, Slovenia, Spain, Sweden, Switzerland, Turkey, United Kingdom and Yugoslavia. The book comes with full colour front and rear covers and the nearly 350 pages includes a selection of black & white photographs and the individual serial number content is in excess of 25,000.

MILITARY AIRCRAFT SERIALS OF EUROPE is available in a handy A5 size and is available in a choice of finish (1) comb bound lay-flat price £9.95; (2) Square bound with duty metal stitching price £9.95; (3) Refill pages for those already have a loose-leaf binder price £9.95: (4) Loose-leaf Binder edition price £13.95.

JET AIRLINER PRODUCTION LIST - Volume 1 - BOEING
NOW AVAILABLE Jet Airliner Production List - Volume 1 - BOEING is completely revised and updated. Jet Airliner Production List gives full production and service histories of EVERY BOEING - BUILT JET AIRLINER that has entered service since the start of the Jet age. Each aircraft is listed by manufacturer and type in contruction number sequence. Each individual entry then lists line number (where applicable), sub-type, and first flight date where known. The entry then goes on to list every registration carried by the airframe, owners and delivery dates, leases, crash or withdrawal from service dates and any other relevant information. There is a complete cross reference of registration to c/n for every type covered. This publication will be available in three formats:- (1) Soft-back in card covers with sewn binding at price £9.95. (2) Comb bound-lay flat at price £9.95; (3) or in a light blue loose-leaf binder at price £13.95.

JET AIRLINER PRODUCTION LIST - Volume 2
To be published in December 1995 Jet Airliner Production List - Volume 2 - is completely revised and updated. Jet Airliner Production List gives full production and service histories of every JET AIRLINER (not covered in Volume one) that has entered service since the start of the Jet age. The types covered in Volume 2 include:- Airbus A.300, Airbus A.310, Airbus A.319/320/321, Airbus A.330/340, British Aerospace 146, British Aircraft Corporation/Aerospatiale Concorde, British Aircraft Corporation 1-11, Canadair Regional Jet, Convair 880, Convair 990, Dassault Mercure, DH.106 Comet 1-4, Douglas DC-8, Douglas DC-9, Douglas DC-10, Fokker F.28, Fokker 100, HS.121 Trident, Lockheed 1011 Tri-Star, McDonnell-Douglas MD-11, ROMBAC 1-11, Sud Aviation SE.210 Caravelle, VFW/Fokker 614 & Vickers VC-10. Each aircraft is listed by manufacturer and type in construction number sequence. Each individual entry then lists line number (where applicable), sub-type, and first flight date where known. The entry then goes on to list every registration carried by the airframe, owners and delivery dates, leases, crash or withdrawal from service dates and any other relevant information. There is a complete cross reference of registration to c/n for every type covered. Over 370 pages. This publication will be available in three formats:- (1) Soft-back in card covers with sewn binding at price £10.95: (2) Comb bound-lay flat at price £10.95; (3) or in a loose-leaf binder at price £14.95.

AIRLINES TO EUROPE 1996
Following the excellent response to the 1st edition of Airlines to Europe, the 1996 edition is now available. As with the first edition we have taken the main date base and stripped out any airlines of aircraft not likely to be seen in Europe. Airlines to Europe only lists 1) Aircraft registration, 2) Aircraft type and 3) Constructors number and line number if applicable. Colour cover and nearly one hundred pages. Price: £3.99.

96 JET & PROP JET - NEW LAY-FLAT EDITION
The only standard reference for the total world-wide corporate fleet identification. Available again by popular demand - in one pocket-sized book. More than 7,700 Jets and 8,600 Projects listed with registration marks, construction numbers and owner identification. Over 250 different models and model derivatives and 43 manufacturers from 143 countries. **Available now £11.95**

FREE CATALOGUES
All our goods are listed in our two free catalogues. Catalogue 1 books, postcards, colour slides and airband radios. Catalogue 2: plastic kits, decals and modelling accessories. Write, ring or fax for your free copy today.

We are just 10 minutes drive from Heathrow Airport, just off the M4/M25 motorways. Bus U3 operates between Heathrow Central and West Drayton BR station, two minutes walk from the shop. All major credit cards accepted. 24hr 'Ansaphone' service.

The Aviation Hobby Shop

(Dept MAM), 4 HORTON PARADE, HORTON ROAD, WEST DRAYTON, MIDDLESEX UB7 8EA
Tel: 01895 442123   Fax: 01895 421412

MILITARY AIRCRAFT MARKINGS 1996

Peter R. March

IAN ALLAN *Publishing*

Contents

Photographs by Peter R. March (PRM) unless otherwise credited

This seventeenth edition published 1996

ISBN 0 7110 2425 1

Published by Ian Allan Publishing

an imprint of Ian Allan Ltd,
Terminal House, Station Approach,
Shepperton, Surrey TW17 8AS.
Printed by Ian Allan Printing Ltd,
Coombelands House, Coombelands Lane,
Addlestone, Surrey KT15 1HY.

Front cover: SEPECAT Jaguar GR1B XX729. *John Dibbs*

Back cover: HS Hawk T1 XX312. *BAe Defence*

Introduction

This seventeenth annual edition of *abc Military Aircraft Markings*, a companion to *abc Civil Aircraft Markings*, lists in alphabetical and numerical order all of the aircraft that carry a United Kingdom military serial, and which are based, or might be seen, in the UK. The term **aircraft** used here covers powered, manned aeroplanes, helicopters, airships and gliders. Included are all the current Royal Air Force, Royal Navy, Army Air Corps, Ministry of Defence (Procurement Executive), Defence Research Agency, manufacturers' test aircraft and civilian-owned aircraft with military markings.

Aircraft withdrawn from operational use but which are retained in the UK for ground training purposes or otherwise preserved by the Services and in museums and collections are listed. The serials of some incomplete aircraft have been included, such as the cockpit sections of machines displayed by the RAF Exhibition Flight, aircraft used by airfield fire sections and for service battle damage repair training (BDRT), together with significant parts of aircraft held by preservation groups and societies. Where only part of the aircraft fuselage remains the abbreviation <ff> for front fuselage/cockpit section or <rf> for rear fuselage is shown after the type. Many of these aircraft are allocated, and sometimes wear, a secondary identity, such as an RAF Support Command 'M' maintenance number. These numbers are listed against those aircraft to which they have been allocated.

A serial 'missing' is either because it was never issued as it formed part of a 'black-out block', or because the aircraft is written off, scrapped, sold, abroad or allocated an alternative marking. Aircraft used as targets on MoD ranges to which access is restricted, and un-manned target drones are omitted, as are UK military aircraft that have been permanently grounded overseas and unlikely to return to Britain.

In the main, the serials listed are those markings presently displayed on the aircraft. Aircraft which bear a false serial are quoted in *italic type*. Very often these serials are carried by replicas, that are denoted by <R> after the type. The manufacturer and aircraft type are given, together with recent alternative, previous, secondary or civil identity shown in round brackets. Complete records of multiple previous identities are only included where space permits. The operating unit and its based location, along with any known unit and base code markings in square brackets, are given as accurately as possible. The unit markings are normally carried boldly on the sides of the fuselage or on the aircraft's fin. In the case of RAF and AAC machines currently in service, they are usually one or two letters or numbers, while the RN continues to use a well-established system of three-figure codes between 000 and 999 together with a fin letter code denoting the aircraft's operational base. RN squadrons, units and bases are allocated blocks of numbers from which individual aircraft codes are issued. To help identification of RN bases and landing platforms on ships, a list of tail-letter codes with their appropriate name, helicopter code number, ship pennant number and type of vessel, is included; as is a helicopter code number/ships' tail-letter code grid cross-reference.

Codes change, for example when aircraft move between units, and therefore the markings currently painted on a particular aircraft might not be those shown in this edition because of subsequent events. The implementation of the Government's continuing Defence Cost Studies and the RAF's Front Line First reductions and re-organisation, again accounts for the large number of changes in this new edition. In particular the closures of Chivenor, Finningley, Scampton, Swanton Morley and Wyton have all had a major effect on the location of aircraft, particularly Hawks, Bulldogs and Tucanos. Those airframes which may not appear in the next edition because of sale, accident, etc, have their fates, where known, given in italic type in the *locations* column.

The Irish Army Air Corps fleet is listed, together with the serials of other overseas air arms whose aircraft might be seen visiting the UK from time to time. The serial numbers are as usually presented on the individual machine or as they are normally identified. Where possible, the aircraft's base and operating unit have been shown.

USAF, US Army and US Navy aircraft based in the UK and in Western Europe, and of types which regularly visit the UK from the USA, are each listed in separate sections by aircraft type. The serial number actually displayed on the aircraft is shown in full, with additional Fiscal Year (FY) or full serial information also provided. Where appropriate, details of the operating wing, squadron allocation and base are added. The USAF is, like the RAF, continuing a major reorganisation which is producing new unit titles, many squadron changes and the closure of bases worldwide. Only details that concern changes effected by December 1995 are shown.

Veteran and Vintage aircraft which carry overseas military markings but which are based in the UK have been separately listed showing their principal means of identification.

Information shown is believed to be correct at 5 February 1996, and significant changes can be monitored through the monthly 'Military Markings' column in *Aircraft Illustrated*.

Acknowledgements

The compiler again wishes to thank the many people who have taken trouble to send comments, criticism and other useful information following the publication of the previous editions of *abc Military Aircraft Markings*. In particular the following correspondents: M. Barclay, D. Braithwaite, P. F. Burton, G. Fraser, H. W. Gandy, A. Helden, I. Logan, P.- J. Martin, A. P. March, D. J. March, E. J. Onley, M. Peaker, A. R. Robinson, M. K. Thompson and P. Wiggins.

This compilation has relied heavily on the publications of the following aviation groups and societies: *Air North, British Aviation Review* (British Aviation Research Group), Macclesfield Historical Aviation Society, *North-West Air News* (Air Britain, Merseyside Branch), *Osprey* (Solent Aviation Society), *Prestwick Airport Letter* (Prestwick Airport Aviation Group), *Scottish Air News* (Central Scotland Aviation Group), *Stansted Aviation Newsletter* (The Stansted Aviation Society) and *Strobe* (MAP).

This fully revised edition of *abc Military Aircraft Markings* would not have been possible without considerable research and collation by Howard Curtis and Ben Dunnell, to whom I am indebted.

PRM   **February 1996**

Tiger Moth T7230 is privately owned G-AFVE. *PRM*

Abbreviations

AAC	Army Air Corps
AACS	Airborne Air Control Squadron
AACTS	Airborne Air Control Training Squadron
AAS	Aeromedical Airlift Squadron
ABS	Air Base Squadron
ACC	Air Combat Command
ACCGS	Air Cadets Central Gliding School
ACCS	Airborne Command and Control Squadron
ACW	Airborne Control Wing
AEF	Air Experience Flight
AES	Air Engineering School
AEW	Airborne Early Warning
AFB	Air Force Base
AFRES	Air Force Reserve
AFSC	Air Force System Command
AG	Airlift Group
AGA	Academia General del Aire
AIU	Accident Investigation Unit
AkG	Aufklärüngsgeschwader (Reconnaissance Wing)
AMC	Air Mobility Command
AMD-BA	Avions Marcel Dassault-Breguet Aviation
AMG	Aircraft Maintenance Group
AMS	Air Movements School
AMW	Air Mobility Wing
ANG	Air National Guard
APS	Aircraft Preservation Society
ARS	Air Refuelling Squadron
ARW	Air Refuelling Wing
ARWS	Advanced Rotary Wing Squadron
AS	Airlift Squadron
ASCW	Airborne Surveillance Control Wing
ASF	Aircraft Servicing Flight
AS&RU	Aircraft Salvage and Repair Unit
ATC	Air Training Corps
ATCC	Air Traffic Control Centre
AvCo	Aviation Company
Avn	Aviation
AW	Airlift Wing
AW	Armstrong Whitworth Aircraft
AWC	Air Warfare Centre
BAC	British Aircraft Corporation
BAe	British Aerospace PLC
BAOR	British Army of the Rhine
BAPC	British Aviation Preservation Council
Batt	Battalion
BATUS	British Army Training Unit Support
BBMF	Battle of Britain Memorial Flight
BDRF	Battle Damage Repair Flight
BDRT	Battle Damage Repair Training
Be	Beech
Bf	Bayerische Flugzeugwerke
BFWF	Basic Fixed Wing Flight
BG	Bomber Group
BGA	British Gliding & Soaring Association
BNFL	British Nuclear Fuels Ltd
BP	Boulton & Paul
BS	Bomber Squadron
B-V	Boeing-Vertol
BW	Bomber Wing
CAC	Commonwealth Aircraft Corporation
CARG	Cotswold Aircraft Restoration Group
CASA	Construcciones Aeronautics SA
Cav	Cavalry
CC	County Council
CCF	Combined Cadet Force/Canadian Car & Foundry Company
CDE	Chemical Defence Establishment
CEAM	Centre d'Expérimentation Aeriennes Militaires
CEV	Centre d'Essais en Vol
CFS	Central Flying School
CGMF	Central Glider Maintenance Flight
CIFAS	Centre d'Instruction des Forces Aériennes Stratégiques
CinC	Commander in Chief
CINCAFSE	Commander in Chief, Allied Forces Southern Europe
CINCLANT	Commander in Chief Atlantic
CIEH	Centre d'Instruction des Equipages d'Hélicoptères
CITac	Centre d'Instruction Tactique
Co	Company
Comp	Composite with
CSDE	Central Servicing Development Establishment
CT	College of Technology
CTE	Central Training Establishment
CTTS	Civilian Technical Training School
CV	Chance-Vought
D-BA	Daimler-Benz Aerospace
D-BD	Dassault-Breguet Dornier
Det	Detachment
DH	de Havilland
DHC	de Havilland Canada
DRA	Defence Research Agency
DTEO	Defence Test and Evaluation Organisation
DTI	Department of Trade and Industry
EA	Escadron Aérien
EAC	Ecole de l'Aviation de Chasse
EAP	European Aircraft Project
EAT	Ecole de l'Aviation de Transport
EB	Escadre de Bombardement
EC	Escadre de Chasse
ECS	Electronic Countermeasures Squadron
EDA	Escadre de Detection Aéroportée
EdC	Escadron de Convoyage
EDCA	Escadron de Détection et de Control Aéroportée
EE	English Electric
EET	Escadron Electronique Tactique
EHI	European Helicopter Industries
EL	Escadre de Liaison
EMA	East Midlands Airport
EMVO	Elementaire Militaire Vlieg Opleiding
ENOSA	Ecole des Navigateurs Operationales Systemes d'Armees
EoN	Elliot's of Newbury
EP&TU	Exhibition, Production & Transportation Unit
EPE	Ecole de Pilotage Elementaire
ER	Escadre de Reconnaissance
ERV	Escadre de Ravitaillement en Vol
ES	Escadrille de Servitude
Esc	Escuadron (Squadron)
Esk	Eskadrille (Squadron)
Eslla	Escuadrilla (Squadron)
Esq	Esquadra (Squadron)
ET	Escadre de Transport
ETE	Escadron de Transport et Entrainment
ETEC	Escadron de Transport d'Entrainement et de Calibration
ETL	Escadron de Transport Légère
ETO	Escadron de Transition Operationnelle
ETOM	Escadron de Transport Outre Mer
ETPS	Empire Test Pilots' School
ETS	Engineering Training School
FAA	Fleet Air Arm/Federal Aviation Administration
FACF	Forward Air Control Flight
FBS	Flugbereitschaftstaffel
FBW	Fly by wire
FC	Forskokcentralen
FE	Further Education
FETC	Fire and Emergency Training Centre
ff	Front fuselage
FG	Fighter Group

FH	Fairchild-Hiller
FI	Falkland Islands
FIWC	Fleet Information Warfare Center
FLGFFB	Fluglehrgruppe Furstenfeldbruck
Flt	Flight
FMA	Fabrica Militar de Aviones
FMV	Forsvarets Materielwerk
FONA	Flag Officer Naval Aviation
FRADU	Fleet Requirements and Air Direction Unit
FRA	FR Aviation
FS	Fighter Squadron
FSCTE	Fire School Central Training Establishment
FTS	Flying Training School
FTW	Flying Training Wing
Fw	Focke Wulf
FW	Fighter Wing/Foster Wickner
FWTS	Fixed Wing Test Squadron
FY	Fiscal Year
F3 OCU	Tornado F3 Operational Conversion Unit
GAL	General Aircraft Ltd
GAM	Groupe Aerien Mixte
GD	General Dynamics
GHL	Groupe d'Helicopteres Legeres
GI	Ground Instruction/Groupement d'Instruction
GT	Grupo de Transporte (Transport Wing)
GTT	Grupo de Transporte de Tropos (Troop Carrier Wing)
HAF	Historic Aircraft Flight
HC	Helicopter Combat Support Squadron
HF	Historic Flying Ltd
HFR	Heeresfliegerregiment (Corps transport regiment)
HFWS	Heeresflieger Waffenschule
Hkp Div	Helikopterdivisionen
HMA	Helicopter Maritime Attack
HMS	Her Majesty's Ship
HOCU	Harrier OCU
HP	Handley-Page
HQ	Headquarters
HS	Hawker Siddeley
HSF	Harrier Servicing Flight
IAF	Israeli Air Force
IHM	International Helicopter Museum
IWM	Imperial War Museum
JATE	Joint Air Transport Establishment
JbG	Jagdbombergeschwader (Fighter Bomber Wing)
JG	Jagdgeschwader (Fighter Wing)
Kridlo	Wing
Letka	Squadron
LTG	Lufttransportgeschwader (Air Transport Wing)
LTV	Ling-Temco-Vought
LVG	Luftwaffen Versorgungs Geschwader (Air Force Maintenance Wing)/Luft Verkehrs Gesellschaft
MARPAT	Maritime Patrouillegroep
MBB	Messerschmitt Bolkow-Blohm
MCAS	Marine Corps Air Station
McD	McDonnell Douglas
Med	Medical
MFG	Marine Flieger Geschwader (Naval Air Wing)
MH	Max Holste
MIB	Military Intelligence Battalion
MiG	Mikoyan — Gurevich
MoD(PE)	Ministry of Defence (Procurement Executive)
Mod	Modified
MR	Maritime Reconnaissance
MRF	Meteorological Research Flight
MS	Morane-Saulnier
MU	Maintenance Unit
NA	North American
NACDS	Naval Air Command Driving School
NAEWF	NATO Airborne Early Warning Force
NAF	Naval Air Facility
NAS	Naval Air Station
NASU	Naval Air Support Unit
NATO	North Atlantic Treaty Organisation
NE	North-East
NI	Northern Ireland
NMSU	Nimrod Major Servicing Unit
NYARC	North Yorks Aircraft Restoration Centre
OCU	Operational Conversion Unit
OEU	Operation Evaluation Unit
OFMC	Old Flying Machine Company
OLUK	Operating Location United Kingdom
PBN	Pilatus Britten-Norman
PRU	Photographic Reconnaissance Unit
R	Replica
RAeS	Royal Aeronautical Society
RAF	Royal Aircraft Factory/Royal Air Force
RAFC	Royal Air Force College
RAFM	Royal Air Force Museum
RAFGSA	Royal Air Force Gliding and Soaring Association
RAOC	Royal Army Ordnance Corps
RCAF	Royal Canadian Air Force
RE	Royal Engineers
Regt	Regiment
REME	Royal Electrical & Mechanical Engineers
rf	Rear fuselage
RJAF	Royal Jordanian Air Force
RM	Royal Marines
RMC of S	Royal Military College of Science
RN	Royal Navy
RNAS	Royal Naval Air Station
RNAW	Royal Naval Aircraft Workshop
RNAY	Royal Naval Aircraft Yard
RNEC	Royal Naval Engineering College
RNGSA	Royal Navy Gliding and Soaring Association
ROF	Royal Ordnance Factory
RQS	Rescue Squadron
R-R	Rolls-Royce
RS	Reid & Sigrist/Reconnaissance Squadron
RSV	Reparto Sperimentale Volo
RW	Reconnaissance Wing
RWTS	Rotary Wing Test Squadron
SA	Scottish Aviation
Saab	Svenska Aeroplan Aktieboleg
SAL	Scottish Aviation Limited
SAM	School of Aviation Medicine
SAOEU	Strike/Attack Operational Evaluation Unit
SAR	Search and Rescue
Saro	Saunders-Roe
SARTU	Search and Rescue Training Unit
SBoLK	Stihacie Bombardovacie Letecké Kridlo
SCW	Sea Control Wing
SEAE	School of Electrical & Aeronautical Engineering
SEPECAT	Société Européenne de Production de l'avion Ecole de Combat et d'Appui Tactique
SFDO	School of Flight Deck Operations
SHAPE	Supreme Headquarters Allied Forces Europe
SIF	Servicing Instruction Flight
SKTU	Sea King Training Unit
Skv	Skvadron
SLK	Stihacie Letecké Kridlo
SLV	School Licht Vliegwezen
Sm	Smaldeel (Squadron)
SNCAN	Société Nationale de Constructions Aéronautiques du Nord
SOES	Station Operations & Engineering Squadron
SOG	Special Operations Group

8

SOS	Special Operations Squadron
SoTT	School of Technical Training
SOW	Special Operations Wing
SPAD	Société Pour les Appareils Deperdussin
Sqn	Squadron
SSF	Station Servicing Flight
SWWAPS	Second World War Aircraft Preservation Society
TA	Territorial Army
T&EE	Test & Evaluation Establishment
TFC	The Fighter Collection
TGp	Test Groep
TMF	Tornado Maintenance Flight
TMTS	Trade Management Training School
TS	Test Squadron
TsAGI	Tsentral'ny Aerogidrodinamicheski Instut (Central Aero & Hydrodynamics Institute)
TSLw	Technische Schule der Luftwaffe
TSW	Tactical Supply Wing
TTTE	Tri-national Tornado Training Establishment
TW	Test Wing
UAS	University Air Squadron
Uberwg	Uberwachunggeschwader
UK	United Kingdom
UKAEA	United Kingdom Atomic Energy Authority
UNFICYP	United Nations' Forces in Cyprus
US	United States
USAF	United States Air Force
USAFE	United States Air Forces in Europe
USAREUR	US Army Europe
USEUCOM	United States European Command
USMC	United States Marine Corps
USN	United States Navy
VFW	Vereinigte Flugtechnische Werke
VGS	Volunteer Gliding School
VMGR	Marine Aerial Refuelling/Transport Squadron
VMGRT	Marine Aerial Refuelling/Transport Training Squadron
VQ	Fleet Air Reconnaissance Squadron
VR	Fleet Logistic Support Squadron
VS	Vickers-Supermarine
VSL	Vycvikové Stredisko Letectva
Wg	Wing
WLT	Weapons Loading Training
WRS	Weather Reconnaissance Squadron
WS	Westland
WTD	Wehrtechnische Dienstelle
WW2	World War II
zDL	základna Dopravního Letectva
ZmDK	Zmiesany Dopravny Kridlo
zSL	základna Skolního Letectva
zTL	základna Taktického Letectva

This section is to assist the reader to locate the places in the United Kingdom where operational military aircraft are based. The term *aircraft* also includes helicopters and gliders.

The alphabetical order listing gives each location in relation to its county and to its nearest classified road(s) (*by* means adjoining; *of* means proximate to), together with its approximate direction and mileage from the centre of a nearby major town or city.

Some civil airports are included where active military units are also based, but **excluded** are MoD sites with non-operational aircraft (eg *gate guardians*), the bases of privately-owned civil aircraft that wear military markings and museums.

User	Base name	County/Region	Location	Distance/direction from (town)
DTEO	Aberporth	Dyfed	N of A487	6m ENE of Cardigan
RAF	Aldergrove/Belfast Airport	Co Antrim	W by A26	13m W of Belfast
RAF/ Hunting	Barkston Heath	Lincolnshire	W by B6404, S of A153	5m NNE of Grantham
RAF	Benson	Oxfordshire	E by A423	1m NE of Wallingford
DTEO/ RAF	Boscombe Down	Wiltshire	S by A303, W of A338	6m N of Salisbury
RAF	Boulmer	Northumberland	E of B1339	4m E of Alnwick
RAF	Brize Norton	Oxfordshire	W of A4095	5m SW of Witney
RAF/ Marshal	Cambridge Airport/ Teversham	Cambridgeshire	S by A1303	2m E of Cambridge
RAF/HM	Chivenor	Devon	S of A361	4m WNW of Barnstaple
RAF	Colerne	Wiltshire	S of A420, E of Fosse Way	5m NE of Bath
RAF	Coltishall	Norfolk	W of B1150	9m NNE of Norwich
RAF	Coningsby	Lincolnshire	S of A153, W by B1192	10m NW of Boston
RAF	Cosford	Shropshire	W of A41, N of A464	9m WNW of Wolverhampton
RAF	Cottesmore	Leicestershire	W of A1, N of B668	9m NW of Stamford
RAF	Cranwell	Lincolnshire	N by A17, S by B1429	5m WNW of Sleaford
RNAS	Culdrose	Cornwall	E by A3083	1m SE of Helston
AAC	Dishforth	Yorkshire North	E by A1	4m E of Ripon
BAe	Dunsfold	Surrey	W of A281, S of B2130	9m S of Guildford
USAF	Fairford	Gloucestershire	S of A417	9m ESE of Cirencester
BAe	Filton	Avon	E by M5 jn 17, W by A38	4m N of Bristol
RNAY	Fleetlands	Hampshire	E by A32	2m SE of Fareham
RAF	Glasgow Airport	Strathclyde	N by M8 jn 28	7m W of city
RAF	Halton	Buckinghamshire	N of A4011, S of B4544	4m ESE of Aylesbury
RAF	Henlow	Bedfordshire	E of A600, W of A6001	1m SW of Henlow
RAF	Honington	Suffolk	E of A134, W of A1088	6m S of Thetford
RAF	Kenley	Greater London	W of A22	1m W of Warlingham
RAF	Kinloss	Grampian	E of B9011, N of B9089	3m NE of Forres
RAF	Kirknewton	Lothian	E by B7031, N by A70	8m SW of Edinburgh
USAF	Lakenheath	Suffolk	W by A1065	8m W of Thetford
RAF	Leeming	Yorkshire North	E by A1	5m SW of Northallerton
RAF	Leuchars	Fife	E of A919	7m SE of Dundee
RAF	Linton-on-Ouse	Yorkshire North	E of B6265	10m NW of York
DTEO	Llanbedr	Gwynedd	W of A496	7m NNW of Barmouth
RAF	Lossiemouth	Grampian	W of B9135, S of B9040	4m N of Elgin
RAF	Lyneham	Wiltshire	W of A3102, S of A420	10m WSW of Swindon
RAF	Machrihanish	Strathclyde	W of A83	3m W of Cambletown
RAF	Manston	Kent	N by A253	3m W of Ramsgate
RAF	Marham	Norfolk	N by A1122	6m W of Swaffham
AAC	Middle Wallop	Hampshire	S by A343	6m SW of Andover
USAF	Mildenhall	Suffolk	S by A1101	9m NNE of Newmarket
RAF	Newton	Nottinghamshire	N of A52, W of A46	7m E of Nottingham
RAF	Northolt	Greater London	N by A40	3m E of M40 jn 1
RAF	Odiham	Hampshire	E of A32	2m S of M3 jn 5
RNAS	Portland	Dorset	E by A354	3m S of Weymouth
RN	Predannack	Cornwall	W by A3083	7m S of Helston
RN	Prestwick Airport	Strathclyde	E by A79	3m N of Ayr
RAF	St Athan	South Glamorgan	W of B4265	13m WSW of Cardiff
RAF	St Mawgan/Newquay Airport	Cornwall	N of A3059	4m ENE of Newquay
RAF	Scampton	Lincolnshire	W by A15	6m N of Lincoln
RAF	Sealand	Clwyd	W by A550	6m WNW of Chester
RAF	Shawbury	Shropshire	W of B5063	7m NNE of Shrewsbury
RAF	South Cerney	Gloucestershire	W by A419	3m SE of Cirencester

User	Base name	County/Region	Location	Distance/direction from (town)
RAF	Swansea Airport/ Fairwood Common	West Glamorgan	W by A4118	6m W of Swansea
RAF/ Shorts	Sydenham/ Belfast City Airport	Co Down	W by A2	2m E of city
RAF	Ternhill	Shropshire	SW by A41	3m SW of Market DTEO
RAF/ AAC	Topcliffe	Yorkshire North	E of A167, W of A168	3m SW of Thirsk
RAF	Upavon	Wiltshire	S by A342	14m WNW of Andover
RAF	Valley	Gwynedd	S of A5 on Anglesey	5m SE of Holyhead
RAF	Waddington	Lincolnshire	E by A607, W by A15	5m S of Lincoln
BAe	Warton	Lancashire	S by A584	8m SE of Blackpool
AAC/ RAF	Wattisham	Suffolk	N of B1078	5m SSW of Stowmarket
DTEO	West Freugh	Dumfries Galloway	& S by A757, W by A715	5m SE of Stranraer
RAF	Weston-on-the-Green	Oxfordshire	E by A43	9m N of Oxford
RAF	Wittering	Cambridgeshire	W by A1, N of A47	3m S of Stamford
RAF	Woodvale	Merseyside	W by A565	5m SSW of Southport
RAF	Wyton	Cambridgeshire	E of A141, N of B1090	3m NE of Huntingdon
WS	Yeovil	Somerset	N of A30, S of A3088	1m W of Yeovil
RNAS	Yeovilton	Somerset	S by B3151, S of A303	5m N of Yeovil

British Military Aircraft Serials

The Committee of Imperial Defence through its Air Committee introduced a standardised system of numbering aircraft in November 1912. The Air Department of the Admiralty was allocated the first batch 1-200 and used these to cover aircraft already in use and those on order. The Army was issued with the next block from 201-800, which included the number 304 which was given to the Cody Biplane now preserved in the Science Museum. By the outbreak of World War 1 the Royal Navy was on its second batch of serials 801-1600 and this system continued with alternating allocations between the Army and Navy until 1916 when number 10000, a Royal Flying Corps BE2C, was reached.

It was decided not to continue with five digit numbers but instead to start again from 1, prefixing RFC aircraft with the letter A and RNAS aircraft with the prefix N. The RFC allocations commenced with A1 an FE2D and before the end of the year had reached A9999 an Armstrong Whitworth FK8. The next group commenced with B1 and continued in logical sequence through the C, D, E and F prefixes. G was used on a limited basis to identify captured German aircraft, while H was the last block of wartime-ordered aircraft. To avoid confusion I was not used, so the new postwar machines were allocated serials in the J range. A further minor change was made in the serial numbering system in August 1929 when it was decided to maintain four numerals after the prefix letter, thus omitting numbers 1 to 999. The new K series therefore commenced at K1000, which was allocated to an AW Atlas.

The Naval N prefix was not used in such a logical way Blocks of numbers were allocated for specific types of aircraft such as seaplanes or flying-boats. By the late 1920s the sequence had largely been used up and a new series using the prefix S was commenced. In 1930 separate naval allocations were stopped and subsequent serials were issued in the 'military' range which had by this time reached the K series. A further change in the pattern of allocations came in the L range. Commencing with L7272 numbers were issued in blocks with smaller blocks of serials between not used. These were known as blackout blocks. It would appear that this policy is being reintroduced at the present time. As M had already been used as a suffix for Maintenance Command instructional airframes it was not used as a prefix. Although N had previously been used for naval aircraft it was used again for serials allocated from 1937.

With the build-up to World War 2 the rate of allocations quickly accelerated and the prefix R was being used when war was declared. The letters O and Q were not allotted, and nor was S which had been used up to S1865 for naval aircraft before integration into the RAF series. By 1940 the serial Z9999 had been reached, as part of a blackout block, with the letters U and Y not used to avoid confusion. The option to recommence serial allocation at A1000 was not taken up; instead it was decided to use an alphabetical two-letter prefix with three numerals running from 100 to 999. Thus AA100 was allocated to a Blenheim IV.

This two-letter, three-numeral serial system which started in 1940 continues today. The letters C, I, O, Q, U and Y were, with the exception of NC, not used. For various reasons the following letter combinations were not issued: DA, DB, DH, EA, GA to GZ, HA, HT, JE, JH, JJ, KR to KT, MR, NW, NZ, SA to SK, SV, TN, TR and VE. The first postwar serials issued were in the VP range while the end of the WZs had been reached by the Korean War. The current new issues are just commencing in the ZJ range. At the current rate of issue the Z range will last well into the 21st century.

Note: Whilst every effort has been made to ensure the accuracy of this publication, no part of the contents has been obtained from official sources. The compiler will be pleased to continue to receive comments, corrections and further information for inclusion in subsequent editions of *Military Aircraft Markings* and the monthly up-date of additions and amendments that is published in *Aircraft Illustrated*. Please send your information to *Military Aircraft Markings*, PO Box 46, Westbury-on-Trym, Bristol BS9 1TF; or fax to 0117 968 3928.

British Military Aircraft Markings

A serial in *italics* denotes that it is not the genuine marking for that airframe.

Serial	Type (other identity) [code]	Owner/operator, location or fate	Notes
164	Bleriot Type XI (BAPC 106/9209M)	RAF Museum Rest'n Centre, Cardington	
168	Sopwith Tabloid Scout <R> (G-BFDE)	RAF Museum, Hendon	
304	Cody Biplane (BAPC 62)	Science Museum, South Kensington	
433	Bleriot Type XXVII (BAPC 107/ 9202M)	RAF Museum, Hendon	
687	RAF BE2b <R> (BAPC 181)	RAF Museum, Hendon	
1197	Bleriot Type XI <R> (G-BPVE)	Privately owned, Booker	
1701	RAF BE2c <R> (BAPC 117)	Brooklands Museum, Weybridge	
2345	Vickers FB5 Gunbus <R> (G-ATVP)	RAF Museum, Hendon	
2699	RAF BE2c	Imperial War Museum, Lambeth	
3066	Caudron GIII (G-AETA/9203M)	RAF Museum, Hendon	
5492	Sopwith Triplane <R> (G-PENY)	Privately owned, Dunkeswell	
5894	DH2 <R> (G-BFVH) [FB2]	Wessex Aviation & Transport, Chalmington	
5964	DH2 <R> (BAPC 112)	Museum of Army Flying, Middle Wallop	
6232	RAF BE2c <R> (BAPC 41)	RAF, stored St Athan	
8359	Short 184 <ff>	FAA Museum, RNAS Yeovilton	
A301	Morane BB (frame)	RAF Museum, Hendon	
A1325	RAF BE2e (G-BVGR)	Privately owned, Rye	
A1742	Bristol Scout D <R> (BAPC 38)	The Aircraft Restoration Co, Duxford	
A4850	RAF SE5 <R> (BAPC 176)	South Yorkshire Aviation Museum, Firbeck	
A7317	Sopwith Pup <R> (BAPC 179)	Midland Air Museum, Coventry	
A8226	Sopwith 1½ Strutter<R>(G-BIDW)	RAF Museum, Hendon	
B1807	Sopwith Pup (G-EAVX) [A7]	Privately owned, Keynsham, Avon	
B6401	Sopwith Camel <R> (G-AWYY)	FAA Museum, RNAS Yeovilton	
B7270	Sopwith Camel <R> (G-BFCZ)	Brooklands Museum, Weybridge	
B9708	Sopwith 1½ Strutter <R>	Macclesfield Historical Av Soc	
C1904	RAF SE5a <R> (G-PFAP) [Z]	Privately owned, Syerston	
C3011	Phoenix Currie Super Wot (G-SWOT) [S]	Privately owned, Breighton	
C4451	Avro 504J <R> (BAPC 210)	Southampton Hall of Aviation	
C4912	Bristol M1C <R> (BAPC 135)	Northern Aeroplane Workshops	
C4940	Bristol M1C <R>	Bygone Times Warehouse, Euxton, Lancs	
C4994	Bristol M1C <R> (G-BLWM)	RAF Museum, Hendon	
C9533	RAF SE5a <R> (G-BUWE) [M]	Privately owned, Boscombe Down	
D2700	RAF SE5a <R> (BAPC 208)	Tangmere Military Aviation Museum	
D3419	Sopwith Camel <R> (BAPC 59)	RAF Cosford Aerospace Museum	
D5329	Sopwith 5F.1 Dolphin	RAF Museum Store, Cardington	
D7560	Avro 504K	Museum of Army Flying, Middle Wallop	
D7889	Bristol F2B Fighter (G-AANM/ BAPC 166)	Privately owned, St Leonards-on-Sea	
D8084	Bristol F2B Fighter (G-ACAA/ F4516) [S]	The Fighter Collection, Old Warden	
D8096	Bristol F2B Fighter (G-AEPH) [D]	The Shuttleworth Collection, Old Warden	
D8781	Avro 504K <R> (G-ECKE)	Privately owned, Rougham	
E373	Avro 504K <R> (BAPC 178)	Privately owned, Eccleston, Lancs	
E449	Avro 504K (G-EBJE/9205M)	RAF Museum, Hendon	
E2466	Bristol F2B Fighter (BAPC 165) [I]	RAF Museum, Hendon	
E2581	Bristol F2B Fighter	Imperial War Museum, Duxford	
F141	RAF SE5a <R> (G-SEVA) [G]	Privately owned, Boscombe Down	
F344	Avro 504K <R>	RAF Museum Store, Henlow	
F542	Sopwith Camel <R> (G-BPOB)	Privately owned, Booker	

F760 – L7775

Notes	Serial	Type (other identity) [code]	Owner/operator, location or fate
	F760	SE5a Microlight <R> [A]	Privately owned, Redhill
	F904	RAF SE5a (G-EBIA)	The Shuttleworth Collection, Old Warden
	F938	RAF SE5a (G-EBIC/9208M)	RAF Museum, Hendon
F943		RAF SE5a <R> (G-BIHF) [S]	Privately owned, White Waltham
F943		RAF SE5a <R> (G-BKDT)	Yorkshire Air Museum, Elvington
	F1010	Airco DH9A [C]	RAF Museum, Hendon
	F3556	RAF RE8	Imperial War Museum, Duxford
F4013		Sopwith Camel <R>	Privately owned, Coventry
	F5447	RAF SE5a <R> (G-BKER) [N]	Privately owned, Cumbernauld
F5459		RAF SE5a <R> (BAPC 142) [11-Y]	
F5459		RAF SE5a <R> (G-INNY) [Y]	Privately owned, Old Sarum
	F6314	Sopwith Camel (9206M) [B]	RAF Museum, Hendon
F8010		RAF SE5a <R> (G-BDWJ) [Z]	Privately owned, Graveley
F8614		Vickers Vimy IV <R> (G-AWAU)	RAF Museum, Hendon
	H1968	Avro 504K <R> (BAPC 42)	RAF, stored St Athan
	H2311	Avro 504K (G-ABAA)	Gr Manchester Mus of Science & Industry
H3426		Hawker Hurricane <R> (BAPC 68)	Midland Air Museum, stored Coventry
	H5199	Avro 504K (BK892/3118M/ G-ACNB/G-ADEV)	The Shuttleworth Collection, Old Warden
	J7326	DH53 Humming Bird (G-EBQP)	Privately owned, Bishops Stortford
	J8067	Westland Pterodactyl 1a	Science Museum, South Kensington
J9941		Hawker Hart 2 (G-ABMR)	RAF Museum, Hendon
	K1786	Hawker Tomtit (G-AFTA)	The Shuttleworth Collection, Old Warden
K2050		Isaacs Fury II (G-ASCM)	Privately owned, Brize Norton
K2059		Isaacs Fury II (G-PFAR)	Privately owned, Dunkeswell
K2075		Isaacs Fury II (G-BEER)	Privately owned, Sturgate
K2227		Bristol 105 Bulldog IIA (G-ABBB) (wreck)	RAF Museum/Skysport Engineering, Biggleswade
K2567		DH82A Tiger Moth (DE306/ 7035M/G-MOTH)	Privately owned, Tadlow
K2571		DH82A Tiger Moth <R>	Privately owned, RAF Hereford
K2572		DH82A Tiger Moth (NM129/ G-AOZH)	Privately owned, Shoreham
K2572		DH82A Tiger Moth <R>	The Aeroplane Collection, Hooton Park
K2587		DH82A Tiger Moth (G-BJAP)	Privately owned, Shoreham
	K3215	Avro 621 Tutor (G-AHSA)	The Shuttleworth Collection, Old Warden
	K3661	Hawker Nimrod II (G-BURZ)	Privately owned, St Leonards on Sea
K3731		Isaacs Fury <R> (G-RODI)	Privately owned, Hailsham
	K4232	Avro 671 Rota I (SE-AZB)	RAF Museum, Hendon
	K4235	Avro 671 Rota I (G-AHMJ) [KX-H]	The Shuttleworth Collection, Old Warden
	K4972	Hawker Hart Trainer IIA (1764M)	RAF Cosford Aerospace Museum
K5054		Supermarine Spitfire <R> (BAPC 214)	The Spitfire Society, Lee-on-Solent
K5054		Supermarine Spitfire <R> (G-BRDV)	Privately owned, Hullavington
K5414		Hawker Hind (G-AENP/ BAPC 78) [XV]	The Shuttleworth Collection, Old Warden
	K5600	Hawker Audax I (2015M/G-BVVI)	Aero Vintage, Paddock Wood
	K6035	Westland Wallace II (2365M)	RAF Museum, Hendon
K7271		Hawker Fury II <R> (BAPC 148)	Tangmere Military Aviation Museum
	K8042	Gloster Gladiator II (8372M)	RAF Museum, Hendon
	K8203	Hawker Demon I (G-BTVE/2292M)	Privately owned, Thorncote Green, Beds
K9926		VS300 Spitfire I <R> (BAPC 217) [JH-C]	RAF Bentley Priory, on display
	K9942	VS300 Spitfire IA (8383M) [SD-V]	RAF Museum, Hendon
L1070		VS300 Spitfire I <R> (BAPC 227) [XT-A]	RAF Turnhouse, on display
	L1592	Hawker Hurricane I [KW-Z]	Science Museum, South Kensington
L1592		Hawker Hurricane I <R> (BAPC 63) [KW-Z]	Kent Battle of Britain Museum, Hawkinge
L1679		Hawker Hurricane I <R> (BAPC 241) [JX-G]	Tangmere Military Aviation Museum
L1710		Hawker Hurricane I <R> (BAPC 219) [AL-D]	RAF Biggin Hill, on display
	L2301	VS Walrus I (G-AIZG)	FAA Museum, RNAS Yeovilton
	L2940	Blackburn Skua I	FAA Museum, RNAS Yeovilton
	L5343	Fairey Battle I [VO-S]	RAF Museum, Hendon
L6906		Miles M14A Magister I (G-AKKY/T9841/BAPC 44)	Museum of Berkshire Aviation, Woodley
	L7775	Vickers Wellington IA (fuselage)	Privately owned, Moreton-in-Marsh

Serial	Type (other identity) [code]	Owner/operator, location or fate	Notes
L8756	Bristol 149 Bolingbroke IVT (RCAF 10001) [XD-E]	RAF Museum, Hendon	
N248	Supermarine S6A	Southampton Hall of Aviation	
N546	Wright Quadruplane 1 <R> (BAPC 164)	Southampton Hall of Aviation	
N1671	Boulton Paul P.82 Defiant I (8370M) [EW-D]	RAF Museum, Hendon	
N1854	Fairey Fulmar II (G-AIBE)	FAA Museum, RNAS Yeovilton	
N2078	Sopwith Baby (8214/8215)	FAA Museum, RNAS Yeovilton	
N2276	Gloster Sea Gladiator II (N5903/ G-GLAD) [H]	The Fighter Collection, Duxford	
N2308	Gloster Gladiator I (L8032/ G-AMRK)[HP-B]	The Shuttleworth Collection, Old Warden	
N2980	Vickers Wellington IA [R]	Brooklands Museum, Weybridge	
N3194	VS300 Spitfire I <R> (BAPC 220) [GR-Z]	RAF Biggin Hill, on display	
N3289	VS300 Spitfire I <R> (BAPC 65) [QV-K]	Kent Battle of Britain Museum, Hawkinge	
N3313	VS300 Spitfire I <R> (BAPC 69) [BO-D]	Kent Battle of Britain Museum, Hawkinge	
N3378	Boulton Paul P.82 Defiant I (wreck)	Boulton Paul Society, Wolverhampton	
N4389	Fairey Albacore [4M] (N4172)	FAA Museum, RNAS Yeovilton	
N4877	Avro 652A Anson I (G-AMDA) [VX-F]	Imperial War Museum, Duxford	
N5182	Sopwith Pup <R> (G-APUP/9213M)	RAF Museum, Hendon	
N5195	Sopwith Pup (G-ABOX)	Museum of Army Flying, Middle Wallop	
N5419	Bristol Scout D <R> (N5419)	Bristol Aircraft Collection, Banwell	
N5492	Sopwith Triplane <R> (BAPC 111)	The Fighter Collection, Duxford	
N5628	Gloster Gladiator II	RAF Museum, Hendon	
N5912	Sopwith Triplane (8385M)	RAF Museum, Hendon	
N6004	Short S29 Stirling I	RAeS Medway Branch, Rochester	
N6037	DH82A Tiger Moth (T6037/ G-ANNB)	Privately owned, Carlisle (rebuild)	
N6181	Sopwith Pup (G-EBKY)	The Shuttleworth Collection, Old Warden	
N6290	Sopwith Triplane <R> (G-BOCK)	The Shuttleworth Collection, Old Warden	
N6452	Sopwith Pup <R> (G-BIAU)	FAA Museum, RNAS Yeovilton	
N6466	DH82A Tiger Moth (G-ANKZ)	Privately owned, Barton	
N6720	DH82A Tiger Moth (7014M) [RUO-B]	No 1940 Sqn ATC, Levenshulme	
N6797	DH82A Tiger Moth (G-ANEH)	Privately owned, Goodwood	
N6812	Sopwith 2F.1 Camel	Imperial War Museum, Lambeth	
N6847	DH82A Tiger Moth (G-APAL)	Privately owned, Little Gransden	
N6848	DH82A Tiger Moth (G-BALX)	Privately owned, Headcorn	
N6965	DH82A Tiger Moth (G-AJTW) [FL-J]	Privately owned, Tibenham	
N6985	DH82A Tiger Moth (G-AHMN)	AAC Historic Aircraft Flt, Middle Wallop	
N9191	DH82A Tiger Moth (G-ALND)	Privately owned, Shobdon	
N9192	DH82A Tiger Moth (G-BSTJ) [RCO-N]	Privately owned, Sywell	
N9389	DH82A Tiger Moth (G-ANJA)	Privately owned, Shipmeadow, Suffolk	
N9899	Supermarine Southampton 1	RAF Museum, Hendon (fuselage)	
N9926	VS300 Spitfire I <R> (BAPC 217) [JH-C]	RAF Bentley Priory, on display	
P1344	HP52 Hampden I (9175M) [PL-K]	RAF Museum Rest'n Centre, Cardington	
P1344	HP52 Hampden I <rf> (parts Hereford L6012)	RAF Museum, Hendon	
P2617	Hawker Hurricane I (8373M) [AF-A]	RAF Museum, Hendon	
P2793	Hawker Hurricane I <R> [SD-M]	Privately owned, Malton	
P2902	Hawker Hurricane I (G-ROBT)	Privately owned, Billingshurst	
P3059	Hawker Hurricane I <R> (BAPC 64) [SD-N]	Kent Battle of Britain Museum, Hawkinge	
P3175	Hawker Hurricane I (wreck)	RAF Museum, Hendon	
P3386	Hawker Hurricane I <R> (BAPC 218) [FT-A]	RAF Bentley Priory, on display	
P3395	Hawker Hurricane IV (KX829)[JX-B]	Birmingham Mus of Science & Technology	
P3554	Hawker Hurricane I (composite)	The Air Defence Collection, Salisbury	
P4139	Fairey Swordfish II (HS618) [5H]	FAA Museum, RNAS Yeovilton	
P5865	CCF T-6J Harvard IV (G-BKCK) [LE-W]	Privately owned, North Weald	
P6382	Miles M14A Hawk Trainer 3 (G-AJRS) [C]	The Shuttleworth Collection, Old Warden	
P7350	VS329 Spitfire IIA (G-AWIJ) [RN-S]	RAF BBMF, Coningsby	

P7540 – W5856

Notes	Serial	Type (other identity) [code]	Owner/operator, location or fate
	P7540	VS329 Spitfire IIA [DU-W]	Dumfries & Galloway Av'n Mus, Tinwald Downs
	P8140	VS329 Spitfire II <R> (BAPC 71) [ZF-K]	Norfolk & Suffolk Av'n Museum, Flixton
	P8448	VS329 Spitfire II <R> (BAPC 225) [UM-D]	RAF Cranwell
	P9444	VS300 Spitfire IA [RN-D]	Science Museum, South Kensington
	R1914	Miles M14A Magister (G-AHUJ)	Privately owned, stored Strathallan
	R4897	DH82A Tiger Moth II (G-ERTY)	Privately owned, Hamstreet
	R4907	DH82A Tiger Moth II (G-ANCS)	Privately owned, Wreningham, Norfolk
	R5250	DH82A Tiger Moth II (G-AODT)	Privately owned, Tibenham
	R5868	Avro Lancaster I (7325M) [PO-S]	RAF Museum, Hendon
	R6915	VS300 Spitfire I	Imperial War Museum, Lambeth
	R9125	Westland Lysander III (8377M) [LX-L]	RAF Museum, Hendon
	R9371	HP59 Halifax II <ff>	Cotswold Aircraft Rest'n Group, Innsworth
	S1287	Fairey Flycatcher <R> (G-BEYB) [5]	Privately owned, Stockbridge
	S1579	Hawker Nimrod I <R> (G-BBVO) [571]	Privately owned, Dunkeswell
	S1595	Supermarine S6B	Science Museum, South Kensington
	T5298	Bristol 156 Beaufighter I <ff>	Midland Air Museum, Coventry
	T5424	DH82A Tiger Moth II (G-AJOA)	Privately owned, Chiseldon
	T5672	DH82A Tiger Moth II (G-ALRI)	Privately owned, Chalmington
	T5854	DH82A Tiger Moth II (G-ANKK)	Privately owned, Halfpenny Green (rebuild)
	T5879	DH82A Tiger Moth II (G-AXBW)	Privately owned, Tongham
	T5968	DH82A Tiger Moth II (G-ANNN)	Privately owned, Hollybush
	T6099	DH82A Tiger Moth II (G-AOGR)	Privately owned, Clacton
	T6256	DH82A Tiger Moth II	Privately owned, Cranfield
	T6296	DH82A Tiger Moth II (8387M)	RAF Museum, Hendon
	T6313	DH82A Tiger Moth II (G-AHVU)	Privately owned, Liphook
	T6390	DH82A Tiger Moth II (G-ANIX)	Island Aeroplane Co, Sandown
	T6818	DH82A Tiger Moth II (G-ANKT) [91]	The Shuttleworth Collection, Old Warden
	T6991	DH82A Tiger Moth II (G-ANOR/ DE694)	Privately owned, Paddock Wood
	T7109	DH82A Tiger Moth II (G-AOIM)	Privately owned, Shobdon
	T7230	DH82A Tiger Moth II (G-AFVE)	Privately owned, Biggin Hill
	T7281	DH82A Tiger Moth II (G-ARTL)	Privately owned, Egton, nr Whitby
	T7404	DH82A Tiger Moth II (G-ANMV)	Privately owned, Booker
	T7471	DH82A Tiger Moth II (G-AJHU)	Privately owned, Compton Abbas
	T7793	DH82A Tiger Moth II (G-ANKV)	Privately owned, Croydon, on display
	T7842	DH82A Tiger Moth II (G-AMTF)	Privately owned, Boughton, Suffolk
	T7909	DH82A Tiger Moth II (G-ANON)	Privately owned, Sherburn-in-Elmet
	T8191	DH82A Tiger Moth II	Privately owned,
	T9707	Miles M14A Magister I (G-AKKR/8378M/T9708)	Gtr Manchester Museum of Science & Industry
	T9738	Miles M14A Magister I (F-AZOR)	Privately owned, Breighton
	V1075	Miles M14A Magister I (G-AKPF)	Privately owned, Shoreham
	V3388	Airspeed AS10 Oxford I (G-AHTW)	Imperial War Museum, Duxford
	V6028	Bristol 149 Bolingbroke IVT (G-MKIV) [GB-D] <rf>	The Aircraft Restoration Co, stored Duxford
	V7350	Hawker Hurricane I (fuselage)	Brenzett Aeronautical Museum
	V7467	Hawker Hurricane I <R> (BAPC 223) [LE-D]	RAF Coltishall, on display
	V7767	Hawker Hurricane I <R> (BAPC 72)	Privately owned, Sopley, Hants
	V9281	WS Lysander IIIA (G-BCWL) [RU-M]	Privately owned, Duxford
	V9441	WS Lysander IIIA (G-AZWT) [AR-A]	Privately owned, stored Strathallan
	V9673	WS Lysander IIIA (V9300/G-LIZY) [MA-J]	Imperial War Museum, Duxford
	W1048	HP59 Halifax II (8465M) [TL-S]	RAF Museum, Hendon
	W2068	Avro 652A Anson I [68]	RAF Museum, Duxford (restoration)
	W2718	VS Walrus I (G-RNLI)	Privately owned, Micheldever
	W4041	Gloster E28/39 [G]	Science Museum, South Kensington
	W4050	DH98 Mosquito	Mosquito Aircraft Museum, St Albans
	W5856	Fairey Swordfish II (G-BMGC) [A2A]	RN Historic Flight, Yeovilton

Serial	Type (other identity) [code]	Owner/operator, location or fate	Notes
W9385	DH87B Hornet Moth (G-ADND) [YG-L]	The Shuttleworth Collection, Old Warden	
X4277	VS361 Spitfire LF XVIE (TB382/7244M) [XT-M]	*Painted as MK673 by June 1995*	
X4474	VS361 Spitfire LF XVIE (TE311/7241M) [QV-I]	RAF EP&TU, St Athan	
X4590	VS300 Spitfire I (8384M) [PR-F]	RAF Museum, Hendon	
X7688	Bristol 156 Beaufighter I (3858M/G-DINT)	Privately owned, Hatch	
Z2033	Fairey Firefly I (G-ASTL) [275]	Imperial War Museum, Duxford	
Z5027	Hawker Hurricane IIb	Privately owned, Audley End	
Z5053	Hawker Hurricane IIb (G-BWHA)	Historic Flying, Audley End	
Z5722	Bristol 149 Bolingbroke IVT (G-BPIV) [WM-Z]	The Aircraft Restoration Company, Duxford	
Z7015	Hawker Sea Hurricane Ib (G-BKTH) [7-L]	The Shuttleworth Collection, Duxford	
Z7197	Percival P30 Proctor III (G-AKZN/8380M)	RAF Museum, Hendon	
Z7381	Hawker Hurricane XIIb (G-HURI) [XR-T]	The Fighter Collection, Duxford	
AA908	VS349 Spitfire VB <R> (BAPC 230) [UM-W]	Eden Camp Theme Park, Malton	
AB130	VS349 Spitfire VA (parts)	Privately owned, Ludham	
AB910	VS349 Spitfire VB (AE-H)	RAF BBMF, Coningsby	
AD540	VS349 Spitfire VB (wreck)	Dumfries and Galloway Av'n Museum	
AE436	HP52 Hampden I (parts)	Lincolnshire Av'n Heritage Centre, E Kirkby	
AE977	Hawker Sea Hurricane Ib (G-TWTD)	Privately owned, Milden	
AL246	Grumman Martlet I	FAA Museum, RNAS Yeovilton	
AM561	Lockheed Hudson V (parts)	Cornwall Aero Park, Helston	
AP506	Cierva C30A (G-ACWM)	IHM, Weston-super-Mare	
AP507	Cierva C30A (G-ACWP) [KX-P]	Science Museum, South Kensington	
AR213	VS300 Spitfire IA (G-AIST) [PR-D]	Privately owned, Booker	
AR501	VS349 Spitfire LF VC (G-AWII) (NN-A]	The Shuttleworth Collection, Old Warden	
AR614	VS349 Spitfire VC (5378M/7555M/ G-BUWA)	The Fighter Collection, Audley End	
BB807	DH82A Tiger Moth (G-ADWO)	Southampton Hall of Aviation	
BE417	Hawker Hurricane XIIb (G-HURR) [AE-K]	Privately owned, Brooklands	
BE421	Hawker Hurricane IIc <R> (BAPC 205) [XP-G]	RAF Museum, Hendon	
BL370	VS349 Spitfire VB	Privately owned, Oxford	
BL614	VS349 Spitfire VB (4354M) [ZD-F]	Medway Aircraft Preservation Society, Rochester	
BL628	VS349 Spitfire F VB (G-BTTN)	*Sold to Australia, April 1995*	
BL655	VS349 Spitfire VB (wreck)	Lincolnshire Av'n Heritage Centre, East Kirkby	
BL924	VS349 Spitfire VB <R> (BAPC 242) [AZ-G]	Tangmere Military Aviation Museum	
BM597	VS349 Spitfire LF VB (5718M/ G-MKVB)[PR-O]	Privately owned, Audley End	
BN230	Hawker Hurricane IIc (LF751/ 5466M) [FT-A]	RAF Manston, Memorial Pavilion	
BR600	VS361 Spitfire IX <R> (BAPC 222) [SH-V]	RAF Uxbridge, on display	
BR600	VS361 Spitfire IX <R> (BAPC 224) [JP-A]	Ambassador Hotel, Norwich	
BW853	Hawker Sea Hurricane XII (G-BRKE)	Privately owned, Milden	
BW881	Hawker Sea Hurricane XIIA (G-KAMM)	Privately owned, Eye, Suffolk	
DD931	Bristol 152 Beaufort VIII (9131M) [L]	RAF Museum, Hendon	
DE208	DH82A Tiger Moth II (G-AGYU)	Privately owned, Ronaldsway	
DE363	DH82A Tiger Moth II (G-ANFC)	Military Aircrft Pres Grp, Hadfield, Derbys	
DE470	DH82A Tiger Moth II (G-ANMY)	Privately owned, Durley, Hants	
DE623	DH82A Tiger Moth II (G-ANFI)	Privately owned, Shobdon	

DE673 – HS503

Notes	Serial	Type (other identity) [code]	Owner/operator, location or fate
	DE673	DH82A Tiger Moth II (6948M/ G-ADNZ)	Privately owned, Hampton
	DE970	DH82A Tiger Moth II (G-AOBJ)	Privately owned, Cardiff
	DE992	DH82A Tiger Moth II (G-AXXV)	Privately owned, Membury
	DF128	DH82A Tiger Moth II (G-AOJJ) [RCO-U]	Privately owned, White Waltham
	DF155	DH82A Tiger Moth II (G-ANFV)	Privately owned, Shempston Fm, Lossiemouth
	DF198	DH82A Tiger Moth II (G-BBRB)	Privately owned, Biggin Hill
	DG202	Gloster F9/40 (5758M) [G]	RAF Cosford Aerospace Museum
	DG590	Miles M2H Hawk Major (8379M/ G-ADMW)	RAF Museum/Skysport Engineering Hatch
	DP872	Fairey Barracuda II (fuselage)	FAA Museum, stored Yeovilton
	DR613	FW Wicko GM1 (G-AFJB)	Privately owned, stored Berkswell
	DV372	Avro 683 Lancaster I <ff>	Imperial War Museum, Lambeth
	EE416	Gloster Meteor F3 <ff>	Science Museum, Wroughton
	EE425	Gloster Meteor F3 <ff>	Rebel Air Museum, Earls Colne
	EE531	Gloster Meteor F4 (7090M)	Midland Air Museum, Coventry
	EE549	Gloster Meteor F4 (7008M)	Tangmere Military Aviation Museum
	EF545	VS349 Spitfire VC <ff>	Privately owned, High Wycombe
	EM720	DH82A Tiger Moth II (G-AXAN)	Privately owned, Little Gransden
	EM727	DH82A Tiger Moth II (G-AOXN)	Privately owned, Yeovil
	EM903	DH82A Tiger Moth II (G-APBI)	Privately owned, Halstead
	EN224	VS366 Spitfire F XII (G-FXII)	Privately owned, Newport Pagnell
	EN343	VS365 Spitfire PR XI <R> (BAPC 226)	RAF Benson, on display
	EN398	VS361 Spitfire F IX <R> (BAPC 190) [JE-J]	Privately owned, Cannock, Staffs
	EP120	VS349 Spitfire LF VB (5377M/ 8070M/G-LFVB) [AE-A]	The Fighter Collection, Audley End
	EX976	NA AT-6D Harvard III	FAA Museum, RNAS Yeovilton
	EZ259	NA AT-6D Harvard III (G-BMJW)	Privately owned, Wakefield
	EZ407	NA AT-6D Harvard III	RN Historic Flight, stored Lee-on-Solent
	FB226	Bonsall Mustang <R> (G-BDWM) [MT-A]	Privately owned, Gamston
	FE695	Noorduyn AT-16 Harvard IIB (G-BTXI)	The Fighter Collection, Duxford
	FE905	Noorduyn AT-16 Harvard IIB (LN-BNM)	RAF Museum, Hendon
	FE992	Noorduyn AT-16 Harvard IIB (G-BDAM) [KT]	Privately owned, Duxford
	FH153	Noorduyn AT-16 Harvard IIB (G-BBHK) [GW-A]	Privately owned, stored Cardiff
	FM118	Avro 683 Lancaster B X <ff>	Privately owned, Gosport, Hants
	FR886	Piper L-4J Cub (G-BDMS)	Privately owned, Old Sarum
	FS728	Noorduyn AT-16 Harvard IIB (G-BAFM) [F]	Privately owned, Goodwood
	FS890	Noorduyn AT-16 Harvard IIB (7554M)	MoD(PE), stored DTEO Boscombe Down
	FT239	CCF T-6J Texan (G-BIWX)	Privately owned, North Weald
	FT323	NA AT-6D Harvard III (FAP 1513)	Privately owned, Cranfield
	FT375	Noorduyn AT-16 Harvard IIB [5]	MoD(PE)/FWTS, DTEO Boscombe Down
	FT391	Noorduyn AT-16 Harvard IIB (G-AZBN)	Privately owned, Shoreham
	FX301	NA AT-6D Harvard III (EX915/ G-JUDI)	Privately owned, Bryngwyn Bach, Clwyd
	FX360	Noorduyn AT-16 Harvard IIB (KF435)	Booker Aircraft Museum
	FX442	Noorduyn AT-16 Harvard IIB [TO-M]	Privately owned, South Gorley, Hants
	FX760	Curtiss P-40N Kittyhawk IV (9150M) [GA-?]	RAF Museum, Hendon
	HB275	Beech C-45 Expeditor II (G-BKGM)	Privately owned, North Weald
	HB751	Fairchild Argus III (G-BCBL)	Privately owned, Little Gransden
	HH379	GAL48 Hotspur II <rf>	Museum of Army Flying, Middle Wallop
	HH982	Taylorcraft Plus D (LB312/G-AHXE)	Privately owned, Shoreham
	HJ711	DH98 Mosquito NF II [VI-C]	Night Fighter Preservation Tm, Elvington
	HM354	Percival P34 Proctor III (G-ANPP)	Privately owned, Stansted
	HM580	Cierva C-30A (G-ACUU)	Imperial War Museum, Duxford
	HS503	Fairey Swordfish IV (BAPC 108)	RAF Cosford Aerospace Museum, stored

Serial	Type (other identity) [code]	Owner/operator, location or fate	Notes
JM135	Bristol 156 Beaufighter XIC (A19-144)	The Fighter Collection, Duxford	
JR505	Hawker Typhoon IB <ff>	Privately owned, Coventry	
JV482	Grumman Wildcat V	Ulster Aviation Society, Langford Lodge	
KB889	Avro Lancaster B X (G-LANC) [NA-I]	Imperial War Museum, Duxford	
KB976	Avro Lancaster B X (G-BCOH)	Aces High, North Weald	
KB994	Avro Lancaster B X (G-BVBP)	Aces High, North Weald	
KD431	CV Corsair IV [E2-M]	FAA Museum, RNAS Yeovilton	
KE209	Grumman Hellcat II	FAA Museum, RNAS Yeovilton	
KE418	Hawker Tempest <rf>	RAF Museum Store, Cardington	
KF183	Noorduyn AT-16 Harvard IIB [3]	MoD(PE)/FWTS, DTEO Boscombe Down	
KF388	Noorduyn AT-16 Harvard IIB <ff>	Privately owned, Bournemouth	
KF435	Noorduyn AT-16 Harvard IIB <ff>	Privately owned, Ottershaw	
KF487	Noorduyn AT-16 Harvard IIB	British Aerial Museum, Duxford, spares use	
KF532	Noorduyn AT-16 Harvard IIB <ff>	Newark Air Museum, Winthorpe	
KG374	Douglas Dakota IV (KN645/8355M) [YS]	RAF Cosford Aerospace Museum	
KG391	Douglas C-47A Dakota III (G-BVOL) [AG]	Airborne Initiative Training, Middle Wallop	
KJ351	Airspeed AS58 Horsa II (TL659/BAPC 80) [23]	Museum of Army Flying, Middle Wallop	
KK995	Sikorsky Hoverfly I [E]	RAF Museum, Hendon	
KL161	NA B-25D Mitchell II (N88972) [VO-B]	The Fighter Collection, Duxford	
KL216	Republic P-47D Thunderbolt (45-49295/9212M) [RS-L]	RAF Cosford Aerospace Museum	
KN448	Douglas Dakota C4 <ff>	Science Museum, South Kensington	
KN751	Consolidated Liberator C VI [F]	RAF Cosford Aerospace Museum	
KP208	Douglas Dakota IV [YS]	Airborne Forces Museum, Aldershot	
KZ191	Hawker Hurricane IV (frame only)	Privately owned, North Weald	
KZ321	Hawker Hurricane IV (G-HURY) (frame only)	The Fighter Collection, Duxford	
LA198	VS356 Spitfire F21 (7118M) [RAI-G]	RAF, stored St Athan	
LA226	VS356 Spitfire F21 (7119M)	RAF, stored At Athan	
LA255	VS356 Spitfire F21 (6490M) [JX-U]	RAF No 1 Sqn, Wittering (preserved)	
LA546	VS Seafire F46 <ff>	Privately owned, Newport Pagnell	
LB294	Taylorcraft Plus D (G-AHWJ)	Museum of Army Flying, Whitchurch	
LB375	Taylorcraft Plus D (G-AHGW)	Privately owned, Edge Hill	
LF363	Hawker Hurricane IIc	RAF, Audley End (on rebuild)	
LF738	Hawker Hurricane IIc (5405M) [UH-A]	RAF Cosford Aerospace Museum	
LF789	DH82 Queen Bee (BAPC 186)	Mosquito Aircraft Museum, London Colney	
LF858	DH82 Queen Bee (G-BLUZ)	Privately owned, Rush Green	
LH208	Airspeed AS51 Horsa I (8596M) (parts only)	Museum of Army Flying, Middle Wallop	
LS326	Fairey Swordfish II (G-AJVH) [L2]	RN Historic Flight, RNAS Yeovilton	
LV907	HP59 Halifax III (HR792) [NP-F]	Yorkshire Air Museum, Elvington	
LZ551	DH100 Vampire [P]	FAA Museum, RNAS Yeovilton	
LZ551	DH100 Vampire FB6 (J-1173/G-DHXX)	Source Classic Jet Flight, Bournemouth	
LZ766	Percival P34 Proctor III (G-ALCK)	Imperial War Museum, Duxford	
LZ842	VS361 Spitfire IX (remains)	Privately owned, Battle, Sussex	
MF628	Vickers Wellington T10 (9210M)	RAF Museum, Hendon	
MH434	VS361 Spitfire LF IXB (G-ASJV) [MN-B]	The Old Flying Machine Company, Duxford	
MH486	VS361 Spitfire LF IX <R> (BAPC 206) [FF-A]	RAF Museum, Hendon	
MH777	VS361 Spitfire IX <R> (BAPC 221) [RF-N]	RAF Northolt, on display	
MJ147	VS361 Spitfire LF IX	Privately owned, Kent	
MJ627	VS509 Spitfire T9 (G-BMSB) [9G-P]	Privately owned, Bruntingthorpe	
MJ730	VS361 Spitfire HF IXE (G-HFIX) [GZ-?]	Privately owned, Staverton	
MJ751	VS361 Spitfire IX <R> (BAPC 209) [DU-V]	D-Day Museum, Shoreham Airport	
MJ832	VS361 Spitfire IX <R> (BAPC 229) [DN-Y]	RAF Digby, on display	
MK356	VS361 Spitfire LF IXC (5690M)	RAF BBMF, St Athan	

MK673 – PP566

Notes	Serial	Type (other identity) [code]	Owner/operator, location or fate
	MK673	VS361 Spitfire LF XVIE (TB382/ X4277/7244M) [SK-E]	RAF EP&TU, St Athan
	MK805	VS361 Spitfire LF IX <R> [SH-B]	Privately owned, Lowestoft
	MK912	VS361 Spitfire LF IXE (G-BRRA) [MN-P]	Privately owned, Paddock Wood
	ML407	VS509 Spitfire T9 (G-LFIX) [OU-V]	Privately owned, Duxford
	ML411	VS361 Spitfire LF IXE	Privately owned, Kent
	ML417	VS361 Spitfire LF IXE (G-BJSG) [2I-T]	The Fighter Collection, Duxford
	ML427	VS361 Spitfire IX (6457M) [I-ST]	Birmingham Museum of Science & Industry
	ML796	Short S25 Sunderland V	Imperial War Museum, Duxford
	ML824	Short S25 Sunderland V [NS-Z]	RAF Museum, Hendon
	MN235	Hawker Typhoon IB	RAF Museum, Hendon
	MP425	Airspeed AS10 Oxford I (G-AITB) [G]	RAF Museum, Hendon
	MT438	Auster III (G-AREI)	Privately owned, Old Sarum
	MT847	VS379 Spitfire FR XIVE (6960M) [AX-H]	Gr Manchester Mus of Science & Industry
	MT928	VS359 Spitfire HF VIIIC (G-BKMI/ MV154)[ZX-M]	Privately owned, Filton
	MV262	VS379 Spitfire FR XIV (G-CCVV)	Privately owned, Booker
	MV293	VS379 Spitfire FR XIV (G-SPIT) [OI-C]	The Fighter Collection, Duxford
	MW376	Hawker Tempest II (G-BSHW)	Privately owned, Audley End
	MW401	Hawker Tempest II (G-PEST)	Privately owned, Brooklands
	MW404	Hawker Tempest II (IAF HA557)	Privately owned
	MW467	VS349 Spitfire V <R> (BAPC 202)	Privately owned, Llanbedr
	MW758	Hawker Tempest II (IAF HA580)	Privately owned
	MW763	Hawker Tempest II (G-TEMT)	Privately owned, Brooklands
	MW800	Hawker Tempest II (G-BSHW/ MW376) [HF-V]	Privately owned, Spanhoe Lodge
	NF370	Fairey Swordfish III	Imperial War Museum, Duxford
	NF389	Fairey Swordfish III [D]	RN Historic Flight, Lee-on-Solent
	NF875	DH89A Dragon Rapide 6 (G-AGTM)	Privately owned, Membury
	NJ673	Auster 5D (G-AOCR)	Privately owned, Wellesbourne Mountford
	NJ695	Auster 4 (G-AJXV)	Privately owned, Tollerton
	NJ703	Auster 5 (G-AKPI)	Privately owned, Croft, Lincs
	NJ719	Auster 5 (TW385/G-ANFU)	Privately owned, Newcastle
	NL750	DH82A Tiger Moth II (T7997/ G-AOBH)	Privately owned, Thruxton
	NL846	DH82A Tiger Moth II (F-BGEQ)	Brooklands Museum, Chessington (rebuild)
	NL985	DH82A Tiger Moth I (7015M/ G-BWIK)	Privately owned, Sywell
	NM181	DH82A Tiger Moth I (G-AZGZ)	Privately owned, Rush Green
	NP181	Percival P31 Proctor IV (G-AOAR)	Privately owned, Biggin Hill
	NP184	Percival P31 Proctor IV (G-ANYP) [K]	Privately owned, Chatteris
	NP294	Percival P31 Proctor IV [TB-M]	Lincolnshire Av'n Heritage Centre, E Kirkby
	NP303	Percival P31 Proctor IV (G-ANZJ)	Privately owned, Byfleet, Surrey
	NV778	Hawker Tempest TT5 (8386M)	RAFM Restoration Centre, Cardington
	NX534	Auster III (G-BUDL)	Privately owned, Middle Wallop
	NX611	Avro 683 Lancaster B VII (8375M/ G-ASXX) [LE-C]	Lincolnshire Av'n Heritage Centre, E Kirkby
	PA474	Avro 683 Lancaster B I [WS-J]	RAF BBMF, Coningsby
	PF179	HS Gnat T1 (XR541/8602M)	Privately owned, Ipswich
	PK624	VS356 Spitfire F22 (8072M) [RAU-T]	The Fighter Collection, Duxford
	PK664	VS356 Spitfire F22 (7759M) [V6-B]	RAF Museum Restoration Centre, Cardington
	PK683	VS356 Spitfire F24 (7150M)	Southampton Hall of Aviation
	PK724	VS356 Spitfire F24 (7288M)	RAF Museum, Hendon
	PL344	VS361 Spitfire LF IXE (G-IXCC) [Y2-B]	Privately owned, Booker
	PL965	VS365 Spitfire PR XI (G-MKXI) [R]	Privately owned, Duxford
	PM631	VS390 Spitfire PR XIX [N]	RAF BBMF, Coningsby
	PM651	VS390 Spitfire PR XIX (7758M) [X]	RAF Museum Restoration Centre, Cardington
	PN323	HP Halifax VII <ff>	Imperial War Museum, Lambeth
	PP566	Fairey Firefly I (fuselage)	South Yorkshire Av'n Museum, Firbeck

Serial	Type (other identity) [code]	Owner/operator, location or fate	Notes
PP972	VS358 Seafire L IIIC (G-BUAR) [6M-D]	Privately owned, East Midlands Airport	
PR536	Hawker Tempest II (IAF HA457) [OQ-H]	RAF Museum, Hendon	
PS853	VS390 Spitfire PR XIX (G-MXIX) [C]	Privately owned, North Weald	
PS915	VS390 Spitfire PR XIX (7548M/ 7711M) [P]	RAF BBMF, Coningsby	
PV202	VS509 Spitfire T9 (G-TRIX) [VZ-M]	Privately owned, Goodwood	
PZ865	Hawker Hurricane IIc (G-AMAU) [J]	RAF BBMF, Coningsby	
RA848	Slingsby Cadet TX1	The Aeroplane Collection, stored Wigan	
RA854	Slingsby Cadet TX1	The Aeroplane Collection, stored Wigan	
RA897	Slingsby Cadet TX1	Newark Air Museum store, Hucknall	
RD253	Bristol 156 Beaufighter TF X (7931M)	RAF Museum, Hendon	
RF342	Avro 694 Lincoln B II (G-29-1/ G-APRJ)	Aces High, North Weald	
RF398	Avro 694 Lincoln B II (8376M)	RAF Cosford Aerospace Museum	
RG333	Miles M38 Messenger IIA (G-AIEK)	Privately owned, Felton, Bristol	
RG333	Miles M38 Messenger IIA (G-AKEZ)	Privately owned, Chelmsford	
RH377	Miles M38 Messenger 4A (G-ALAH)	Privately owned, Stretton, Cheshire	
RH746	Bristol 164 Brigand TF1	North-East Aircraft Museum, Usworth	
RL962	DH89A Dominie II (G-AHED)	RAF Museum Store, Cardington	
RM221	Percival P31 Proctor IV (G-ANXR)	Privately owned, Biggin Hill	
RN218	Isaacs Spitfire <R> (G-BBJI) [N]	Privately owned, Langham	
RR232	VS361 Spitfire HF IXC (G-BRSF)	Privately owned, Lancing, Sussex	
RR299	DH98 Mosquito T III (G-ASKH) [HT-E]	British Aerospace, Hawarden	
RT486	Auster 5 (G-AJGJ) [PF-A]	Privately owned, Old Sarum	
RT520	Auster 5 (G-ALYB)	South Yorkshire Av'n Museum, Firbeck	
RW388	VS361 Spitfire LF XVIE (6946M) [U4-U]	Stoke-on-Trent City Museum, Hanley	
RW393	VS361 Spitfire LF XVIE (7293M) [XT-A]	RAF Cosford Aerospace Museum	
RX168	VS358 Seafire L IIIC (G-BWEM)	Privately owned, High Wycombe	
SL674	VS361 Spitfire LF IX (8392M) [RAS-H]	RAF Museum Restoration Centre, Cardington	
SM520	VS361 Spitfire LF IX	Privately owned, Audley End	
SM832	VS379 Spitfire F XIVE (G-WWII) [YB-A]	The Fighter Collection, Duxford	
SM845	VS394 Spitfire FR XVIII (G-BUOS)	Privately owned, Audley End	
SX137	VS384 Seafire F XVII	FAA Museum, RNAS Yeovilton	
SX300	VS384 Seafire F XVII	Privately owned, Warwick	
SX336	VS384 Seafire F XVII (G-BRMG)	Privately owned, Twyford, Bucks	
TA122	DH98 Mosquito FB VI [UP-G]	Mosquito Aircraft Museum, London Colney	
TA634	DH98 Mosquito TT35 (G-AWJV) [8K-K]	Mosquito Aircraft Museum, London Colney	
TA639	DH98 Mosquito TT35 (7806M) [AZ-E]	RAF Cosford Aerospace Museum	
TA719	DH98 Mosquito TT35 (G-ASKC)	Imperial War Museum, Duxford	
TA805	VS361 Spitfire IX (remains)	Privately owned, Sandown, IOW	
TB252	VS361 Spitfire LF XVIE (G-XVIE) [GW-H]	Privately owned, Audley End	
TB752	VS361 Spitfire LF XVIE (8086M) [KH-Z]	RAF Manston, Memorial Pavilion	
TB885	VS361 Spitfire LF XVIE	Shoreham Aircraft Preservation Society	
TD248	VS361 Spitfire LF XVIE (7246M/ G-OXVI) [D]	Privately owned, North Weald	
TD314	VS361 Spitfire LF IX (N601DA)	Privately owned, Ludham, Norfolk	
TE184	VS361 Spitfire LF XVIE (6850M/ G-MXVI)	Privately owned, Audley End	
TE462	VS361 Spitfire LF XVIE (7243M)	Royal Scottish Mus'm of Flight, E Fortune	
TE566	VS361 Spitfire LF IXE (G-BLCK) [DU-A]	Historic Aircraft Collection, Duxford	
TG263	Saro SR.A1 (G-12-1) [P]	Southampton Hall of Aviation	
TG511	HP67 Hastings C1 (8554M)	RAF Cosford Aerospace Museum	
TG517	HP67 Hastings T5	Newark Air Museum, Winthorpe	
TG528	HP67 Hastings C1A	Imperial War Museum, Duxford	
TJ118	DH98 Mosquito TT35 <ff>	Mosquito Aircraft Museum, stored	

Notes	Serial	Type (other identity) [code]	Owner/operator, location or fate
	TJ138	DH98 Mosquito B35 (7607M) [VO-L]	RAF Museum, Hendon
	TJ324	Auster 5 (G-APAH)	Privately owned, Cumbernauld
	TJ343	Auster 5 (G-AJXC)	Privately owned, stored Hook
	TJ398	Auster 5 (BAPC 70)	Aircraft Pres'n Soc of Scotland, E Fortune
	TJ569	Auster 5 (G-AKOW)	Museum of Army Flying, Middle Wallop
	TJ672	Auster 5D (G-ANIJ)	Privately owned, RAF Swanton Morley
	TJ704	Beagle A.61 Terrier 2 (G-ASCD) [JA]	Yorkshire Air Museum, Elvington
	TJ707	Auster 5 (frame)	Air Service Training, Perth
	TK718	GAL59 Hamilcar I	Royal Tank Museum, Bovington
	TK777	GAL59 Hamilcar I (fuselage)	Museum of Army Flying, Middle Wallop
	TL615	Airspeed AS58 Horsa II	Robertsbridge Aviation Society
	TP367	VS394 Spitfire XVIII	Privately owned, Hatch
	TS291	Slingsby Cadet TX1 (BGA852)	Royal Scottish Mus'm of Flight, E Fortune
	TS423	Douglas C-47A Dakota C3 (G-DAKS)	Aces High Ltd, North Weald
	TS798	Avro 685 York C1 (G-AGNV)	RAF Cosford Aerospace Museum
	TV959	DH98 Mosquito T III [AF-V]	The Fighter Collection, stored Duxford
	TV959	DH98 Mosquito T III <R>	Privately owned, Heald Green, Cheshire
	TW384	Auster 5 (G-ANHZ)	Privately owned, Headcorn
	TW439	Auster 5 (G-ANRP)	Privately owned, Breighton
	TW448	Auster 5 (G-ANLU)	Privately owned, Hedge End
	TW462	Beagle A.61 Terrier 1 (G-ARLO)	Privately owned, Chandlers Ford, Hants
	TW467	Auster 5 (G-ANIE)	Privately owned, Middle Wallop
	TW511	Auster 5 (G-APAF)	Privately owned, North Coates
	TW536	Auster AOP6 (7704M/G-BNGE) [TS-V]	Privately owned, Middle Wallop
	TW591	Auster 6A (G-ARIH) [N]	Privately owned, Abbots Bromley
	TW641	Beagle A.61 Terrier 2 (G-ATDN)	Privately owned, Biggin Hill
	TX183	Avro 652A Anson C19 (G-BSMF)	Privately owned, Arbroath
	TX213	Avro 652A Anson C19 (G-AWRS)	North-East Aircraft Museum, Usworth
	TX214	Avro 652A Anson C19 (7817M)	RAF Cosford Aerospace Museum
	TX226	Avro 652A Anson C19 (7865M)	Imperial War Museum, stored Duxford
	TX228	Avro 652A Anson C19	Scrapped, 1992
	TX235	Avro 652A Anson C19	Caernarfon Air World
	VD165	Slingsby T7 Kite (BGA 400)	Privately owned, Dunstable
	VF301	DH100 Vampire F1 (7060M) [RAL-B]	Midland Air Museum, Coventry
	VF512	Auster 6A (G-ARRX) [PF-M]	Privately owned, White Waltham
	VF516	Beagle A.61 Terrier 2 (G-ASMZ) [T]	Privately owned, Bagby
	VF526	Auster 6A (G-ARXU) [T]	Privately owned, Middle Wallop
	VF548	Beagle A.61 Terrier 1 (G-ASEG)	Privately owned, Dunkeswell
	VH127	Fairey Firefly TT4 [200/R]	FAA Museum, stored RNAS Yeovilton
	VL348	Avro 652A Anson C19 (G-AVVO)	Newark Air Museum, Winthorpe
	VL349	Avro 652A Anson C19 (G-AWSA)	Norfolk & Suffolk Aviation Mus'm, Flixton
	VM325	Avro 652A Anson C19	Midland Air Museum, Coventry
	VM360	Avro 652A Anson C19 (G-APHV)	Royal Scottish Mus'm of Flight, E Fortune
	VM791	Slingsby Cadet TX3 (XA312/ 8876M)	No 450 Sqn ATC, RAF Kenley
	VN148	Grunau Baby IIb (BAPC 33/ BGA2400)	Privately owned, Dunstable
	VN485	VS356 Spitfire F24 (7326M)	Imperial War Museum, Duxford
	VP293	Avro 696 Shackleton T4 <ff>	Lincolnshire Av'n Heritage Centre, E Kirkby
	VP519	Avro 652A Anson C19 (G-AVVR) <ff>	The Aeroplane Collection, Hooton Park
	VP952	DH104 Devon C2 (8820M)	RAF Cosford Aerospace Museum
	VP955	DH104 Devon C2 (G-DVON)	Privately owned, Old Sarum
	VP957	DH104 Devon C2 (8822M) <ff>	No 1137 Sqn ATC, Belfast
	VP959	DH104 Devon C2 (G-BWFB) [L]	Privately owned, Little Staughton
	VP967	DH104 Devon C2 (G-KOOL)	East Surrey Technical College, Redhill
	VP968	DH104 Devon C2	DTEO Boscombe Down, derelict
	VP971	DH104 Devon C2 (8824M)	FSCTE, RAF Manston
	VP975	DH104 Devon C2 [M]	Science Museum, Wroughton
	VP978	DH104 Devon C2 (8553M)	RAF Brize Norton, instructional use
	VP981	DH104 Devon C2	RAF, stored Coningsby
	VR137	Westland Wyvern TF1	FAA Museum, stored RNAS Yeovilton
	VR192	Percival P40 Prentice T1 (G-APIT)	SWWAPS, Lasham
	VR249	Percival P40 Prentice T1 (G-APIY) [FA-EL]	Newark Air Museum, Winthorpe
	VR259	Percival P40 Prentice T1 (G-APJB)	Air Antique, Coventry

Serial	Type (other identity) [code]	Owner/operator, location or fate	Notes
VR930	Hawker Sea Fury FB11 (8382M)	RN Historic Flight, Brough	
VS356	Percival P40 Prentice T1 (G-AOLU)	Privately owned, Stonehaven	
VS517	Avro 652A Anson T20	RN, stored Lee-on-Solent	
VS562	Avro 652A Anson T21 (8012M)	Maes Artro Craft Village, Llanbedr	
VS610	Percival P40 Prentice T1 (G-AOKL) [K-L]	Privately owned, Bassingbourn	
VS623	Percival P40 Prentice T1 (G-AOKZ) [KQ-F]	Midland Air Museum, Coventry	
VT260	Gloster Meteor F4 (8813M) [67]	Imperial War Museum, stored Duxford	
VT409	Fairey Firefly AS5 (mostly WD889)	North-East Aircraft Museum, Usworth	
VT812	DH100 Vampire F3 (7200M) [N]	RAF Museum, Hendon	
VT935	Boulton Paul P111A (VT769)	Midland Air Museum, Coventry	
VT987	Auster AOP6 (G-BKXP)	Privately owned, Little Gransden, Cambs	
VV106	Supermarine 510 (7175M)	FAA Museum, stored Wroughton	
VV217	DH100 Vampire FB5 (7323M)	North-East Aircraft Museum, Usworth	
VV901	Avro 652A Anson T21	Yorkshire Air Museum, Elvington	
VW453	Gloster Meteor T7 (8703M) [Z]	RAF Innsworth, on display	
VW985	Auster AOP6 (G-ASEF)	Privately owned, Upper Arncott, Oxon	
VX118	Auster AOP6 (G-ASNB)	Privately owned, Kingston Deverill	
VX147	Alon A2 Aircoupe (G-AVIL)	Privately owned, Headcorn	
VX185	EE Canberra B(I)8 (7631M) <ff>	Science Museum, Wroughton	
VX250	DH103 Sea Hornet 21 [48] <rf>	Mosquito Aircraft Museum, London Colney	
VX272	Hawker P1052 (7174M)	FAA Museum, stored Wroughton	
VX275	Slingsby T21B Sedbergh TX1 (8884M/BGA 572)	RAF Museum Restoration Centre, Cardington	
VX461	DH100 Vampire FB5 (7646M)	RAF Cosford Aerospace Museum, stored	
VX573	Vickers Valetta C2 (8389M)	RAF Cosford Aerospace Museum, stored	
VX577	Vickers Valetta C2	North-East Aircraft Museum, Usworth	
VX580	Vickers Valetta C2	Norfolk & Suffolk Av'n Museum, Flixton	
VX595	WS51 Dragonfly HR1 [29]	Gosport Aviation Society, HMS Sultan	
VX653	Hawker Sea Fury FB11 (G-BUCM) [062]	The Fighter Collection, Duxford	
VX665	Hawker Sea Fury FB11 <rf>	RN Historic Flight, at BAe Brough	
VX926	Auster T7 (G-ASKJ)	Privately owned, Little Gransden	
VZ304	DH100 Vampire FB6 (J-1167/ G-MKVI) [A-T]	Vintage Aircraft Team, Bruntingthorpe	
VZ345	Hawker Sea Fury T20S	RN Historic Flight, Brough (on rebuild)	
VZ462	Gloster Meteor F8	SWWAPS, stored Lasham	
VZ467	Gloster Meteor F8 (G-METE) [01]	Classic Jets Flying Museum, Biggin Hill	
VZ477	Gloster Meteor F8 (7741M) <ff>	Midland Air Museum, Coventry	
VZ608	Gloster Meteor FR9	Newark Air Museum, Winthorpe	
VZ634	Gloster Meteor T7 (8657M)	Newark Air Museum, Winthorpe	
VZ638	Gloster Meteor T7 (G-JETM) [HF]	Privately owned, Charlwood, Surrey	
VZ728	RS4 Desford Trainer (G-AGOS)	Snibston Discovery Park, stored Coalville	
VZ962	WS51 Dragonfly HR1 [904]	IHM, Weston-super-Mare	
VZ965	WS51 Dragonfly HR5	FAA Museum, at RNAS Culdrose	
WA473	VS Attacker F1 [102/J]	FAA Museum, RNAS Yeovilton	
WA576	Bristol 171 Sycamore 3 (7900M/G-ALSS)	Dumfries & Galloway Av'n Mus, Tinwald Downs	
WA577	Bristol 171 Sycamore 3 (7718M/G-ALST)	North-East Aircraft Museum, Usworth	
WA591	Gloster Meteor T7 (7917M) [W]	Meteor Flight, Yatesbury	
WA630	Gloster Meteor T7 [69] <ff>	Robertsbridge Aviation Museum, Mayfield	
WA634	Gloster Meteor T7/8	RAF Cosford Aerospace Museum	
WA638	Gloster Meteor T7	Martin Baker Aircraft, Chalgrove	
WA662	Gloster Meteor T7	South Yorkshire Aviation Museum, Firbeck	
WA984	Gloster Meteor F8 [A]	Tangmere Military Aviation Museum	
WB188	Hawker Hunter F3 (7154M)	Tangmere Military Aviation Museum	
WB271	Fairey Firefly AS5 [204/R]	RN Historic Flight, RNAS Yeovilton	
WB440	Fairey Firefly AS6 <ff>	South Yorkshire Aviation Museum, Firbeck	
WB491	Avro 706 Ashton 2 (TS897/ G-AJJW) <ff>	Avro Aircraft Rest' Society, BAe Woodford	
WB550	DHC1 Chipmunk T10 [D]	RAF, stored Newton	
WB556	DHC1 Chipmunk T10	RAFGSA, Bicester	
WB560	DHC1 Chipmunk T10	RAF, stored Newton	
WB565	DHC1 Chipmunk T10 [X]	AAC BFWF, Middle Wallop	
WB567	DHC1 Chipmunk T10	RAF, stored Newton	
WB569	DHC1 Chipmunk T10 [R]	RAF, stored Newton	
WB571	DHC1 Chipmunk T10 (G-AOSF) [34]	Privately owned,	
WB575	DHC1 Chipmunk T10 [907]	Sold to France as F-AZPD, March 1995	
WB584	DHC1 Chipmunk T10 (7706M) <ff>	No 327 Sqn ATC, Kilmarnock	

Notes	Serial	Type (other identity) [code]	Owner/operator, location or fate
	WB585	DHC1 Chipmunk T10 (G-AOSY) [RCU-X]	Privately owned, Blackbushe
	WB586	DHC1 Chipmunk T10 [A]	RAF, stored Newton
	WB588	DHC1 Chipmunk T10 (G-AOTD) [D]	Privately owned, Biggin Hill
	WB615	DHC1 Chipmunk T10 [E]	AAC BFWF, Middle Wallop
	WB624	DHC1 Chipmunk T10 <ff>	South Yorkshire Air Museum, Firbeck
	WB626	DHC1 Chipmunk T10 <ff>	Privately owned, Swanton Morley
	WB627	DHC1 Chipmunk T10 [N]	RAF, stored Newton
	WB645	DHC1 Chipmunk T10	RAFGSA, Bicester, spares use
	WB647	DHC1 Chipmunk T10 [R]	AAC BFWF, Middle Wallop
	WB652	DHC1 Chipmunk T10 [V]	RAF, stored Newton
	WB654	DHC1 Chipmunk T10 [T]	AAC BFWF, Middle Wallop
	WB657	DHC1 Chipmunk T10 [908]	RN Historic Flight, Yeovilton
	WB660	DHC1 Chipmunk T10 (G-ARMB)	Privately owned, Shipdham
	WB670	DHC1 Chipmunk T10 (8361M) <ff>	No 1312 Sqn ATC, Southend
	WB671	DHC1 Chipmunk T10 [910]	Privately owned, Husbands Bosworth
	WB685	DHC1 Chipmunk T10 <ff>	North-East Aircraft Museum, Usworth
	WB693	DHC1 Chipmunk T10 [S]	AAC BFWF, Middle Wallop
	WB697	DHC1 Chipmunk T10 [95]	RAF, stored Newton
	WB702	DHC1 Chipmunk T10 (G-AOFE)	Privately owned, Goodwood
	WB703	DHC1 Chipmunk T10 (G-ARMC)	Privately owned, White Waltham
	WB711	DHC1 Chipmunk T10 (G-APPM)	The Aircraft Restoration Co, Duxford
	WB739	DHC1 Chipmunk T10 [8]	RAF, stored Newton
	WB754	DHC1 Chipmunk T10 [H]	AAC BFWF, Middle Wallop
	WB758	DHC1 Chipmunk T10 (7729M) [P]	Privately owned, Torbay
	WB763	DHC1 Chipmunk T10 (G-BBMR) [14]	Privately owned, Ottershaw
	WB922	Slingsby T21B Sedburgh	Privately owned, stored Rufforth
	WB981	Slingsby T21B Sedburgh (BGA 3238)	Privately owned, Aston Down
	WD286	DHC1 Chipmunk T10 (G-BBND) [J]	Privately owned, Bourn
	WD288	DHC1 Chipmunk T10 (G-AOSO) [38]	Privately owned, Charlton Park, Wilts
	WD289	DHC1 Chipmunk T10 [E]	RAF, stored Newton
	WD292	DHC1 Chipmunk T10 (G-BCRX)	Privately owned, Old Sarum
	WD293	DHC1 Chipmunk T10 (7645M) <ff>	No 1367 Sqn ATC, Caerleon
	WD305	DHC1 Chipmunk T10 (G-ARGG)	Privately owned, Coventry
	WD310	DHC1 Chipmunk T10 [B]	RAF, stored Newton
	WD318	DHC1 Chipmunk T10 (8207M) <ff>	RAF Halton
	WD325	DHC1 Chipmunk T10 [N]	AAC BFWF, Middle Wallop
	WD331	DHC1 Chipmunk T10 [J]	RAF, stored Newton
	WD355	DHC1 Chipmunk T10 (WD335) <ff>	No 1955 Sqn ATC, Wells, Somerset
	WD356	DHC1 Chipmunk T10 (7625M)	Privately owned, St Ives, Cambridgeshire
	WD363	DHC1 Chipmunk T10 (G-BCIH) [5]	Privately owned, Andrewsfield
	WD370	DHC1 Chipmunk T10 <ff>	No 176 Sqn ATC, Hove
	WD373	DHC1 Chipmunk T10 [12]	RAF No 2 AEF, Bournemouth
	WD374	DHC1 Chipmunk T10 [903]	*Sold to Australia as VH-BSR, November 1994*
	WD377	DHC1 Chipmunk T10	Dumfries & Galloway Av'n Mus, Tinwald Downs
	WD379	DHC1 Chipmunk T10 (WB696/ G-APLO) [K]	Privately owned, Jersey
	WD386	DHC1 Chipmunk T10 <ff>	Vintage Aircraft Team, Cranfield
	WD388	DHC1 Chipmunk T10 (G-BDIC)	Privately owned, Woodvale
	WD390	DHC1 Chipmunk T10 [68]	RAF, stored Newton
	WD413	Avro 652A Anson T21 (7881M/ G-BFIR)	Privately owned, Lee-on-Solent
	WD646	Gloster Meteor TT20 (8189M) [R]	Privately owned, North Weald
	WD686	Gloster Meteor NF11	Muckleburgh Collection, Weybourne
	WD790	Gloster Meteor NF11 (8743M)<ff>	North-East Aircraft Museum, Usworth
	WD931	EE Canberra B2 <ff>	RAF Cosford Aerospace Museum
	WD935	EE Canberra B2 (8440M) <ff>	Privately owned, Bridgnorth
	WD954	EE Canberra B2 <ff>	Privately owned, Romford, Essex
	WD955	EE Canberra T17A [EM]	*To R Norwegian AF Museum, Bodø 27 April 1995*
	WE113	EE Canberra T4 <ff>	Privately owned, Woodhurst, Cambridgeshire
	WE122	EE Canberra TT18 [845] <ff>	Privately owned, North Weald
	WE139	EE Canberra PR3 (8369M)	RAF Museum, Hendon
	WE168	EE Canberra PR3 (8049M) <ff>	Privately owned, Colchester
	WE173	EE Canberra PR3 (8740M) <ff>	Privately owned, Stock, Essex

Serial	Type (other identity) [code]	Owner/operator, location or fate	Notes
WE188	EE Canberra T4	Solway Aviation Society, Carlisle	
WE192	EE Canberra T4 <ff>	Jet Aviation Preservation Grp, Long Marston	
WE199	FE Canberra T4 <ff>	Macclesfield Historic Avn Soc, Barton	
WE275	DH112 Venom FB50 (J-1601/ G-VIDI)	Source Classic Jet Flight, Bournemouth	
WE402	DH112 Venom FB50 (J-1523/ G-VENI)	Source Classic Jet Flight, Bournemouth	
WE569	Auster T7 (G-ASAJ)	Privately owned, Bassingbourn	
WE600	Auster T7(mod) (7602M)	RAF Cosford Aerospace Museum	
WE925	Gloster Meteor F8	Classic Jet Aircraft Group, Loughborough	
WE982	Slingsby T30B Prefect TX1 (8781M)	RAF Cosford Aerospace Museum	
WE990	Slingsby T30B Prefect TX1 (BGA 2583)	Privately owned, RAF Swanton Morley	
WF118	Percival P57 Sea Prince T1 (G-DACA)	Privately owned, Charlwood, Surrey	
WF122	Percival P57 Sea Prince T1 [575/CU]	Flambards Village Theme Park, Helston	
WF125	Percival P57 Sea Prince T1 [576]	RN Predannack Fire School	
WF128	Percival P57 Sea Prince T1 (8611M)	Norfolk & Suffolk Aviation Museum, Flixton	
WF137	Percival P57 Sea Prince C1	SWWAPS, Lasham	
WF145	Hawker Sea Hawk F1 <ff>	Privately owned, Eaglescott	
WF225	Hawker Sea Hawk F1 [CU]	RNAS Culdrose, at main gate	
WF259	Hawker Sea Hawk F2 [171/A]	Royal Scottish Mus'm of Flight,E Fortune	
WF369	Vickers Varsity T1 [F]	Newark Air Museum, Winthorpe	
WF372	Vickers Varsity T1 [A]	Brooklands Museum, Weybridge	
WF376	Vickers Varsity T1	Bristol Airport Fire Section	
WF408	Vickers Varsity T1 (8395M)	RAF Northolt, for ground instruction	
WF410	Vickers Varsity T1 [F]	Brunel Technical College, Lulsgate	
WF643	Gloster Meteor F8 [X]	Norfolk & Suffolk Aviation Museum, Flixton	
WF714	Gloster Meteor F8 (WK914)	The Old Flying Machine Co, stored Duxford	
WF784	Gloster Meteor T7 (7895M)	RAF Quedgeley, at main gate	
WF825	Gloster Meteor T7 (8359M) [A]	Avon Avn Museum, stored Malmesbury	
WF877	Gloster Meteor T7 (G-BPOA)	39 Restoration Group, North Weald	
WF911	EE Canberra B2 <ff>	Pennine Aviation Museum, store	
WF916	EE Canberra T17 [EL]	*Scrapped at Wyton, February 1995*	
WF922	EE Canberra PR3	Midland Air Museum, Coventry	
WG300	DHC1 Chipmunk T10 <ff>	RAFGSA, Bicester	
WG303	DHC1 Chipmunk T10 (8208M) <ff>	RAFGSA, Bicester	
WG307	DHC1 Chipmunk T10 (G-BCYJ)	Privately owned, Shempston Fm, Lossiemouth	
WG308	DHC1 Chipmunk T10 [8]	RAF No 8 AEF, Shawbury	
WG316	DHC1 Chipmunk T10 (G-BCAH)	Privately owned, Shoreham	
WG321	DHC1 Chipmunk T10 [G]	AAC BFWF, Middle Wallop	
WG323	DHC1 Chipmunk T10 [F]	AAC BFWF, Middle Wallop	
WG348	DHC1 Chipmunk T10 (G-BBMV)	Privately owned, Moulton St Mary	
WG350	DHC1 Chipmunk T10 (G-BPAL)	Privately owned, Thruxton	
WG362	DHC1 Chipmunk T10 (8437M/ 8630M) <ff>		
WG403	DHC1 Chipmunk T10 [O] (wreck)	AAC, Middle Wallop, spares use	
WG407	DHC1 Chipmunk T10	RAF, stored Newton	
WG418	DHC1 Chipmunk T10 (8209M/ G-ATDY) <ff>	RAF, stored Newton	
WG419	DHC1 Chipmunk T10 (8206M) <ff>	No 1053 Sqn ATC, Armthorpe	
WG422	DHC1 Chipmunk T10 (8394M/ G-BFAX) [116]	The Aircraft Restoration Co, Duxford	
WG430	DHC1 Chipmunk T10 [3]	RAF No 1 AEF, Manston	
WG432	DHC1 Chipmunk T10 [L]	AAC BFWF, Middle Wallop	
WG458	DHC1 Chipmunk T10 [B]	RAF, stored Newton	
WG463	DHC1 Chipmunk T10 (8363M/ G-ATDX) <ff>	No 188 Sqn ATC, Ipswich	
WG465	DHC1 Chipmunk T10 (G-BCEY)	Privately owned, White Waltham	
WG469	DHC1 Chipmunk T10 [72]	RAF, stored Newton	
WG471	DHC1 Chipmunk T10 (8210M) <ff>	No 301 Sqn ATC, Bury St Edmunds	
WG472	DHC1 Chipmunk T10 (G-AOTY)	Privately owned, Netherthorpe	
WG477	DHC1 Chipmunk T10 (8362M/ G-ATDP) <ff>	No 281 Sqn ATC, Birkdale	
WG478	DHC1 Chipmunk T10	Privately owned,	
WG479	DHC1 Chipmunk T10 [F]	RAF, stored Newton	

Notes	Serial	Type (other identity) [code]	Owner/operator, location or fate
	WG480	DHC1 Chipmunk T10 [D]	RAF, stored Newton
	WG486	DHC1 Chipmunk T10	RAF BBMF, stored Newton
	WG511	Avro 696 Shackleton T4 (fuselage)	Flambards Village Theme Park, Helston
	WG718	WS51 Dragonfly HR3 [934]	Privately owned, East Yorkshire
	WG719	WS51 Dragonfly HR5 (G-BRMA) [902]	IHM, Weston-super-Mare
	WG724	WS51 Dragonfly HR5 [932]	North-East Aircraft Museum, Usworth
	WG751	WS51 Dragonfly HR5	Privately owned, Ramsgreave, Lancs
	WG754	WS51 Dragonfly HR3 (WG725/ 7703M) [912/CU]	Flambards Village Theme Park, Helston
	WG760	EE P1A (7755M)	RAF Cosford Aerospace Museum
	WG763	EE P1A (7816M)	Gtr Manchester Mus'm of Science & Industry
	WG768	Short SB5 (8005M)	RAF Cosford Aerospace Museum
	WG774	BAC 221	Science Museum, RNAS Yeovilton
	WG777	Fairey FD2 (7986M)	RAF Cosford Aerospace Museum
	WG789	EE Canberra B2/6 <ff>	Privately owned, Mendlesham, Suffolk
	WH132	Gloster Meteor T7 (7906M) [J]	No 276 Sqn ATC, Chelmsford
	WH166	Gloster Meteor T7 (8052M)	Privately owned, Birlingham, Worcs
	WH291	Gloster Meteor F8	SWWAPS, Lasham
	WH301	Gloster Meteor F8 (7930M) [T]	RAF Museum, Hendon
	WH364	Gloster Meteor F8 (8169M)	Avon Aviation Museum, stored Yatesbury
	WH453	Gloster Meteor D16 [L]	MoD(PE), stored DTEO Llanbedr
	WH646	EE Canberra T17A <ff>	Midland Air Museum, Coventry
	WH657	EE Canberra B2	Brenzett Aeronautical Museum
	WH665	EE Canberra T17 (8763M) [J]	BAe Filton, Fire Section
	WH699	EE Canberra B2T (WJ637/8755M)	RAFC Cranwell
	WH725	EE Canberra B2	Imperial War Museum, Duxford
	WH734	EE Canberra B2(mod)	MoD(PE), DTEO Llanbedr
	WH740	EE Canberra T17 (8762M) [K]	East Midlands Airport Aero Park
	WH773	EE Canberra PR7 (8696M)	Privately owned, Charlwood, Surrey
	WH774	EE Canberra PR7 (fuselage)	Scrapped at Farnborough, 1994
	WH775	EE Canberra PR7 (8128M/ 8868M) <ff>	Phoenix Aviation, Bruntingthorpe
	WH779	EE Canberra PR7 [BP]	RAF No 39(1 PRU) Sqn, Marham
	WH780	EE Canberra T22 <ff>	Privately owned, Stock, Essex
	WH780	EE Canberra T22 <rf>	RAF St Athan, Fire Section
	WH791	EE Canberra PR7 (8165M/8176M/ 8187M)	RAF Cottesmore, at main gate
	WH796	EE Canberra PR7 <ff>	Privately owned, Stock, Essex
	WH797	EE Canberra T22 <ff>	Privately owned, Stock, Essex
	WH797	EE Canberra T22 <rf>	RAF St Athan, Fire Section
	WH801	EE Canberra T22 <ff>	Privately owned, Stock, Essex
	WH803	EE Canberra T22 <ff>	Privately owned, Stock, Essex
	WH840	EE Canberra T4 (8350M) <ff>	Privately owned, Flixton
	WH846	EE Canberra T4	Yorkshire Air Museum, Elvington
	WH849	EE Canberra T4 [BE]	FR Aviation, Bournemouth
	WH850	EE Canberra T4 <ff>	Macclesfield Historical Av'n Soc, Barton
	WH854	EE Canberra T4 <ff>	Martin Baker Aircraft, Chalgrove
	WH863	EE Canberra T17 (8693M) <ff>	Newark Air Museum, Winthorpe
	WH876	EE Canberra B2(mod)	MoD(PE), DTEO Aberporth, instructional use
	WH887	EE Canberra TT18 [847]	MoD(PE), stored DTEO Llanbedr
	WH902	EE Canberra T17A [EK]	RAF Wyton
	WH903	EE Canberra B2 (8584M) <ff>	Yorkshire Air Museum, Elvington
	WH904	EE Canberra T19	Newark Air Museum, Winthorpe
	WH946	EE Canberra B6(mod) (8185M) <ff>	Privately owned, Tetney, Grimsby
	WH952	EE Canberra B6	Royal Arsenal, Woolwich
	WH953	EE Canberra B6(mod)	Scrapped at Farnborough, January 1995
	WH957	EE Canberra E15 (8869M) <ff> East Kirkby	Lincolnshire Av'n Heritage Centre,
	WH960	EE Canberra B15 (8344M) <ff>	Privately owned, Hucknall
	WH964	EE Canberra E15 (8870M) <ff>	Phoenix Aviation, Bruntingthorpe
	WH984	EE Canberra B15 (8101M) <ff>	Phoenix Aviation, Bruntingthorpe
	WH991	WS51 Dragonfly HR3	Privately owned, Elvington
	WJ231	Hawker Sea Fury FB11 (WE726) [115/O]	FAA Museum, Yeovilton
	WJ237	WAR Sea Fury <R> (G-BLTG) [113/O]	Privately owned, Langham
	WJ358	Auster AOP6 (G-ARYD)	Museum of Army Flying, stored Middle Wallop

Serial	Type (other identity) [code]	Owner/operator, location or fate	Notes
WJ565	EE Canberra T17 (8871M) <ff>	Phoenix Aviation, Bruntingthorpe	
WJ567	EE Canberra B2 <ff>	Privately owned, Houghton, Cambs	
WJ576	EE Canberra T17	Wales Aircraft Museum, Cardiff	
WJ603	EE Canberra B2 (8664M) <ff>	Privately owned, Stock, Essex	
WJ607	EE Canberra T17A (G-BVWU) [EB]	*Sold to South Africa as ZU-AUE, April 1995*	
WJ614	EE Canberra TT18 (N76765) [846]	Privately owned, St Athan	
WJ630	EE Canberra T17 [ED]	RAF, stored Wyton	
WJ633	EE Canberra T17A [EF]	RAF Wyton, Fire Section	
WJ636	EE Canberra TT18 [CX]	RAF Wyton, Fire Section	
WJ639	EE Canberra TT18 [39]	North-East Aircraft Museum, Usworth	
WJ640	EE Canberra B2 <ff>	Privately owned, Guildford	
WJ676	EE Canberra B2 (7796M) <ff>	Privately owned, Liverpool	
WJ677	EE Canberra B2 <ff>	RNAS Culdrose, Fire Section	
WJ680	EE Canberra TT18 (G-BURM) [CT]	Canberra Flight, North Weald	
WJ717	EE Canberra TT18 (9052M)	RAF CTTS, St Athan	
WJ721	EE Canberra TT18 [21]	Pennine Aviation Museum, Bacup	
WJ731	EE Canberra B2T [BK] <ff>	Derby World War 2 Avionics Museum	
WJ775	EE Canberra B6 (8581M) [J] (fuselage)	FSCTE, RAF Manston	
WJ821	EE Canberra PR7 (8668M)	Army, Bassingbourn, on display	
WJ863	EE Canberra T4 <ff>	Cambridge Airport Fire Section	
WJ865	EE Canberra T4	*Scrapped at Farnborough, January 1995*	
WJ866	EE Canberra T4 [AV]	RAF No 39(1 PRU) Sqn, Marham	
WJ872	EE Canberra T4 (8492M) <ff>	No 327 Sqn ATC, Kilmarnock	
WJ874	EE Canberra T4 [AS]	RAF, stored Shawbury	
WJ876	EE Canberra T4 <ff>		
WJ880	EE Canberra T4 (8491M) <ff>	Dumfries & Galloway Av'n Mus, Tinwald Downs	
WJ893	Vickers Varsity T1	T&EE Aberporth Fire Section	
WJ903	Vickers Varsity T1 [C] <ff>	Dumfries & Galloway Av'n Mus, Tinwald Downs	
WJ945	Vickers Varsity T1 (G-BEDV) [21]	Imperial War Museum, Duxford	
WJ975	EE Canberra T19 [S]	Bomber County Aviation Museum, Hemswell	
WJ981	EE Canberra T17A [EN]	RAF Wyton, Fire Section	
WJ986	EE Canberra T17 [EP]	*Scrapped at Wyton, February 1995*	
WJ992	EE Canberra T4	FR Aviation, Bournemouth	
WK102	EE Canberra T17 (8780M) <ff>	Privately owned, Welshpool	
WK118	EE Canberra TT18 <ff>	Privately owned, Worcester	
WK119	EE Canberra B2 <ff>	RAF Wyton, Fire Section	
WK122	EE Canberra TT18 [22]	Flambards Village Theme Park, Helston	
WK124	EE Canberra TT18 (9093M) [CR]	FSCTE, RAF Manston	
WK126	EE Canberra TT18 (N2138J) [843]	Gloucestershire Aviation Collection, Staverton	
WK127	EE Canberra T17 (8985M) <ff>	Air Scouts, Bassingbourn	
WK128	EE Canberra B2	MoD(PE), DTEO Llanbedr	
WK142	EE Canberra TT18 (N76764) [848]	Privately owned, St Athan	
WK143	EE Canberra B2	DTEO Llanbedr Fire Section	
WK144	EE Canberra B2 (8689M) <ff>	Privately owned, Stock, Essex	
WK163	EE Canberra B6(mod) (G-BVWC)	Classic Aviation Projects, Bruntingthorpe	
WK198	VS Swift F4 (7428M) (fuselage)	North-East Aircraft Museum, Usworth	
WK275	VS Swift F4	Privately owned, Upper Hill, nr Leominster	
WK277	VS Swift FR5 (7719M) [N]	Newark Air Museum, Winthorpe	
WK281	VS Swift FR5 (7712M) [S]	Tangmere Military Aviation Museum	
WK511	DHC1 Chipmunk T10 (G-BVBT) [905]	Kennet Aviation, Cranfield	
WK512	DHC1 Chipmunk T10 [A]	AAC BFWF, Middle Wallop	
WK517	DHC1 Chipmunk T10 [84]	RAF, stored Newton	
WK518	DHC1 Chipmunk T10	RAF BBMF, Coningsby	
WK522	DHC1 Chipmunk T10 (G-BCOU)	Privately owned, High Easter	
WK549	DHC1 Chipmunk T10 (G-BTWF) [Y]	Privately owned, Rufforth	
WK550	DHC1 Chipmunk T10 [G]	RAF No 8 AEF, Shawbury	
WK554	DHC1 Chipmunk T10 [4]	RAF No 1 AEF, Manston	
WK558	DHC1 Chipmunk T10 (G-ARMG)	Privately owned, Wellesbourne Mountford	
WK559	DHC1 Chipmunk T10 [M]	AAC BFWF, Middle Wallop	
WK562	DHC1 Chipmunk T10 [91]	RAF, stored Newton	
WK570	DHC1 Chipmunk T10 (8211M) <ff>	No 424 Sqn ATC, Southampton	
WK572	DHC1 Chipmunk T10 [92]	RAF, stored Newton	
WK574	DHC1 Chipmunk T10 (G-BVPC)	*Sold to Australia, December 1994*	
WK576	DHC1 Chipmunk T10 (8357M) <ff>	No 1206 Sqn ATC, Lichfield	

Notes	Serial	Type (other identity) [code]	Owner/operator, location or fate
	WK584	DHC1 Chipmunk T10 (7556M) <ff>	No 216 Sqn ATC, Bawtry
	WK585	DHC1 Chipmunk T10	RAF, stored Newton
	WK586	DHC1 Chipmunk T10 [V]	AAC BFWF, Middle Wallop
	WK589	DHC1 Chipmunk T10 [C]	Privately owned,
	WK590	DHC1 Chipmunk T10 [69]	RAF, stored Newton
	WK608	DHC1 Chipmunk T10 [906]	RN Historic Flt, Yeovilton
	WK609	DHC1 Chipmunk T10 [93]	RAF, stored Newton
	WK611	DHC1 Chipmunk T10 (G-ARWB)	Privately owned, White Waltham
	WK613	DHC1 Chipmunk T10 [P]	Pennine Aviation Museum, Bacup
	WK620	DHC1 Chipmunk T10 [T] (fuselage)	AAC, Middle Wallop, spares use
	WK621	DHC1 Chipmunk T10 (G-BDBL)	*Sold as ZK-UAS, September 1994*
	WK622	DHC1 Chipmunk T10 (G-BCZH)	Privately owned, Horsford
	WK624	DHC1 Chipmunk T10 (G-BWHI) [M]	The Aircraft Restoration Co, Duxford
	WK626	DHC1 Chipmunk T10 (8213M) <ff>	Wiltshire Historic Aviation Grp, Salisbury
	WK628	DHC1 Chipmunk T10 (G-BBMW)	Privately owned, Shoreham
	WK630	DHC1 Chipmunk T10 [11]	RAF No 2 AEF, Bournemouth
	WK633	DHC1 Chipmunk T10 [B]	Privately owned,
	WK634	DHC1 Chipmunk T10 [902]	*Sold to Canada, January 1995*
	WK635	DHC1 Chipmunk T10	RN, stored Shawbury
	WK638	DHC1 Chipmunk T10 (G-BWJZ)	Privately owned, Spanhoe Lodge
	WK639	DHC1 Chipmunk T10 (G-BWJU)]	Privately owned, Blackburn
	WK640	DHC1 Chipmunk T10 [C]	RAF, stored Newton
	WK642	DHC1 Chipmunk T10 [94]	RAF, stored Newton
	WK643	DHC1 Chipmunk T10 [G]	RAF CFS, Scampton
	WK654	Gloster Meteor F8 (8092M) [X]	City of Norwich Aviation Museum
	WK800	Gloster Meteor D16 [Z]	MoD(PE), DTEO Llanbedr
WK864	Gloster Meteor F8 (WL168/ 7750M) [C]	RAF Finningley on display
	WK935	Gloster Meteor Prone Pilot (7869M)	RAF Cosford Aerospace Museum
	WK991	Gloster Meteor F8 (7825M)	Imperial War Museum, Duxford
	WL131	Gloster Meteor F8 (7751M) <ff>	4th Guernsey Air Scouts, Guernsey Airport
	WL181	Gloster Meteor F8 [X]	North-East Aircraft Museum, Usworth
	WL332	Gloster Meteor T7 [888]	Privately owned, Long Marston
	WL345	Gloster Meteor T7	Privately owned, Hollington, E Sussex
	WL349	Gloster Meteor T7 [Z]	Gloucestershire Airport, on display
	WL360	Gloster Meteor T7 (7920M) [G]	Gloucestershire Av'n Coll, Staverton
	WL375	Gloster Meteor T7	Dumfries & Galloway Av'n Mus, Tinwald Downs
	WL405	Gloster Meteor T7	Martin Baker Aircraft, Chalgrove, spares use
	WL419	Gloster Meteor T7	Martin Baker Aircraft, Chalgrove
	WL505	DH100 Vampire FB9 (7705M/ G-FBIX)	Vintage Aircraft Team, Bruntingthorpe
	WL626	Vickers Varsity T1 (G-BHDD) [P]	East Midlands Airport Aero Park
	WL627	Vickers Varsity T1 (8488M) [D] <ff>	Privately owned, Preston, Humberside
	WL635	Vickers Varsity T1	RAF Machrihanish Police School
	WL679	Vickers Varsity T1 (9155M)	RAF Cosford Aerospace Museum
	WL732	BP P108 Sea Balliol T21	RAF Cosford Aerospace Museum
	WL756	Avro 696 Shackleton AEW2 (9101M)	RAF St Mawgan, Fire Section
	WL795	Avro 696 Shackleton MR2C (8753M) [T]	RAF St Mawgan, on display
WL925	Slingsby T31B Cadet TX3 (WV925) <ff>	RAF No 633 VGS, Cosford
	WM145	AW Meteor NF11 <ff>	N Yorks Aircraft Recovery Centre, Chop Gate
	WM167	AW Meteor NF11 (G-LOSM)	Jet Heritage Ltd, Bournemouth
	WM223	AW Meteor TT20	SWWAPS, Lasham
	WM267	Gloster Meteor NF11 <ff>	Night Fighter Preservation Group, Elvington
	WM292	AW Meteor TT20 [841]	Wales Aircraft Museum, Cardiff
WM311	AW Meteor TT20 (WM224/8177M)	Privately owned, North Weald
WM366	AW Meteor NF13 (4X-FNA)	SWWAPS, Lasham
	WM367	AW Meteor NF13 <ff>	Privately owned, North Weald
	WM571	DH112 Sea Venom FAW21 [VL]	Southampton Hall of Aviation
	WM729	DH113 Vampire NF10 [A] <ff>	Mosquito Aircraft Museum, London Colney
	WM913	Hawker Sea Hawk FB5 (8162M) [456/J]	Newark Air Museum, Winthorpe
	WM961	Hawker Sea Hawk FB5 [J]	Caernarfon Air World
	WM969	Hawker Sea Hawk FB5 [10/Z]	Imperial War Museum, Duxford
	WM993	Hawker Sea Hawk FB5 [034]	Privately owned, Peasedown St John

Serial	Type (other identity) [code]	Owner/operator, location or fate	Notes
WM994	Hawker Sea Hawk FB5 (G-SEAH)	Sold to the USA as N994WM, December 1994	
WN105	Hawker Sea Hawk FB3 (WF299/ 8164M)	Privately owned, Birlingham, Worcs	
WN108	Hawker Sea Hawk FB5 [033]	Ulster Aviation Society, Langford Lodge	
WN149	BP P108 Balliol T2 <ff>	Boulton-Paul Society, Wolverhampton	
WN411	Fairey Gannet AS1 (fuselage)	Privately owned, Southampton	
WN493	WS51 Dragonfly HR5	FAA Museum, RNAS Yeovilton	
WN499	WS51 Dragonfly HR5 [Y]	Caernarfon Air World	
WN516	BP P108 Balliol T2 <ff>	North-East Aircraft Museum, Usworth	
WN534	BP P108 Balliol T2 <ff>	Boulton-Paul Society, Wolverhampton	
WN890	Hawker Hunter F2 <ff>	Robertsbridge Aviation Society	
WN904	Hawker Hunter F2 (7544M) [3]	RE 39 Regt, Waterbeach, on display	
WN907	Hawker Hunter F2 (7416M) <ff>	Blyth Valley Aviation Collection, Walpole	
WP180	Hawker Hunter F5 (WP190/ 7582M/8473M) [K]	Gloucestershire Aviation Collection, Staverton	
WP185	Hawker Hunter F5 (7583M)	Privately owned, RAF Cosford	
WP250	DH113 Vampire NF10 <ff>	Privately owned, Tamworth	
WP255	DH113 Vampire NF10 <ff>	South Yorkshire Aviation Museum, Firbeck	
WP270	EoN Eton TX1 (8598M)	Gtr Manchester Mus'm of Science & Industry	
WP271	EoN Eton TX1	Privately owned, stored Keevil	
WP309	Percival P57 Sea Prince T1 [570/CU]	Privately owned, Carlisle	
WP313	Percival P57 Sea Prince T1 [568/CU]	FAA Museum, stored Wroughton	
WP314	Percival P57 Sea Prince T1 (8634M) [573/CU]	Privately owned, Carlisle Airport	
WP321	Percival P57 Sea Prince T1 (G-BRFC) [750/CU]	Aces High, North Weald	
WP503	WS51 Dragonfly HR3 [901]	Privately owned, Storwood, East Yorks	
WP515	EE Canberra B2 <ff>	Wales Aircraft Museum, Cardiff	
WP772	DHC1 Chipmunk T10 [Q] (wreck)	Privately owned, St Athan	
WP776	DHC1 Chipmunk T10 [817/CU]	RN, stored Shawbury	
WP784	DHC1 Chipmunk T10 <ff>	Privately owned, Boston	
WP786	DHC1 Chipmunk T10 [G]	RAF, stored Newton	
WP788	DHC1 Chipmunk T10 (G-BCHL)	Privately owned, Sleap	
WP790	DHC1 Chipmunk T10 (G-BBNC) [T]	Mosquito Aircraft Museum, London Colney	
WP795	DHC1 Chipmunk T10 (G-BVZZ) [901]	Privately owned, Lee-on-Solent	
WP800	DHC1 Chipmunk T10 (G-BCXN) [2]	Privately owned, Halton	
WP801	DHC1 Chipmunk T10 [911]	Sold to Canada, January 1995	
WP803	DHC1 Chipmunk T10 [C]	RAF, stored Newton	
WP805	DHC1 Chipmunk T10 [D]	Privately owned,	
WP808	DHC1 Chipmunk T10 (G-BDEU)	Privately owned, Binham	
WP809	DHC1 Chipmunk T10 (G-BVTX) [778]	Privately owned, Husbands Bosworth	
WP831	DHC1 Chipmunk T10 (G-BBMT)	Privately owned, Little Gransden	
WP833	DHC1 Chipmunk T10 [A]	RAF, stored Newton	
WP835	DHC1 Chipmunk T10 (G-BDCB)	Sold to Germany, August 1995	
WP837	DHC1 Chipmunk T10 [L]	RAF, stored Newton	
WP839	DHC1 Chipmunk T10 [A]	RAF No 8 AEF, Shawbury	
WP840	DHC1 Chipmunk T10 [9]	RAF No 2 AEF, Bournemouth	
WP843	DHC1 Chipmunk T10 (G-BDBP)	Privately owned, Booker	
WP844	DHC1 Chipmunk T10 [85]	RAF, stored Newton	
WP845	DHC1 Chipmunk T10 <ff>	Vintage Aircraft Team, Bruntingthorpe	
WP855	DHC1 Chipmunk T10 [5]	RAF No 1 AEF, Manston	
WP856	DHC1 Chipmunk T10 (G-BVWP) [904]	Privately owned, Cuckfield	
WP857	DHC1 Chipmunk T10 (G-BDRJ) [24]	Privately owned, Elstree	
WP859	DHC1 Chipmunk T10 [E]	RAF No 8 AEF, Shawbury	
WP860	DHC1 Chipmunk T10	RAF, stored Newton	
WP863	DHC1 Chipmunk T10 (8360M/ G-ATJI) <ff>	No 2293 Sqn ATC, Marlborough	
WP864	DHC1 Chipmunk T10 (8214M) <ff>	RAF, stored Newton	
WP869	DHC1 Chipmunk T10 (8215M) <ff>	RAF	
WP871	DHC1 Chipmunk T10 [W]	AAC BFWF, Middle Wallop	
WP872	DHC1 Chipmunk T10	RAF, stored Newton	

Notes	Serial	Type (other identity) [code]	Owner/operator, location or fate
	WP896	DHC1 Chipmunk T10 [M]	Privately owned,
	WP900	DHC1 Chipmunk T10 [V]	Privately owned,
	WP901	DHC1 Chipmunk T10 [B]	RAF, stored Newton
	WP903	DHC1 Chipmunk T10 (G-BCGC)	RN Gliding Club, Culdrose
	WP904	DHC1 Chipmunk T10 [909]	Sold to Canada, January 1995
	WP906	DHC1 Chipmunk T10 [816/CU]	RN, stored Shawbury
	WP907	DHC1 Chipmunk T10 <ff> (7970M)	Privately owned, Reading
	WP912	DHC1 Chipmunk T10 (8467M)	RAF Cosford Aerospace Museum
	WP914	DHC1 Chipmunk T10 [E]	RAF, stored Newton
	WP920	DHC1 Chipmunk T10 [10]	RAF No 2 AEF, Bournemouth
	WP921	DHC1 Chipmunk T10 <ff>	No 1924 Sqn ATC, Croydon
	WP925	DHC1 Chipmunk T10 [C]	AAC BFWF, Middle Wallop
	WP927	DHC1 Chipmunk T10 (8216M/ G-ATJK) <ff>	RAF, stored Newton
	WP928	DHC1 Chipmunk T10 [D]	AAC BFWF, Middle Wallop
	WP929	DHC1 Chipmunk T10 [F]	RAF No 8 AEF, Shawbury
	WP930	DHC1 Chipmunk T10 [J]	AAC BFWF, Middle Wallop
	WP962	DHC1 Chipmunk T10 [C]	RAF, stored Newton
	WP964	DHC1 Chipmunk T10 [Y]	AAC BFWF, Middle Wallop
	WP967	DHC1 Chipmunk T10	RAF, stored Newton
	WP970	DHC1 Chipmunk T10 [T]	RAF, stored Newton
	WP971	DHC1 Chipmunk T10 (G-ATHD)	Privately owned, Denham
	WP972	DHC1 Chipmunk T10 (8667M) <ff>	
	WP974	DHC1 Chipmunk T10 [9R]	RAF, stored Newton
	WP976	DHC1 Chipmunk T10 (WP791/ G-APTS)	Privately owned, Booker
	WP977	DHC1 Chipmunk T10 (G-BHRD) [N]	Privately owned, Kidlington
	WP978	DHC1 Chipmunk T10 (7467M) <ff>	RAF No 2 AEF, Bournemouth
	WP981	DHC1 Chipmunk T10 [D]	RAF, stored Newton
	WP983	DHC1 Chipmunk T10 [B]	AAC BFWF, Middle Wallop
	WP984	DHC1 Chipmunk T10 [H]	RAF, stored Newton
	WR410	DH112 Venom FB54 (J-1790/ G-BLKA) [N]	Vintage Aircraft Team, Bruntingthorpe
	WR539	DH112 Venom FB4 (8399M) [F]	Mosquito Aircraft Museum, London Colney
	WR960	Avro 696 Shackleton AEW2 (8772M)	Gtr Manchester Mus'm of Science & Industry
	WR963	Avro 696 Shackleton AEW2	Air Antique, Coventry
	WR971	Avro 696 Shackleton MR3 (8119M) [Q]	Privately owned, Narborough, Norfolk
	WR974	Avro 696 Shackleton MR3 (8117M) [K]	Privately owned, Charlwood, Surrey
	WR977	Avro 696 Shackleton MR3 (8186M) [B]	Newark Air Museum, Winthorpe
	WR982	Avro 696 Shackleton MR3 (8106M) [J]	Privately owned, Charlwood, Surrey
	WR985	Avro 696 Shackleton MR3 (8103M) [H]	Privately owned, Long Marston
	WS103	Gloster Meteor T7 [709/VL]	FAA Museum, Crawley College
	WS692	Gloster Meteor NF12 (7605M) [C]	Newark Air Museum, Winthorpe
	WS726	Gloster Meteor NF14 (7960M) [G]	No 1855 Sqn ATC, Royton
	WS739	Gloster Meteor NF14 (7961M)	Newark Air Museum, Winthorpe
	WS760	Gloster Meteor NF14 (7964M)	Meteor Flight, stored Yatesbury
	WS774	Gloster Meteor NF14 (7959M)	Privately owned, Fearn, Highlands
	WS776	Gloster Meteor NF14 (7716M) [K]	RAF North Luffenham, at main gate
	WS788	Gloster Meteor NF14 (7967M) [Z]	Yorkshire Air Museum, Elvington
	WS792	Gloster Meteor NF14 (7965M) [K]	Privately owned, Brighouse Bay, D&G
	WS807	Gloster Meteor NF14 (7973M) [N]	Meteor Flight, stored Yatesbury
	WS832	Gloster Meteor NF14 [W]	Solway Aviation Society, Carlisle Airport
	WS838	Gloster Meteor NF14	Midland Air Museum, Coventry
	WS843	Gloster Meteor NF14 (7937M) [Y]	RAF Museum, Hendon
	WT121	Douglas Skyraider AEW1 (WT983) [415/CU]	FAA Museum, stored RNAS Yeovilton
	WT308	EE Canberra B(I)6	RN, Predannack Fire School
	WT309	EE Canberra B(I)6	DTEO Boscombe Down, Apprentice School
	WT327	EE Canberra B(I)8	Classic Aviation Projects, Bruntingthorpe
	WT333	EE Canberra B6(mod) (G-BVXC)	Classic Aviation Projects, Bruntingthorpe
	WT339	EE Canberra B(I)8 (8198M)	RAF Barkston Heath Fire Section
	WT480	EE Canberra T4 [AT]	RAF No 39(1 PRU) Sqn, Marham

Serial	Type (other identity) [code]	Owner/operator, location or fate	Notes
WT482	EE Canberra T4 <f>	Privately owned, Long Marston	
WT483	EE Canberra T4 [83]	Privately owned, Long Marston	
WT486	EE Canberra T4 (8102M) [C]	*Scrapped Belfast Airport, June 1995*	
WT488	EE Canberra T4	BAe Dunsfold Fire Section	
WT507	EE Canberra PR7 (8131M/8548M) [44] <f>	No 384 Sqn ATC, Mansfield	
WT509	EE Canberra PR7 [BR]	RAF No 39(1 PRU) Sqn, Marham	
WT510	EE Canberra T22 <f>	Privately owned, Stock, Essex	
WT519	EE Canberra PR7 [CH]	RAF Wyton, Fire Section	
WT520	EE Canberra PR7 (8094M/ 8184M) <f>	Privately owned, Burntwood, Staffs	
WT525	EE Canberra T22 <f>	Privately owned, South Woodham Ferrers	
WT532	EE Canberra PR7 (8728M/ 8890M) [Z]	Bournemouth Int'l Airport, Fire Section	
WT534	EE Canberra PR7 (8549M) <f>	No 492 Sqn ATC, Shirley, W. Midlands	
WT536	EE Canberra PR7 (8063M) <f>	Privately owned, Bruntingthorpe	
WT537	EE Canberra PR7	BAe Samlesbury, on display	
WT555	Hawker Hunter F1 (7499M)	Privately owned, Greenford, London	
WT569	Hawker Hunter F1 (7491M)	No 2117 Sqn ATC, Kenfig Hill, Mid-Glamorgan	
WT612	Hawker Hunter F1 (7496M)	RAF Henlow on display	
WT619	Hawker Hunter F1 (7525M)	Gtr Manchester Mus'm of Science & Industry	
WT648	Hawker Hunter F1 (7530M) <f>	The Air Defence Collection, Salisbury	
WT651	Hawker Hunter F1 [C]	Newark Air Museum, Winthorpe	
WT660	Hawker Hunter F1 (7421M) [C]	Privately owned, New Byth, Grampian	
WT680	Hawker Hunter F1 (7533M) [Z]	No 1429 Sqn ATC, at T&EE Aberporth	
WT684	Hawker Hunter F1 (7422M)	Jet Aviation Preservation Grp, Long Marston	
WT694	Hawker Hunter F1 (7510M)	Caernarfon Air World	
WT711	Hawker Hunter GA11 [833/DD]	Caernarfon Air World	
WT720	Hawker Hunter F51 (RDAF E-408/ 8565M) [B]	RAF Sealand, on display	
WT722	Hawker Hunter T8C (G-BWGN) [878/VL]	Classic Jet Aircraft Co, Exeter	
WT723	Hawker Hunter PR11 [866/VL,3]	SFDO, RNAS Culdrose	
WT744	Hawker Hunter GA11 [868/VL]	Privately owned, Eaglescott	
WT746	Hawker Hunter F4 (7770M) [A]	Army, Saighton, Chester	
WT799	Hawker Hunter T8C [879/VL]	Privately owned, Ipswich	
WT804	Hawker Hunter GA11 [831/DD]	FETC, Moreton-in-Marsh	
WT806	Hawker Hunter GA11	RN, stored Shawbury	
WT859	Supermarine 544 <f>	Brooklands Aviation Museum, Weybridge	
WT867	Slingsby T31B Cadet TX3	Privately owned, Eaglescott	
WT899	Slingsby T31B Cadet TX3	Privately owned, Rush Green	
WT902	Slingsby T31B Cadet TX3 (BGA 3147)	Privately owned, Lleweni Parc, Clwyd	
WT905	Slingsby T31B Cadet TX3	Privately owned, Bridge of Don, Grampian	
WT910	Slingsby T31B Cadet TX3 (BGA 3953)	Privately owned, Challock	
WT933	Bristol 171 Sycamore 3 (G-ALSW/ 7709M)	Newark Air Museum, Winthorpe	
WV106	Douglas Skyraider AEW1 [427/C]	Flambards Village Theme Park, Helston	
WV198	Sikorsky S55 Whirlwind HAR21 (G-BJWY) [K]	Solway Aviation Society, Carlisle	
WV256	Hawker Hunter GA11 [862/VL]	RN, stored Shawbury	
WV276	Hawker Hunter F4 (7847M) [D]	DRA Avionics & Sensors Dept, Farnborough	
WV318	Hawker Hunter T7B	Privately owned, Cranfield	
WV322	Hawker Hunter T8C (9096M) [Y]	SIF, RAFC Cranwell	
WV332	Hawker Hunter F4 (7673M) <f>	No 1254 Sqn ATC, Godalming	
WV372	Hawker Hunter T7 [877/VL,1]	SFDO, RNAS Culdrose	
WV381	Hawker Hunter GA11 [732/VL]	UKAEA, Culham, Oxon	
WV382	Hawker Hunter GA11 [830/VL]	Jet Avn Preservation Grp, Long Marston	
WV383	Hawker Hunter T7	MoD(PE)/DRA, DTEO Boscombe Down	
WV395	Hawker Hunter F4 (8001M)	BAe Dunsfold, Fire Section	
WV396	Hawker Hunter T8C [879/VL]	RN, stored Shawbury	
WV483	Percival P56 Provost T1 (7693M) [N-E]	Privately owned	
WV486	Percival P56 Provost T1 (7694M) [N-D]	Privately owned, Grazeley, Berks	
WV493	Percival P56 Provost T1 (G-BDYG/7696M)	Royal Scottish Mus'm of Flight, E Fortune	

Notes	Serial	Type (other identity) [code]	Owner/operator, location or fate
	WV499	Percival P56 Provost T1 (7698M) [P-G]	Privately owned, North Weald
	WV562	Percival P56 Provost T1 (7606M) [P-C]	RAF Cosford Aerospace Museum, stored
	WV605	Percival P56 Provost T1 [T-B]	Norfolk & Suffolk Aviation Museum, Flixton
	WV606	Percival P56 Provost T1 (7622M) [P-B]	Newark Air Museum, Winthorpe
	WV666	Percival P56 Provost T1 (7925M/ G-BTDH) [O-D]	Privately owned, Shoreham
	WV679	Percival P56 Provost T1 (7615M) [O-J]	Privately owned, Wellesbourne Mountford
	WV703	Percival P66 Pembroke C1 (8108M/G-IIIM)	Privately owned, Tattershall Thorpe
	WV705	Percival P66 Pembroke C1 <ff>	Southampton Hall of Aviation, stored
	WV740	Percival P66 Pembroke C1 (G-BNPH)	Privately owned, Jersey
	WV746	Percival P66 Pembroke C1 (8938M)	RAF Cosford Aerospace Museum
	WV753	Percival P66 Pembroke C1 (8113M)	Cardiff Airport Fire Section
	WV781	Bristol 171 Sycamore HR12 (G-ALTD/7839M)	Caernarfon Air World
	WV783	Bristol 171 Sycamore HR12 (G-ALSP/7841M)	RAF Museum Restoration Centre, Cardington
	WV787	EE Canberra B2/8 (8799M)	Newark Air Museum, Winthorpe
	WV795	Hawker Sea Hawk FGA6 (8151M)	Privately owned, Bournemouth
	WV797	Hawker Sea Hawk FGA6 (8155M) [491/J]	Midland Air Museum, Coventry
	WV798	Hawker Sea Hawk FGA6 [026/CU]	SWWAPS, Lasham
	WV826	Hawker Sea Hawk FGA6 [147/Z]	Wales Aircraft Museum, Cardiff
	WV843	Hawker Sea Hawk FGA6 <ff>	*Actually WF145*
	WV856	Hawker Sea Hawk FGA6 [163]	FAA Museum, RNAS Yeovilton
	WV903	Hawker Sea Hawk FGA4 (8153M) [128/C]	RN Historic Flight, at BAe Dunsfold
	WV908	Hawker Sea Hawk FGA6 (8154M) [188/A]	RN Historic Flight, at BAe Dunsfold
	WW138	DH112 Sea Venom FAW22 [227/Z]	FAA Museum, RNAS Yeovilton
	WW145	DH112 Sea Venom FAW22 [680/LM]	Royal Scottish Mus'm of Flight,E Fortune
	WW217	DH112 Sea Venom FAW22 [736]	Newark Air Museum, Winthorpe
	WW388	Percival P56 Provost T1 (7616M) [O-F]	South Yorkshire Aviation Museum, Firbeck
	WW421	Percival P56 Provost T1 (7688M) [P-B]	Lincolnshire Av'n Heritage Centre, East Kirkby
	WW442	Percival P56 Provost T1 (7618M) [N]	Privately owned, Kings Langley
	WW444	Percival P56 Provost T1 [D]	Privately owned
	WW447	Percival P56 Provost T1	Privately owned, Grazeley, Berks
	WW453	Percival P56 Provost T1 (G-TMKI) [W-S]	Kennet Aviation, Cranfield
	WW654	Hawker Hunter GA11 [834/DD]	Privately owned, Portsmouth
WX660		Hover-Air HA-5 Hoverhawk III (XW660)	Privately owned, Cheltenham
	WX788	DH112 Venom NF3	Night Fighter Preservation Team, Elvington
	WX853	DH112 Venom NF3 (7443M)	Mosquito Aircraft Museum, London Colney
	WX905	DH112 Venom NF3 (7458M)	Newark Air Museum, Winthorpe
	WZ415	DH115 Vampire T11 [72]	No 2 Sqn ATC, Leavesden
	WZ425	DH115 Vampire T11	Privately owned, Birlingham
	WZ450	DH115 Vampire T11 <ff>	Lashenden Air Warfare Museum, Headcorn
	WZ458	DH115 Vampire T11 (7728M) [31] <ff>	Blyth Valley Aviation Collection, Walpole
	WZ464	DH115 Vampire T11 (N62430) [40]	Vintage Aircraft Team, Bruntingthorpe
	WZ507	DH115 Vampire T11 (G-VTII)	Vintage Aircraft Team, Bruntingthorpe
	WZ514	DH115 Vampire T11	*Scrapped*
	WZ515	DH115 Vampire T11 [60]	Solway Aviation Society, Carlisle
	WZ518	DH115 Vampire T11	North-East Aircraft Museum, Usworth
	WZ549	DH115 Vampire T11 (8118M) [F]	Ulster Heritage Centre, Langford Lodge
	WZ550	DH115 Vampire T11 (7902M) [NF]	*Sold to Malta, October 1995*

Serial	Type (other identity) [code]	Owner/operator, location or fate	Notes
WZ553	DH115 Vampire T11 (G-DHYY) [40]	Source Classic Jet Flight, Bruntingthorpe	
WZ557	DH115 Vampire T11	N Yorks Aircraft Recovery Centre, Chop Gate	
WZ559	DH115 Vampire T11 (7736M) [45] <ff>	RAF Halton Fire Section	
WZ581	DH115 Vampire T11 <ff>	Privately owned, Hemel Hempstead	
WZ584	DH115 Vampire T11 [K]	St Albans College of Further Education	
WZ589	DH115 Vampire T11 [19]	Lashenden Air Warfare Museum, Headcorn	
WZ590	DH115 Vampire T11 [19]	Imperial War Museum, Duxford	
WZ608	DH115 Vampire T11 [56] <ff>	Privately owned, Romford	
WZ620	DH115 Vampire T11 [68]	Avon Aviation Museum, Yatesbury	
WZ662	Auster AOP9 (G-BKVK)	Privately owned, Middle Wallop	
WZ706	Auster AOP9 (7851M/G-BURR)	Privately owned, Middle Wallop	
WZ711	Auster AOP9/Beagle E3 (G-AVHT)	Privately owned, Middle Wallop	
WZ721	Auster AOP9	Museum of Army Flying, Middle Wallop	
WZ724	Auster AOP9 (7432M)	AAC Middle Wallop, at main gate	
WZ736	Avro 707A (7868M)	Gtr Manchester Mus'm of Science & Industry	
WZ744	Avro 707C (7932M)	RAF Cosford Aerospace Museum	
WZ753	Slingsby T38 Grasshopper TX1	Southampton Hall of Aviation	
WZ765	Slingsby T38 Grasshopper TX1	RAFGSA, Bicester	
WZ767	Slingsby T38 Grasshopper TX1	North-East Aircraft Museum, Usworth	
WZ769	Slingsby T38 Grasshopper TX1	Privately owned, stored Rufforth	
WZ779	Slingsby T38 Grasshopper TX1	Privately owned, Old Sarum	
WZ791	Slingsby T38 Grasshopper TX1 (8944M)	RAF Museum, Hendon	
WZ792	Slingsby T38 Grasshopper TX1	Privately owned, Falgunzeon, D&G	
WZ793	Slingsby T38 Grasshopper TX1	Whitgift School, Croydon	
WZ796	Slingsby T38 Grasshopper TX1	Privately owned, Nympsfield, stored	
WZ822	Slingsby T38 Grasshopper TX1 (BGA 3875)	Robertsbridge Aviation Society, Mayfield	
WZ826	Vickers Valiant B(K)1 (XD826/ 7872M) <ff>	Privately owned, Rayleigh, Essex	
WZ829	Slingsby T38 Grasshopper TX1	RAFGSA, stored Bicester	
WZ831	Slingsby T38 Grasshopper TX1	Privately owned, Nympsfield	
WZ845	DHC1 Chipmunk T10 [6]	RAF No 1 AEF, Manston	
WZ846	DHC1 Chipmunk T10 (G-BCSC/ 8439M) <ff>	No 1404 Sqn ATC, Chatham	
WZ847	DHC1 Chipmunk T10 [F]	RAF, stored Newton	
WZ856	DHC1 Chipmunk T10	RAF, stored Newton	
WZ862	DHC1 Chipmunk T10 [A]	RAF, stored Newton	
WZ866	DHC1 Chipmunk T10 (8217M/ G-ATEB) <ff>	Dumfries & Galloway Av'n Mus, Tinwald Downs	
WZ868	DHC1 Chipmunk T10 (G-BCIW) [H]	Privately owned, Fownhope, H&W	
WZ868	DHC1 Chipmunk T10 (WG322/ G-ARMF) [H]	Privately owned, Audley End	
WZ869	DHC1 Chipmunk T10 (8019M) [R] <ff>	No 395 Sqn ATC, Handforth	
WZ872	DHC1 Chipmunk T10 [E]	RAF, stored Newton	
WZ876	DHC1 Chipmunk T10 (G-BBWN)	Privately owned, Netherthorpe	
WZ877	DHC1 Chipmunk T10	RAF, stored Newton	
WZ878	DHC1 Chipmunk T10 [86]	RAF, stored Newton	
WZ879	DHC1 Chipmunk T10 [73]	RAF, stored Newton	
WZ882	DHC1 Chipmunk T10 [K]	AAC BFWF, Middle Wallop	
WZ884	DHC1 Chipmunk T10 [P]	AAC BFWF, Middle Wallop	
XA109	DH115 Sea Vampire T22	Royal Scottish Mus'm of Flight, E Fortune	
XA127	DH115 Sea Vampire T22 <ff>	FAA Museum, stored RNAS Yeovilton	
XA129	DH115 Sea Vampire T22	FAA Museum, stored Wroughton	
XA225	Slingsby T38 Grasshopper TX1	Churchers College, Petersfield, Hants	
XA230	Slingsby T38 Grasshopper TX1 (BGA 4098)	Uppingham School, Leics	
XA231	Slingsby T38 Grasshopper TX1 (8888M)	E Cheshire & S Manchester Wg ATC, Sealand	
XA243	Slingsby T38 Grasshopper TX1 (8886M)	RAF, stored St Athan	
XA244	Slingsby T38 Grasshopper TX1	RAF, stored Cosford	
XA282	Slingsby T31B Cadet TX3	Caernarfon Air World	
XA286	Slingsby T31B Cadet TX3	Privately owned, stored Rufforth	
XA289	Slingsby T31B Cadet TX3	Privately owned, Eaglescott	
XA290	Slingsby T31B Cadet TX3	Privately owned, stored Rufforth	

Notes	Serial	Type (other identity) [code]	Owner/operator, location or fate
	XA292	Slingsby T31B Cadet TX3 (BGA3350)	*Sold to the USA as N81653, May 1995*
	XA293	Slingsby T31B Cadet TX3	Privately owned, Breighton
	XA302	Slingsby T31B Cadet TX3 (BGA3786)	Privately owned, Winthorpe
	XA454	Fairey Gannet COD4	RNAS Yeovilton Fire Section
	XA459	Fairey Gannet ECM6 [E]	Privately owned, Cirencester
	XA460	Fairey Gannet ECM6 [768/BY]	NE Wales Institute of HE, Connah's Quay
	XA466	Fairey Gannet COD4 [777/LM]	FAA Museum, stored Wroughton
	XA508	Fairey Gannet T2 [627/GN]	Midland Air Museum, Coventry
	XA553	Gloster Javelin FAW1 (7470M)	RAF Stanmore Park, on display
	XA564	Gloster Javelin FAW1 (7464M)	RAF Cosford Aerospace Museum
	XA571	Gloster Javelin FAW1 (7663M/ 7722M) <ff>	Privately owned, Catford
	XA634	Gloster Javelin FAW4 (7641M) [L]	RAF Leeming, on display
	XA699	Gloster Javelin FAW5 (7809M)	Midland Air Museum, Coventry
	XA801	Gloster Javelin FAW2 (7739M) <ff>	Privately owned, Stock, Essex
	XA847	EE P1B (8371M)	Privately owned, Southampton Docks
	XA862	WS55 Whirlwind HAR1 (G-AMJT) [9]	IHM, Weston-super-Mare
	XA864	WS55 Whirlwind HAR1	FAA Museum, stored
	XA868	WS55 Whirlwind HAR1	IHM, Weston-super-Mare
	XA870	WS55 Whirlwind HAR1	Flambards Village Theme Park, Helston
	XA880	DH104 Devon C2 (G-BVXR)	Privately owned, Staverton
	XA893	Avro 698 Vulcan B1 (8591M) <ff>	RAF Cosford Aerospace Museum
	XA903	Avro 698 Vulcan B1 <ff>	Privately owned, Sidcup, Kent
	XA909	Avro 698 Vulcan B1 <ff>	Privately owned, Reigate
	XB259	Blackburn B101 Beverley C1 (G-AOAI)	Museum of Army Transport, Beverley
	XB261	Blackburn B101 Beverley C1 <ff>	Imperial War Museum, Duxford
	XB446	Grumman TBM-3 Avenger	FAA Museum, Yeovilton
	XB480	Hiller HT1 [537]	FAA Museum, stored Wroughton
	XB733	Canadair CL-13 Sabre 4 (G-ATBF)	Privately owned
	XB812	Canadair CL-13 Sabre F4 (9227M) [U]	RAF Museum, Hendon
	XD145	Saro SR53	RAF Cosford Aerospace Museum
	XD163	WS55 Whirlwind HAR10 (8645M) [X]	IHM, Weston-super-Mare
	XD165	WS55 Whirlwind HAR10 (8673M) [B]	AAC Netheravon, instructional use
	XD186	WS55 Whirlwind HAR10 (8730M)	
	XD215	VS Scimitar F1 <ff>	Privately owned, Cheltenham
	XD234	VS Scimitar F1 [834]	DRA, derelict Farnborough
	XD235	VS Scimitar F1 <ff>	No 424 Sqn ATC, Southampton
	XD244	VS Scimitar F1 <ff>	Privately owned, Ottershaw
	XD317	VS Scimitar F1 [112/R]	FAA Museum, RNAS Yeovilton
	XD332	VS Scimitar F1 [194/C]	Flambards Village Theme Park, Helston
	XD375	DH115 Vampire T11 (7887M) [72]	City of Norwich Aviation Museum
	XD377	DH115 Vampire T11 (8203M) [A] <ff>	Yorkshire Air Museum, Elvington
	XD382	DH115 Vampire T11 (8033M)	Privately owned, Ripley, Derbys
	XD425	DH115 Vampire T11 [16]	Dumfries & Galloway Av'n Mus, stored
	XD434	DH115 Vampire T11 [25]	Fenland Aviation Museum, Wisbech
	XD435	DH115 Vampire T11 [26] <ff>	Privately owned, Lapworth, Warwicks
	XD445	DH115 Vampire T11 [51]	Bomber County Aviation Museum, Hemswell
	XD447	DH115 Vampire T11 [50]	Jet Aircraft Pres'n Grp., Long Marston
	XD452	DH115 Vampire T11 (7990M) [47] <ff>	Privately owned, Chester
	XD453	DH115 Vampire T11 (7890M) [64]	No 58 Sqn ATC, Elvington
	XD459	DH115 Vampire T11 [63] <ff>	Phoenix Aviation, Bruntingthorpe
	XD463	DH115 Vampire T11 (8023M)	No 1360 Sqn ATC, Stapleford, Notts
	XD506	DH115 Vampire T11 (7983M)	RAF Swinderby
	XD515	DH115 Vampire T11 (7998M/ XM515)	Newark Air Museum, Winthorpe
	XD525	DH115 Vampire T11 (7882M) <ff>	Campbell College CCF, Belfast
	XD528	DH115 Vampire T11 (8159M)	South Yorkshire Air Museum, Firbeck
	XD534	DH115 Vampire T11 [41]	Military Aircraft Pres'n Grp, Barton
	XD535	DH115 Vampire T11 <ff>	Macclesfield Historical Av'n Soc
	XD536	DH115 Vampire T11 (7734M) [H]	Alleyn's School CCF, Northolt
	XD542	DH115 Vampire T11 (7604M)[28]	RAF Edzell, Scotland, on display

Serial	Type (other identity) [code]	Owner/operator, location or fate	Notes
XD547	DH115 Vampire T11 [Z] (composite)	Dumfries & Galloway Av'n Mus, Tinwald Downs	
XD593	DH115 Vampire T11 [50]	Newark Air Museum, Winthorpe	
XD595	DH115 Vampire T11 <ff>	Privately owned, Glentham, Lincs	
XD596	DH115 Vampire T11 (7939M)	Southampton Hall of Aviation	
XD599	DH115 Vampire T11	Caernarfon Air World	
XD602	DH115 Vampire T11 (7737M) <ff>	Privately owned, Brands Hatch	
XD614	DH115 Vampire T11 (8124M) <ff>	Privately owned, Southampton	
XD616	DH115 Vampire T11 [56]	Mosquito Aircraft Museum, London Colney	
XD622	DH115 Vampire T11 (8160M)	No 2214 Sqn ATC, Usworth	
XD624	DH115 Vampire T11 [O]	Macclesfield Technical College	
XD626	DH115 Vampire T11 [Q]	Midland Air Museum, Coventry	
XD674	Hunting Jet Provost T1 (7570M)[T]	RAF Cosford Aerospace Museum	
XD816	Vickers Valiant B(K)1 <ff>	Brooklands Museum, Weybridge	
XD818	Vickers Valiant B(K)1 (7894M)	RAF Museum, Hendon	
XD857	Vickers Valiant B(K)1 <ff>	Privately owned, Rayleigh, Essex	
XD875	Vickers Valiant B(K)1 <ff>	British Aviation Heritage, Bruntingthorpe	
XE317	Bristol 171 Sycamore HR14 (G-AMWO) [S-N]	Newark Air Museum, Winthorpe	
XE327	Hawker Sea Hawk FGA6 [644/LH]	Privately owned, Kings Langley, Herts	
XE339	Hawker Sea Hawk FGA6 (8156M) [149/E]	BAe Dunsfold (under restoration)	
XE340	Hawker Sea Hawk FGA6 [131/Z]	Montrose Air Station Museum, Montrose	
XE368	Hawker Sea Hawk FGA6 [200/J]	Flambards Village Theme Park, Helston	
XE489	Hawker Sea Hawk FGA6 (G-JETH)	Privately owned, Charlwood, Surrey	
XE521	Fairey Rotodyne Y (parts)	IHM, Weston-super-Mare	
XE584	Hawker Hunter FGA9 <ff>	Macclesfield Historical Av'n Soc, Barton	
XE597	Hawker Hunter FGA9 (8874M) <ff>	RAF Halton	
XE601	Hawker Hunter FGA9	MoD(PE)/FWTS, DTEO Boscombe Down	
XE624	Hawker Hunter FGA9 (8875M) [G]	RAF Brawdy, on display	
XE627	Hawker Hunter F6A [T]	Imperial War Museum, Duxford	
XE643	Hawker Hunter FGA9 (8586M) <ff>	RAF EP&TU, Aldergrove	
XE650	Hawker Hunter FGA9 (G-9-449) <ff>	Macclesfield Historical Av'n Soc	
XE653	Hawker Hunter F6A (8829M/ G-BVWV) [S]	*Sold to South Africa as ZU-AUJ, August 1995*	
XE656	Hawker Hunter F6 (8678M)	Privately owned, Ipswich	
XE665	Hawker Hunter T8C (G-BWGM) [876/VL]	Classic Jet Aircraft Co, Exeter	
XE668	Hawker Hunter GA11 [832/DD]	RN Predannack Fire School	
XE670	Hawker Hunter F4 (7762M/8585M) <ff>	RAF EP&TU, St Athan	
XE677	Hawker Hunter F4 (G-HHUN)	Jet Heritage Ltd, Bournemouth	
XE685	Hawker Hunter GA11 (G-GAII) [861/VL]	Classic Jet Aircraft Co, Exeter	
XE689	Hawker Hunter GA11 (G-BWGK) [864/VL]	Classic Jet Aircraft Co, Exeter	
XE707	Hawker Hunter GA11 (G-BVYH) [865/VL]	*To USA as N707XE, 10 July 1995*	
XE712	Hawker Hunter GA11 [708]	RN Predannack Fire School	
XE793	Slingsby T31B Cadet TX3 (8666M)	RAF St Athan, instructional use	
XE799	Slingsby T31B Cadet TX3 (8943M) [R]	RAF ACCGS Syerston, preserved	
XE802	Slingsby T31B Cadet TX3	Privately owned, Cupar, Fife	
XE807	Slingsby T31B Cadet TX3 (BGA3545)	Privately owned, Bath	
XE849	DH115 Vampire T11 (7928M) [V3]	Jet Aviation Preservation Grp, Long Marston	
XE852	DH115 Vampire T11 [H]	No 2247 Sqn ATC, Hawarden	
XE855	DH115 Vampire T11 <ff>	Midland Air Museum, Coventry	
XE856	DH115 Vampire T11	Privately owned, Catfoss	
XE864	DH115 Vampire T11 (composite with XD435)	Privately owned, Stretton, Cheshire	
XE872	DH115 Vampire T11 [62]	Midland Air Museum, Coventry	
XE874	DH115 Vampire T11 (8582M) [61]	Privately owned, New Byth, Grampian	
XE897	DH115 Vampire T11 (XD403)	Privately owned, Errol	
XE920	DH115 Vampire T11 (8196M/ G-VMPR) [D]	Privately owned, RAF Valley	
XE921	DH115 Vampire T11 [64] <ff>	South Yorkshire Air Museum, Firbeck	
XE935	DH115 Vampire T11 [30]	South Yorkshire Air Museum, Firbeck	
XE946	DH115 Vampire T11 (7473M) <ff>	RAF Museum Restoration Centre, Cardington	

XE956 – XG226

Notes	Serial	Type (other identity) [code]	Owner/operator, location or fate
	XE956	DH115 Vampire T11 (G-OBLN)	Privately owned, Bridgend
	XE979	DH115 Vampire T11 [54]	Privately owned, Birlingham, Worcs
	XE982	DH115 Vampire T11 (7564M) [01]	Privately owned, Dunkeswell
	XE985	DH115 Vampire T11 (*WZ476*)	Mosquito Aircraft Museum, London Colney
	XE993	DH115 Vampire T11 (8161M)	Privately owned, Cosford
	XE995	DH115 Vampire T11 [53]	Privately owned, High Halden, Kent
	XE998	DH115 Vampire T11 (*U-1215*)	Brooklands Museum, Weybridge
	XF113	VS Swift F7 [19] <ff>	The Air Defence Collection, Salisbury
	XF114	VS Swift F7 (G-SWIF)	Jet Heritage Ltd, Bournemouth
	XF289	Hawker Hunter T8C (G-BVYI) [875/VL]	*To USA as N289XF, 10 July 1995*
	XF300	Hawker Hunter GA11 [860/VL]	RN, stored Shawbury
	XF301	Hawker Hunter GA11 [834/VL]	Privately owned, Bournemouth
	XF310	Hawker Hunter T8C [869/VL,2]	SFDO, RNAS Culdrose
	XF314	Hawker Hunter F51 (RDAF E-412) [N]	Tangmere Military Aviation Museum
	XF321	Hawker Hunter T7	RNAS Yeovilton, BDRT
	XF324	Hawker Hunter F51 (RDAF E-427) [D]	Privately owned, Bruntingthorpe
	XF357	Hawker Hunter T8C (G-BWGL) [871/VL]	Classic Jet Aircraft Co, Exeter
	XF358	Hawker Hunter T8C [870/VL]	RN, stored Shawbury
	XF368	Hawker Hunter GA11 [863/VL]	RN, stored Shawbury
	XF375	Hawker Hunter F6A (8736M/ G-BUEZ) [05]	The Old Flying Machine Co, Duxford
	XF382	Hawker Hunter F6A [15]	Midland Air Museum, Coventry
	XF383	Hawker Hunter F6 (8706M) <ff>	Privately owned, Oxford
	XF383	Hawker Hunter F51 (RDAF E-409)	*Markings removed, October 1995*
	XF509	Hawker Hunter F6 (8708M)	Humbrol Paints, Hull
	XF515	Hawker Hunter F6A (8830M) [C]	Kennet Aviation, Cranfield
	XF516	Hawker Hunter F6A (8685M/ G-BVVC) [66,F]	*Sold to South Africa, November 1995*
	XF519	Hawker Hunter FGA9 (8677M/ 8738M/9183M) (composite with XJ695) [J]	FSCTE, RAF Manston
	XF522	Hawker Hunter F6 <ff>	No 1365 Sqn ATC, Aylesbury
	XF526	Hawker Hunter F6 (8679M) [78/E]	RAF St Athan Fire Section
	XF527	Hawker Hunter F6 (8680M)	RAF Halton, on display
	XF545	Percival P56 Provost T1 (7957M) [O-K]	Privately owned, Cranfield
	XF597	Percival P56 Provost T1 (G-BKFW) [AH]	Privately owned, Aldermaston
	XF603	Percival P56 Provost T1 [H]	Kennet Aviation, Cranfield
	XF690	Percival P56 Provost T1 (8041M/ G-MOOS)	Kennet Aviation, Cranfield
	XF708	Avro 716 Shackleton MR3 [203/C]	Imperial War Museum, Duxford
	XF785	Bristol 173 (7648M/G-ALBN)	RAF Museum Restoration Centre, Cardington
	XF836	Percival P56 Provost T1 (8043M/ G-AWRY) [JG]	Privately owned, Thatcham
	XF844	Percival P56 Provost T1 [70]	*Sold to the USA, November 1994*
	XF877	Percival P56 Provost T1 (G-AWVF) [JX]	Privately owned, Goodwood
	XF926	Bristol 188 (8368M)	RAF Cosford Aerospace Museum
	XF967	Hawker Hunter T8C (9186M) [T]	SIF, RAFC Cranwell
	XF994	Hawker Hunter T8C [873/VL]	RN, stored Shawbury
	XF995	Hawker Hunter T8B (9237M) [K]	SIF, RAFC Cranwell
	XG154	Hawker Hunter FGA9 (8863M) [54]	RAF Museum, Hendon
	XG160	Hawker Hunter F6A (8831M/ G-BWAF) [U]	RJAF Historic Flight, Bournemouth
	XG164	Hawker Hunter F6 (8681M)	RAF Halton
	XG172	Hawker Hunter F6A (8832M) [A]	Privately owned, Ipswich
	XG194	Hawker Hunter FGA9 (8839M) [55] <rf>	RAF North Luffenham Training Area
	XG195	Hawker Hunter FGA9 (comp with XG297)	Bomber County Aviation Museum, Hemswell
	XG196	Hawker Hunter F6A (8702M) [31]	RAF Bracknell, on display
	XG209	Hawker Hunter F6 (8709M) [69]	RAF Halton Fire Section
	XG210	Hawker Hunter F6	Privately owned, Beck Row, Suffolk
	XG225	Hawker Hunter F6A (8713M) [S]	RAF Cosford on display
	XG226	Hawker Hunter F6A (8800M)	Privately owned, Long Marston

Serial	Type (other identity) [code]	Owner/operator, location or fate	Notes
XG226	Hawker Hunter F6A (8800M) [28] <ff>	Privately owned, Faygate	
XG252	Hawker Hunter FGA9 (8840M) [U]	RAF Credenhill, on display	
XG254	Hawker Hunter FGA9 (8881M)	RAF Coltishall Fire Section	
XG274	Hawker Hunter F6 (8710M) [71]	Privately owned, Ipswich	
XG290	Hawker Hunter F6 (8711M) [74] (fuselage)	Jet Heritage Ltd, Bournemouth	
XG297	Hawker Hunter FGA9 <ff>	Pennine Aviation Museum, stored Bacup	
XG325	EE Lightning F1 <ff>	Privately owned, Rayleigh, Essex	
XG329	EE Lightning F1 (8050M)	Norfolk & Suffolk Aviation Museum, Flixton	
XG331	EE Lightning F1 <ff>	Macclesfield Historical Av'n Soc	
XG337	EE Lightning F1 (8056M) [M]	RAF Cosford Aerospace Museum	
XG452	Bristol 192 Belvedere HC1 (7997M/G-BRMB)	IHM, Weston-super-Mare	
XG454	Bristol 192 Belvedere HC1 (8366M)	Gr Manchester Museum of Science & Industry	
XG462	Bristol 192 Belvedere HC1 <ff>	IHM, stored Weston-super-Mare	
XG474	Bristol 192 Belvedere HC1 (8367M) [O]	RAF Museum, Hendon	
XG496	DH104 Devon C2 (G-ANDX)	Solway Aviation Society, Carlisle	
XG502	Bristol 171 Sycamore HR14	Museum of Army Flying, Middle Wallop	
XG506	Bristol 171 Sycamore HR14 (7852M)	Bomber County Aviation Museum, Hemswell	
XG518	Bristol 171 Sycamore HR14 (8009M) [S-E]	North-East Aircraft Museum, Usworth	
XG523	Bristol 171 Sycamore HR14 <ff>	North-East Aircraft Museum, Usworth	
XG540	Bristol 171 Sycamore HR14 (7899M/8345M) [Y-S]	Privately owned, Preston, Lancs	
XG544	Bristol 171 Sycamore HR14	Privately owned, Lower Tremar	
XG547	Bristol 171 Sycamore HR14 (G-HAPR) [S-T]	IHM, Weston-super-Mare	
XG574	WS55 Whirlwind HAR3	FAA Museum, stored Wroughton	
XG577	WS55 Whirlwind HAR3 (9050M)	RAF Leconfield Crash Rescue Training	
XG594	WS55 Whirlwind HAS7 [517/PO]	Royal Scottish Mus'm of Flight, E Fortune	
XG596	WS55 Whirlwind HAS7 [66]	IHM/Westland, Yeovil (under restoration)	
XG613	DH112 Sea Venom FAW21	Imperial War Museum, Duxford	
XG629	DH112 Sea Venom FAW21 <ff>	Privately owned, Long Marston	
XG680	DH112 Sea Venom FAW22 [735/VL]	North-East Aircraft Museum, Usworth	
XG691	DH112 Sea Venom FAW22 [93/J]	Gloucestershire Aviation Collection, Staverton	
XG692	DH112 Sea Venom FAW22 [668/LM]	Midland Warplane Museum, Warwick	
XG730	DH112 Sea Venom FAW22 [499/A]	Mosquito Aircraft Museum, London Colney	
XG736	DH112 Sea Venom FAW22	Ulster Aviation Society, Newtownards	
XG737	DH112 Sea Venom FAW22 [220/Z]	Jet Aircraft Pres'n Grp., Long Marston	
XG743	DH115 Sea Vampire T22 [597/LM]	Wymondham College, Norfolk	
XG775	DH115 Vampire T55 (U-1219/ G-DHWW)	Source Classic Jet Flight, Bournemouth	
XG797	Fairey Gannet ECM6 [277]	Imperial War Museum, Duxford	
XG831	Fairey Gannet ECM6 [396]	Flambards Village Theme Park, Helston	
XG882	Fairey Gannet T5 (8754M) [771/LM]	Privately owned, Errol	
XG883	Fairey Gannet T5 [773/BY]	Wales Aircraft Museum, Cardiff	
XG888	Fairey Gannet T5 [LM]	*To Australia, August 1995*	
XG900	Short SC1	FAA Museum, RNAS Yeovilton	
XG905	Short SC1	Ulster Folk & Transpt Mus, Holywood, Co Down	
XH131	EE Canberra PR9 [AA]	RAF No 39(1 PRU) Sqn, Marham	
XH132	Short SC9 Canberra (8915M) <ff>	Privately owned, St Austell	
XH133	EE Canberra PR9 <ff>	Privately owned, Stock, Essex	
XH134	EE Canberra PR9 [AA]	RAF No 39(1 PRU) Sqn, Marham	
XH135	EE Canberra PR9 [AC]	RAF No 39(1 PRU) Sqn, Marham	
XH136	EE Canberra PR9 (8782M) <ff>	Phoenix Aviation, Bruntingthorpe	
XH165	EE Canberra PR9 <ff>	Blyth Valley Aviation Collection, Walpole	
XH168	EE Canberra PR9	RAF No 39(1 PRU) Sqn, Marham	
XH169	EE Canberra PR9	RAF No 39(1 PRU) Sqn, Marham	
XH170	EE Canberra PR9 (8739M)	RAF Wyton, on display	
XH171	EE Canberra PR9 (8746M) [U]	RAF Cosford Aerospace Museum	
XH174	EE Canberra PR9 <ff>	RAF, stored St Athan	

XH175 – XJ772

Notes	Serial	Type (other identity) [code]	Owner/operator, location or fate
	XH175	EE Canberra PR9 <ff>	Privately owned, Stock, Essex
	XH177	EE Canberra PR9 <ff>	Privately owned, Stock, Essex
	XH278	DH115 Vampire T11 (8595M/7866M)	Privately owned, Felton, Northumberland
	XH312	DH115 Vampire T11 [18]	Privately owned, Dodleston, Cheshire
	XH313	DH115 Vampire T11 [E]	St Albans College of FE
	XH328	DH115 Vampire T11	Jet Heritage Ltd, Bournemouth (dismantled)
	XH330	DH115 Vampire T11 [73]	Privately owned, Bridgnorth
	XH537	Avro 698 Vulcan B2MRR (8749M) <ff>	Privately owned, Sidcup, Kent
	XH558	Avro 698 Vulcan B2 (G-VLCN)	British Aviation Heritage, Bruntingthorpe
	XH560	Avro 698 Vulcan K2 <ff>	Privately owned, Romford
	XH563	Avro 698 Vulcan B2MRR <ff>	Privately owned, Banchory
	XH567	EE Canberra B6(mod)	Sold abroad, January 1996
	XH568	EE Canberra B6(mod) (G-BVIC)	Classic Aviation Projects, Bruntingthorpe
	XH584	EE Canberra T4 (G-27-374) <ff>	South Yorkshire Air Museum, Firbeck
	XH592	HP80 Victor K1A (8429M) <ff>	Phoenix Aviation, Bruntingthorpe
	XH648	HP80 Victor K1A	Imperial War Museum, Duxford
	XH669	HP80 Victor K2 (9092M) <ff>	Privately owned, Southend Airport
	XH670	HP80 Victor SR2 <ff>	Privately owned, Romford, Essex
	XH672	HP80 Victor K2	RAF Cosford Aerospace Museum
	XH673	HP80 Victor K2 (8911M)	RAF Marham, on display
	XH767	Gloster Javelin FAW9 (7955M) [A]	City of Norwich Aviation Museum
	XH837	Gloster Javelin FAW7 (8032M) <ff>	Caernarfon Air World
	XH892	Gloster Javelin FAW9 (7982M) [J]	Norfolk & Suffolk Aviation Museum, Flixton
	XH897	Gloster Javelin FAW9	Imperial War Museum, Duxford
	XH903	Gloster Javelin FAW9 (7938M)	Gloucestershire Aviation Collection, Staverton
	XH980	Gloster Javelin FAW8 (7867M) <ff>	Privately owned, Stock, Essex
	XH992	Gloster Javelin FAW8 (7829M) [P]	Newark Air Museum, Winthorpe
	XJ314	RR Thrust Measuring Rig	FAA Museum, RNAS Yeovilton
	XJ380	Bristol 171 Sycamore HR14 (8628M)	Privately owned, New Byth, Grampian
	XJ389	Fairey Jet Gyrodyne (XD759/ G-AJJP)	Museum of Berkshire Aviation, Woodley
	XJ393	WS55 Whirlwind HAR3	Privately owned, Codmore Hill, Sussex
	XJ409	WS55 Whirlwind HAR10	
	XJ435	WS55 Whirlwind HAR10 (8671M) [V]	AAC Netheravon, instructional use
	XJ476	DH110 Sea Vixen FAW1 <ff>	No 424 Sqn ATC, Southampton Hall of Av'n
	XJ481	DH110 Sea Vixen FAW1 [VL]	RNAY Fleetlands Museum
	XJ482	DH110 Sea Vixen FAW1 [713/VL]	Norfolk & Suffolk Aviation Museum, Flixton
	XJ488	DH110 Sea Vixen FAW1 <ff>	Privately owned, New Milton, Hants
	XJ494	DH110 Sea Vixen FAW2	Privately owned, Kings Langley, Herts
	XJ560	DH110 Sea Vixen FAW2 (8142M) [242]	Newark Air Museum, Winthorpe
	XJ565	DH110 Sea Vixen FAW2 [127/E]	Mosquito Aircraft Museum, London Colney
	XJ571	DH110 Sea Vixen FAW2 (8140M) [242/R]	Brooklands Museum
	XJ575	DH110 Sea Vixen FAW2 <ff>	Wellesbourne Wartime Museum
	XJ579	DH110 Sea Vixen FAW2 <ff>	Midland Air Museum, Coventry
	XJ580	DH110 Sea Vixen FAW2 [131/E]	Christchurch Memorial Group
	XJ607	DH110 Sea Vixen FAW2 (8171M) [701/VL]	Privately owned, Dunsfold
	XJ634	Hawker Hunter F6A (8684M) [29]	Privately owned, Ipswich Airport
	XJ639	Hawker Hunter F6A (8687M) [H]	Privately owned, Ipswich Airport
	XJ676	Hawker Hunter F6A (8844M)	The Old Flying Machine Co, Duxford
	XJ690	Hawker Hunter FGA9 <ff>	Privately owned, Market Drayton
	XJ714	Hawker Hunter FR10	Jet Aviation Pres'n Grp., Long Marston
	XJ723	WS55 Whirlwind HAR10	Montrose Air Station Museum, Montrose
	XJ726	WS55 Whirlwind HAR10	Caernarfon Air World
	XJ727	WS55 Whirlwind HAR10 (8661M) [L]	AAC Dishforth, BDRT
	XJ729	WS55 Whirlwind HAR10 (8732M/ G-BVGE)	Privately owned, Cricklade
	XJ758	WS55 Whirlwind HAR10 (8464M) <ff>	Privately owned, Oswestry
	XJ763	WS55 Whirlwind HAR10 (G-BKHA) [P]	Privately owned stored, Thornicombe, Dorset
	XJ772	DH115 Vampire T11 [H]	Mosquito Aircraft Museum, London Colney

Serial	Type (other identity) [code]	Owner/operator, location or fate	Notes
XJ823	Avro 698 Vulcan B2A	Solway Aviation Society, Carlisle Airport	
XJ824	Avro 698 Vulcan B2A	Imperial War Museum, Duxford	
XJ917	Bristol 171 Sycamore HR14 [H-S]	Bristol Aero Collection, Banwell	
XJ918	Bristol 171 Sycamore HR14 (8190M)	RAF Cosford Aerospace Museum	
XK149	Hawker Hunter F6A (8714M) [L]	British Aviation Heritage, Bruntingthorpe	
XK378	Auster AOP9 (TAD200)	Privately owned, Dale, Dyfed	
XK416	Auster AOP9 (7855M/G-AYUA)	Vintage Aircraft Team, Cranfield	
XK417	Auster AOP9 (G-AVXY)	Privately owned, Leicester East	
XK418	Auster AOP9 (7976M)	SWWAPS, Lasham	
XK421	Auster AOP9 (8365M) (frame)	British Classic Aircraft Rest'n, Hedge End	
XK482	Saro Skeeter AOP12 (7840M/ G-BJWC) [C]	Privately owned, Blackpool	
XK488	Blackburn NA39 Buccaneer S1	FAA Museum, RNAS Yeovilton	
XK526	Blackburn NA39 Buccaneer S2 (8648M)	RAF Honington, at main gate	
XK527	Blackburn NA39 Buccaneer S2D (8818M) <ff>	Privately owned, New Milton, Hants	
XK530	Blackburn NA39 Buccaneer S1	DRA Bedford Fire Section	
XK532	Blackburn NA39 Buccaneer S1 (8867M) [632/LM]	The Fresson Trust, Inverness Airport	
XK533	Blackburn NA39 Buccaneer S1 <ff>	Royal Scottish Mus'm of Flight, E Fortune	
XK590	DH115 Vampire T11 [V]	Wellesbourne Wartime Museum	
XK623	DH115 Vampire T11 (G-VAMP) [56]	Caernarfon Air World	
XK624	DH115 Vampire T11 [32]	Norfolk & Suffolk Aviation Museum, Flixton	
XK625	DH115 Vampire T11 [12]	Brenzett Aeronautical Museum	
XK627	DH115 Vampire T11	Pennine Aviation Museum, Bacup	
XK632	DH115 Vampire T11 [67]	No 2 Sqn ATC, Leavesden	
XK637	DH115 Vampire T11 [56]	No 1855 Sqn ATC, Royton, Greater Manchester	
XK655	DH106 Comet C2(RC) <ff>	Privately owned, Maryport	
XK659	DH106 Comet C2(RC) <ff>	Privately owned, Elland, W. Yorks	
XK695	DH106 Comet C2(RC) (9164M) (fuselage)	Scrapped at Newton, 1995	
XK699	DH106 Comet C2 (7971M)	RAF Lyneham on display	
XK724	Folland Gnat F1 (7715M)	RAF Cosford Aerospace Museum	
XK740	Folland Gnat F1 (8396M)	Southampton Hall of Aviation	
XK741	Folland Gnat F1 (fuselage)	Midland Air Museum, Coventry	
XK776	ML Utility 1	Museum of Army Flying, Middle Wallop	
XK789	Slingsby T38 Grasshopper TX1	Warwick School, Warwick	
XK790	Slingsby T38 Grasshopper TX1	Privately owned, stored Husbands Bosworth	
XK819	Slingsby T38 Grasshopper TX1	The Real Aeroplane Company, Breighton	
XK820	Slingsby T38 Grasshopper TX1	Lancing School, West Sussex	
XK822	Slingsby T38 Grasshopper TX1	Privately owned, West Malling	
XK895	DH104 Sea Devon C20 (G-SDEV) [19/CU]	Privately owned, Cambridge	
XK896	DH104 Sea Devon C20 (G-RNAS)	Privately owned, stored Staverton	
XK907	WS55 Whirlwind HAS7 [U]	Midland Air Museum, Coventry	
XK911	WS55 Whirlwind HAS7 [519/PO]	Privately owned, Ipswich	
XK936	WS55 Whirlwind HAS7 [62]	Imperial War Museum, Duxford	
XK944	WS55 Whirlwind HAS7	No 617 Sqn ATC, Malpas School, Cheshire	
XK968	WS55 Whirlwind HAR10 (8445M) [E]	FSCTE, RAF Manston	
XK987	WS55 Whirlwind HAR10 (8393M)	MoD Swynnerton, Staffs	
XK988	WS55 Whirlwind HAR10 [D]	AAC Middle Wallop, Fire Section	
XL149	Blackburn B101 Beverley C1 (7988M) <ff>	Newark Air Museum, Winthorpe	
XL160	HP80 Victor K2 (8910M) <ff>	Blyth Valley Aviation Collection, Walpole	
XL161	HP80 Victor K2 (9214M)	RAF Lyneham Fire Section	
XL162	HP80 Victor K2 (9114M)	Scrapped at Manston, April 1995	
Xl 163	HP80 Victor K2 (8916M)	Privately owned, Stock, Essex	
XL164	HP80 Victor K2 (9215M) <ff>	Privately owned, Charlwood, Surrey	
XL188	HP80 Victor K2 (9100M) (fuselage)	RAF Kinloss Fire Section	
XL190	HP80 Victor K2 (9216M)	RAF St Mawgan Fire Section	
XL192	HP80 Victor K2 (9024M)	RAF Marham Fire Section	
XL231	HP80 Victor K2	Yorkshire Air Museum, Elvington	
XL318	Avro 698 Vulcan B2 (8733M)	RAF Museum, Hendon	
XL319	Avro 698 Vulcan B2	North-East Aircraft Museum, Usworth	

XL360 – XL993

| --- | --- | --- | --- |
	XL360	Avro 698 Vulcan B2A	Midland Air Museum, Coventry
	XL388	Avro 698 Vulcan B2 <ff>	Blyth Valley Aviation Collection, Walpole
	XL391	Avro 698 Vulcan B2	Privately owned, Blackpool
	XL426	Avro 698 Vulcan B2 (G-VJET)	Vulcan Restoration Trust, Southend
	XL427	Avro 698 Vulcan B2 (8756M)	*Scrapped at Machrihanish, April 1995*
	XL445	Avro 698 Vulcan K2 (8811M) <ff>	Blyth Valley Aviation Collection, Walpole
	XL449	Fairey Gannet AEW3	Wales Aircraft Museum, Cardiff
	XL472	Fairey Gannet AEW3 [044/R]	Privately owned, Charlwood, Surrey
	XL497	Fairey Gannet AEW3 [041/R]	RN, Prestwick, on display
	XL500	Fairey Gannet AEW3 [LM]	RNAS Culdrose, for display
	XL502	Fairey Gannet AEW3 (8610M/ G-BMYP)	Privately owned, Sandtoft, S Yorks
	XL503	Fairey Gannet AEW3 [070/E]	FAA Museum, RNAS Yeovilton
	XL563	Hawker Hunter T7	Privately owned, on display Farnborough
	XL564	Hawker Hunter T7 [4]	MoD(PE)/ETPS, DTEO Boscombe Down
	XL565	Hawker Hunter T7 (parts of WT745)	Privately owned, Lincolnshire
	XL567	Hawker Hunter T7 (8723M) [84]	Privately owned, Exeter
	XL568	Hawker Hunter T7A (9224M) [C]	SIF, RAFC Cranwell
	XL569	Hawker Hunter T7 (8833M) [80]	East Midlands Airport Aero Park
	XL572	Hawker Hunter T7 (G-HNTR) [83]	Yorkshire Air Museum, Elvington
	XL573	Hawker Hunter T7 (G-BVGH)	Classic Jet Aircraft Co, Exeter Airport
	XL577	Hawker Hunter T7 (8676M) [W]	Flight Simulator Centre, Navenby, Lincs
	XL578	Hawker Hunter T7	Privately owned, Cranfield
	XI 580	Hawker Hunter T8M [723]	FAAM, stored RNAS Yeovilton
	XL586	Hawker Hunter T7 <rf>	RNAY Fleetlands Apprentice School
	XL587	Hawker Hunter T7 (8807M) [Z]	Privately owned,
	XL591	Hawker Hunter T7	Privately owned, Lincolnshire
	XL592	Hawker Hunter T7 (8836M) [Y]	Privately owned
	XL598	Hawker Hunter T8C (G-BVWG)	*To South Africa, April 1995*
	XL600	Hawker Hunter T7 (G-BVWN) [Y/FL]	Privately owned, Southall
	XL601	Hawker Hunter T7 [874/VL,4]	SFDO, RNAS Culdrose
	XL602	Hawker Hunter T8M (G-BWFT)	Classic Jet Aircraft Co, Exeter
	XL603	Hawker Hunter T8M [724]	British Aviation Heritage, Bruntingthorpe
	XL612	Hawker Hunter T7 [2]	MoD(PE)/ETPS, DTEO Boscombe Down
	XL613	Hawker Hunter T7 (G-BVMB)	Classic Jet Aircraft Co, Exeter
	XL614	Hawker Hunter T7	Privately owned
	XL616	Hawker Hunter T7 (9223M/ G-BWIE)	Privately owned, Cranfield
	XL618	Hawker Hunter T7 (8892M) [05]	Caernarfon Air World
	XL623	Hawker Hunter T7 (8770M) [90]	RAF Newton
	XL629	EE Lightning T4	DTEO Boscombe Down, at main gate
	XL703	SAL Pioneer CC1 (8034M)	RAF Cosford Aerospace Museum, stored
	XL728	WS58 Wessex HAS1	RAF Brawdy, Fire Section
	XL735	Saro Skeeter AOP12	Privately owned
	XL738	Saro Skeeter AOP12 (7860M)	Museum of Army Flying, Middle Wallop
	XL739	Saro Skeeter AOP12	AAC Wattisham, on display
	XL762	Saro Skeeter AOP12 (8017M)	Royal Scottish Mus'm of Flight, E Fortune
	XL763	Saro Skeeter AOP12	Privately owned, Ottershaw
	XL764	Saro Skeeter AOP12 (7940M)	Newark Air Museum, Winthorpe
	XL765	Saro Skeeter AOP12	Privately owned, Pimlico
	XL770	Saro Skeeter AOP12 (8046M)	Southampton Hall of Aviation
	XL809	Saro Skeeter AOP12 (G-BLIX)	Privately owned, Wilden, Beds
	XL811	Saro Skeeter AOP12	IHM, Weston-super-Mare
	XL812	Saro Skeeter AOP12 (G-SARO)	Privately owned, Old Buckenham
	XL813	Saro Skeeter AOP12	Museum of Army Flying, Middle Wallop
	XL814	Saro Skeeter AOP12	AAC Historic Aircraft Flight, Middle Wallop
	XL824	Bristol 171 Sycamore HR14 (8021M)	Gr Manchester Mus'm of Science & Industry
	XL829	Bristol 171 Sycamore HR14	Bristol Industrial Museum
	XL836	WS55 Whirlwind HAS7 [65]	RN Predannack Fire School
	XL840	WS55 Whirlwind HAS7	Privately owned, Long Marston
	XL847	WS55 Whirlwind HAS7 [83]	AAC Middle Wallop, Fire Section
	XL853	WS55 Whirlwind HAS7 [LS]	RNAY Fleetlands Museum
	XL875	WS55 Whirlwind HAR9	Air Service Training, Perth
	XL880	WS55 Whirlwind HAR9 [35]	RN Predannack Fire School
	XL929	Percival P66 Pembroke C1 (G-BNPU)	D-Day Museum, Shoreham Airport
	XL954	Percival P66 Pembroke C1 (9042M/N4234C)	Air Antique, Coventry
	XL993	SAL Twin Pioneer CC1 (8388M)	RAF Cosford Aerospace Museum

Serial	Type (other identity) [code]	Owner/operator, location or fate	Notes
XM135	BAC Lightning F1 [135]	Imperial War Museum, Duxford	
XM169	BAC Lightning F1A (8422M) <ff>	N Yorks Aircraft Recovery Centre, Chop Gate	
XM172	BAC Lightning F1A (8427M) [B]	RAF Coltishall, gate guard	
XM173	BAC Lightning F1A (8414M) [A]	RAF Bentley Priory, at main gate	
XM191	BAC Lightning F1A (7854M/ 8590M) <ff>	RAF EP&TU, St Athan	
XM192	BAC Lightning F1A (8413M) [K]	Privately owned, Binbrook	
XM223	DH104 Devon C2 [J]	MoD(PE), DTEO West Freugh	
XM279	EE Canberra B(I)8 <ff>	Privately owned, Flixton	
XM300	WS58 Wessex HAS1	Welsh Industrial & Maritime Mus'm, Cardiff	
XM327	WS58 Wessex HAS3 [401/KE]	College of Nautical Studies, Warsash	
XM328	WS58 Wessex HAS3	SFDO, RNAS Culdrose	
XM329	WS58 Wessex HAS1	*Burnt at Predannack by August 1995*	
XM330	WS58 Wessex HAS1	IHM, Weston-super-Mare	
XM349	Hunting Jet Provost T3A (9046M) [T]	RAF No 1 SoTT, Cosford	
XM350	Hunting Jet Provost T3A (9036M) [89]		
XM351	Hunting Jet Provost T3 (8078M)		
XM355	Hunting Jet Provost T3 (8229M) [D]	Arbury College, Cambridge	
XM358	Hunting Jet Provost T3A (8987M) [53]	Privately owned, RAF Cosford	
XM362	Hunting Jet Provost T3 (8230M)	RAF No 1 SoTT, Cosford	
XM363	Hunting Jet Provost T3 <ff>	RAF Cranwell	
XM365	Hunting Jet Provost T3A [37]	Global Aviation, Binbrook	
XM367	Hunting Jet Provost T3 (8083M) [Z]	Privately owned	
XM369	Hunting Jet Provost T3 (8084M) [C]	Privately owned, New Byth, Grampian	
XM370	Hunting Jet Provost T3A (G-BVSP) [10]	Privately owned, Manchester	
XM372	Hunting Jet Provost T3A (8917M) [55]	RAF Linton-on-Ouse Fire Section	
XM374	Hunting Jet Provost T3A [18]	*Sold to USA as N374XM, April 1995*	
XM375	Hunting Jet Provost T3 (8231M) [B]	RAF Cottesmore Fire Section	
XM376	Hunting Jet Provost T3A (G-BWDR) [27]	Global Aviation, Binbrook	
XM378	Hunting Jet Provost T3A [34]	Global Aviation, Binbrook	
XM379	Hunting Jet Provost T3		
XM381	Hunting Jet Provost T3 (8232M) [A]	RAF Marham Fire Section	
XM383	Hunting Jet Provost T3A [90]	Newark Air Museum, Winthorpe	
XM386	Hunting Jet Provost T3 (8076M) [08]	*To Stanford PTA, 1994*	
XM387	Hunting Jet Provost T3A [I]	*Sold to USA as N387TW, July 1995*	
XM401	Hunting Jet Provost T3A [17]		
XM402	Hunting Jet Provost T3 (8055AM) [J]	Privately owned, Narborough, Norfolk	
XM403	Hunting Jet Provost T3A (9048M)	RAF No 1 SoTT, Cosford	
XM404	Hunting Jet Provost T3 (8055BM)	FETC, Moreton-in-Marsh	
XM405	Hunting Jet Provost T3A (G-TORE) [42]	Kennet Aviation, Cranfield	
XM408	Hunting Jet Provost T3 (8333M) [D]	Privately owned, Bruntingthorpe	
XM409	Hunting Jet Provost T3 (8082M) <rf>	RAF, stored St Athan	
XM410	Hunting Jet Provost T3 (8054AM) [B]	RAF North Luffenham Training Area	
XM412	Hunting Jet Provost T3A (9011M) [41]	Privately owned, North Weald	
XM414	Hunting Jet Provost T3A (8996M)	Flight Experience Workshop, Belfast	
XM417	Hunting Jet Provost T3 (8054BM)	RAF North Luffenham Training Area	
XM419	Hunting Jet Provost T3A (8990M) [102]	RAF CTTS, St Athan	
XM424	Hunting Jet Provost T3A (G-BWDS)	Global Aviation, Binbrook	
XM425	Hunting Jet Provost T3A (8995M) [88]	Privately owned, Bruntingthorpe	
XM426	Hunting Jet Provost T3 (XN511) [64] <ff>	Robertsbridge Aviation Museum, Mayfield	

XM455 – XN239

Notes	Serial	Type (other identity) [code]	Owner/operator, location or fate
	XM455	Hunting Jet Provost T3A (8960M) [K]	Global Aviation, Binbrook
	XM459	Hunting Jet Provost T3A [F] (fuselage)	RAF, stored Shawbury
	XM463	Hunting Jet Provost T3A [38]	RAF Museum, Hendon
	XM464	Hunting Jet Provost T3A [23]	Privately owned, Colsterworth, Lincs
	XM465	Hunting Jet Provost T3A [55]	
	XM467	Hunting Jet Provost T3 (8085M)	
	XM468	Hunting Jet Provost T3 (8081M)	Privately owned, King's Lynn
	XM470	Hunting Jet Provost T3A [12]	Global Aviation, Binbrook
	XM471	Hunting Jet Provost T3A (8968M) [L,93]	RAF No 1 SoTT, Cosford
	XM473	Hunting Jet Provost T3A (8974M/ G-TINY)	Privately owned, Norwich
	XM474	Hunting Jet Provost T3 (8121M)	No 1330 Sqn ATC, Warrington
	XM475	Hunting Jet Provost T3A (9112M) [44]	FSCTE, RAF Manston
	XM478	Hunting Jet Provost T3A (8983M) [33]	Global Aviation, Binbrook
	XM479	Hunting Jet Provost T3A (G-BVEZ)	Privately owned, Newcastle
	XM480	Hunting Jet Provost T3 (8080M)	RAF Finningley
	XM529	Saro Skeeter AOP12 (7979M/ G-BDNS)	Privately owned, Handforth
	XM553	Saro Skeeter AOP12 (G-AWSV)	Privately owned, Middle Wallop
	XM555	Saro Skeeter AOP12 (0027M)	HAF Cosford Aerospace Museum, stored
	XM556	Saro Skeeter AOP12 (7870M/ G-HELI)	To Germany, 1995
	XM561	Saro Skeeter AOP12 (7980M)	South Yorkshire Air Museum, Firbeck
	XM564	Saro Skeeter AOP12	Royal Armoured Corps Museum, Bovington
	XM569	Avro 698 Vulcan B2	Wales Aircraft Museum, Cardiff
	XM575	Avro 698 Vulcan B2A (G-BLMC)	East Midlands Airport Aero Park
	XM594	Avro 698 Vulcan B2	Newark Air Museum, Winthorpe
	XM597	Avro 698 Vulcan B2	Royal Scottish Mus'm of Flight, E Fortune
	XM598	Avro 698 Vulcan B2 (8778M)	RAF Cosford Aerospace Museum
	XM602	Avro 698 Vulcan B2 (8771M) <ff>	Avro Aircraft Restoration Society, Woodford
	XM603	Avro 698 Vulcan B2	Avro Aircraft Restoration Society, Woodford
	XM607	Avro 698 Vulcan B2 (8779M)	RAF Waddington, on display
	XM612	Avro 698 Vulcan B2	City of Norwich Aviation Museum
	XM652	Avro 698 Vulcan B2 <ff>	Privately owned, Burntwood, Staffs
	XM655	Avro 698 Vulcan B2 (G-VULC)	Privately owned, Wellesbourne Mountford
	XM656	Avro 698 Vulcan B2 (8757M) <ff>	Privately owned, Stock, Essex
	XM660	WS55 Whirlwind HAS7 [78]	North-East Aircraft Museum, Usworth
	XM685	WS55 Whirlwind HAS7 (G-AYZJ) [513/PO]	Newark Air Museum, Winthorpe
	XM693	HS Gnat T1 (7891M)	BAe Hamble on display
	XM693	HS Gnat T1 (8618M/XP504/ G-TIMM)	Kennet Aviation, Cranfield
	XM694	HS Gnat T1	Privately owned, Portsmouth
	XM697	HS Gnat T1 (G-NAAT)	Jet Heritage Ltd, Bournemouth
	XM708	HS Gnat T1 (8573M)	RAF Locking, on display
	XM709	HS Gnat T1 (8617M) [67]	Privately owned
	XM715	HP80 Victor K2	British Aviation Heritage, Bruntingthorpe
	XM717	HP80 Victor K2 <ff>	RAF Museum Restoration Centre, Cardington
	XM819	Lancashire EP9 Prospector (G-APXW)	Museum of Army Flying, Middle Wallop
	XM833	WS58 Wessex HAS3	SWWAPS, Lasham
	XM838	WS58 Wessex HAS3 [05]	Burnt at Predannack by August 1995
	XM843	WS58 Wessex HAS1 [527]	RNAS Lee-on-Solent, BDRT
	XM868	WS58 Wessex HAS1 [517]	RN Predannack Fire School
	XM870	WS58 Wessex HAS3	RNAS Lee-on-Solent, BDRT
	XM874	WS58 Wessex HAS1 [521/CU]	RN Predannack Fire School
	XM927	WS58 Wessex HAS3 (8814M) [660/PO]	RAF Shawbury, Fire Section
	XN126	WS55 Whirlwind HAR10 (8655M) [S]	RAF Benson BDRT
	XN137	Hunting Jet Provost T3 <ff>	Privately owned, Ottershaw
	XN198	Slingsby T31B Cadet TX3	Privately owned, Challock Lees
	XN238	Slingsby T31B Cadet TX3 <ff>	Robertsbridge Aviation Society, Mayfield
	XN239	Slingsby T31B Cadet TX3 (8889M) [G]	Imperial War Museum, Duxford

Serial	Type (other identity) [code]	Owner/operator, location or fate	Notes
XN243	Slingsby T31B Cadet TX3 (BGA 3145)	RAFGSA, Bicester	
XN246	Slingsby T31B Cadet TX3	Southampton Hall of Aviation	
XN258	WS55 Whirlwind HAR9 [589/CU]	North-East Aircraft Museum, Usworth	
XN259	WS55 Whirlwind HAS7	London City Airport, Fire Section	
XN263	WS55 Whirlwind HAS7	Privately owned, Chichester	
XN297	WS55 Whirlwind HAR9 (XN311) [12]	Privately owned, Hull	
XN298	WS55 Whirlwind HAR9 [810/LS]	International Fire Training Centre, Chorley	
XN299	WS55 Whirlwind HAS7 [ZZ]	Royal Marines' Museum, Portsmouth	
XN302	WS55 Whirlwind HAS7 (9037M)	RAF Finningley, Fire Section	
XN304	WS55 Whirlwind HAS7 [64]	Norfolk & Suffolk Aviation Museum, Flixton	
XN332	Saro P531 (G-APNV) [759]	FAA Museum, stored Wroughton	
XN334	Saro P531	FAA Museum, Crawley College of Technology	
XN341	Saro Skeeter AOP12 (8022M)	Privately owned, Luton Airport	
XN344	Saro Skeeter AOP12 (8018M)	Science Museum, South Kensington	
XN351	Saro Skeeter AOP12 (G-BKSC)	Privately owned, Shempston Fm, Lossiemouth	
XN359	WS55 Whirlwind HAR9 [34/ED]	RNAS Lee-on-Solent, Fire Section	
XN380	WS55 Whirlwind HAS7	Lashenden Air Warfare Museum, Headcorn	
XN385	WS55 Whirlwind HAS7	Privately owned, Bournemouth	
XN386	WS55 Whirlwind HAR9 [435/ED]		
XN412	Auster AOP9	Cotswold Aircraft Rest'n Grp, Innsworth	
XN435	Auster AOP9 (G-BGBU)	Privately owned, Egham	
XN437	Auster AOP9 (G-AXWA)	Privately owned, Welling	
XN441	Auster AOP9 (G-BGKT)	Privately owned, Reymerston Hall	
XN458	Hunting Jet Provost T3 (8234M)	Wales Aircraft Museum, Cardiff	
XN459	Hunting Jet Provost T3A [N]	Global Aviation, Binbrook	
XN461	Hunting Jet Provost T3A (G-BVBE)	Privately owned, Sandtoft	
XN462	Hunting Jet Provost T3A [17]	RAF, stored Shawbury	
XN466	Hunting Jet Provost T3A [29] <ff>	No 1005 Sqn ATC, Radcliffe, Gtr Manchester	
XN467	Hunting Jet Provost T4 (8559M) [B]	To Otterburn ranges by December 1994	
XN470	Hunting Jet Provost T3A [41]	Global Aviation, Binbrook	
XN472	Hunting Jet Provost T3A (8959M) [J,86]	RAF No 1 SoTT, Cosford	
XN473	Hunting Jet Provost T3A (8862M) [98] <ff>		
XN492	Hunting Jet Provost T3 (8079M)		
XN494	Hunting Jet Provost T3A (9012M) [43]	AAC Middle Wallop, Fire Section	
XN495	Hunting Jet Provost T3A (8786M) [102]	RAF Finningley, Fire Section	
XN497	Hunting Jet Provost T3A [52]	RAF St Athan	
XN498	Hunting Jet Provost T3A [16]	Global Aviation, Binbrook	
XN500	Hunting Jet Provost T3A [48]	CSE Ltd, Oxford, ground instruction	
XN501	Hunting Jet Provost T3A (8958M) [G]	RAF No 1 SoTT, Cosford	
XN502	Hunting Jet Provost T3A [D]	Sold as N502GW, January 1995	
XN503	Hunting Jet Provost T3	Wiltshire Historic Av'n Group, Salisbury	
XN505	Hunting Jet Provost T3A [25]		
XN508	Hunting Jet Provost T3A [47]	RAF St Athan	
XN509	Hunting Jet Provost T3A [50]	Privately owned, Colsterworth, Lincs	
XN510	Hunting Jet Provost T3A [40]	Global Aviation, Binbrook	
XN512	Hunting Jet Provost T3 (8435M)	Phoenix Aviation Museum, Bruntingthorpe	
XN549	Hunting Jet Provost T3 (8235M) [32,P]	RAF Shawbury Fire Section	
XN551	Hunting Jet Provost T3A (8984M)	RAF CTTS, St Athan	
XN554	Hunting Jet Provost T3 (8436M) [K]	RAF North Luffenham Training Area	
XN573	Hunting Jet Provost T3 [E] <ff>	Newark Air Museum, Winthorpe	
XN577	Hunting Jet Provost T3A (8956M) [89,F]	RAF No 1 SoTT, Cosford	
XN579	Hunting Jet Provost T3A (9137M) [14]	RAF North Luffenham Training Area	

Notes	Serial	Type (other identity) [code]	Owner/operator, location or fate
	XN582	Hunting Jet Provost T3A (8957M) [95,H]	Privately owned, Cambridge
	XN584	Hunting Jet Provost T3A (9014M) [E]	Phoenix Aviation, Bruntingthorpe
	XN586	Hunting Jet Provost T3A (9039M) [91,S]	Brooklands Technical College
	XN589	Hunting Jet Provost T3A (9143M) [46]	RAF Linton-on-Ouse, on display
	XN592	Hunting Jet Provost T3 <ff>	No 1105 Sqn ATC, Winchester
	XN593	Hunting Jet Provost T3A (8988M) [97,Q]	
	XN594	Hunting Jet Provost T3 (8077M) [W]	Privately owned
	XN595	Hunting Jet Provost T3A [43]	Privately owned, Peterborough
	XN597	Hunting Jet Provost T3 (7984M) <ff>	South Yorkshire Air Museum, Firbeck
	XN600	Hunting Jet Provost T3A <ff>	To the Aviodome Museum, Holland
	XN602	Hunting Jet Provost T3 (8088M)	FSCTE, RAF Manston
	XN607	Hunting Jet Provost T3 <ff>	N Yorks Aircraft Recovery Centre, Chop Gate
	XN629	Hunting Jet Provost T3A (G-BVEG) [49]	Transair (UK) Ltd, North Weald
	XN632	Hunting Jet Provost T3 (8352M)	Privately owned, Eaglescott
	XN634	Hunting Jet Provost T3A <ff>	Privately owned, Ipswich
	XN634	Hunting Jet Provost T3A [53] <rf>	BAe Warton Fire Section
	XN636	Hunting Jet Provost T3A (9045M) [15]	Privately owned
	XN637	Hunting Jet Provost T3 (G-BKOU) [3]	Privately owned, North Weald
	XN641	Hunting Jet Provost T3A (8865M) [47]	RAF Newton Fire Section
	XN643	Hunting Jet Provost T3A (8704M) <ff>	SIF, RAFC Cranwell
	XN647	DH110 Sea Vixen FAW2 [707/VL]	Flambards Village Theme Park, Helston
	XN649	DH110 Sea Vixen FAW2 [126]	MoD(PE), stored DRA Farnborough
	XN650	DH110 Sea Vixen FAW2 [VL]	Wales Aircraft Museum, Cardiff
	XN651	DH110 Sea Vixen FAW2 <ff>	Privately owned, Pucklechurch, Avon
	XN657	DH110 Sea Vixen D3 [TR-1]	Privately owned
	XN685	DH110 Sea Vixen FAW2 (8173M) [03/VL]	Midland Air Museum, Coventry
	XN688	DH110 Sea Vixen FAW2 (8141M) [511]	DRA Farnborough Fire Section
	XN691	DH110 Sea Vixen FAW2 (8143M) [247/H]	Aces High, North Weald
	XN692	DH110 Sea Vixen FAW2 [125/E]	Privately owned, Stock, Essex
	XN696	DH110 Sea Vixen FAW2 <ff>	Blyth Valley Aviation Collection, Walpole
	XN714	Hunting H126	RAF Cosford Aerospace Museum
	XN724	EE Lightning F2A (8513M) [F]	Privately owned, Newcastle-upon-Tyne
	XN728	EE Lightning F2A (8546M) [V]	Privately owned, Balderton, Notts
	XN734	EE Lightning F3A (8346M/ G-BNCA) <ff>	Privately owned, Cranfield
	XN769	EE Lightning F2 (8402M) <ff>	Privately owned, Stock, Essex
	XN774	EE Lightning F2A (8551M) [F]	Coningsby, derelict
	XN776	EE Lightning F2A (8535M) [C]	Royal Scottish Mus'm of Flight,E Fortune
	XN817	AW660 Argosy C1	MoD(PE), DTEO West Freugh Fire Section
	XN819	AW660 Argosy C1 (8205M) <ff>	Newark Air Museum, Winthorpe
	XN923	HS Buccaneer S1 [13]	Privately owned, Charlwood, Surrey
	XN928	HS Buccaneer S1 (8179M) [353]	Wales Aircraft Museum, Cardiff
	XN929	HS Buccaneer S1 (8051M) <ff>	SIF, RAFC Cranwell
	XN930	HS Buccaneer S1 (8180M) [632/LM] <ff>	Privately owned, Stock, Essex
	XN934	HS Buccaneer S1 [631] (fuselage)	RN Predannack Fire School
	XN953	HS Buccaneer S1 (8182M)	RN Predannack Fire School
	XN957	HS Buccaneer S1 [630/LM]	FAA Museum, stored RNAS Yeovilton
	XN964	HS Buccaneer S1 [613/LM]	Newark Air Museum, Winthorpe
	XN967	HS Buccaneer S1 <ff>	Privately owned
	XN972	HS Buccaneer S1 (8183M/ XN962) <ff>	RAF EP&TU, St Athan
	XN974	HS Buccaneer S2A	Yorkshire Air Museum, Elvington
	XN979	HS Buccaneer S2 <ff>	ATC, RAF Stanbridge
	XP110	WS58 Wessex HAS3 [55/FL]	RNAS Lee-on-Solent
	XP137	WS58 Wessex HAS3 [CU]	RNAS Culdrose, BDRT

Serial	Type (other identity) [code]	Owner/operator, location or fate	Notes
XP140	WS58 Wessex HAS3 (8806M) [653/PO]	RAF Chilmark, BDRT	
XP142	WS58 Wessex HAS3	FAA Museum, stored Wroughton	
XP150	WS58 Wessex HAS3	FETC, Moreton-in-Marsh	
XP151	WS58 Wessex HAS1 [047/R]	RN Predannack Fire School	
XP157	WS58 Wessex HAS1 [AN]	RNAS Yeovilton, Fire Section	
XP158	WS58 Wessex HAS1 [522]	RNAS Culdrose, Fire Section	
XP159	WS58 Wessex HAS1 (8877M) [047/R]	Privately owned, Brands Hatch	
XP160	WS58 Wessex HAS1 [521/CU]	RN Predannack Fire School	
XP165	WS Scout AH1	IHM, Weston-super-Mare	
XP166	WS Scout AH1 (G-APVL)	Privately owned, Old Buckenham	
XP190	WS Scout AH1	South Yorkshire Aviation Museum, Firbeck	
XP191	WS Scout AH1	AAC Middle Wallop, BDRT	
XP226	Fairey Gannet AEW3 [073/E]	Newark Air Museum, Winthorpe	
XP241	Auster AOP9	Rebel Air Museum, Andrewsfield	
XP242	Auster AOP9 (G-BUCI)	AAC Historic Aircraft Flight, Middle Wallop	
XP244	Auster AOP9 (7864M/*M7922*)		
XP248	Auster AOP9 (7863M/WZ679)	Privately owned, Little Gransden	
XP254	Auster AOP11 (G-ASCC)	Privately owned, Turweston	
XP279	Auster AOP9 (G-BWKK)	Privately owned, Popham	
XP280	Auster AOP9	Snibston Discovery Park, Coalville	
XP281	Auster AOP9	Imperial War Museum, Duxford	
XP282	Auster AOP9 (G-BGTC)	Privately owned, Widmerpool	
XP283	Auster AOP9 (7859M)	Privately owned, Lichfield	
XP299	WS55 Whirlwind HAR10 (8726M)	RAF Cosford Aerospace Museum	
XP329	WS55 Whirlwind HAR10 (8791M) [V]	Privately owned, Tattershall Thorpe	
XP330	WS55 Whirlwind HAR10	CAA Fire School, Teesside Airport	
XP344	WS55 Whirlwind HAR10 (8764M) [X]	RAF North Luffenham	
XP345	WS55 Whirlwind HAR10 (8792M)	Privately owned, Storwood, East Yorks	
XP346	WS55 Whirlwind HAR10 (8793M)	Privately owned, Long Marston	
XP350	WS55 Whirlwind HAR10	Flambards Village Theme Park, Helston	
XP351	WS55 Whirlwind HAR10 (8672M) [Z]	RAF Shawbury, on display	
XP353	WS55 Whirlwind HAR10 (8720M)	Privately owned, Brands Hatch	
XP354	WS55 Whirlwind HAR10 (8721M)	Privately owned, Cricklade, Wilts	
XP355	WS55 Whirlwind HAR10 (8463M/G-BEBC)	City of Norwich Aviation Museum	
XP359	WS55 Whirlwind HAR10 (8447M)	RAF Stafford, Fire Section	
XP360	WS55 Whirlwind HAR10 [V]	Privately owned, Upper Hill, Hereford	
XP361	WS55 Whirlwind HAR10 (8731M)	RAF Coltishall, Fire Section	
XP395	WS55 Whirlwind HAR10 (8674M) [A]	Privately owned, Tattershall Thorpe	
XP398	WS55 Whirlwind HAR10 (8794M)	Privately owned, Charlwood, Surrey	
XP399	WS55 Whirlwind HAR10	Privately owned, Chelmsford, Essex	
XP404	WS55 Whirlwind HAR10 (8682M)	IHM, Weston-super-Mare	
XP405	WS55 Whirlwind HAR10 (8656M) [Y]	Junior Infantry Reg't, Shorncliffe, Kent	
XP411	AW660 Argosy C1 (8442M) [C]	RAF Cosford Aerospace Museum	
XP454	Slingsby T38 Grasshopper TX1	Wellingborough School, Wellingborough	
XP458	Slingsby T38 Grasshopper TX1	City of Norwich Aviation Museum	
XP463	Slingsby T38 Grasshopper TX1	Privately owned, stored Rufforth	
XP488	Slingsby T38 Grasshopper TX1	Fenland Aviation Museum, Wisbech	
XP490	Slingsby T38 Grasshopper TX1	Ipswich School, Ipswich	
XP493	Slingsby T38 Grasshopper TX1	Privately owned, stored Aston Down	
XP494	Slingsby T38 Grasshopper TX1	Privately owned, Breighton	
XP502	HS Gnat T1 (8576M)	RAF CTTS, St Athan	
XP503	HS Gnat T1 (8568M) [73]	Phoenix Aviation, Bruntingthorpe	
XP505	HS Gnat T1	Science Museum, Wroughton	
XP516	HS Gnat T1 (8580M) [16]	DRA Structures Dept, Farnborough	
XP534	HS Gnat T1 (8620M/G-BVPP) [64]	*Painted as XR993 by September 1995*	
XP540	HS Gnat T1 (8608M) [62]	Privately owned, Bruntingthorpe	
XP542	HS Gnat T1 (8575M) [42]	R Military Coll of Science, Shrivenham	
XP547	Hunting Jet Provost T4 (8992M) [N,03]	Global Aviation, Binbrook	
XP556	Hunting Jet Provost T4 (9027M) [B]	Phoenix Aviation, Bruntingthorpe	
XP557	Hunting Jet Provost T4 (8494M)	South Yorkshire Air Museum, Firbeck	
XP558	Hunting Jet Provost T4 (8627M) [20]	RAF St Athan Fire Section	

XP563 – XR137

Notes	Serial	Type (other identity) [code]	Owner/operator, location or fate
	XP563	Hunting Jet Provost T4 (9028M) [C]	Phoenix Aviation, Bruntingthorpe
	XP567	Hunting Jet Provost T4 (8510M) [23]	*Sold to the USA as N8782M, May 1995*
	XP568	Hunting Jet Provost T4	Jet Aviation Pres'n Grp., Long Marston
	XP573	Hunting Jet Provost T4 (8236M) [19]	Jersey Airport Fire Section
	XP585	Hunting Jet Provost T4 (8407M) [24]	NE Wales Institute, Wrexham
	XP627	Hunting Jet Provost T4	North-East Aircraft Museum, Usworth
	XP629	Hunting Jet Provost T4 (9026M) [P]	RAF North Luffenham Training Area
	XP638	Hunting Jet Provost T4 (9034M) [A]	RAF Waddington, BDRT
	XP640	Hunting Jet Provost T4 (8501M) [D]	Yorkshire Air Museum, Elvington
	XP672	Hunting Jet Provost T4 (8458M/ G-RAFI) [27]	Privately owned, Ramsey, Isle of Man
	XP677	Hunting Jet Provost T4 (8587M) <ff>	No 2530 Sqn ATC, Headley Court, Uckfield
	XP680	Hunting Jet Provost T4 (8460M)	RAF St Athan, Fire Section
	XP686	Hunting Jet Provost T4 (8401M/ 8502M) [G]	RAF North Luffenham Training Area
	XP688	Hunting Jet Provost T4 (9031M) [E]	Phoenix Aviation, Bruntingthorpe
	XP693	BAC Lightning F6 (G-FSIX)	Lightning Flying Club, Exeter Airport
	XP701	BAC Lightning F3 (8924M) <ff>	Robertsbridge Aviation Society, Mayfield
	XP703	BAC Lightning F3 <ff>	Lightning Preservation Grp, Bruntingthorpe
	XP706	BAC Lightning F3 (8925M)	Lincs Lightning Pres'n Soc, Strubby
	XP741	BAC Lightning F3 (8939M) [AR]	FSCTE, RAF Manston
	XP745	BAC Lightning F3 (8453M) [H]	Privately owned, Greenford, West London
	XP772	DHC2 Beaver AL1 (G-BUCJ)	The Aircraft Restoration Co, Duxford
	XP775	DHC2 Beaver AL1	Privately owned
	XP806	DHC2 Beaver AL1	Museum of Army Flying, Middle Wallop
	XP820	DHC2 Beaver AL1	AAC Historic Aircraft Flight, Middle Wallop
	XP821	DHC2 Beaver AL1 [MCO]	Museum of Army Flying, Middle Wallop
	XP822	DHC2 Beaver AL1	Privately owned
	XP831	Hawker P1127 (8406M)	Science Museum, South Kensington
	XP841	Handley-Page HP115	FAA Museum, RNAS Yeovilton
	XP846	WS Scout AH1 [B,H] (fuselage)	RE 39 Regiment, Waterbeach, instructional use
	XP847	WS Scout AH1	Museum of Army Flying, Middle Wallop
	XP848	WS Scout AH1	Army Apprentice College, Arborfield, on display
	XP849	WS Scout AH1	MoD(PE)/ETPS, DTEO Boscombe Down
	XP850	WS Scout AH1 (fuselage)	AAC, stored Dishforth
	XP853	WS Scout AH1	AAC SEAE, Arborfield
	XP854	WS Scout AH1 (7898M/TAD043)	AAC SEAE, Arborfield
	XP855	WS Scout AH1	Army Apprentice College, Arborfield
	XP856	WS Scout AH1	AAC Middle Wallop, BDRT
	XP857	WS Scout AH1	AAC Middle Wallop Fire Section
	XP883	WS Scout AH1	MoD(PE)/ETPS, DTEO Boscombe Down
	XP884	WS Scout AH1	AAC SEAE, Arborfield
	XP886	WS Scout AH1	Army Apprentice College, Arborfield
	XP888	WS Scout AH1	AAC SEAE, Arborfield
	XP890	WS Scout AH1 [G] (fuselage)	AAC, stored RNAW Almondbank
	XP891	WS Scout AH1 [S]	*Sold to New Zealand, October 1995*
	XP893	WS Scout AH1	AAC, stored Middle Wallop
	XP899	WS Scout AH1 [D]	Army Apprentice College, Arborfield
	XP902	WS Scout AH1	AAC Netheravon
	XP905	WS Scout AH1	AAC SEAE, Arborfield
	XP907	WS Scout AH1 (G-SROE)	Privately owned, Ipswich
	XP908	WS Scout AH1 [Y]	AAC, stored Sek Kong
	XP910	WS Scout AH1	AAC SEAE, Arborfield
	XP919	DH110 Sea Vixen FAW2 (8163M) [706/VL]	Blyth Valley Aviation Collection, Walpole
	XP924	DH110 Sea Vixen D3	Privately owned
	XP925	DH110 Sea Vixen FAW2 [752] <ff>	DRA Farnborough, Fire Section
	XP956	DH110 Sea Vixen FAW2	Privately owned, Dunsfold
	XP980	Hawker P.1127	FAA Museum, RNAS Yeovilton
	XP984	Hawker P.1127	BAe Dunsfold (under restoration)
	XR137	AW660 Argosy E1	Caernarfon Air World

Serial	Type (other identity) [code]	Owner/operator, location or fate	Notes
XR220	BAC TSR2 (7933M)	RAF Cosford Aerospace Museum	
XR222	BAC TSR2	Imperial War Museum, Duxford	
XR232	Sud Alouette AH2 (F-WEIP)	Museum of Army Flying, Middle Wallop	
XR240	Auster AOP9 (G-BDFH)	Privately owned, Cambridge	
XR241	Auster AOP9 (G-AXRR)	The Aircraft Restoration Co, Duxford	
XR244	Auster AOP9	AAC Historic Aircraft Flight, Middle Wallop	
XR246	Auster AOP9 (7862M/G-AZBU)	Privately owned, Reymerston Hall	
XR267	Auster AOP9 (G-BJXR)	Cotswold Aircraft Rest'n Grp, Innsworth	
XR271	Auster AOP9	Museum of Artillery, Woolwich	
XR371	SC5 Belfast C1	RAF Cosford Aerospace Museum	
XR379	Sud Alouette AH2	AAC Historic Aircraft Flight, Middle Wallop	
XR436	Saro Scout AH1	AAC Middle Wallop, BDRT	
XR453	WS55 Whirlwind HAR10 (8873M) [A]	RAF Odiham, on gate	
XR458	WS55 Whirlwind HAR10 (8662M) [H]	Museum of Army Flying, Middle Wallop	
XR485	WS55 Whirlwind HAR10 [Q]	Norfolk & Suffolk Aviation Museum, Flixton	
XR486	WS55 Whirlwind HCC12 (8727M/G-RWWW)	Privately owned, Redhill	
XR497	WS58 Wessex HC2 [F]	RAF No 72 Sqn, Aldergrove	
XR498	WS58 Wessex HC2 [X]	RAF No 60 Sqn, Benson	
XR499	WS58 Wessex HC2 [W]	RAF No 72 Sqn, Aldergrove	
XR501	WS58 Wessex HC2	RAF	
XR502	WS58 Wessex HC2 [Z]	RAF No 60 Sqn, Benson	
XR503	WS58 Wessex HC2	MoD(PE)/ETPS, DTEO Boscombe Down	
XR504	WS58 Wessex HC2 [Joker]	RAF No 84 Sqn, Akrotiri	
XR505	WS58 Wessex HC2 [WA]	RAF No 2 FTS, Shawbury	
XR506	WS58 Wessex HC2 [V]	RAF No 60 Sqn, Benson	
XR507	WS58 Wessex HC2	RAF SARTU, Valley	
XR508	WS58 Wessex HC2	RAF No 60 Sqn, Benson	
XR511	WS58 Wessex HC2 [L]	RAF, stored Benson	
XR515	WS58 Wessex HC2 [B]	RAF No 28 Sqn, Sek Kong	
XR516	WS58 Wessex HC2 [WB]	RAF No 2 FTS, Shawbury	
XR517	WS58 Wessex HC2 [N]	RAF No 60 Sqn, Benson	
XR518	WS58 Wessex HC2 [O]	RAF No 72 Sqn, Aldergrove	
XR520	WS58 Wessex HC2	RAF SARTU, Valley	
XR521	WS58 Wessex HC2 [WD]	RAF No 2 FTS, Shawbury	
XR522	WS58 Wessex HC2 [A]	RAF No 28 Sqn, Sek Kong	
XR523	WS58 Wessex HC2 [M]	RAF No 60 Sqn, Benson	
XR525	WS58 Wessex HC2 [G]	RAF No 60 Sqn, Benson	
XR526	WS58 Wessex HC2 (8147M)	Westlands, Yeovil, instructional use	
XR527	WS58 Wessex HC2 [K]	RAF No 72 Sqn, Aldergrove	
XR528	WS58 Wessex HC2 [T]	RAF No 72 Sqn, Aldergrove	
XR529	WS58 Wessex HC2 [E]	RAF No 72 Sqn, Aldergrove	
XR534	HS Gnat T1 (8578M) [65]	RAF Valley	
XR535	HS Gnat T1 (8569M) [05]	RAF Halton	
XR537	HS Gnat T1 (8642M/G-NATY) [T]	Jet Heritage Ltd, Bournemouth	
XR538	HS Gnat T1 (8621M/G-RORI) [69]	Privately owned, Cranfield	
XR569	HS Gnat T1 (8560M) [08]	Phoenix Aviation, Bruntingthorpe	
XR571	HS Gnat T1 (8493M)	RAF Red Arrows, Scampton, on display	
XR574	HS Gnat T1 (8631M) [72]	RAF No 1 SoTT, Cosford	
XR588	WS58 Wessex HC2 [Hearts]	RAF No 84 Sqn, Akrotiri	
XR595	WS Scout AH1 (G-BWHU) [M]	Privately owned, Plymouth	
XR597	WS Scout AH1	AAC SEAE, Arborfield	
XR600	WS Scout AH1 (fuselage)	AAC Netheravon, BDRT	
XR601	WS Scout AH1	Army Apprentice College, Arborfield	
XR627	WS Scout AH1 [X]	AAC SEAE, Arborfield	
XR628	WS Scout AH1	AAC, stored RNAW Almondbank	
XR629	WS Scout AH1 (fuselage)	AAC, stored RNAW Almondbank	
XR630	WS Scout AH1 [U]	AAC Middle Wallop, BDRT	
XR632	WS Scout AH1	Privately owned, Hawarden	
XR635	WS Scout AH1	RNAS Yeovilton	
XR639	WS Scout AH1 [X] (fuselage)	AAC, stored RNAW Almondbank	
XR650	Hunting Jet Provost T4 (8459M) [28]	MoD(PE), DTEO Boscombe Down, GI use	
XR651	Hunting Jet Provost T4 (8431M) [A]		
XR654	Hunting Jet Provost T4 [34]	Macclesfield Hist Av'n Society, Barton	
XR658	Hunting Jet Provost T4 (8192M)	N Wales Inst of HE, Connah's Quay	
XR662	Hunting Jet Provost T4 (8410M)	RAF Finningley	
XR670	Hunting Jet Provost T4 (8498M)	RAF Odiham, Fire Section	

Notes	Serial	Type (other identity) [code]	Owner/operator, location or fate
	XR672	Hunting Jet Provost T4 (8495M) [50]	RAF Halton, Fire Section
	XR673	Hunting Jet Provost T4 (9032M) [L]	Privately owned, North Weald
	XR674	Hunting Jet Provost T4 (G-TOMG/ 9030M)	Painted as XW428
	XR679	Hunting Jet Provost T4 (8991M) [M,04]	Global Aviation, Binbrook
	XR681	Hunting Jet Provost T4 (8588M) <ff>	No 1218 Sqn ATC, Manston
	XR700	Hunting Jet Provost T4 (8589M) <ff>	RAF EP&TU, Aldergrove
	XR701	Hunting Jet Provost T4 (9025M) [K,21]	Sold to the USA as N8272W, May 1995
	XR704	Hunting Jet Provost T4 (8506M) [30]	Sold to the USA as N8272Y, May 1995
	XR713	BAC Lightning F3 (8935M) [C]	RAF Leuchars, BDRT
	XR718	BAC Lightning F6 (8932M) [DA]	Blyth Valley Aviation Collection, Walpole
	XR724	BAC Lightning F6 (G-BTSY)	Privately owned, Binbrook
	XR725	BAC Lightning F6	Privately owned, Binbrook
	XR726	BAC Lightning F6 <ff>	Privately owned, Harrogate
	XR728	BAC Lightning F6 [JS]	Lightning Preservation Grp, Bruntingthorpe
	XR747	BAC Lightning F6 <ff>	Privately owned, Plymouth
	XR749	BAC Lightning F3 (8934M) [DA]	Teeside Airport, on display
	XR751	BAC Lightning F3	Privately owned, Lower Tremar, Cornwall
	XH753	BAC Lightning F6 (8969M) [BP]	RAF Leeming on display
	XR754	BAC Lightning F6 (8972M) <ff>	Blyth Valley Aviation Collection, Walpole
	XR755	BAC Lightning F6	Privately owned, Callington, Cornwall
	XR757	BAC Lightning F6 <ff>	NATO Aircraft Museum, New Waltham, Humberside
	XR759	BAC Lightning F6 <ff>	Privately owned, Haxey, Humberside
	XR770	BAC Lightning F6 [JS]	NATO Aircraft Museum, New Waltham, Humberside
	XR771	BAC Lightning F6 [BM]	Midland Air Museum, Coventry
	XR773	BAC Lightning F6 (G-OPIB)	Lightning Flying Club, Exeter Airport
	XR777	WS Scout AH1 (really XT625)	AAC, stored Middle Wallop
	XR806	BAC VC10 C1K	RAF No 10 Sqn, Brize Norton
	XR807	BAC VC10 C1K	RAF No 10 Sqn, Brize Norton
	XR808	BAC VC10 C1K	RAF No 10 Sqn, Brize Norton
	XR810	BAC VC10 C1K	RAF No 10 Sqn, Brize Norton
	XR944	Wallis WA116 (G-ATTB)	RAF Museum, Hendon
	XR953	HS Gnat T1 (8609M) [63]	RAF Halton
	XR954	HS Gnat T1 (8570M) [30]	Privately owned, Ipswich
	XR955	HS Gnat T1 [SAH-2]	Privately owned, Leavesden
	XR977	HS Gnat T1 (8640M) [3]	RAF Cosford Aerospace Museum
	XR980	HS Gnat T1 (8622M) [70]	Sold to the USA as N936FC, October 1994
	XR985	HS Gnat T1 (7886M)	Vintage Aircraft Team, Bruntingthorpe
	XR991	HS Gnat T1 (8624M/XS102/ G-MOUR)	Intrepid Aviation Co, North Weald
	XR993	HS Gnat T1 (8620M/XP534/ G-BVPP)	Kennet Aviation, Cranfield
	XR998	HS Gnat T1 (8623M) [71]	Sold to the USA as N998XR, May 1995
	XS101	HS Gnat T1 (8638M) (G-GNAT)	Privately owned, Cranfield
	XS122	WS58 Wessex HAS3 [655/PO]	RNAS Lee-on-Solent
	XS128	WS58 Wessex HAS1 [37]	RNAS Yeovilton, Fire Section
	XS149	WS58 Wessex HAS3 [661/GL]	IHM, Weston-super-Mare
	XS165	Hiller UH12E (G-ASAZ) [37]	Privately owned, Luton
	XS176	Hunting Jet Provost T4 (8514M) [N]	University of Salford, Manchester
	XS177	Hunting Jet Provost T4 (9044M) [N]	RAF Valley Fire Section
	XS178	Hunting Jet Provost T4 (8994M) [P,05]	Sold to Australia, April 1994
	XS179	Hunting Jet Provost T4 (8237M) [20]	University of Salford, Manchester
	XS180	Hunting Jet Provost T4 (8238M) [21]	RAF St Athan (dismantled)
	XS181	Hunting Jet Provost T4 (9033M) [F]	Phoenix Aviation, Bruntingthorpe
	XS183	Hunting Jet Provost T4 <ff>	Imperial War Museum, stored Duxford
	XS186	Hunting Jet Provost T4 (8408M) [M]	RAF North Luffenham Training Area

Serial	Type (other identity) [code]	Owner/operator, location or fate	Notes
XS209	Hunting Jet Provost T4 (8409M) [29]	RAF Halton	
XS215	Hunting Jet Provost T4 (8507M) [17]	RAF Halton, dismantled	
XS216	Hunting Jet Provost T4 <ff>	RAF Finningley Fire Section	
XS217	Hunting Jet Provost T4 (9029M) [O]	Privately owned, Bruntingthorpe	
XS218	Hunting Jet Provost T4 (8508M) <ff>	Museum of Berkshire Aviation, Woodley	
XS230	BAC Jet Provost T5P (G-BVWF)	Transair (UK) Ltd, North Weald	
XS231	BAC Jet Provost T5 (G-ATAJ)	Phoenix Aviation, Bruntingthorpe	
XS235	DH106 Comet 4C	MoD(PE)/FWTS, DTEO Boscombe Down	
XS416	BAC Lightning T5 <ff>	NATO Aircraft Museum, New Waltham, Humberside	
XS417	BAC Lightning T5	Newark Air Museum, Winthorpe	
XS420	BAC Lightning T5	Fenland Air Museum, Wisbech	
XS422	BAC Lightning T5	Privately owned, Southampton Docks	
XS451	BAC Lightning T5 (8503M/ G-LTNG)	Lightning Flying Club, Plymouth	
XS452	BAC Lightning T5 (G-BPFE) [BT]	Privately owned, Cranfield	
XS456	BAC Lightning T5	Privately owned, Wainfleet	
XS457	BAC Lightning T5 <ff>	NATO Aircraft Museum, New Waltham, Humberside	
XS458	BAC Lightning T5 [DY]	Privately owned, Cranfield	
XS459	BAC Lightning T5	Fenland Air Museum, Wisbech	
XS463	WS Wasp HAS1 (XT431)	IHM, Weston-super-Mare	
XS463	WS Wasp HAS1	RN Predannack Fire School	
XS479	WS58 Wessex HU5 (8819M) [XF]	JATE, RAF Brize Norton	
XS481	WS58 Wessex HU5	AAC Dishforth, BDRT	
XS482	WS58 Wessex HU5 [A-D]	Privately owned, RAF Manston	
XS483	WS58 Wessex HU5 [T/VL]	RNAS Lee-on-Solent, BDRT	
XS484	WS58 Wessex HU5 [821/CU]	RAF Finningley, Fire Section	
XS485	WS58 Wessex HC5C [*Hearts*]	RAF, stored Shawbury	
XS486	WS58 Wessex HU5 [524/CU,F]	RN Recruiting Team, Lee-on-Solent	
XS488	WS58 Wessex HU5 (9056M) [XK]	RAF No 1 SoTT, Cosford	
XS489	WS58 Wessex HU5 [R]	RAF Odiham, instructional use	
XS491	WS58 Wessex HU5 [XM]	RAF No 16 MU Stafford, Fire Section	
XS492	WS58 Wessex HU5 [623]	RN, stored	
XS493	WS58 Wessex HU5	RN, stored Fleetlands	
XS496	WS58 Wessex HU5 [625/PO]	RN AES, *HMS Sultan*, Gosport	
XS498	WS58 Wessex HC5C [*Joker*]	RAF, stored Shawbury	
XS507	WS58 Wessex HU5 [627/PO]	RN AES, *HMS Sultan*, Gosport	
XS508	WS58 Wessex HU5	FAA Museum, RNAS Yeovilton	
XS509	WS58 Wessex HU5	MoD(PE)/ETPS, DTEO Boscombe Down	
XS510	WS58 Wessex HU5 [626/PO]	BAe Warton, instructional use	
XS511	WS58 Wessex HU5 [M]	RN AES, *HMS Sultan*, Gosport	
XS513	WS58 Wessex HU5 [419/PO]	RNAS Lee-on-Solent, BDRT	
XS514	WS58 Wessex HU5 [L]	RN AES, *HMS Sultan*, Gosport	
XS515	WS58 Wessex HU5 [N]	RN AES, *HMS Sultan*, Gosport	
XS516	WS58 Wessex HU5 [Q]	RNAS Lee-on-Solent	
XS517	WS58 Wessex HC5C [*Diamonds*]	RAF, stored Shawbury	
XS520	WS58 Wessex HU5 [F]	RN AES, *HMS Sultan*, Gosport	
XS521	WS58 Wessex HU5	Army, Saighton, Cheshire	
XS522	WS58 Wessex HU5 [ZL]	RNAS Lee-on-Solent	
XS523	WS58 Wessex HU5 [824/CU]	RNAS Lee-on-Solent, BDRT	
XS527	WS Wasp HAS1	FAA Museum, RNAS Yeovilton	
XS529	WS Wasp HAS1 [461]	RNAS Culdrose, BDRT	
XS535	WS Wasp HAS1 [432]	RAOC, West Moors, Dorset	
XS538	WS Wasp HAS1 [451]	*Burnt at Predannack by August 1995*	
XS539	WS Wasp HAS1 [435]	RNAY Fleetlands Apprentice School	
XS545	WS Wasp HAS1 [635]	RNAS Lee-on-Solent	
XS567	WS Wasp HAS1 [434/E]	Imperial War Museum, Duxford	
XS568	WS Wasp HAS1 [441]	RNAY Fleetlands Apprentice School	
XS569	WS Wasp HAS1	RNAY Fleetlands Apprentice School	
XS570	WS Wasp HAS1 [445/P]	Warship Preservation Trust, Birkenhead	
XS572	WS Wasp HAS1 (8845M) [414]	RAF No 16 MU Stafford, Fire Section	
XS576	DH110 Sea Vixen FAW2 [125/E]	Imperial War Museum, Duxford	
XS577	DH110 Sea Vixen D3	Privately owned	
XS587	DH110 Sea Vixen FAW(TT)2 (8828M/G-VIXN)	Privately owned, Charlwood, Surrey	
XS590	DH110 Sea Vixen FAW2 [131/E]	FAA Museum, RNAS Yeovilton	
XS596	HS Andover C1(PR)	MoD(PE)/FWTS, DTEO Boscombe Down	
XS597	HS Andover C1	*Sold as 3D-ATS, November 1994*	

Notes	Serial	Type (other identity) [code]	Owner/operator, location or fate
	XS598	HS Andover C1 (fuselage)	FETC, Moreton-in-Marsh
	XS603	HS Andover E3	Hunting Air Services, East Midlands Airport
	XS605	HS Andover E3	RAF Northolt Fire Section
	XS606	HS Andover C1	MoD(PE)/ETPS, DTEO Boscombe Down
	XS607	HS Andover C1 (G-BEBY)	MoD(PE)/DRA, DTEO Boscombe Down
	XS610	HS Andover E3	Hunting Air Services, East Midlands Airport
	XS639	HS Andover E3A	RAF Cosford Aerospace Museum
	XS640	HS Andover E3	Hunting Air Services, East Midlands Airport
	XS641	HS Andover C1(PR) (9198M) [Z]	RAF No 1 SoTT, Cosford
	XS343	HS Andover E3A	MoD(PE), DTEO Boscombe Down, wfu
	XS646	HS Andover C1(mod)	MoD(PE)/DRA, DTEO Boscombe Down
	XS674	WS58 Wessex HC2 [R]	RAF No 60 Sqn, Benson
	XS675	WS58 Wessex HC2 [Spades]	RAF No 84 Sqn, Akrotiri
	XS676	WS58 Wessex HC2 [WJ]	RAF No 2 FTS, Shawbury
	XS677	WS58 Wessex HC2 [WK]	RAF No 2 FTS, Shawbury
	XS679	WS58 Wessex HC2 [WG]	RAF No 2 FTS, Shawbury
	XS695	HS Kestrel FGA1	RAF Museum Restoration Centre, Cardington
	XS709	HS125 Dominie T1 [M]	RAF No 3 FTS, Cranwell
	XS710	HS125 Dominie T1 [O]	RAF No 3 FTS, Cranwell
	XS711	HS125 Dominie T1 [L]	RAF No 3 FTS, Cranwell
	XS712	HS125 Dominie T2 [A]	RAF No 3 FTS, Cranwell
	XS713	HS125 Dominie T2 [C]	RAF No 3 FTS, Cranwell
	XS714	HS125 Dominie T1 [P]	FSCTE, RAF Manston
	XS726	HS125 Dominie T1 [T]	RAF No 3 FTS, Cranwell
	XS727	HS125 Dominie T1 [D]	RAF No 3 FTS, Cranwell
	XS728	HS125 Dominie T2 [E]	MoD(PE)/FWTS, DTEO Boscombe Down
	XS729	HS125 Dominie T1 [G]	RAF No 3 FTS, Cranwell
	XS730	HS125 Dominie T2 [H]	RAF No 3 FTS, Cranwell
	XS731	HS125 Dominie T2 [J]	RAF No 3 FTS, Cranwell
	XS732	HS125 Dominie T1 [B] (fuselage)	DERA, Fort Halstead, Kent
	XS733	HS125 Dominie T1 [Q]	RAF No 3 FTS, Cranwell
	XS734	HS125 Dominie T2 [N]	RAF No 3 FTS, Cranwell
	XS735	HS125 Dominie T1 [R]	RAF No 3 FTS, Cranwell
	XS736	HS125 Dominie T2 [S]	RAF No 3 FTS, Cranwell
	XS737	HS125 Dominie T2 [K]	RAF No 3 FTS, Cranwell
	XS738	HS125 Dominie T1 [U]	RAF No 3 FTS, Cranwell
	XS739	HS125 Dominie T2 [F]	RAF No 3 FTS, Cranwell
	XS743	Beagle B206Z Basset CC1	MoD(PE)/ETPS, DTEO Boscombe Down
	XS770	Beagle B206Z Basset CC1 (G-HRHI)	Privately owned, Cranfield
	XS789	HS748 Andover CC2	Sold as D2-MAG, April 1995
	XS790	HS748 Andover CC2	MoD(PE)/DRA, DTEO Boscombe Down
	XS791	HS748 Andover CC2	Phoenix Aviation, Bruntingthorpe
	XS792	HS748 Andover CC2	Sold as G-BVZS, March 1995
	XS793	HS748 Andover CC2 (9178M) [Y]	RAF No 1 SoTT, Cosford
	XS794	HS748 Andover CC2	Sold as D2-MAF, April 1995
	XS862	WS58 Wessex HAS3	NB&C Defence Centre, Winterbourne Gunner
	XS863	WS58 Wessex HAS1	Imperial War Museum, Duxford
	XS866	WS58 Wessex HAS1 [520/CU]	SFDO, RNAS Culdrose
	XS868	WS58 Wessex HAS1	RNAS Lee-on-Solent
	XS870	WS58 Wessex HAS1 [PO]	RN Portland, Fire Section
	XS871	WS58 Wessex HAS1 (8457M) [AI]	RAF Odiham, Fire Section
	XS872	WS58 Wessex HAS1 [572/CU]	RNAY Fleetlands Apprentice School
	XS873	WS58 Wessex HAS1	Burnt at Predannack by August 1995
	XS876	WS58 Wessex HAS1 [523]	RNAS Culdrose, Fire Section
	XS877	WS58 Wessex HAS1 [516/PO]	RN Predannack Fire School
	XS881	WS58 Wessex HAS1 [046/CU]	RNAS Yeovilton, BDRT
	XS885	WS58 Wessex HAS1 [12/CU]	SFDO, RNAS Culdrose
	XS886	WS58 Wessex HAS1 [527/CU]	Sea Scouts, Evesham, Worcs
	XS887	WS58 Wessex HAS1 [403/FI]	Flambards Village Theme Park, Helston
	XS888	WS58 Wessex HAS1 [521]	Guernsey Airport, Fire Section
	XS897	BAC Lightning F6	South Yorkshire Aviation Museum, Firbeck
	XS898	BAC Lightning F6 <ff>	Phoenix Aviation, Bruntingthorpe
	XS899	BAC Lightning F6 <ff>	Phoenix Aviation, Bruntingthorpe
	XS903	BAC Lightning F6 [BA]	Yorkshire Air Museum, Elvington
	XS904	BAC Lightning F6 [BQ]	Lightning Preservation Grp, Bruntingthorpe
	XS919	BAC Lightning F6	Privately owned, Lower Tremar, Cornwall
	XS922	BAC Lightning F6 (8973M) <ff>	Wilts Historic Aircraft Group, Salisbury

Serial	Type (other identity) [code]	Owner/operator, location or fate	Notes
XS923	BAC Lightning F6 <ff>	Privately owned, Cranfield	
XS925	BAC Lightning F6 (8961M) [BA]	RAF Museum, Hendon	
XS928	BAC Lightning F6	BAe, Warton, stored	
XS932	BAC Lightning F6 <ff>	Phoenix Aviation, Bruntingthorpe	
XS933	BAC Lightning F6 <ff>	Privately owned, Terrington St Clement	
XS936	BAC Lightning F6	Privately owned, Liskeard, Cornwall	
XT108	Agusta-Bell 47G-3 Sioux AH1 [U]	Museum of Army Flying, Middle Wallop	
XT123	WS Sioux AH1 (XT176) [D]	RM, stored Yeovilton	
XT131	Agusta-Bell 47G-3 Sioux AH1 [B]	AAC Historic Aircraft Flight, Middle Wallop	
XT133	Agusta-Bell 47G-3 Sioux AH1 (7923M)	Royal Engineers' Museum, Chatham, stored	
XT140	Agusta-Bell 47G-3 Sioux AH1	Air Service Training, Perth	
XT148	Agusta-Bell 47G-3 Sioux AH1	IHM, Weston-super-Mare	
XT150	Agusta-Bell 47G-3 Sioux AH1 (7883M) [R]	AAC Netheravon, on display	
XT151	WS Sioux AH1 [W]	Museum of Army Flying, stored Middle Wallop	
XT175	WS Sioux AH1 (TAD175)	CSE Oxford for ground instruction	
XT176	WS Sioux AH1 [U]	Painted as XT123 by July 1995	
XT190	WS Sioux AH1	IHM, Weston-super-Mare	
XT200	WS Sioux AH1 [F]	Newark Air Museum, Winthorpe	
XT236	WS Sioux AH1 (frame only)	North-East Aircraft Museum, Usworth	
XT242	WS Sioux AH1 (composite) [12]	The Aeroplane Collection, Firbeck	
XT255	WS58 Wessex HAS3 (8751M)	RAF No 14 MU, Carlisle, BDRT	
XT257	WS58 Wessex HAS3 (8719M)	RAF No 1 SoTT, Cosford	
XT272	HS Buccaneer S2	DRA Farnborough Fire Section	
XT277	HS Buccaneer S2A (8853M) <ff>	Privately owned, Welshpool	
XT284	HS Buccaneer S2A (8855M)	RAF St Athan, BDRT	
XT288	HS Buccaneer S2B (9134M)	Royal Scottish Museum of Flight, E Fortune	
XT415	WS Wasp HAS1 [FIR3]	Sold to RNZAF	
XT420	WS Wasp HAS1 [606]	Privately owned, Ipswich	
XT422	WS Wasp HAS1 [324]	Privately owned, Burgess Hill	
XT427	WS Wasp HAS1 [606]	Flambards Village Theme Park, Helston	
XT434	WS Wasp HAS1 [455]	RNAY Fleetlands Apprentice School	
XT437	WS Wasp HAS1 [423]	RNAS Lee-on-Solent	
XT439	WS Wasp HAS1 [605]	Kennet Aviation, Cranfield	
XT443	WS Wasp HAS1 [422/AU]	IHM, Weston-super-Mare	
XT449	WS58 Wessex HU5 [C]	RN, Lee-on-Solent, Fire Section	
XT450	WS58 Wessex HU5	RN, Predannack Fire School	
XT453	WS58 Wessex HU5 [A/B]	RNAS Yeovilton	
XT455	WS58 Wessex HU5 [U]	RN AES, HMS Sultan, Gosport	
XT456	WS58 Wessex HU5 (8941M) [XZ]	RAF Aldergrove, BDRT	
XT458	WS58 Wessex HU5 [622]	RNAS Lee-on-Solent	
XT460	WS58 Wessex HU5 [K]	RNAS Lee-on-Solent, BDRT	
XT463	WS58 Wessex HC5C [Clubs]	RAF, stored Shawbury	
XT466	WS58 Wessex HU5 (8921M) [XV]		
XT468	WS58 Wessex HU5 [628]	RNAS Lee-on-Solent	
XT469	WS58 Wessex HU5 (8920M)	RAF No 16 MU, Stafford, ground instruction	
XT470	WS58 Wessex HU5 [A]	AAC, Netheravon, Fire Section	
XT471	WS58 Wessex HU5	AAC, 9 Regt Dishforth, BDRT	
XT472	WS58 Wessex HU5 [XC]	IHM, Weston-super-Mare	
XT475	WS58 Wessex HU5 (9108M) [624]	FSCTE, RAF Manston	
XT480	WS58 Wessex HU5 [468/RG]	RNAY Fleetlands, on display	
XT481	WS58 Wessex HU5	RN Predannack Fire School	
XT482	WS58 Wessex HU5 [ZM/VL]	FAA Museum, RNAS Yeovilton	
XT484	WS58 Wessex HU5 [H]	RNAS Lee-on-Solent	
XT485	WS58 Wessex HU5	RN AES, HMS Sultan, Gosport	
XT486	WS58 Wessex HU5 (8919M) [XR]	RAF JATE, preserved Brize Norton	
XT550	WS Sioux AH1 [D]	AAC Wattisham, on display	
XT575	Vickers Viscount 837 <ff>	Privately owned, Stock, Essex	
XT595	McD F-4K Phantom FG1 (8851M) <ff>	RAF EP&TU, St Athan	
XT596	McD F-4K Phantom FG1	FAA Museum, RNAS Yeovilton	
XT597	McD F-4K Phantom FG1	MoD(PE), DTEO Boscombe Down, for lightning tests	
XT601	WS58 Wessex HC2	RAF No 22 Sqn, C Flt, Valley	
XT602	WS58 Wessex HC2	RAF, stored RNAY Fleetlands	
XT603	WS58 Wessex HC2 [WF]	RAF No 2 FTS, Shawbury	
XT604	WS58 Wessex HC2	RAF, stored RNAY Fleetlands	
XT605	WS58 Wessex HC2 [E]	RAF No 28 Sqn, Sek Kong	

XT606 – XT895

Notes	Serial	Type (other identity) [code]	Owner/operator, location or fate
	XT606	WS58 Wessex HC2 [WL]	RAF No 2 FTS, Shawbury
	XT607	WS58 Wessex HC2 [P]	RAF No 72 Sqn, Aldergrove
	XT616	WS Scout AH1 (fuselage)	AAC, stored RNAW Almondbank
	XT617	WS Scout AH1	AAC, stored RNAW Almondbank
	XT620	WS Scout AH1	AAC Dishforth, BDRT
	XT621	WS Scout AH1	R. Military College of Science, Shrivenham
	XT623	WS Scout AH1	Army Apprentice College, Arborfield
	XT624	WS Scout AH1 [D]	Privately owned, Lincolnshire
	XT626	WS Scout AH1 [Q]	AAC Historic Aircraft Flt, Middle Wallop
	XT630	WS Scout AH1 [X]	Privately owned, Lincolnshire
	XT631	WS Scout AH1 [D]	MoD(PE), DTEO Boscombe Down
	XT632	WS Scout AH1	Privately owned, Hawarden
	XT633	WS Scout AH1	Army Apprentice College, Arborfield
	XT634	WS Scout AH1 [T]	Privately owned, Hawarden
	XT636	WS Scout AH1 [F]	*Withdrawn from use at Brunei*
	XT637	WS Scout AH1 (fuselage)	RNAS Yeovilton, Fire Section
	XT638	WS Scout AH1 [N]	AAC Middle Wallop, at gate
	XT639	WS Scout AH1 [Y] (fuselage)	AAC, stored RNAW Almondbank
	XT640	WS Scout AH1	RNAS Lee-on-Solent, BDRT
	XT642	WS Scout AH1 (fuselage)	AAC, stored RNAW Almondbank
	XT643	WS Scout AH1 [Z]	RE 39 Reg't, Waterbeach, instruct'l use
	XT644	WS Scout AH1 [Y]	Privately owned, Hawarden
	XT645	WS Scout AH1 (fuselage)	AAC Thorney Island, DDRT
	XT646	WS Scout AH1 [Z]	*Sold to New Zealand, October 1995*
	XT649	WS Scout AH1	*Sold to New Zealand, October 1995*
	XT661	Vickers Viscount 838 <ff>	Phoenix Aviation, Bruntingthorpe
	XT668	WS58 Wessex HC2 [S]	RAF No 72 Sqn, Aldergrove
	XT669	WS58 Wessex HC2 (8894M) [T]	RAF Aldergrove, Fire Section
	XT670	WS58 Wessex HC2	RAF SARTU, Valley
	XT671	WS58 Wessex HC2 [D]	RAF No 60 Sqn, Benson
	XT672	WS58 Wessex HC2 [WE]	RAF No 2 FTS, Shawbury
	XT673	WS58 Wessex HC2 [G]	RAF No 28 Sqn, Sek Kong
	XT675	WS58 Wessex HC2 [C]	RAF No 28 Sqn, Sek Kong
	XT676	WS58 Wessex HC2 [I]	RAF No 72 Sqn, Aldergrove
	XT677	WS58 Wessex HC2 (8016M)	RAF Brize Norton Fire Section
	XT678	WS58 Wessex HC2 [H]	RAF No 28 Sqn, Sek Kong
	XT680	WS58 Wessex HC2 [*Diamonds*]	RAF No 84 Sqn, Akrotiri
	XT681	WS58 Wessex HC2 [U]	RAF No 72 Sqn, Aldergrove
	XT752	Fairey Gannet T5 (WN365/ G-APYO)	*Sold to the USA, November 1994*
	XT755	WS58 Wessex HU5 (9053M) [V]	Phoenix Aviation, Bruntingthorpe
	XT756	WS58 Wessex HU5 [ZJ]	RN, Lee-on-Solent, Fire Section
	XT759	WS58 Wessex HU5 [XY]	RN Fleetlands, derelict
	XT760	WS58 Wessex HU5 [418]	RN
	XT761	WS58 Wessex HU5	RN AES, *HMS Sultan*, Gosport
	XT762	WS58 Wessex HU5	SFDO, RNAS Culdrose
	XT765	WS58 Wessex HU5 [J]	RN AES, *HMS Sultan*, Gosport
	XT766	WS58 Wessex HU5 (9054M) [822/CU]	Privately owned, Shawell, Leics
	XT769	WS58 Wessex HU5 [823]	FAA Museum, stored RNAS Yeovilton
	XT770	WS58 Wessex HU5 (9055M)	RAF Halton
	XT771	WS58 Wessex HU5 [620/PO]	RN AES, *HMS Sultan*, Gosport
	XT772	WS58 Wessex HU5 (8805M)	SARTU RAF Valley, ground instruction
	XT773	WS58 Wessex HU5 (9123M)	RAF St Athan, BDRT
	XT778	WS Wasp HAS1 [430]	RNAS Lee-on-Solent
	XT780	WS Wasp HAS1 [636]	RNAY Fleetlands Apprentice School
	XT788	WS Wasp HAS1 [442] (G-BMIR)	Privately owned, Charlwood, Surrey
	XT793	WS Wasp HAS1 [456]	Privately owned, Bruntingthorpe
	XT803	WS Sioux AH1 [Y]	Privately owned, Panshanger
	XT827	WS Sioux AH1 [D] (spares)	AAC Historic Aircraft Flight, Middle Wallop
	XT852	McD YF-4M Phantom FGR2	MoD(PE), DTEO West Freugh, Fire Section
	XT853	McD YF-4M Phantom FGR2 (9071M)	*Scrapped at Scampton, October 1995*
	XT858	McD F-4K Phantom FG1	MoD(PE), stored Aston Down
	XT864	McD F-4K Phantom FG1 (8998M/ XT684) [BJ]	RAF Leuchars on display
	XT867	McD F-4K Phantom FG1 (9064M) [BH]	RAF Leuchars BDRT
	XT891	McD F-4M Phantom FGR2 (9136M)	RAF Coningsby, on display
	XT895	McD F-4M Phantom FGR2 (9171M) [Q]	RAF Valley, Fire Section

Serial	Type (other identity) [code]	Owner/operator, location or fate	Notes
XT896	McD F-4M Phantom FGR2 [V]	*Scrapped at Shawbury, August 1995*	
XT897	McD F-4M Phantom FGR2 [N]	*Scrapped at Shawbury, August 1995*	
XT900	McD F-4M Phantom FGR2 (9099M) [CO]	RAF Honington, BDRT	
XT903	McD F-4M Phantom FGR2 [X]	RAF Leuchars, BDRT	
XT905	McD F-4M Phantom FGR2 [P]	RAF Coningsby, stored	
XT907	McD F-4M Phantom FGR2 (9151M) [W]	Defence School, Chattenden	
XT910	McD F-4M Phantom FGR2	*Scrapped at Shawbury, August 1995*	
XT911	McD F-4M Phantom FGR2 <ff>	Wales Aircraft Museum, Cardiff	
XT914	McD F-4M Phantom FGR2 [Z]	RAF Leeming, decoy	
XV101	BAC VC10 C1K	RAF No 10 Sqn, Brize Norton	
XV102	BAC VC10 C1K	RAF No 10 Sqn, Brize Norton	
XV103	BAC VC10 C1K	RAF No 10 Sqn, Brize Norton	
XV104	BAC VC10 C1K	RAF No 10 Sqn, Brize Norton	
XV105	BAC VC10 C1K	RAF No 10 Sqn, Brize Norton	
XV106	BAC VC10 C1K	RAF No 10 Sqn, Brize Norton	
XV107	BAC VC10 C1K	RAF No 10 Sqn, Brize Norton	
XV108	BAC VC10 C1K	RAF No 10 Sqn, Brize Norton	
XV109	BAC VC10 C1K	RAF No 10 Sqn, Brize Norton	
XV118	WS Scout AH1 (9141M)	RAF Air Movements School, Brize Norton	
XV119	WS Scout AH1 [T]	AAC, Netheravon, BDRT	
XV121	WS Scout AH1	Privately owned, Hawarden	
XV122	WS Scout AH1 [D]	AAC, stored RNAW Almondbank	
XV123	WS Scout AH1	IHM, Weston-super-Mare	
XV124	WS Scout AH1 [W]	AAC SEAE, Arborfield	
XV126	WS Scout AH1 [X]	Privately owned, Hawarden	
XV127	WS Scout AH1	Army, Middle Wallop (children's playground)	
XV128	WS Scout AH1	*Sold to New Zealand, October 1995*	
XV129	WS Scout AH1 [V]	*Sold to New Zealand, October 1995*	
XV130	WS Scout AH1 (G-BWJW) [R]	*Privately owned, Cricklade, Wilts*	
XV131	WS Scout AH1 [Y]	AAC Middle Wallop, BDRT	
XV134	WS Scout AH1 [P]	Privately owned, Ipswich	
XV135	WS Scout AH1	AAC	
XV136	WS Scout AH1 [X]	AAC Netheravon, on display	
XV137	WS Scout AH1	Privately owned,	
XV138	WS Scout AH1	AAC, stored RNAW Almondbank	
XV139	WS Scout AH1	Army Apprentice College, Arborfield	
XV140	WS Scout AH1 (G-KAXL) [K]	Kennet Aviation, Cranfield	
XV141	WS Scout AH1	Army Apprentice College, Arborfield	
XV147	HS Nimrod MR1(mod)	MoD(PE)/BAe Warton	
XV148	HS Nimrod MR1(mod)	MoD(PE)/BAe Woodford	
XV163	HS Buccaneer S2A <ff>	Phoenix Aviation, Bruntingthorpe	
XV165	HS Buccaneer S2B <ff>	Gloucestershire Aviation Collection, Staverton	
XV168	HS Buccaneer S2B	BAe Brough, on display	
XV176	Lockheed C-130K Hercules C3	RAF Lyneham Transport Wing	
XV177	Lockheed C-130K Hercules C3	RAF Lyneham Transport Wing	
XV178	Lockheed C-130K Hercules C1	RAF Lyneham Transport Wing	
XV179	Lockheed C-130K Hercules C1	RAF Lyneham Transport Wing	
XV181	Lockheed C-130K Hercules C1	RAF Lyneham Transport Wing	
XV182	Lockheed C-130K Hercules C1	RAF Lyneham Transport Wing	
XV183	Lockheed C-130K Hercules C3	RAF Lyneham Transport Wing	
XV184	Lockheed C-130K Hercules C3	RAF Lyneham Transport Wing	
XV185	Lockheed C-130K Hercules C1	RAF Lyneham Transport Wing	
XV186	Lockheed C-130K Hercules C1	RAF Lyneham Transport Wing	
XV187	Lockheed C-130K Hercules C1	RAF Lyneham Transport Wing	
XV188	Lockheed C-130K Hercules C3	RAF Lyneham Transport Wing	
XV189	Lockheed C-130K Hercules C3	RAF Lyneham Transport Wing	
XV190	Lockheed C-130K Hercules C3	RAF Lyneham Transport Wing	
XV191	Lockheed C-130K Hercules C1	RAF Lyneham Transport Wing	
XV192	Lockheed C-130K Hercules C1	RAF Lyneham Transport Wing	
XV195	Lockheed C-130K Hercules C1	RAF Lyneham Transport Wing	
XV196	Lockheed C-130K Hercules C1	RAF Lyneham Transport Wing	
XV197	Lockheed C-130K Hercules C3	RAF Lyneham Transport Wing	
XV199	Lockheed C-130K Hercules C3	RAF Lyneham Transport Wing	
XV200	Lockheed C-130K Hercules C1	RAF Lyneham Transport Wing	
XV201	Lockheed C-130K Hercules C1K	RAF Lyneham Transport Wing	
XV202	Lockheed C-130K Hercules C3	RAF Lyneham Transport Wing	
XV203	Lockheed C-130K Hercules C1K	RAF Lyneham Transport Wing	
XV204	Lockheed C-130K Hercules C1K	RAF Lyneham Transport Wing	

Notes	Serial	Type (other identity) [code]	Owner/operator, location or fate
	XV205	Lockheed C-130K Hercules C1	RAF Lyneham Transport Wing
	XV206	Lockheed C-130K Hercules C1	RAF Lyneham Transport Wing
	XV207	Lockheed C-130K Hercules C3	RAF Lyneham Transport Wing
	XV208	Lockheed C-130K Hercules W2	MoD(PE)/MRF, DTEO Boscombe Down
	XV209	Lockheed C-130K Hercules C3	RAF Lyneham Transport Wing
	XV210	Lockheed C-130K Hercules C1	RAF Lyneham Transport Wing
	XV211	Lockheed C-130K Hercules C1	MoD(PE)/FWTS, DTEO Boscombe Down
	XV212	Lockheed C-130K Hercules C3	RAF Lyneham Transport Wing
	XV213	Lockheed C-130K Hercules C1K	RAF Lyneham Transport Wing
	XV214	Lockheed C-130K Hercules C3	RAF, stored Cambridge
	XV215	Lockheed C-130K Hercules C1	RAF Lyneham Transport Wing
	XV217	Lockheed C-130K Hercules C3	RAF Lyneham Transport Wing
	XV218	Lockheed C-130K Hercules C1	RAF Lyneham Transport Wing
	XV219	Lockheed C-130K Hercules C3	RAF Lyneham Transport Wing
	XV220	Lockheed C-130K Hercules C3	RAF Lyneham Transport Wing
	XV221	Lockheed C-130K Hercules C3	RAF Lyneham Transport Wing
	XV222	Lockheed C-130K Hercules C3	RAF Lyneham Transport Wing
	XV223	Lockheed C-130K Hercules C3	RAF Lyneham Transport Wing
	XV226	HS Nimrod MR2	RAF No 120 Sqn, Kinloss
	XV227	HS Nimrod MR2	RAF No 120 Sqn, Kinloss
	XV228	HS Nimrod MR2	RAF No 201 Sqn, Kinloss
	XV229	HS Nimrod MR2	RAF No 206 Sqn, Kinloss
	XV230	HS Nimrod MR2	RAF No 201 Sqn, Kinloss
	XV231	HS Nimrod MR2	HAF No 206 Sqn, Kinloss
	XV232	HS Nimrod MR2	RAF No 201 Sqn, Kinloss
	XV233	HS Nimrod MR2	RAF No 206 Sqn, Kinloss
	XV234	HS Nimrod MR2	RAF, stored Kinloss
	XV235	HS Nimrod MR2	RAF No 120 Sqn, Kinloss
	XV236	HS Nimrod MR2	RAF No 42(R) Sqn, Kinloss
	XV238	HS Nimrod <R> (parts of G-ALYW)	RAF EP&TU, St Athan
	XV239	HS Nimrod MR2	*Written off, Lake Ontario, Canada, 2 Sep 1995*
	XV240	HS Nimrod MR2	RAF No 120 Sqn, Kinloss
	XV241	HS Nimrod MR2	RAF No 201 Sqn, Kinloss
	XV242	HS Nimrod MR2	RAF, stored Kinloss
	XV243	HS Nimrod MR2	RAF No 120 Sqn, Kinloss
	XV244	HS Nimrod MR2	RAF No 201 Sqn, Kinloss
	XV245	HS Nimrod MR2	RAF No 201 Sqn, Kinloss
	XV246	HS Nimrod MR2	RAF No 201 Sqn, Kinloss
	XV247	HS Nimrod MR2	RAF, stored Kinloss
	XV248	HS Nimrod MR2	RAF No 206 Sqn, Kinloss
	XV249	HS Nimrod R	MoD(PE)/BAe Woodford (conversion)
	XV250	HS Nimrod MR2	RAF No 120 Sqn, Kinloss
	XV251	HS Nimrod MR2	RAF No 206 Sqn, Kinloss
	XV252	HS Nimrod MR2	RAF No 201 Sqn, Kinloss
	XV254	HS Nimrod MR2	RAF No 201 Sqn, Kinloss
	XV255	HS Nimrod MR2	RAF Kinloss MR Wing
	XV258	HS Nimrod MR2	RAF No 206 Sqn, Kinloss
	XV260	HS Nimrod MR2	RAF No 120 Sqn, Kinloss
	XV263	BAe Nimrod AEW3P (8967M)	RAF Air Engineer Sqn, Finningley
	XV268	DHC2 Beaver AL1 (G-BVER)	Privately owned
	XV277	HS Harrier GR1	RNAS Yeovilton
	XV279	HS Harrier GR1 (8566M) [44]	RAF Wittering WLT
	XV280	HS Harrier GR1 <ff>	RNAS Yeovilton, Fire Section
	XV281	HS Harrier GR3	BAe Warton, instructional use
	XV290	Lockheed C-130K Hercules C3	RAF Lyneham Transport Wing
	XV291	Lockheed C-130K Hercules C1	RAF Lyneham Transport Wing
	XV292	Lockheed C-130K Hercules C1	RAF Lyneham Transport Wing
	XV293	Lockheed C-130K Hercules C1	RAF Lyneham Transport Wing
	XV294	Lockheed C-130K Hercules C3	RAF Lyneham Transport Wing
	XV295	Lockheed C-130K Hercules C1	RAF Lyneham Transport Wing
	XV296	Lockheed C-130K Hercules C1K	*Scrapped at Cambridge, December 1995*
	XV297	Lockheed C-130K Hercules C1	RAF Lyneham Transport Wing
	XV298	Lockheed C-130K Hercules C1	MoD(PE)/FWTS, DTEO Boscombe Down
	XV299	Lockheed C-130K Hercules C3	RAF Lyneham Transport Wing
	XV300	Lockheed C-130K Hercules C1	RAF Lyneham Transport Wing
	XV301	Lockheed C-130K Hercules C3	RAF Lyneham Transport Wing
	XV302	Lockheed C-130K Hercules C3	RAF Lyneham Transport Wing
	XV303	Lockheed C-130K Hercules C3	RAF Lyneham Transport Wing
	XV304	Lockheed C-130K Hercules C3	RAF Lyneham Transport Wing
	XV305	Lockheed C-130K Hercules C3	RAF Lyneham Transport Wing
	XV306	Lockheed C-130K Hercules C1	RAF Lyneham Transport Wing
	XV307	Lockheed C-130K Hercules C3	RAF Lyneham Transport Wing

Serial	Type (other identity) [code]	Owner/operator, location or fate
XV328	BAC Lightning T5 <ff>	Privately owned, Bruntingthorpe
XV332	HS Buccaneer S2B	RAF Marham, Fire Section
XV333	HS Buccaneer S2B [234/H]	FAA Museum, RNAS Yeovilton
XV337	HS Buccaneer S2C (8852M)	RAF St Athan, BDRT
XV338	HS Buccaneer S2A (8774M) <ff>	RAF EP&TU, St Athan
XV344	HS Buccaneer S2C	MoD(PE), stored DTEO Boscombe Down
XV350	HS Buccaneer S2B	East Midlands Aero Park
XV352	HS Buccaneer S2B <ff>	RAF, stored St Athan
XV353	HS Buccaneer S2B (9144M) <ff>	Privately owned,
XV359	HS Buccaneer S2B	RN Predannack Fire School
XV361	HS Buccaneer S2B	Ulster Aviation Society, Langford Lodge
XV370	Sikorsky S61D-2	RNAS Lee-on-Solent
XV371	WS61 Sea King HAS1	RN AES, *HMS Sultan*, Gosport
XV372	WS61 Sea King HAS1	RAF St Mawgan, instructional use
XV393	McD F-4M Phantom FGR2 [Q]	RAF Marham, WLT
XV399	McD F-4M Phantom FGR2 <ff>	Privately owned, Stock, Essex
XV401	McD F-4M Phantom FGR2 [I]	MoD(PE), DTEO Boscombe Down, GI use
XV402	McD F-4M Phantom FGR2 <ff>	Privately owned, Stock, Essex
XV406	McD F-4M Phantom FGR2 (9098M) [CK]	RAF Carlisle, on display
XV408	McD F-4M Phantom FGR2 (9165M) [Z]	RAF Cranwell, on display
XV411	McD F-4M Phantom FGR2 (9103M) [L]	FSCTE, RAF Manston
XV415	McD F-4M Phantom FGR2 (9163M) [E]	RAF Boulmer, on display
XV420	McD F-4M Phantom FGR2 [O]	RAF Neatishead, main gate
XV422	McD F-4M Phantom FGR2] (9157M) [T	Stornoway Airport, on display
XV423	McD F-4M Phantom FGR2 [Y]	RAF Leeming, BDRT
XV424	McD F-4M Phantom FGR2 (9152M) [I]	RAF Museum, Hendon
XV426	McD F-4M Phantom FGR2 [P]	RAF Coningsby, BDRT
XV433	McD F-4M Phantom FGR2 [E]	*Scrapped at Shawbury, August 1995*
XV435	McD F-4M Phantom FGR2 [R]	DTEO Llanbedr, Fire Section
XV460	McD F-4M Phantom FGR2 [R]	RAF Coningsby
XV465	McD F-4M Phantom FGR2 [S]	RAF Leeming, decoy
XV467	McD F-4M Phantom FGR2 (9158M) [F]	Benbecula Airport, on display
XV468	McD F-4M Phantom FGR2 (9159M) [H]	RAF Woodvale, on display
XV469	McD F-4M Phantom FGR2	*Scrapped at Shawbury, August 1995*
XV474	McD F-4M Phantom FGR2 [T]	The Old Flying Machine Company, Duxford
XV482	McD F-4M Phantom FGR2 (9107M) [T]	RAF Leuchars, Fire Section
XV487	McD F-4M Phantom FGR2 [G]	*Scrapped at Shawbury, August 1995*
XV489	McD F-4M Phantom FGR2 <ff>	Privately owned, Bruntingthorpe
XV490	McD F-4M Phantom FGR2 <ff>	Privately owned, Bruntingthorpe
XV497	McD F-4M Phantom FGR2 [W]	RAF High Wycombe, on display
XV499	McD F-4M Phantom FGR2	RAF Leeming, WLT
XV500	McD F-4M Phantom FGR2 (9113M)	RAF St Athan, on display
XV577	McD F-4K Phantom FG1 (9065M) [AM]	RAF Leuchars, BDRT
XV581	McD F-4K Phantom FG1 (9070M) [AE]	RAF Buchan, on display
XV582	McD F-4K Phantom FG1 (9066M) [M]	RAF Leuchars on display
XV585	McD F-4K Phantom FG1 [AP]	RAF Leuchars
XV586	McD F-4K Phantom FG1 (9067M) [AJ]	RAF Leuchars BDRT
XV588	McD F-4K Phantom FG1 [007] <ff>	RN Predannack Fire School
XV591	McD F-4K Phantom FG1 <ff>	RAF Cosford Aerospace Museum
XV625	WS Wasp HAS1 [471]	RN AES, *HMS Sultan*, Gosport
XV629	WS Wasp HAS1	AAC Middle Wallop, BDRT
XV642	WS61 Sea King HAS2A	RNAS Lee-on-Solent
XV643	WS61 Sea King HAS6 [703/PW]	RN No 819 Sqn, Prestwick
XV644	WS61 Sea King HAS1 [643]	*Burnt at Predannack 1995*
XV647	WS61 Sea King HAR5 [820/CU]	RN No 771 Sqn, Culdrose
XV648	WS61 Sea King HAR5 [827/CU]	RN, stored Fleetlands
XV649	WS61 Sea King AEW2A [186/N]	RN No 849 Sqn, Culdrose
XV650	WS61 Sea King AEW2A [184/L]	RN No 849 Sqn, Culdrose

XV651 – XV804

Notes	Serial	Type (other identity) [code]	Owner/operator, location or fate
	XV651	WS61 Sea King HAR5	RNAY Fleetlands (conversion)
	XV653	WS61 Sea King HAS6 [500]	RN No 810 Sqn, Culdrose
	XV654	WS61 Sea King HAS6 [705/PW] (wreck)	RNAY Fleetlands, stored
	XV655	WS61 Sea King HAS5 [701/PW]	RN AMG, Culdrose
	XV656	WS61 Sea King AEW2A [180]	RN No 849 Sqn, Culdrose
	XV657	WS61 Sea King HAS5 [132]	RN ETS, Culdrose
	XV659	WS61 Sea King HAS6 [268/N]	RN No 814 Sqn, Culdrose
	XV660	WS61 Sea King HAS6 [511/CL]	RN No 810 Sqn, Culdrose
	XV661	WS61 Sea King HAR5 [824/CU]	RN No 771 Sqn, Culdrose
	XV663	WS61 Sea King HAS6 [501/CU]	RN No 810 Sqn, Culdrose
	XV664	WS61 Sea King AEW2A [181/CU]	RN No 849 Sqn, Culdrose
	XV665	WS61 Sea King HAS6 [505/CU]	RN No 810 Sqn, Culdrose
	XV666	WS61 Sea King HAR5 [823/CU]	RNAY Fleetlands
	XV669	WS61 Sea King HAS1 [10]	RN ETS, Culdrose
	XV670	WS61 Sea King HAS6	RN No 819 Sqn, Prestwick
	XV671	WS61 Sea King AEW2A [188/CU]	RNAY Fleetlands
	XV672	WS61 Sea King AEW2A [182/L]	RN No 849 Sqn, Culdrose
	XV673	WS61 Sea King HAR5	RNAY Fleetlands (conversion)
	XV674	WS61 Sea King HAS6 [705/PW]	RN No 819 Sqn, Prestwick
	XV675	WS61 Sea King HAS6 [598/CU]	RN No 706 Sqn, Culdrose
	XV676	WS61 Sea King HAS6 [515/CM]	RN No 810 Sqn, Culdrose
	XV677	WS61 Sea King HAS6 [269/N]	RN No 814 Sqn, Culdrose
	XV696	WS61 Sea King HAS6 [708/PW]	RN No 819 Sqn, Prestwick
	XV697	WS61 Sea King AEW2A [181/CU]	RN No 849 Sqn, Culdrose
	XV699	WS61 Sea King HAR5 [826/CU]	RN, stored Fleetlands
	XV700	WS61 Sea King HAS6 [008/CU]	RN AMG, Culdrose
	XV701	WS61 Sea King HAS6 [010/L]	RN AMG, Culdrose
	XV703	WS61 Sea King HAS6 [265/N]	RN No 814 Sqn, Culdrose
	XV704	WS61 Sea King AEW2A [183/L]	RN No 849 Sqn, Culdrose
	XV705	WS61 Sea King HAR5 [821/CU]	RN No 771 Sqn, Culdrose
	XV706	WS61 Sea King HAS6 [583/CU]	RN No 706 Sqn, Culdrose
	XV707	WS61 Sea King AEW2A [185/N]	RN No 849 Sqn, Culdrose
	XV708	WS61 Sea King HAS6 [510/CU]	RN No 810 Sqn, Culdrose
	XV709	WS61 Sea King HAS6 [585]	RN No 706 Sqn, Culdrose
	XV710	WS61 Sea King HAS6 [012/L]	RN No 820 Sqn, Culdrose
	XV711	WS61 Sea King HAS6 [709/PW]	RN No 819 Sqn, Prestwick
	XV712	WS61 Sea King HAS6 [266/N]	RN No 814 Sqn, Culdrose
	XV713	WS61 Sea King HAS6 [018/L]	RN No 820 Sqn, Culdrose
	XV714	WS61 Sea King AEW2A [187/N]	RN No 849 Sqn, Culdrose
	XV720	WS58 Wessex HC2	RAF SARTU, Valley
	XV721	WS58 Wessex HC2 [H]	RAF No 72 Sqn, Aldergrove
	XV722	WS58 Wessex HC2 [WH]	RAF No 2 FTS, Shawbury
	XV723	WS58 Wessex HC2 [Q]	RAF No 72 Sqn, Aldergrove
	XV724	WS58 Wessex HC2	RAF No 22 Sqn, C Flt, Valley
	XV725	WS58 Wessex HC2 [C]	RAF No 72 Sqn, Aldergrove
	XV726	WS58 Wessex HC2 [J]	RAF No 72 Sqn, Aldergrove
	XV728	WS58 Wessex HC2 [A]	RAF No 72 Sqn, Aldergrove
	XV729	WS58 Wessex HC2	RAF SARTU, Valley
	XV730	WS58 Wessex HC2 [Clubs]	RAF No 84 Sqn, Akrotiri
	XV731	WS58 Wessex HC2 [Y]	RAF No 72 Sqn, Aldergrove
	XV732	WS58 Wessex HCC4	RAF No 32(The Royal) Sqn, Northolt
	XV733	WS58 Wessex HCC4	RAF No 32(The Royal) Sqn, Northolt
	XV738	HS Harrier GR3 (9074M) [B]	Phoenix Aviation, Bruntingthorpe
	XV741	HS Harrier GR3 [1,5]	SFDO, RNAS Culdrose
	XV744	HS Harrier GR3 (9167M) [3K]	Royal Military College of Science, Shrivenham
	XV747	HS Harrier GR3 (8979M) (fuselage)	No 1803 Sqn ATC, Hucknall
	XV748	HS Harrier GR3 [3D]	Cranfield College of Aeronautics
	XV751	HS Harrier GR3	*Scrapped at Leicester, October 1995*
	XV752	HS Harrier GR3 (9078M) [B,HF]	RAF No 1 SoTT, Cosford
	XV753	HS Harrier GR3 (9075M) [3F,4]	SFDO, RNAS Culdrose
	XV755	HS Harrier GR3 [M]	RNAS Yeovilton, Fire Section
	XV760	HS Harrier GR3 [VL]	RNAS Yeovilton, ETS
	XV779	HS Harrier GR3 (8931M) [01,A]	RAF Wittering on display
	XV783	HS Harrier GR3 [N]	RN AES, *HMS Sultan*, Gosport
	XV784	HS Harrier GR3 (8909M) <ff>	DTEO, Boscombe Down, GI use
	XV786	HS Harrier GR3 <ff>	RNAS Culdrose
	XV786	HS Harrier GR3 [S] <rf>	RN, Predannack Fire School
	XV798	HS Harrier GR1(mod)	Bristol Aero Collection, Banwell
	XV804	HS Harrier GR3	Defence NBC Centre, Winterbourne Gunner

Serial	Type (other identity) [code]	Owner/operator, location or fate	Notes
XV806	HS Harrier GR3 [E]	SFDO, RNAS Culdrose	
XV808	HS Harrier GR3 (9076M) [3J,6]	SFDO, RNAS Culdrose	
XV810	HS Harrier GR3 (9038M) [K]	RAF St Athan, BDRT	
XV814	DH106 Comet 4	MoD(PE), DTEO Boscombe Down, spares use	
XV863	HS Buccaneer S2B (9115M/ 9139M/9145M) [S]	RAF Lossiemouth, on display	
XV864	HS Buccaneer S2B	FSCTE, RAF Manston	
XV865	HS Buccaneer S2B (9226M)	RAF Coningsby, Fire Section	
XV867	HS Buccaneer S2B	RAF Lossiemouth	
XW175	HS Harrier T4A(mod)	MoD(PE), Cranfield Institute of Technology	
XW198	WS Puma HC1	RAF No 230 Sqn, Aldergrove	
XW199	WS Puma HC1 [NB]	RAF No 27(R) Sqn, Odiham	
XW200	WS Puma HC1	RAF No 230 Sqn, Aldergrove	
XW201	WS Puma HC1	RAF No 27(R) Sqn, Odiham	
XW202	WS Puma HC1 [NE]	RAF No 27(R) Sqn, Odiham	
XW204	WS Puma HC1	RAF No 18 Sqn, Laarbruch	
XW206	WS Puma HC1 [NG]	RAF No 27(R) Sqn, Odiham	
XW207	WS Puma HC1	RAF No 230 Sqn, Aldergrove	
XW208	WS Puma HC1	RAF No 230 Sqn, Aldergrove	
XW209	WS Puma HC1 [NH]	RAF No 27(R) Sqn, Odiham	
XW210	WS Puma HC1	RAF Odiham (on repair)	
XW211	WS Puma HC1 [CH]	RAF No 27(R) Sqn, Odiham	
XW212	WS Puma HC1	RAF No 230 Sqn, Aldergrove	
XW213	WS Puma HC1	RAF No 18 Sqn, Laarbruch	
XW214	WS Puma HC1	RAF No 230 Sqn, Aldergrove	
XW215	WS Puma HC1 [R]	Westland, Yeovil (on rebuild)	
XW216	WS Puma HC1 [BY]	RAF No 18 Sqn, Laarbruch	
XW217	WS Puma HC1 [NK]	RAF No 27 Sqn, Odiham	
XW218	WS Puma HC1 [BW]	RAF No 18 Sqn, Laarbruch	
XW219	WS Puma HC1	RAF No 33 Sqn, Odiham	
XW220	WS Puma HC1 [CZ]	RAF No 27(R) Sqn, Odiham	
XW221	WS Puma HC1	RAF No 230 Sqn, Aldergrove	
XW222	WS Puma HC1	RAF No 33 Sqn, Odiham	
XW223	WS Puma HC1	RAF No 33 Sqn, Odiham	
XW224	WS Puma HC1 [BZ]	RAF No 18 Sqn, Laarbruch	
XW225	WS Puma HC1	RAF No 230 Sqn, Aldergrove	
XW226	WS Puma HC1	RAF No 230 Sqn, Aldergrove	
XW227	WS Puma HC1	RAF No 33 Sqn, Odiham	
XW229	WS Puma HC1	RAF No 33 Sqn, Odiham	
XW231	WS Puma HC1 [NM]	RAF No 27(R) Sqn, Odiham	
XW232	WS Puma HC1 [DJ]	RAF No 230 Sqn, Aldergrove	
XW234	WS Puma HC1	RAF No 230 Sqn, Aldergrove	
XW235	WS Puma HC1	RAF No 33 Sqn, Odiham	
XW236	WS Puma HC1 [NO]	RAF No 27(R) Sqn, Odiham	
XW237	WS Puma HC1	RAF No 230 Sqn, Aldergrove	
XW241	Sud SA330E Puma	DRA Avionics & Sensors Dept, Farnborough	
XW249	Cushioncraft CC7	Flambards Village Theme Park, Helston	
XW264	HS Harrier T2 <ff>	Gloucestershire Aviation Collection, Staverton	
XW265	HS Harrier T4A [W]	RAF, stored Shawbury	
XW266	HS Harrier T4N	MoD(PE)/FWTS, DTEO Boscombe Down	
XW267	HS Harrier T4	RAF, stored DTEO Boscombe Down	
XW268	HS Harrier T4N (fuselage)	RNAS Yeovilton, spares recovery	
XW269	HS Harrier T4 [BD]	RAF Wittering	
XW270	HS Harrier T4 (fuselage)	Cranfield Institute of Technology	
XW271	HS Harrier T4 [X,1]	SFDO, RNAS Culdrose	
XW272	HS Harrier T4 (8783M) <ff>		
XW276	Aérospatiale SA341 Gazelle	North-East Aircraft Museum, Usworth	
XW281	WS Scout AH1 [U]	Privately owned, Hawarden	
XW282	WS Scout AH1 [W]	Sold to New Zealand, October 1995	
XW283	WS Scout AH1 [U]	RM, stored Yeovilton	
XW284	WS Scout AH1 [A] (fuselage)	AAC, stored RNAW Almondbank	
XW289	BAC Jet Provost T5A (G-BVXT/ G-JPVA)	Kennet Aircraft, Cranfield	
XW290	BAC Jet Provost T5A (9199M) [41,MA]	RAF No 1 SoTT, Cosford	
XW291	BAC Jet Provost T5 [N]		
XW292	BAC Jet Provost T5A (9128M) [32]	RAF No 1 SoTT, Cosford	
XW293	BAC Jet Provost T5 (G-BWCS) [Z]	Downbird UK Ltd, Tatenhill	

Notes	Serial	Type (other identity) [code]	Owner/operator, location or fate
	XW294	BAC Jet Provost T5A (9129M) [45]	RAF No 1 SoTT, Cosford
	XW299	BAC Jet Provost T5A (9146M) [60,MB]	RAF No 1 SoTT, Cosford
	XW301	BAC Jet Provost T5A (9147M) [63,MC]	RAF No 1 SoTT, Cosford
	XW302	BAC Jet Provost T5 [T]	
	XW303	BAC Jet Provost T5A (9119M) [127]	RAF No 1 SoTT, Cosford
	XW304	BAC Jet Provost T5 (9172M) [MD]	RAF No 1 SoTT, Cosford
	XW305	BAC Jet Provost T5A [42]	Privately owned, Ipswich
	XW306	BAC Jet Provost T5 [O]	
	XW309	BAC Jet Provost T5 (9179M) [V,ME]	RAF No 1 SoTT, Cosford
	XW310	BAC Jet Provost T5A (G-BWGS) [37]	Privately owned, Ipswich
	XW311	BAC Jet Provost T5 (9180M) [W,MF]	RAF No 1 SoTT, Cosford
	XW312	BAC Jet Provost T5A (9109M) [64]	RAF No 1 SoTT, Cosford
	XW313	BAC Jet Provost T5A (G-BVTB) [85]	Sold to the USA, 1995
	XW315	BAC Jet Provost T5A	Privately owned, Long Marston
	XW317	BAC Jet Provost T5A [79]	
	XW318	BAC Jet Provost T5A (9190M) [78,MG]	RAF No 1 SoTT, Cosford
	XW319	BAC Jet Provost T5A [76]	Sold to the USA, 1994
	XW320	BAC Jet Provost T5A (9015M) [71]	RAF No 1 SoTT, Cosford
	XW321	BAC Jet Provost T5A (9154M) [62,MH]	RAF No 1 SoTT, Cosford
	XW322	BAC Jet Provost T5B [D]	Sold to the USA, 1994
	XW323	BAC Jet Provost T5A (9166M) [86]	RAF Museum, Hendon
	XW324	BAC Jet Provost T5 [U]	Global Aviation, Binbrook
	XW325	BAC Jet Provost T5B (G-BWGF) [E]	Global Aviation, Binbrook
	XW326	BAC Jet Provost T5A [62]	Sold to the USA, July 1995
	XW327	BAC Jet Provost T5A (9130M) [62]	RAF No 1 SoTT, Cosford
	XW328	BAC Jet Provost T5A (9177M) [75,MI]	RAF No 1 SoTT, Cosford
	XW330	BAC Jet Provost T5A (9195M) [82,MJ]	RAF No 1 SoTT, Cosford
	XW333	BAC Jet Provost T5A (G-BVTC/ G-JPRO)	Global Aviation, Binbrook
	XW335	BAC Jet Provost T5A (9061M) [74]	RAF No 1 SoTT, Cosford
	XW336	BAC Jet Provost T5A [67]	Sold to the USA, 1994
	XW351	BAC Jet Provost T5A (9062M) [31]	RAF Halton
	XW352	BAC Jet Provost T5 [R]	Privately owned, stored Tamworth
	XW353	BAC Jet Provost T5A (9090M) [3]	RAF Cranwell, on display
	XW355	BAC Jet Provost T5A [20]	Downbird UK Ltd, Tatenhill
	XW358	BAC Jet Provost T5A (9181M) [59,MK]	RAF No 1 SoTT, Cosford
	XW360	BAC Jet Provost T5A (9153M) [61,ML]	RAF No 1 SoTT, Cosford
	XW361	BAC Jet Provost T5A (9192M) [81,MM]	RAF No 1 SoTT, Cosford
	XW363	BAC Jet Provost T5A [36]	BAe Training School, Warton
	XW364	BAC Jet Provost T5A (9188M) [35,MN]	RAF No 1 SoTT, Cosford
	XW365	BAC Jet Provost T5A (9018M) [73]	RAF No 1 SoTT, Cosford
	XW366	BAC Jet Provost T5A (9097M) [75]	RAF No 1 SoTT, Cosford
	XW367	BAC Jet Provost T5A (9193M) [64,MO]	RAF No 1 SoTT, Cosford
	XW370	BAC Jet Provost T5A (9196M) [72,MP]	RAF No 1 SoTT, Cosford
	XW372	BAC Jet Provost T5A [M]	Privately owned, Ipswich
	XW375	BAC Jet Provost T5A (9149M) [52]	RAF Halton
	XW404	BAC Jet Provost T5A (9049M)	RAF CTTS, St Athan
	XW405	BAC Jet Provost T5A (9187M) [J,MQ]	RAF No 1 SoTT, Cosford
	XW406	BAC Jet Provost T5A [23]	To The Netherlands, 21 March 1995
	XW409	BAC Jet Provost T5A (9047M)	RAF CTTS, St Athan

Serial	Type (other identity) [code]	Owner/operator, location or fate	Notes
XW410	BAC Jet Provost T5A (9125M) [80,MR]	RAF No 1 SoTT, Cosford	
XW412	BAC Jet Provost T5A [74]	*Sold to the USA, 1994*	
XW413	BAC Jet Provost T5A (9126M) [69]	RAF No 1 SoTT, Cosford	
XW416	BAC Jet Provost T5A (9191M) [84,MS]	RAF No 1 SoTT, Cosford	
XW418	BAC Jet Provost T5A (9173M) [MT]	RAF No 1 SoTT, Cosford	
XW419	BAC Jet Provost T5A (9120M) [125]	RAF Halton	
XW420	BAC Jet Provost T5A (9194M) [83,MU]	RAF No 1 SoTT, Cosford	
XW421	BAC Jet Provost T5A (9111M) [60]	RAF No 1 SoTT, Cosford	
XW422	BAC Jet Provost T5A (G-BWEB) [3]	Privately owned, North Weald	
XW423	BAC Jet Provost T5A [14]		
XW425	BAC Jet Provost T5A (9200M) [H,MV]	RAF No 1 SoTT, Cosford	
XW427	BAC Jet Provost T5A (9124M) [67]	RAF No 1 SoTT, Cosford	
XW428	BAC Jet Provost T5A [39]	*Sold to the USA as N4311M, December 1994*	
XW428	Hunting Jet Provost T4 (XR674/ G-TOMG/9030M)	Privately owned, North Weald	
XW429	BAC Jet Provost T5B [C]	Global Aviation, Binbrook	
XW430	BAC Jet Provost T5A (9176M) [77,MW]	RAF No 1 SoTT, Cosford	
XW431	BAC Jet Provost T5B (G-BWBS) [A]	Downbird UK Ltd, Tatenhill	
XW432	BAC Jet Provost T5A (9127M) [76,MX]	RAF No 1 SoTT, Cosford	
XW433	BAC Jet Provost T5A [63]		
XW434	BAC Jet Provost T5A (9091M) [78,MY]	RAF No 1 SoTT, Cosford	
XW436	BAC Jet Provost T5A (9148M) [68]	RAF No 1 SoTT, Cosford	
XW437	BAC Jet Provost T5A [71]	*Sold to the USA as N80873, March 1995*	
XW438	BAC Jet Provost T5B [B]		
XW527	HS Buccaneer S2B <ff>	Privately owned, Wittering	
XW528	HS Buccaneer S2B (8861M) [C]	RAF Coningsby Fire Section	
XW530	HS Buccaneer S2B	Privately owned, Elgin	
XW544	HS Buccaneer S2B (8857M) [Y]	Privately owned	
XW547	HS Buccaneer S2B (9095M/ 9169M) [R]	RAF Cosford Aerospace Museum	
XW549	HS Buccaneer S2B (8860M) (fuselage)	RAF Kinloss, BDRT	
XW550	HS Buccaneer S2B <ff>	Privately owned, West Horndon, Essex	
XW566	SEPECAT Jaguar T2	DRA Avionics & Sensors Dept, Farnborough	
XW612	WS Scout AH1 [A]	Privately owned, Lincolnshire	
XW613	WS Scout AH1 [W]	Privately owned, Lincolnshire	
XW614	WS Scout AH1	AAC Historic Flight, Middle Wallop	
XW616	WS Scout AH1	AAC No 70 MU, Middle Wallop	
XW630	HS Harrier GR3	RN AES, *HMS Sultan*, Gosport	
XW635	Beagle D5/180 (G-AWSW)	Privately owned, Spanhoe Lodge	
XW664	HS Nimrod R1	RAF No 51 Sqn, Waddington	
XW665	HS Nimrod R1	RAF No 51 Sqn, Waddington	
XW666	HS Nimrod R1	*Crashed, Moray Firth, 16 May 1995*	
XW750	HS748 Series 107	MoD(PE)/DRA, DTEO Boscombe Down	
XW763	HS Harrier GR3 (9002M/9041M) (fuselage)	Imperial War Museum, stored Duxford	
XW764	HS Harrier GR3 (8981M)	RAF Leeming, Fire Section	
XW768	HS Harrier GR3 (9072M) [N]	RAF No 1 SoTT, Cosford	
XW784	Mitchell-Procter Kittiwake I (G-BBRN)	Privately owned, Haverfordwest	
XW795	WS Scout AH1 (fuselage)	AAC, stored Middle Wallop	
XW796	WS Scout AH1 [X]	AAC SEAE, Arborfield	
XW798	WS Scout AH1	AAC, Middle Wallop	
XW799	WS Scout AH1	*Sold to New Zealand, October 1995*	
XW835	WS Lynx	AAC Dishforth, GI use	
XW836	WS Lynx	DERA, Lasham	
XW837	WS Lynx (fuselage)	IHM, stored Weston-super-Mare	
XW838	WS Lynx [TAD 009]	AAC SEAE, Arborfield	

Notes	Serial	Type (other identity) [code]	Owner/operator, location or fate
	XW839	WS Lynx	IHM, Weston-super-Mare
	XW843	WS Gazelle AH1	AAC SEAE, Arborfield
	XW844	WS Gazelle AH1	AAC 1 Regiment, Gütersloh
	XW845	WS Gazelle HT2 [47/CU]	RN No 705 Sqn, Culdrose
	XW846	WS Gazelle AH1 [M]	AAC No 670 Sqn, Middle Wallop
	XW847	WS Gazelle AH1	AAC No 665 Sqn, Aldergrove
	XW848	WS Gazelle AH1 [D]	AAC No 670 Sqn, Middle Wallop
	XW849	WS Gazelle AH1 [G]	RM No 847 Sqn, Yeovilton
	XW851	WS Gazelle AH1 [H]	RM No 847 Sqn, Yeovilton
	XW852	WS Gazelle HCC4	RAF No 32(The Royal) Sqn, Northolt
	XW853	WS Gazelle HT2 [53/CU]	RN No 705 Sqn, Culdrose
	XW854	WS Gazelle HT2 [46/CU]	RN No 705 Sqn, Culdrose
	XW855	WS Gazelle HCC4	RAF No 32(The Royal) Sqn, Northolt
	XW856	WS Gazelle HT2 [49/CU]	RN No 705 Sqn, Culdrose
	XW857	WS Gazelle HT2 [55/CU]	RN No 705 Sqn, Culdrose
	XW858	WS Gazelle HT3 [C]	RAF No 2 FTS, Shawbury
	XW860	WS Gazelle HT2	AAC SEAE, Arborfield
	XW861	WS Gazelle HT2 [52/CU]	RN No 705 Sqn, Culdrose
	XW862	WS Gazelle HT3 [D]	RAF No 2 FTS, Shawbury
	XW863	WS Gazelle HT2 [42/CU]	AAC SEAE, Arborfield
	XW864	WS Gazelle HT2 [54/CU]	RN No 705 Sqn, Culdrose
	XW865	WS Gazelle AH1 [C]	AAC No 670 Sqn, Middle Wallop
	XW866	WS Gazelle HT3 [E]	RAF No 2 FTS, Shawbury
	XW868	WS Gazelle HT2 [50/CU]	RN No 705 Sqn, Culdrose
	XW870	WS Gazelle HT3 [F]	RAF No 2 FTS, Shawbury
	XW871	WS Gazelle HT2 [44/CU]	RN No 705 Sqn, Culdrose
	XW884	WS Gazelle HT2 [41/CU]	RN No 705 Sqn, Culdrose
	XW885	WS Gazelle AH1	AAC No 667 Sqn, Middle Wallop
	XW887	WS Gazelle HT2 [FL]	RNAY Fleetlands Station Flight
	XW888	WS Gazelle AH1	AAC SEAE, Arborfield
	XW889	WS Gazelle AH1	AAC SEAE, Arborfield
	XW890	WS Gazelle HT2	RNAS Yeovilton, on display
	XW891	WS Gazelle HT2 [49] (fuselage)	RNAS Culdrose, Fire Section
	XW892	WS Gazelle AH1	AAC No 658 Sqn, Netheravon
	XW893	WS Gazelle AH1	AAC No 665 Sqn, Aldergrove
	XW894	WS Gazelle HT2 [37/CU]	RN No 705 Sqn, Culdrose
	XW895	WS Gazelle HT2 [51/CU]	RN No 705 Sqn, Culdrose
	XW897	WS Gazelle AH1 [Z]	AAC No 670 Sqn, Middle Wallop
	XW898	WS Gazelle HT3 [G]	RAF No 2 FTS, Shawbury
	XW899	WS Gazelle AH1 [Z]	AAC No 658 Sqn, Netheravon
	XW900	WS Gazelle AH1 (TAD-900)	AAC SEAE, Arborfield
	XW902	WS Gazelle HT3 [H]	RAF No 2 FTS, Shawbury
	XW903	WS Gazelle AH1	AAC No 3 (TA) Flt, Turnhouse
	XW904	WS Gazelle AH1 [H1]	AAC No 670 Sqn, Middle Wallop
	XW906	WS Gazelle HT3 [J]	RAF No 2 FTS, Shawbury
	XW907	WS Gazelle HT2 [48/CU]	RN No 705 Sqn, Culdrose
	XW908	WS Gazelle AH1 [E]	AAC No 670 Sqn, Middle Wallop
	XW909	WS Gazelle AH1	AAC 1 Regiment, Gütersloh
	XW910	WS Gazelle HT3 [K]	RAF No 2 FTS, Shawbury
	XW911	WS Gazelle AH1 [I]	AAC No 670 Sqn, Middle Wallop
	XW912	WS Gazelle AH1	AAC, stored RNAW Almondbank
	XW913	WS Gazelle AH1 [E]	AAC No 663 Sqn, Wattisham
	XW916	HS Harrier GR3 [W]	RAF Wittering, Fire Section
	XW919	HS Harrier GR3 [W]	SFDO, RNAS Culdrose
	XW923	HS Harrier GR3 (8724M) <ff>	RAF Wittering for rescue training
	XW927	HS Harrier T4 [02]	RAF Laarbruch
	XW930	HS125-1B	BAe Dunsfold, spares reclamation
	XW934	HS Harrier T4 [Y]	DERA Farnborough
	XW986	HS Buccaneer S2B	Jet Aviation Preservation Group, Long Marston
	XW987	HS Buccaneer S2B	Lincolnshire Military Collection
	XW988	HS Buccaneer S2B	*Sold to South Africa as ZU-AVI*
	XX101	Cushioncraft CC7	IHM, Weston-super-Mare
	XX102	Cushioncraft CC7	Museum of Army Transport, Beverley
	XX105	BAC 1-11/201AC (G-ASJD)	MoD(PE)/DRA, DTEO Boscombe Down
	XX108	SEPECAT Jaguar GR1 [A]	RAF No 16(R) Sqn, Lossiemouth
	XX109	SEPECAT Jaguar GR1 (8918M) [US]	RAF Coltishall, ground instruction
	XX110	SEPECAT Jaguar GR1 <R> (BAPC 169)	RAF Halton
	XX110	SEPECAT Jaguar GR1 (8955M) [EP]	RAF No 1 SoTT, Cosford

Serial	Type (other identity) [code]	Owner/operator, location or fate	Notes
XX112	SEPECAT Jaguar GR1A [EC]	RAF, stored Shawbury	
XX115	SEPECAT Jaguar GR1 (8821M) (fuselage)	RAF No 1 SoTT, Cosford	
XX116	SEPECAT Jaguar GR1A	RAF No 16(R) Sqn, Lossiemouth	
XX117	SEPECAT Jaguar GR1A [06]	MoD(PE)/DRA, DTEO Boscombe Down	
XX119	SEPECAT Jaguar GR1A (8898M) [E]	RAF No 16(R) Sqn, Lossiemouth	
XX121	SEPECAT Jaguar GR1 [EQ]	RAF, No 1 SoTT, Cosford	
XX139	SEPECAT Jaguar T2A [T]	RAF No 16(R) Sqn, Lossiemouth	
XX140	SEPECAT Jaguar T2 (9008M) [D,JJ]	RAF No 1 SoTT, Cosford	
XX141	SEPECAT Jaguar T2A [Z]	SIF, RAFC Cranwell	
XX143	SEPECAT Jaguar T2B [GS]	RAF St Athan (conversion)	
XX144	SEPECAT Jaguar T2A [U]	RAF No 16(R) Sqn, Lossiemouth	
XX145	SEPECAT Jaguar T2	MoD(PE)/ETPS, DTEO Boscombe Down	
XX146	SEPECAT Jaguar T2A [X]	RAF No 16(R) Sqn, Lossiemouth	
XX150	SEPECAT Jaguar T2A [W]	RAF No 16(R) Sqn, Lossiemouth	
XX154	HS Hawk T1	MoD(PE), DTEO Llanbedr	
XX156	HS Hawk T1	MoD(PE), DTEO Boscombe Down	
XX157	HS Hawk T1A	RN FRADU, Culdrose	
XX158	HS Hawk T1A [PA]	RAF No 4 FTS/19(R) Sqn, Valley	
XX159	HS Hawk T1A	RAF No 4 FTS/19(R) Sqn, Valley	
XX160	HS Hawk T1	MoD(PE), DTEO Llanbedr	
XX161	HS Hawk T1 [DQ]	RAF No 4 FTS/208(R) Sqn, Valley	
XX162	HS Hawk T1	MoD(PE)/SAM, DTEO Boscombe Down	
XX163	HS Hawk T1 [PH] (wreck)	RAF Valley, for gate	
XX164	HS Hawk T1 [CN]	RAF No 4 FTS/74(R) Sqn, Valley	
XX165	HS Hawk T1	RN FRADU, Culdrose	
XX167	HS Hawk T1	RAF No 4 FTS/74(R) Sqn, Valley	
XX168	HS Hawk T1 [CR]	RAF No 100 Sqn/JFACSTU, Leeming	
XX169	HS Hawk T1	RAF No 4 FTS/74(R) Sqn, Valley	
XX170	HS Hawk T1 [DS]	MoD(PE), DTEO Llanbedr	
XX171	HS Hawk T1 [DW]	RAF No 4 FTS/208(R) Sqn, Valley	
XX172	HS Hawk T1	RAF St Athan Station Flight	
XX173	HS Hawk T1	RAF No 4 FTS/74(R) Sqn, Valley	
XX174	HS Hawk T1	RAF No 4 FTS/74(R) Sqn, Valley	
XX175	HS Hawk T1	RN FRADU, Culdrose	
XX176	HS Hawk T1 [DS]	RAF No 4 FTS/208(R) Sqn, Valley	
XX177	HS Hawk T1 [CP]	RAF No 4 FTS/74(R) Sqn, Valley	
XX178	HS Hawk T1 [PQ]	RAF No 4 FTS/19(R) Sqn, Valley	
XX179	HS Hawk T1 [PR]	RAF No 4 FTS/19(R) Sqn, Valley	
XX181	HS Hawk T1 [CB]	RAF No 4 FTS/19(R) Sqn, Valley	
XX183	HS Hawk T1	RN FRADU, Culdrose	
XX184	HS Hawk T1	RAF St Athan Station Flight	
XX185	HS Hawk T1 [TM]	RAF No 4 FTS/74(R) Sqn, Valley	
XX186	HS Hawk T1A	RAF No 4 FTS/19(R) Sqn, Valley	
XX187	HS Hawk T1A	RAF No 4 FTS/74(R) Sqn, Valley	
XX188	HS Hawk T1A [CG]	RAF No 100 Sqn, Leeming	
XX189	HS Hawk T1A	RAF No 4 FTS/19(R) Sqn, Valley	
XX190	HS Hawk T1A	RAF, stored Shawbury	
XX191	HS Hawk T1A [DT]	RAF No 4 FTS/208(R) Sqn, Valley	
XX193	HS Hawk T1A [CB]	RAF No 100 Sqn, Leeming	
XX194	HS Hawk T1A [CO]	RAF No 100 Sqn, Leeming	
XX195	HS Hawk T1A [CA]	RAF No 100 Sqn, Leeming	
XX196	HS Hawk T1A [DB]	RAF No 4 FTS/208(R) Sqn, Valley	
XX198	HS Hawk T1A [DC]	RAF, stored Shawbury	
XX199	HS Hawk T1A [TG]	RAF No 4 FTS/74(R) Sqn, Valley	
XX200	HS Hawk T1A [CF]	RAF No 100 Sqn, Leeming	
XX201	HS Hawk T1A [N]	RAF, stored Shawbury	
XX202	HS Hawk T1A	RAF, stored Shawbury	
XX203	HS Hawk T1A	RAF, stored Shawbury	
XX204	HS Hawk T1A [PC]	RAF No 4 FTS/19(R) Sqn, Valley	
XX205	HS Hawk T1A	RN FRADU, Culdrose	
XX217	HS Hawk T1A	RAF, stored Shawbury	
XX218	HS Hawk T1A	RAF, stored Shawbury	
XX219	HS Hawk T1A	RAF, stored Shawbury	
XX220	HS Hawk T1A [PD]	RAF, stored Shawbury	
XX221	HS Hawk T1A [DG]	RAF No 4 FTS/208(R) Sqn, Valley	
XX222	HS Hawk T1A [TJ]	RAF No 4 FTS/74(R) Sqn, Valley	
XX223	HS Hawk T1 (fuselage)	Privately owned, Charlwood, Surrey	
XX224	HS Hawk T1 [PM]	RAF No 4 FTS/19(R) Sqn, Valley	
XX225	HS Hawk T1 [PN]	RAF No 4 FTS/19(R) Sqn, Valley	
XX226	HS Hawk T1 [74]	RAF No 4 FTS/74(R) Sqn, Valley	

Notes	Serial	Type (other identity) [code]	Owner/operator, location or fate
	XX227	HS Hawk T1A	RAF *Red Arrows*, Cranwell
	XX228	HS Hawk T1A [CC]	RAF No 100 Sqn, Leeming
	XX230	HS Hawk T1A	RAF, stored Shawbury
	XX231	HS Hawk T1W	RAF No 4 FTS/19(R) Sqn, Valley
	XX232	HS Hawk T1	RAF No 4 FTS/74(R) Sqn, Valley
	XX233	HS Hawk T1	RAF *Red Arrows*, Cranwell
	XX234	HS Hawk T1 [DV]	RN FRADU, Culdrose
	XX235	HS Hawk T1	RAF No 4 FTS/19(R) Sqn, Valley
	XX236	HS Hawk T1 [PK]	RAF No 4 FTS/19(R) Sqn, Valley
	XX237	HS Hawk T1	RAF *Red Arrows*, Cranwell
	XX238	HS Hawk T1	RAF No 4 FTS/19(R) Sqn, Valley
	XX239	HS Hawk T1 [DZ]	RAF No 4 FTS/208(R) Sqn, Valley
	XX240	HS Hawk T1	RAF No 4 FTS, Valley
	XX242	HS Hawk T1 [Y]	RN FRADU, Culdrose
	XX244	HS Hawk T1	RAF No 4 FTS/19(R) Sqn, Valley
	XX245	HS Hawk T1	RN FRADU, Culdrose
	XX246	HS Hawk T1A	RAF, stored Shawbury
	XX247	HS Hawk T1A [CM]	RAF No 100 Sqn, Leeming
	XX248	HS Hawk T1A [CJ]	RAF No 100 Sqn, Leeming
	XX249	HS Hawk T1W	RAF No 4 FTS/19(R) Sqn, Valley
	XX250	HS Hawk T1 [CS]	RAF No 100 Sqn/JFACSTU, Leeming
	XX252	HS Hawk T1A	RAF *Red Arrows*, Cranwell
	XX253	HS Hawk T1A	RAF *Red Arrows*, Cranwell
XX253	HS Hawk T1 <R> (BAPC 171)	RAF EP&TU, St Athan
	XX254	HS Hawk T1A	MoD(PE)/BAe Brough
	XX255	HS Hawk T1A [TE]	RAF, stored Shawbury
	XX256	HS Hawk T1A	RAF, stored Shawbury
	XX258	HS Hawk T1A [PE]	RAF No 4 FTS/19(R) Sqn, Valley
	XX260	HS Hawk T1A	RAF *Red Arrows*, Cranwell
	XX261	HS Hawk T1A	RAF, stored Shawbury
	XX263	HS Hawk T1A	RN FRADU, Culdrose
XX263	HS Hawk T1 <R> (BAPC 152)	RAF EP&TU, St Athan
	XX264	HS Hawk T1A	RAF *Red Arrows*, Cranwell
	XX265	HS Hawk T1A [CN]	RAF No 100 Sqn, Leeming
	XX266	HS Hawk T1A	RAF *Red Arrows*, Cranwell
	XX278	HS Hawk T1A	RAF No 4 FTS/19(R) Sqn, Valley
	XX280	HS Hawk T1A	RAF, stored Shawbury
	XX281	HS Hawk T1A	RAF No 4 FTS/19(R) Sqn, Valley
	XX282	HS Hawk T1A	RAF, stored Shawbury
	XX283	HS Hawk T1 [DY]	RAF No 4FTS/208(R) Sqn, Valley
	XX284	HS Hawk T1A [CL]	RAF No 100 Sqn, Leeming
	XX285	HS Hawk T1A [CH]	RAF No 100 Sqn, Leeming
	XX286	HS Hawk T1A	RN, stored Shawbury
	XX287	HS Hawk T1A	RAF No 4 FTS/19(R) Sqn, Valley
	XX288	HS Hawk T1W [DX]	*Written off, RAF Mona, 10 August 1995*
	XX289	HS Hawk T1A [CI]	RAF No 100 Sqn, Leeming
	XX290	HS Hawk T1 [DV]	RAF No 4 FTS/208(R) Sqn, Valley
	XX292	HS Hawk T1W	RAF *Red Arrows*, Cranwell
	XX294	HS Hawk T1	RAF *Red Arrows*, Cranwell
	XX295	HS Hawk T1 [DA]	RAF No 4 FTS/208(R) Sqn, Valley
	XX296	HS Hawk T1 [DR]	RAF No 4 FTS/208(R) Sqn, Valley
	XX297	HS Hawk T1A (8933M)	RAF Finningley Fire Section
XX297	HS Hawk T1 <R> (BAPC 171)	*Painted as XX253 by July 1995*
	XX299	HS Hawk T1W [DO]	RAF No 4 FTS/208(R) Sqn, Valley
	XX301	HS Hawk T1A	RN FRADU, Culdrose
	XX302	HS Hawk T1A	RAF No 4 FTS/74(R) Sqn, Valley
	XX303	HS Hawk T1A	RAF No 4 FTS/74(R) Sqn, Valley
	XX304	HS Hawk T1A (fuselage)	RAF, stored Shawbury
	XX306	HS Hawk T1A	RAF *Red Arrows*, Cranwell
	XX307	HS Hawk T1	RAF *Red Arrows*, Cranwell
	XX308	HS Hawk T1	RAF *Red Arrows*, Cranwell
	XX309	HS Hawk T1	RAF No 4 FTS/74(R) Sqn, Valley
	XX310	HS Hawk T1W	RAF No 4 FTS/19(R) Sqn, Valley
	XX311	HS Hawk T1	RN FRADU, Culdrose
	XX312	HS Hawk T1 [CF]	RAF No 4 FTS/74(R) Sqn, Valley
	XX313	HS Hawk T1 [DX]	RAF No 4 FTS/208(R) Sqn, Valley
	XX314	HS Hawk T1 [DU]	RAF No 4 FTS/208(R) Sqn, Valley
	XX315	HS Hawk T1A [DA]	RN FRADU, Culdrose
	XX316	HS Hawk T1A [DF]	RAF No 4 FTS/208(R) Sqn, Valley
	XX317	HS Hawk T1A	RAF No 4 FTS/208(R) Sqn, Valley
	XX318	HS Hawk T1A [PG]	RAF No 4 FTS/19(R) Sqn, Valley
	XX319	HS Hawk T1A [TF]	RAF No 4 FTS/74(R) Sqn, Valley
	XX320	HS Hawk T1A	RAF, stored Shawbury

Serial	Type (other identity) [code]	Owner/operator, location or fate	Notes
XX321	HS Hawk T1A [DH]	RAF No 4 FTS/208(R) Sqn, Valley	
XX322	HS Hawk T1A [W]	RAF, stored Shawbury	
XX323	HS Hawk T1A [TD]	RAF No 4 FTS/74(R) Sqn, Valley	
XX324	HS Hawk T1A [DM]	RAF No 4 FTS/208(R) Sqn, Valley	
XX325	HS Hawk T1A [CE]	RAF No 100 Sqn, Leeming	
XX326	HS Hawk T1A [PH]	RAF No 4 FTS/19(R) Sqn, Valley	
XX327	HS Hawk T1	MoD(PE)/SAM, DTEO Boscombe Down	
XX329	HS Hawk T1A [PJ]	RAF No 4 FTS/19(R) Sqn, Valley	
XX330	HS Hawk T1A [DE]	RAF No 4 FTS/208(R) Sqn, Valley	
XX331	HS Hawk T1A [CK]	RAF No 100 Sqn, Leeming	
XX332	HS Hawk T1A [TW]	RAF No 4 FTS/74(R) Sqn, Valley	
XX335	HS Hawk T1A [CD]	RAF No 100 Sqn, Leeming	
XX337	HS Hawk T1A	RN FRADU, Culdrose	
XX338	HS Hawk T1W [PV]	RAF No 4 FTS/19(R) Sqn, Valley	
XX339	HS Hawk T1A	RAF No 4 FTS/74(R) Sqn, Valley	
XX341	HS Hawk T1 ASTRA [1]	MoD(PE)/ETPS, DTEO Boscombe Down	
XX342	HS Hawk T1 [2]	MoD(PE)/ETPS, DTEO Boscombe Down	
XX343	HS Hawk T1 [3]	MoD(PE)/ETPS, DTEO Boscombe Down	
XX344	HS Hawk T1 (8847M) (fuselage)	DRA Farnborough Fire Section	
XX345	HS Hawk T1A [DJ]	RAF No 4 FTS/208(R) Sqn, Valley	
XX346	HS Hawk T1A	RN FRADU, Culdrose	
XX348	HS Hawk T1A [DN]	RAF No 4 FTS/208(R) Sqn, Valley	
XX349	HS Hawk T1W [TL]	RAF No 4 FTS/74(R) Sqn, Valley	
XX350	HS Hawk T1A [TC]	RAF No 4 FTS/74(R) Sqn, Valley	
XX351	HS Hawk T1A [DP]	RAF No 4 FTS/208(R) Sqn, Valley	
XX352	HS Hawk T1A [CP]	RAF No 100 Sqn, Leeming	
XX370	WS Gazelle AH1	AAC No 665 Sqn, Aldergrove	
XX371	WS Gazelle AH1	AAC No 12 Flt, Laarbruch	
XX372	WS Gazelle AH1 [1]	AAC No 656 Sqn, Dishforth	
XX375	WS Gazelle AH1 [E1]	AAC No 670 Sqn, Middle Wallop	
XX378	WS Gazelle AH1 [Q]	AAC No 670 Sqn, Middle Wallop	
XX379	WS Gazelle AH1	AAC No 658 Sqn, Netheravon	
XX380	WS Gazelle AH1 [A]	RM No 847 Sqn, Yeovilton	
XX381	WS Gazelle AH1	AAC No 2(TA) Flt, Netheravon	
XX382	WS Gazelle HT3 [M]	RAF No 2 FTS, Shawbury	
XX383	WS Gazelle AH1 [E]	AAC No 658 Sqn, Netheravon	
XX384	WS Gazelle AH1	AAC No 652 Sqn, Gütersloh	
XX385	WS Gazelle AH1 [X]	AAC No 670 Sqn, Middle Wallop	
XX386	WS Gazelle AH1	AAC, RNAY Fleetlands	
XX387	WS Gazelle AH1	AAC SEAE, Arborfield	
XX388	WS Gazelle AH1	AAC No 652 Sqn, Gütersloh	
XX389	WS Gazelle AH1	AAC No 652 Sqn, Gütersloh	
XX391	WS Gazelle HT2 [56/CU]	RN No 705 Sqn, Culdrose	
XX392	WS Gazelle AH1 [A1]	AAC No 670 Sqn, Middle Wallop	
XX393	WS Gazelle AH1	AAC 4 Regiment, Wattisham	
XX394	WS Gazelle AH1 [X]	AAC No 2(TA) Flt, Netheravon	
XX395	WS Gazelle AH1	AAC No 657 Sqn, Dishforth	
XX396	WS Gazelle HT3 (8718M) [N]	RAF EP&TU, Henlow	
XX398	WS Gazelle AH1 [2]	AAC No 656 Sqn, Dishforth	
XX399	WS Gazelle AH1 [Y]	AAC No 2(TA) Flt, Netheravon	
XX403	WS Gazelle AH1 [U]	AAC No 670 Sqn, Middle Wallop	
XX405	WS Gazelle AH1 [C1]	AAC No 670 Sqn, Middle Wallop	
XX406	WS Gazelle HT3 [P]	RAF No 7 Sqn, Odiham	
XX407	WS Gazelle AH1 [D1]	AAC No 670 Sqn, Middle Wallop	
XX408	WS Gazelle AH1	AAC No 654 Sqn, Wattisham	
XX409	WS Gazelle AH1	AAC No 669 Sqn, Wattisham	
XX410	WS Gazelle HT2 [58/CU]	RNAS Lee-on-Solent	
XX411	WS Gazelle AH1 [X]	AAC Middle Wallop, BDRT	
XX411	WS Gazelle AH1 <rf>	FAA Museum, RNAS Yeovilton	
XX412	WS Gazelle AH1 [B]	RM No 847 Sqn, Yeovilton	
XX413	WS Gazelle AH1 [C]	RM No 847 Sqn, Yeovilton	
XX414	WS Gazelle AH1	AAC No 661 Sqn, Gütersloh	
XX416	WS Gazelle AH1	AAC No 657 Sqn, Dishforth	
XX417	WS Gazelle AH1	AAC No 667 Sqn, Middle Wallop	
XX418	WS Gazelle AH1	AAC No 651 Sqn, Gütersloh	
XX419	WS Gazelle AH1 [D]	AAC 3 Regiment, Wattisham	
XX431	WS Gazelle HT2 [VL]	RN FONA, Yeovilton	
XX432	WS Gazelle AH1	AAC No 665 Sqn, Aldergrove	
XX433	WS Gazelle AH1	AAC No 663 Sqn, Wattisham	
XX435	WS Gazelle AH1	AAC No 653 Sqn, Wattisham	
XX436	WS Gazelle HT2 [39/CU]	RN No 705 Sqn, Culdrose	
XX437	WS Gazelle AH1	AAC No 661 Sqn, Gütersloh	
XX438	WS Gazelle AH1 [N]	AAC No 661 Sqn, Gütersloh	

Notes	Serial	Type (other identity) [code]	Owner/operator, location or fate
	XX439	WS Gazelle AH1	AAC No 651 Sqn, Gütersloh
	XX440	WS Gazelle AH1	AAC No 665 Sqn, Aldergrove
	XX441	WS Gazelle HT2 [38/CU]	RN, damaged July 1995, stored Shawbury
	XX442	WS Gazelle AH1 [E]	AAC No 658 Sqn, Netheravon
	XX443	WS Gazelle AH1 [Y]	AAC No 658 Sqn, Netheravon
	XX444	WS Gazelle AH1 [E]	AAC, stored Fleetlands
	XX445	WS Gazelle AH1 [T]	AAC No 664 Sqn, Dishforth
	XX446	WS Gazelle HT2 [57/CU]	RN No 705 Sqn, Culdrose
	XX447	WS Gazelle AH1	AAC No 658 Sqn, Netheravon
	XX448	WS Gazelle AH1	AAC No 654 Sqn, Wattisham
	XX449	WS Gazelle AH1 [Y]	AAC No 657 Sqn, Dishforth
	XX450	WS Gazelle AH1 [D]	RM No 847 Sqn, Yeovilton
	XX451	WS Gazelle HT2 [58/CU]	*Written off near Chepstow, 5 October 1995*
	XX452	WS Gazelle AH1	AAC Middle Wallop Fire Section
	XX453	WS Gazelle AH1 [3]	AAC No 656 Sqn, Dishforth
	XX454	WS Gazelle AH1	AAC No 656 Sqn, Dishforth
	XX455	WS Gazelle AH1	AAC No 661 Sqn, Gütersloh
	XX456	WS Gazelle AH1	AAC No 3(TA) Flt, Turnhouse
	XX457	WS Gazelle AH1 [Z]	AAC No 2(TA) Flt, Netheravon
	XX460	WS Gazelle AH1	AAC No 654 Sqn, Wattisham
	XX462	WS Gazelle AH1	AAC No 669 Sqn, Wattisham
	XX466	HS Hunter T66B/T7 (XL620) [830/DD]	RN Predannack Fire School
	XX467	HS Hunter T66B/T7 (XL605)	Air Service Training, Perth
	XX469	WS Lynx HAS2 (G-DNCL)	Lancashire Fire Brigade, Lancaster
	XX475	HP137 Jetstream T2 (N1036S) [572]	MoD(PE), DTEO West Freugh
	XX476	HP137 Jetstream T2 (N1037S) [561/CU]	RN No 750 Sqn, Culdrose
	XX477	HP137 Jetstream T1 (G-AXXS/ 8462M) <ff>	RAF Finningley for ground instruction
	XX478	HP137 Jetstream T2 (G-AXXT) [564/CU]	RN No 750 Sqn, Culdrose
	XX479	HP137 Jetstream T2 (G-AXUR) [563/CU]	RN No 750 Sqn, Culdrose
	XX480	HP137 Jetstream T2 (G-AXXU) [565/CU]	RN No 750 Sqn, Culdrose
	XX481	HP137 Jetstream T2 (G-AXUP) [560/CU]	RN No 750 Sqn, Culdrose
	XX482	SA Jetstream T1 [J]	RAF No 3 FTS/45(R) Sqn, Cranwell
	XX483	SA Jetstream T2 [562/CU]	RN No 750 Sqn, Culdrose
	XX484	SA Jetstream T2 [566/CU]	RN No 750 Sqn, Culdrose
	XX485	SA Jetstream T2 [567/CU]	RN No 750 Sqn, Culdrose
	XX486	SA Jetstream T2 [569/CU]	RN No 750 Sqn, Culdrose
	XX487	SA Jetstream T2 [568/CU]	RN No 750 Sqn, Culdrose
	XX488	SA Jetstream T2 [571/CU]	RN No 750 Sqn, Culdrose
	XX490	SA Jetstream T2 [570/CU]	RN No 750 Sqn, Culdrose
	XX491	SA Jetstream T1 [K]	RAF No 3 FTS/45(R) Sqn, Cranwell
	XX492	SA Jetstream T1 [A]	RAF No 3 FTS/45(R) Sqn, Cranwell
	XX493	SA Jetstream T1 [L]	RAF No 3 FTS/45(R) Sqn, Cranwell
	XX494	SA Jetstream T1 [B]	RAF No 3 FTS/45(R) Sqn, Cranwell
	XX495	SA Jetstream T1 [C]	RAF No 3 FTS/45(R) Sqn, Cranwell
	XX496	SA Jetstream T1 [D]	RAF No 3 FTS/45(R) Sqn, Cranwell
	XX497	SA Jetstream T1 [E]	RAF No 3 FTS/45(R) Sqn, Cranwell
	XX498	SA Jetstream T1 [F]	RAF No 3 FTS/45(R) Sqn, Cranwell
	XX499	SA Jetstream T1 [G]	RAF No 3 FTS/45(R) Sqn, Cranwell
	XX500	SA Jetstream T1 [H]	RAF No 3 FTS/45(R) Sqn, Cranwell
	XX507	HS125 CC2	RAF No 32(The Royal) Sqn, Northolt
	XX508	HS125 CC2	RAF No 32(The Royal) Sqn, Northolt
	XX510	WS Lynx HAS2 [69/LS]	RN Lynx Training School, Lee-on-Solent
	XX513	SA Bulldog T1 [10]	RAF No 3 FTS, Cranwell
	XX515	SA Bulldog T1 [2]	RAF No 3 FTS, Cranwell
	XX516	SA Bulldog T1 [C]	RAF Cambridge UAS/No 5 AEF, Cambridge
	XX518	SA Bulldog T1 [Z]	RAF Cambridge UAS/No 5 AEF, Cambridge
	XX519	SA Bulldog T1 [14]	RAF No 3 FTS, Cranwell
	XX520	SA Bulldog T1	RAF East Midlands UAS/No 7 AEF, Newton
	XX521	SA Bulldog T1 [01]	RAF East Lowlands UAS, Turnhouse
	XX522	SA Bulldog T1 [11]	RAF No 3 FTS, Cranwell
	XX523	SA Bulldog T1 [X]	RAF Liverpool UAS, Woodvale
	XX524	SA Bulldog T1 [04]	RAF London UAS/No 6 AEF, Benson

Serial	Type (other identity) [code]	Owner/operator, location or fate	Notes
XX525	SA Bulldog T1 [03]	RAF East Lowlands UAS, Turnhouse	
XX526	SA Bulldog T1 [C]	RAF Oxford UAS, Benson	
XX527	SA Bulldog T1 [D]	RAF Aberdeen, Dundee & St Andrews UAS, Leuchars	
XX528	SA Bulldog T1 [D]	RAF Oxford UAS, Benson	
XX529	SA Bulldog T1	RAF Cambridge UAS/No 5 AEF, Cambridge	
XX531	SA Bulldog T1 [06]	RAF Wales UAS, St Athan	
XX532	SA Bulldog T1 [7]	RAF No 3 FTS, Cranwell	
XX533	SA Bulldog T1 [U]	RAF Northumbrian UAS/No 11 AEF, Leeming	
XX534	SA Bulldog T1 [B]	RAF Birmingham UAS, Cosford	
XX535	SA Bulldog T1 [S]	RAF East Midlands UAS/No 7 AEF, Newton	
XX536	SA Bulldog T1 [6]	RAF Manchester UAS/No 10 AEF, Woodvale	
XX537	SA Bulldog T1 [02]	RAF East Lowlands UAS, Turnhouse	
XX538	SA Bulldog T1 [X]	RAF No 3 FTS, Cranwell	
XX539	SA Bulldog T1 [L]	RAF Liverpool UAS, Woodvale	
XX540	SA Bulldog T1 [15]	RAF No 3 FTS, Cranwell	
XX541	SA Bulldog T1 [F]	RAF Bristol UAS/No 3 AEF , Colerne	
XX543	SA Bulldog T1 [F]	RAF Yorkshire UAS/No 9 AEF, Church Fenton	
XX544	SA Bulldog T1 [01]	RAF London UAS/No 6 AEF, Benson	
XX545	SA Bulldog T1 [02]	RAF East Lowlands UAS, Turnhouse, GI use	
XX546	SA Bulldog T1 [03]	RAF London UAS/No 6 AEF, Benson	
XX547	SA Bulldog T1 [05]	RAF London UAS/No 6 AEF, Benson	
XX548	SA Bulldog T1 [06]	RAF London UAS/No 6 AEF, Benson	
XX549	SA Bulldog T1	RAF Southampton UAS, DTEO Boscombe Down	
XX550	SA Bulldog T1 [Z]	RAF Northumbrian UAS/No 11 AEF, Leeming	
XX551	SA Bulldog T1 [E]	RAF Oxford UAS, Benson	
XX552	SA Bulldog T1 [08]	RAF London UAS/No 6 AEF, Benson	
XX553	SA Bulldog T1 [07]	RAF London UAS/No 6 AEF, Benson	
XX554	SA Bulldog T1 [09]	RAF London UAS/No 6 AEF, Benson	
XX555	SA Bulldog T1 [U]	RAF Liverpool UAS, Woodvale	
XX556	SA Bulldog T1 [M]	RAF East Midlands UAS/No 7 AEF, Newton	
XX557	SA Bulldog T1	RAF Linton-on-Ouse, ground instruction	
XX558	SA Bulldog T1 [A]	RAF Birmingham UAS, Cosford	
XX559	SA Bulldog T1	RAF Glasgow & Strathclyde UAS, Glasgow	
XX560	SA Bulldog T1	RAF Glasgow & Strathclyde UAS, Glasgow	
XX561	SA Bulldog T1 [A]	RAF Aberdeen, Dundee & St Andrews UAS, Leuchars	
XX562	SA Bulldog T1 [E]	RAF Queen's UAS, Sydenham	
XX611	SA Bulldog T1	RAF Glasgow & Strathclyde UAS, Glasgow	
XX612	SA Bulldog T1 [05]	RAF Wales UAS, St Athan	
XX614	SA Bulldog T1 [6]	RAF No 3 FTS, Cranwell	
XX615	SA Bulldog T1 [2]	RAF Manchester UAS/No 10 AEF, Woodvale	
XX616	SA Bulldog T1 [3]	RAF Manchester UAS/No 10 AEF, Woodvale	
XX617	SA Bulldog T1 [4]	RAF, stored Shawbury	
XX619	SA Bulldog T1 [B]	RAF Yorkshire UAS/No 9 AEF, Church Fenton	
XX620	SA Bulldog T1 [C]	RAF Yorkshire UAS/No 9 AEF, Church Fenton	
XX621	SA Bulldog T1 [87]	RAF Yorkshire UAS/No 9 AEF, Church Fenton	
XX622	SA Bulldog T1 [88]	RAF Yorkshire UAS/No 9 AEF, Church Fenton	
XX623	SA Bulldog T1 [M]	RAF, stored Newton	
XX624	SA Bulldog T1 [T]	RAF Northumbrian UAS/No 11 AEF, Leeming	
XX625	SA Bulldog T1 [01]	RAF Wales UAS, St Athan	
XX626	SA Bulldog T1 [02]	RAF Wales UAS, St Athan	
XX627	SA Bulldog T1 [03]	RAF Wales UAS, St Athan	
XX628	SA Bulldog T1 [04]	RAF Wales UAS, St Athan	

Notes	Serial	Type (other identity) [code]	Owner/operator, location or fate
	XX629	SA Bulldog T1 [V]	RAF Northumbrian UAS/No 11 AEF, Leeming
	XX630	SA Bulldog T1 [A]	RAF Liverpool UAS, Woodvale
	XX631	SA Bulldog T1 [W]	RAF Northumbrian UAS/No 11 AEF, Leeming
	XX632	SA Bulldog T1 [D]	RAF Bristol UAS/No 3 AEF , Colerne
	XX633	SA Bulldog T1 [X]	RAF Northumbrian UAS/No 11 AEF, Leeming
	XX634	SA Bulldog T1 [1]	RAF No 3 FTS, Cranwell
	XX635	SA Bulldog T1 (8767M)	RAF CTTS, St Athan
	XX636	SA Bulldog T1 [Y]	RAF Northumbrian UAS/No 11 AEF, Leeming
	XX637	SA Bulldog T1 (9197M) [U]	SERCO, RAF St Athan
	XX638	SA Bulldog T1	RAF No 3 FTS, Cranwell
	XX639	SA Bulldog T1 [02]	RAF London UAS/No 6 AEF, Benson
	XX640	SA Bulldog T1 [B]	RAF Queen's UAS, Sydenham
	XX653	SA Bulldog T1 [E]	RAF Bristol UAS/No 3 AEF , Colerne
	XX654	SA Bulldog T1 [A]	RAF Bristol UAS/No 3 AEF , Colerne
	XX655	SA Bulldog T1 [B]	RAF Bristol UAS/No 3 AEF , Colerne
	XX656	SA Bulldog T1 [C]	RAF Bristol UAS/No 3 AEF , Colerne
	XX657	SA Bulldog T1 [U]	RAF Cambridge UAS/No 5 AEF, Cambridge
	XX658	SA Bulldog T1 [A]	RAF Cambridge UAS/No 5 AEF, Cambridge
	XX059	SA Bulldog I 1 [S]	RAF Cambridge UAS/No 5 AEF, Cambridge
	XX661	SA Bulldog T1 [B]	RAF Oxford UAS, Benson
	XX663	SA Bulldog T1 [B]	RAF Aberdeen, Dundee & St Andrews UAS, Leuchars
	XX664	SA Bulldog T1 [04]	RAF East Lowlands UAS, Turnhouse
	XX665	SA Bulldog T1	RAF Aberdeen, Dundee & St Andrews UAS, Leuchars
	XX666	SA Bulldog T1 [A]	RAF Queen's UAS, Sydenham
	XX667	SA Bulldog T1 [16]	RAF No 3 FTS, Cranwell
	XX668	SA Bulldog T1 [1]	RAF Manchester UAS/No 10 AEF, Woodvale
	XX669	SA Bulldog T1 (8997M) [B]	Phoenix Aviation, Bruntingthorpe
	XX670	SA Bulldog T1 [C]	RAF Birmingham UAS, Cosford
	XX671	SA Bulldog T1 [D]	RAF Birmingham UAS, Cosford
	XX672	SA Bulldog T1 [E]	RAF Birmingham UAS, Cosford
	XX685	SA Bulldog T1 [C]	RAF Aberdeen, Dundee & St Andrews UAS, Leuchars
	XX686	SA Bulldog T1	RAF Glasgow & Strathclyde UAS, Glasgow
	XX687	SA Bulldog T1 [A]	RAF East Midlands UAS/No 7 AEF, Newton
	XX688	SA Bulldog T1 [S]	RAF, stored Shawbury
	XX689	SA Bulldog T1 [3]	RAF No 3 FTS, Cranwell
	XX690	SA Bulldog T1 [5]	RAF No 3 FTS, Cranwell
	XX691	SA Bulldog T1	RAF Oxford UAS & London UAS/No 6 AEF, Benson
	XX692	SA Bulldog T1 [A]	RAF Yorkshire UAS/No 9 AEF, Church Fenton
	XX693	SA Bulldog T1 [4]	RAF No 3 FTS, Cranwell
	XX694	SA Bulldog T1 [E]	RAF East Midlands UAS/No 7 AEF, Newton
	XX695	SA Bulldog T1 [A]	RAF Oxford UAS, Benson
	XX696	SA Bulldog T1 [8]	RAF No 3 FTS, Cranwell
	XX697	SA Bulldog T1 [C]	RAF Queen's UAS, Sydenham
	XX698	SA Bulldog T1 [9]	RAF No 3 FTS, Cranwell
	XX699	SA Bulldog T1 [F]	RAF Birmingham UAS, Cosford
	XX700	SA Bulldog T1 [17]	RAF No 3 FTS, Cranwell
	XX701	SA Bulldog T1 [01]	RAF Southampton UAS, DTEO Boscombe Down
	XX702	SA Bulldog T1	RAF East Midlands UAS/No 7 AEF, Newton
	XX704	SA Bulldog T1 [U]	RAF East Midlands UAS/No 7 AEF, Newton
	XX705	SA Bulldog T1 [05]	RAF Southampton UAS, DTEO Boscombe Down
	XX706	SA Bulldog T1	RAF Southampton UAS, DTEO Boscombe Down

Serial	Type (other identity) [code]	Owner/operator, location or fate	Notes
XX707	SA Bulldog T1 [04]	RAF Southampton UAS, DTEO Boscombe Down	
XX708	SA Bulldog T1 [03]	RAF Southampton UAS, DTEO Boscombe Down	
XX709	SA Bulldog T1 [E]	RAF Yorkshire UAS/No 9 AEF, Church Fenton	
XX710	SA Bulldog T1 [5]	RAF, stored Shawbury	
XX711	SA Bulldog T1 [D]	RAF Queen's UAS, Sydenham	
XX713	SA Bulldog T1 [Z]	RAF Yorkshire UAS/No 9 AEF, Church Fenton	
XX714	SA Bulldog T1 [D]	RAF Yorkshire UAS/No 9 AEF, Church Fenton	
XX719	SEPECAT Jaguar GR1A [EE]	BAe Warton (for Oman)	
XX720	SEPECAT Jaguar GR1A [GB]	RAF No 54 Sqn, Coltishall	
XX722	SEPECAT Jaguar GR1 [EF]	RAF St Athan	
XX723	SEPECAT Jaguar GR1A [GQ]	RAF No 54 Sqn, Coltishall	
XX724	SEPECAT Jaguar GR1A [GA]	RAF, stored Shawbury	
XX725	SEPECAT Jaguar GR1B [GU]	RAF No 54 Sqn, Coltishall	
XX725	SEPECAT Jaguar GR1 <R> (BAPC 150) [25]	RAF EP&TU, St Athan	
XX726	SEPECAT Jaguar GR1 (8947M) [EB]	RAF No 1 SoTT, Cosford	
XX727	SEPECAT Jaguar GR1 (8951M) [ER]	RAF No 1 SoTT, Cosford	
XX729	SEPECAT Jaguar GR1B [EL]	RAF No 6 Sqn, Coltishall	
XX730	SEPECAT Jaguar GR1 (8952M) [EC]	RAF No 1 SoTT, Cosford	
XX733	SEPECAT Jaguar GR1A [ER]	RAF St Athan	
XX736	SEPECAT Jaguar GR1 (9110M)	RAF Coltishall, BDRT	
XX737	SEPECAT Jaguar GR1A [EE]	RAF No 6 Sqn, Coltishall	
XX738	SEPECAT Jaguar GR1A [GG]	RAF No 54 Sqn, Coltishall	
XX739	SEPECAT Jaguar GR1 (8902M) [I]	RAF No 1 SoTT, Cosford	
XX741	SEPECAT Jaguar GR1A [04]	RAF, stored Shawbury	
XX743	SEPECAT Jaguar GR1 (8949M) [EG]	RAF No 1 SoTT, Cosford	
XX744	SEPECAT Jaguar GR1 [DJ]	RAF No 1 SoTT, Cosford	
XX745	SEPECAT Jaguar GR1A [EG]	RAF No 6 Sqn, Coltishall	
XX746	SEPECAT Jaguar GR1A (8895M) [07]	RAF No 1 SoTT, Cosford	
XX747	SEPECAT Jaguar GR1 (8903M)	ATF, RAFC Cranwell	
XX748	SEPECAT Jaguar GR1B [GK]	MoD(PE)/DRA, DTEO Boscombe Down	
XX751	SEPECAT Jaguar GR1 (8937M) [10]	RAF No 1 SoTT, Cosford	
XX752	SEPECAT Jaguar GR1A [EQ]	RAF No 6 Sqn, Coltishall	
XX753	SEPECAT Jaguar GR1 (9087M) <ff>	RAF EP&TU, St Athan	
XX756	SEPECAT Jaguar GR1 (8899M) [AM]	RAF No 1 SoTT, Cosford	
XX757	SEPECAT Jaguar GR1 (8948M) [CU]	RAF No 1 SoTT, Cosford	
XX761	SEPECAT Jaguar GR1 (8600M) <ff>	BAe Warton, instructional use	
XX763	SEPECAT Jaguar GR1 (9009M)	RAF CTTS, St Athan	
XX764	SEPECAT Jaguar GR1 (9010M)	RAF CTTS, St Athan	
XX765	SEPECAT Jaguar ACT	Loughborough University	
XX766	SEPECAT Jaguar GR1A [EA]	RAF No 6 Sqn, Coltishall	
XX767	SEPECAT Jaguar GR1B [GE]	RAF St Athan (conversion)	
XX818	SEPECAT Jaguar GR1 (8945M) [DE]	RAF No 1 SoTT, Cosford	
XX819	SEPECAT Jaguar GR1 (8923M) [CE]	RAF No 1 SoTT, Cosford	
XX821	SEPECAT Jaguar GR1 (8896M) [P]	SIF, RAFC Cranwell	
XX824	SEPECAT Jaguar GR1 (9019M) [AD]	RAF Halton	
XX825	SEPECAT Jaguar GR1 (9020M) [BN]	RAF Halton	
XX826	SEPECAT Jaguar GR1 (9021M) [34,JH]	RAF No 1 SoTT, Cosford	
XX829	SEPECAT Jaguar T2A [Y]	RAF No 16(R) Sqn, Lossiemouth	
XX830	SEPECAT Jaguar T2	MoD(PE)/ETPS, DTEO Boscombe Down	
XX832	SEPECAT Jaguar T2A [Z]	RAF No 16(R) Sqn, Lossiemouth	
XX833	SEPECAT Jaguar T2B	RAF AWC/SAOEU, Boscombe Down	

Notes	Serial	Type (other identity) [code]	Owner/operator, location or fate
	XX835	SEPECAT Jaguar T2B [FY]	RAF No 41 Sqn, Coltishall
	XX836	SEPECAT Jaguar T2A	RAF, stored Shawbury
	XX837	SEPECAT Jaguar T2 (8978M) [Z]	RAF No 1 SoTT, Cosford
	XX838	SEPECAT Jaguar T2A [X]	RAF, stored Shawbury
	XX839	SEPECAT Jaguar T2A [GW]	RAF St Athan
	XX840	SEPECAT Jaguar T2A [X]	RAF, stored Shawbury
	XX841	SEPECAT Jaguar T2A [ES]	RAF No 6 Sqn, Coltishall
	XX842	SEPECAT Jaguar T2A [EW]	RAF, stored Shawbury
	XX844	SEPECAT Jaguar T2 (9023M) [F,JF]	RAF No 1 SoTT, Cosford
	XX845	SEPECAT Jaguar T2A [ET]	RAF No 6 Sqn, Coltishall
	XX846	SEPECAT Jaguar T2A [V]	RAF No 16(R) Sqn, Lossiemouth
	XX847	SEPECAT Jaguar T2A [FX]	RAF No 41 Sqn, Coltishall
	XX885	HS Buccaneer S2B (9225M)	RAF Lossiemouth, BDRT
	XX886	HS Buccaneer S2B	RAF Honington, WLT use
	XX888	HS Buccaneer S2B <ff>	Privately owned, Dundonald
	XX889	HS Buccaneer S2B	RAF, stored St Athan
	XX894	HS Buccaneer S2B [020/R]	British Aviation Heritage, Bruntingthorpe
	XX895	HS Buccaneer S2B	Privately owned, Woking
	XX897	HS Buccaneer S2B	Privately owned, Bournemouth
	XX899	HS Buccaneer S2B <ff>	*Scrapped at St Athan, October 1994*
	XX900	HS Buccaneer S2B	British Aviation Heritage, Bruntingthorpe
	XX901	HS Buccaneer S2B	Gloucestershire Av'n Coll'n, stored Kemble
	XX907	WS Lynx AH1	DERA Structures Dept, Farnborough
	XX910	WS Lynx HAS2	DERA Structures Dept, Farnborough
	XX914	BAC VC10-1103 (8777M) <rf>	RAF AMS, Brize Norton
	XX919	BAC 1-11/402AP (PI-C1121)	MoD(PE)/DRA, DTEO Boscombe Down
	XX946	Panavia Tornado (P02) (8883M)	RAF Museum, Hendon
	XX947	Panavia Tornado (P03) (8797M)	RAF, stored St Athan
	XX948	Panavia Tornado (P06) (8879M) [P]	RAF No 1 SoTT, Cosford
	XX955	SEPECAT Jaguar GR1A [GK]	RAF, stored Shawbury
	XX956	SEPECAT Jaguar GR1 (8950M) [BE]	RAF No 1 SoTT, Cosford
	XX958	SEPECAT Jaguar GR1 (9022M) [BK,JG]	RAF No 1 SoTT, Cosford
	XX959	SEPECAT Jaguar GR1 (8953M) [CJ]	RAF No 1 SoTT, Cosford
	XX962	SEPECAT Jaguar GR1B [EK]	MoD(PE)/DRA, DTEO Boscombe Down
	XX965	SEPECAT Jaguar GR1A [C]	RAF No 16(R) Sqn, Lossiemouth
	XX966	SEPECAT Jaguar GR1A (8904M) [EL]	RAF No 1 SoTT, Cosford
	XX967	SEPECAT Jaguar GR1 (9006M) [AC,JD]	RAF No 1 SoTT, Cosford
	XX968	SEPECAT Jaguar GR1 (9007M) [AJ,JE]	RAF No 1 SoTT, Cosford
	XX969	SEPECAT Jaguar GR1A (8897M) [01]	RAF No 1 SoTT, Cosford
	XX970	SEPECAT Jaguar GR1B [EH]	RAF No 6 Sqn, Coltishall
	XX974	SEPECAT Jaguar GR1A [GH]	RAF No 54 Sqn, Coltishall
	XX975	SEPECAT Jaguar GR1 (8905M) [07]	RAF No 1 SoTT, Cosford
	XX976	SEPECAT Jaguar GR1 (8906M) [BD]	RAF No 1 SoTT, Cosford
	XX977	SEPECAT Jaguar GR1 (9132M) [DL,05]	RAF St Athan, BDRT
	XX979	SEPECAT Jaguar GR1A	MoD(PE)/FWTS, DTEO Boscombe Down
	XZ101	SEPECAT Jaguar GR1A [D]	RAF No 16(R) Sqn, Lossiemouth
	XZ103	SEPECAT Jaguar GR1A [P]	RAF No 41 Sqn, Coltishall
	XZ104	SEPECAT Jaguar GR1A [FM]	RAF No 41 Sqn, Coltishall
	XZ106	SEPECAT Jaguar GR1A [FR]	RAF No 41 Sqn, Coltishall
	XZ107	SEPECAT Jaguar GR1A [H]	RAF No 41 Sqn, Coltishall
	XZ108	SEPECAT Jaguar GR1A	RAF No 16(R) Sqn, Lossiemouth
	XZ109	SEPECAT Jaguar GR1A [EN]	RAF No 6 Sqn, Coltishall
	XZ111	SEPECAT Jaguar GR1A	RAF St Athan
	XZ112	SEPECAT Jaguar GR1A [GA]	RAF No 54 Sqn, Coltishall
	XZ113	SEPECAT Jaguar GR1A [FD]	RAF No 41 Sqn, Coltishall
	XZ114	SEPECAT Jaguar GR1A [FB]	RAF, stored Shawbury
	XZ115	SEPECAT Jaguar GR1A [FC]	RAF, stored Shawbury
	XZ117	SEPECAT Jaguar GR1A [GG]	RAF, stored Shawbury
	XZ118	SEPECAT Jaguar GR1A [FF]	RAF No 41 Sqn, Coltishall

Serial	Type (other identity) [code]	Owner/operator, location or fate	Notes
XZ119	SEPECAT Jaguar GR1A [FG]	RAF No 41 Sqn, Coltishall	
XZ129	HS Harrier GR3 [ETS]	RN ETS, Yeovilton	
XZ130	HS Harrier GR3 (9079M) [A,HE]	RAF No 1 SoTT, Cosford	
XZ131	HS Harrier GR3 (9174M) <ff>	RAF EP&TU, St Athan	
XZ132	HS Harrier GR3 (9168M) [C]	ATF, RAFC Cranwell	
XZ133	HS Harrier GR3 [10]	Imperial War Museum, Duxford	
XZ135	HS Harrier GR3 (8848M) <ff>	RAF EP&TU, St Athan	
XZ138	HS Harrier GR3 (9040M) <ff>	RAFC Cranwell, Trenchard Hall	
XZ145	HS Harrier T4 [T]	RAF, stored Shawbury	
XZ146	HS Harrier T4 [S]	RAF, stored Shawbury	
XZ170	WS Lynx AH7(mod)	MoD(PE)/Westland, Yeovil	
XZ171	WS Lynx AH7 [UN]	AAC No 664 Sqn, Dishforth	
XZ172	WS Lynx AH7	AAC No 655 Sqn, Aldergrove	
XZ173	WS Lynx AH7 [W]	AAC No 663 Sqn, Wattisham	
XZ174	WS Lynx AH7	AAC No 655 Sqn, Aldergrove	
XZ175	WS Lynx AH7 [Z]	AAC No 671 Sqn, Middle Wallop	
XZ176	WS Lynx AH7 [O]	AAC No 663 Sqn, Wattisham	
XZ177	WS Lynx AH7	AAC, stored RNAY Fleetlands	
XZ178	WS Lynx AH7 [1]	AAC No 656 Sqn, Dishforth	
XZ179	WS Lynx AH7	AAC No 654 Sqn, Wattisham	
XZ180	WS Lynx AH7 [R]	RM No 847 Sqn, Yeovilton	
XZ181	WS Lynx AH1	AAC, stored RNAY Fleetlands	
XZ182	WS Lynx AH7 [M]	RM No 847 Sqn, Yeovilton	
XZ183	WS Lynx AH7	AAC No 654 Sqn, Wattisham	
XZ184	WS Lynx AH7 [W]	AAC, stored RNAY Fleetlands	
XZ185	WS Lynx AH7	AAC No 654 Sqn, Wattisham	
XZ186	WS Lynx AH7 (wreckage)	AAC, RNAY Fleetlands	
XZ187	WS Lynx AH7	AAC No 667 Sqn, Middle Wallop	
XZ188	WS Lynx AH7	AAC No 662 Sqn, Wattisham	
XZ190	WS Lynx AH7 [V]	AAC No 663 Sqn, Wattisham	
XZ191	WS Lynx AH7 [X]	AAC, stored RNAY Fleetlands	
XZ192	WS Lynx AH7	AAC No 655 Sqn, Aldergrove	
XZ193	WS Lynx AH7 [I]	AAC No 671 Sqn, Middle Wallop	
XZ194	WS Lynx AH7	AAC No 654 Sqn, Wattisham	
XZ195	WS Lynx AH7 [T]	AAC SEAE, Arborfield	
XZ196	WS Lynx AH7 [A]	AAC, RNAY Fleetlands (conversion)	
XZ197	WS Lynx AH7	AAC No 669 Sqn, Wattisham	
XZ198	WS Lynx AH7	AAC No 655 Sqn, Aldergrove	
XZ199	WS Lynx AH7	AAC No 657 Sqn, Dishforth	
XZ203	WS Lynx AH7	AAC, stored RNAY Fleetlands	
XZ205	WS Lynx AH7	AAC No 655 Sqn, Aldergrove	
XZ206	WS Lynx AH7	AAC, stored RNAY Fleetlands	
XZ207	WS Lynx AH7	AAC No 669 Sqn, Wattisham	
XZ208	WS Lynx AH7 [Z]	AAC No 664 Sqn, Dishforth	
XZ209	WS Lynx AH1 [T]	AAC, stored RNAY Fleetlands	
XZ210	WS Lynx AH7 [X]	AAC No 663 Sqn, Wattisham	
XZ211	WS Lynx AH7	AAC No 651 Sqn, Gütersloh	
XZ212	WS Lynx AH7	AAC, stored RNAY Fleetlands	
XZ213	WS Lynx AH1 [TAD 213]	RNAY Fleetlands Apprentice School	
XZ214	WS Lynx AH7	AAC No 657 Sqn, Dishforth	
XZ215	WS Lynx AH7	AAC No 655 Sqn, Aldergrove	
XZ216	WS Lynx AH7 [4]	AAC No 656 Sqn, Dishforth	
XZ217	WS Lynx AH7	AAC No 661 Sqn, Gütersloh	
XZ218	WS Lynx AH7	AAC No 655 Sqn, Aldergrove	
XZ219	WS Lynx AH7	AAC 1 Regiment, Gütersloh	
XZ220	WS Lynx AH7	AAC No 669 Sqn, Wattisham	
XZ221	WS Lynx AH7	AAC No 651 Sqn, Gütersloh	
XZ222	WS Lynx AH7 [P]	AAC No 657 Sqn, Dishforth	
XZ228	WS Lynx HAS3S	RN AMG, Portland	
XZ229	WS Lynx HAS3S [338/CT]	RN No 815 Sqn, Portland	
XZ230	WS Lynx HAS3S [336/CV]	RN No 815 Sqn, Portland	
XZ231	WS Lynx HAS3	RN AMG, Portland	
XZ232	WS Lynx HAS3S [410/GC]	RN No 815 Sqn, Portland	
XZ233	WS Lynx HAS3 [435/ED]	RNAY Fleetlands	
XZ234	WS Lynx HAS3S [444]	RN No 815 Sqn, Portland	
XZ235	WS Lynx HAS3S [635]	RN No 702 Sqn, Portland	
XZ236	WS Lynx HMA8	MoD(PE)/RWTS, DTEO Boscombe Down	
XZ237	WS Lynx HAS3S [330/BZ]	RN No 815 Sqn, Portland	
XZ238	WS Lynx HAS3S [434/ED]	RN No 815 Sqn, Portland	
XZ239	WS Lynx HAS3 [305]	RN No 815 Sqn, Portland	
XZ241	WS Lynx HAS3S [365/AY]	RN No 815 Sqn, Portland	
XZ243	WS Lynx HAS3 (wreck)	RN Portland, GI use	
XZ245	WS Lynx HAS3S [306]	RN No 815 Sqn, Portland	

Notes	Serial	Type (other identity) [code]	Owner/operator, location or fate
	XZ246	WS Lynx HAS3 [435/ED]	RN No 815 Sqn, Portland
	XZ248	WS Lynx HAS3S [345/NC]	RN No 815 Sqn, Portland
	XZ250	WS Lynx HAS3S [645]	RNAY Fleetlands
	XZ252	WS Lynx HAS3	RN, stored Fleetlands
	XZ254	WS Lynx HAS3S [308]	RN No 815 Sqn, Portland
	XZ255	WS Lynx HAS3S [631]	RN No 702 Sqn, Portland
	XZ256	WS Lynx HMA8 [671]	RN No 815 Sqn OEU, Portland
	XZ257	WS Lynx HAS3S	RN No 815 Sqn, Portland
	XZ258	*WS Lynx HAS3S [633]*	*Repainted as ZD258 by July 1995*
		(really ZD258)	
	XZ284	HS Nimrod MR2	RAF No 42(R) Sqn, Kinloss
	XZ287	BAe Nimrod AEW3 (9140M)	RAF TSW, Stafford
		(fuselage)	
	XZ290	WS Gazelle AH1 [F]	AAC No 670 Sqn, Middle Wallop
	XZ291	WS Gazelle AH1	AAC No 12 Flt, Laarbruch
	XZ292	WS Gazelle AH1 [4]	AAC No 656 Sqn, Dishforth
	XZ294	WS Gazelle AH1	AAC No 669 Sqn, Wattisham
	XZ295	WS Gazelle AH1	AAC No 6(TA) Flt, Shawbury
	XZ296	WS Gazelle AH1	AAC No 654 Sqn, Wattisham
	XZ298	WS Gazelle AH1 [X]	AAC No 657 Sqn, Dishforth
	XZ299	WS Gazelle AH1	AAC No 665 Sqn, Aldergrove
	XZ300	WS Gazelle AH1 [L]	AAC No 670 Sqn, Middle Wallop
	XZ301	WS Gazelle AH1 [A]	AAC No 663 Sqn, Wattisham
	XZ302	WS Gazelle AH1	AAC, stored RNAY Fleetlands
	XZ303	WS Gazelle AH1 [4]	AAC No 656 Sqn, Dishforth
	XZ304	WS Gazelle AH1	AAC No 6(TA) Flt, Shawbury
	XZ305	WS Gazelle AH1	AAC 3 Regiment, Wattisham
	XZ307	WS Gazelle AH1	AAC, stored RNAY Fleetlands
	XZ308	WS Gazelle AH1 [V]	AAC No 657 Sqn, Dishforth
	XZ309	WS Gazelle AH1	AAC No 6(TA) Flt, Shawbury
	XZ310	WS Gazelle AH1 [U]	AAC No 670 Sqn, Middle Wallop
	XZ311	WS Gazelle AH1	AAC No 6(TA) Flt, Shawbury
	XZ312	WS Gazelle AH1	AAC No 2(TA) Flt, Netheravon
	XZ313	WS Gazelle AH1 [S]	AAC No 663 Sqn, Wattisham
	XZ314	WS Gazelle AH1 [A]	AAC No 666(TA) Sqn, Netheravon
	XZ315	WS Gazelle AH1	AAC No 665 Sqn, Aldergrove
	XZ316	WS Gazelle AH1 [B]	AAC No 658 Sqn, Netheravon
	XZ317	WS Gazelle AH1 [R]	AAC No 670 Sqn, Middle Wallop
	XZ318	WS Gazelle AH1	AAC No 664 Sqn, Dishforth
	XZ320	WS Gazelle AH1	RM, stored Fleetlands
	XZ321	WS Gazelle AH1	AAC No 665 Sqn, Aldergrove
	XZ322	WS Gazelle AH1 [N]	AAC No 670 Sqn, Middle Wallop
	XZ323	WS Gazelle AH1	AAC, RNAY Fleetlands
	XZ324	WS Gazelle AH1	AAC No 3(TA) Flt, Turnhouse
	XZ325	WS Gazelle AH1 [T]	AAC No 670 Sqn, Middle Wallop
	XZ326	WS Gazelle AH1	RM, stored Fleetlands
	XZ327	WS Gazelle AH1 [B1]	AAC No 670 Sqn, Middle Wallop
	XZ328	WS Gazelle AH1	AAC No 654 Sqn, Wattisham
	XZ329	WS Gazelle AH1 [J]	AAC No 670 Sqn, Middle Wallop
	XZ330	WS Gazelle AH1 [Y]	AAC No 670 Sqn, Middle Wallop
	XZ331	WS Gazelle AH1 [C]	AAC No 663 Sqn, Wattisham
	XZ332	WS Gazelle AH1 [O]	AAC No 670 Sqn, Middle Wallop
	XZ333	WS Gazelle AH1 [A]	AAC No 670 Sqn, Middle Wallop
	XZ334	WS Gazelle AH1 [S]	AAC No 670 Sqn, Middle Wallop
	XZ335	WS Gazelle AH1	AAC, RNAY Fleetlands
	XZ337	WS Gazelle AH1 [5]	AAC No 656 Sqn, Dishforth
	XZ338	WS Gazelle AH1	AAC No 661 Sqn, Gütersloh
	XZ339	WS Gazelle AH1	AAC No 667 Sqn, Middle Wallop
	XZ340	WS Gazelle AH1	AAC No 29 Flt, BATUS, Suffield, Canada
	XZ341	WS Gazelle AH1	AAC No 3(TA) Flt, Turnhouse
	XZ342	WS Gazelle AH1	AAC, stored RNAY Fleetlands
	XZ343	WS Gazelle AH1	AAC No 659 Sqn, Wattisham
	XZ344	WS Gazelle AH1 [F1]	AAC No 670 Sqn, Middle Wallop
	XZ345	WS Gazelle AH1	AAC No 669 Sqn, Wattisham
	XZ346	WS Gazelle AH1	AAC No 665 Sqn, Aldergrove
	XZ347	WS Gazelle AH1	AAC No 664 Sqn, Dishforth
	XZ348	WS Gazelle AH1 (wreckage)	AAC, stored RNAY Fleetlands
	XZ349	WS Gazelle AH1 [G1]	AAC No 670 Sqn, Middle Wallop
	XZ355	SEPECAT Jaguar GR1A [FJ]	RAF No 41 Sqn, Coltishall
	XZ356	SEPECAT Jaguar GR1A [EP]	RAF No 6 Sqn, Coltishall
	XZ357	SEPECAT Jaguar GR1A [FK]	RAF No 41 Sqn, Coltishall
	XZ358	SEPECAT Jaguar GR1A [FL]	RAF No 41 Sqn, Coltishall
	XZ360	SEPECAT Jaguar GR1A [FN]	RAF No 41 Sqn, Coltishall

Serial	Type (other identity) [code]	Owner/operator, location or fate	Notes
XZ361	SEPECAT Jaguar GR1A [T]	RAF No 41 Sqn, Coltishall	
XZ362	SEPECAT Jaguar GR1B [GC]	RAF No 54 Sqn, Coltishall	
XZ363	SEPECAT Jaguar GR1A [O]	RAF, stored Shawbury	
XZ363	SEPECAT Jaguar GR1A <R> (BAPC 151) [A]	RAF EP&TU, St Athan	
XZ364	SEPECAT Jaguar GR1A [GJ]	RAF No 54 Sqn, Coltishall	
XZ366	SEPECAT Jaguar GR1A [FS]	RAF No 41 Sqn, Coltishall	
XZ367	SEPECAT Jaguar GR1A [GP]	RAF No 54 Sqn, Coltishall	
XZ368	SEPECAT Jaguar GR1 [8900M] [AG]	RAF No 1 SoTT, Cosford	
XZ369	SEPECAT Jaguar GR1B [EF]	RAF No 6 Sqn, Coltishall	
XZ370	SEPECAT Jaguar GR1 (9004M) [JB]	RAF No 1 SoTT, Cosford	
XZ371	SEPECAT Jaguar GR1 (8907M) [AP]	RAF No 1 SoTT, Cosford	
XZ372	SEPECAT Jaguar GR1A [ED]	RAF No 6 Sqn, Coltishall	
XZ373	SEPECAT Jaguar GR1A [GF]	*Written off Adriatic Sea, 21 June 1995*	
XZ374	SEPECAT Jaguar GR1 (9005M) [JC]	RAF No 1 SoTT, Cosford	
XZ375	SEPECAT Jaguar GR1B [GR]	RAF St Athan (conversion)	
XZ377	SEPECAT Jaguar GR1A [EB]	RAF No 6 Sqn, Coltishall	
XZ378	SEPECAT Jaguar GR1A [EP]	RAF, stored Shawbury	
XZ381	SEPECAT Jaguar GR1B [EC]	MoD(PE)/DRA, DTEO Boscombe Down	
XZ382	SEPECAT Jaguar GR1 (8908M) [AE]	RAF Coltishall BDRF	
XZ383	SEPECAT Jaguar GR1 (8901M) [AF]	RAF No 1 SoTT, Cosford	
XZ384	SEPECAT Jaguar GR1 (8954M) [BC]	RAF No 1 SoTT, Cosford	
XZ385	SEPECAT Jaguar GR1A [F]	RAF No 16(R) Sqn, Lossiemouth	
XZ389	SEPECAT Jaguar GR1 (8946M) [BL]	RAF Halton	
XZ390	SEPECAT Jaguar GR1A (9003M) [35,JA]	RAF No 1 SoTT, Cosford	
XZ391	SEPECAT Jaguar GR1A [GM]	RAF No 54 Sqn, Coltishall	
XZ392	SEPECAT Jaguar GR1A [GQ]	RAF, stored Shawbury	
XZ394	SEPECAT Jaguar GR1A [GN]	RAF No 54 Sqn, Coltishall	
XZ396	SEPECAT Jaguar GR1A [EM]	RAF No 6 Sqn, Coltishall	
XZ398	SEPECAT Jaguar GR1A [FA]	RAF No 41 Sqn, Coltishall	
XZ399	SEPECAT Jaguar GR1A [EJ]	RAF No 6 Sqn, Coltishall	
XZ400	SEPECAT Jaguar GR1A [EG]	RAF, stored Shawbury	
XZ431	HS Buccaneer S2B	RAF Marham, Fire Section	
XZ439	BAe Sea Harrier FA2	MoD(PE)/FWTS, DTEO Boscombe Down	
XZ440	BAe Sea Harrier FA2	MoD(PE)/BAe Brough (on rebuild)	
XZ445	BAe Harrier T4A [721]	RN No 899 Sqn, Yeovilton	
XZ455	BAe Sea Harrier FA2 [001]	RN No 801 Sqn, Yeovilton	
XZ457	BAe Sea Harrier FA2 [714]	*Written off Yeovilton, 20 Oct 1995*	
XZ459	BAe Sea Harrier FA2 [126]	RN No 800 Sqn, Yeovilton	
XZ492	BAe Sea Harrier FA2 [127]	RN No 800 Sqn, Yeovilton	
XZ493	BAe Sea Harrier FRS1 [126]	FAA Museum, RNAS Yeovilton	
XZ494	BAe Sea Harrier FA2 [122]	MoD(PE)/BAe Dunsfold (conversion)	
XZ497	BAe Sea Harrier FA2 [712/R]	MoD(PE)/FWTS, DTEO Boscombe Down	
XZ499	BAe Sea Harrier FA2 [123]	MoD(PE)/BAe Dunsfold (conversion)	
XZ559	Slingsby T61F Venture T2 (G-BUEK)	Privately owned, Tibenham	
XZ570	WS61 Sea King HAS5(mod)	MoD(PE)/RWTS, DTEO Boscombe Down	
XZ571	WS61 Sea King HAS6 [014/L]	RN No 820 Sqn, Culdrose	
XZ574	WS61 Sea King HAS6 [704/PW]	RN No 819 Sqn, Prestwick	
XZ575	WS61 Sea King HAS5 [599]	RN No 706 Sqn, Culdrose	
XZ576	WS61 Sea King HAS6	MoD(PE)/RWTS, DTEO Boscombe Down	
XZ578	WS61 Sea King HAS5 [581]	RN , stored Fleetlands	
XZ579	WS61 Sea King HAS6 [706/PW]	RN No 819 Sqn, Prestwick	
XZ580	WS61 Sea King HAS6 [267/N]	RN No 814 Sqn, Culdrose	
XZ581	WS61 Sea King HAS6 [514]	RN No 810 Sqn OEU, DTEO Boscombe Down	
XZ585	WS61 Sea King HAR3	RAF No 202 Sqn, A Flt, Boulmer	
XZ586	WS61 Sea King HAR3 [S]	RAF No 202 Sqn, D Flt, Lossiemouth	
XZ587	WS61 Sea King HAR3	RAF No 22 Sqn, B Flt, Wattisham	
XZ588	WS61 Sea King HAR3	RAF St Mawgan	
XZ589	WS61 Sea King HAR3	RAF SKTU/No 205(R) Sqn, St Mawgan	
XZ590	WS61 Sea King HAR3	RAF No 22 Sqn, B Flt, Wattisham	
XZ591	WS61 Sea King HAR3	RAF No 202 Sqn, D Flt, Lossiemouth	
XZ592	WS61 Sea King HAR3	RAF St Mawgan	

Notes	Serial	Type (other identity) [code]	Owner/operator, location or fate
	XZ593	WS61 Sea King HAR3	RAF No 202 Sqn, A Flt, Boulmer
	XZ594	WS61 Sea King HAR3	RAF No 22 Sqn, A Flt, Chivenor
	XZ595	WS61 Sea King HAR3	RAF SKTU/No 205(R) Sqn, St Mawgan
	XZ596	WS61 Sea King HAR3	RAF No 22 Sqn, A Flt, Chivenor
	XZ597	WS61 Sea King HAR3	RAF No 78 Sqn, Mount Pleasant, FI
	XZ598	WS61 Sea King HAR3	RAF St Mawgan
	XZ599	WS61 Sea King HAR3 [S]	RAF St Mawgan
	XZ605	WS Lynx AH7 [Y]	RM No 847 Sqn, Yeovilton
	XZ606	WS Lynx AH7	AAC No 667 Sqn, Middle Wallop
	XZ607	WS Lynx AH7 [M]	AAC, Wattisham
	XZ608	WS Lynx AH7 [1]	AAC No 656 Sqn, Dishforth
	XZ609	WS Lynx AH7	AAC No 669 Sqn, Wattisham
	XZ610	WS Lynx AH7	AAC 1 Regiment, Gütersloh
	XZ611	WS Lynx AH7	AAC 1 Regiment, Gütersloh
	XZ612	WS Lynx AH7 [N]	RM No 847 Sqn, Yeovilton
	XZ613	WS Lynx AH7 [F]	AAC SEAE, Arborfield
	XZ614	WS Lynx AH7 [X]	RM No 847 Sqn, Yeovilton
	XZ615	WS Lynx AH7	AAC No 655 Sqn, Aldergrove
	XZ616	WS Lynx AH7 [2]	AAC No 656 Sqn, Dishforth
	XZ617	WS Lynx AH7 [UN]	AAC 9 Regiment, Dishforth
	XZ631	Panavia Tornado GR4	MoD(PE)/BAe Warton
	XZ641	WS Lynx AH7 [G]	AAC No 671 Sqn, Middle Wallop
	XZ642	WS Lynx AH7	AAC 1 Regiment, Gütersloh
	XZ643	WS Lynx AH7	AAC, Wattisham
	XZ644	WS Lynx AH7 (wreck)	AAC
	XZ645	WS Lynx AH7 [Z]	AAC No 663 Sqn, Wattisham
	XZ646	WS Lynx AH7	AAC 1 Regiment, Gütersloh
	XZ647	WS Lynx AH7	AAC No 655 Sqn, Aldergrove
	XZ648	WS Lynx AH7	AAC 1 Regiment, Gütersloh
	XZ649	WS Lynx AH7	AAC No 655 Sqn, Aldergrove
	XZ650	WS Lynx AH7	AAC 1 Regiment, Gütersloh
	XZ651	WS Lynx AH7	AAC No 657 Sqn, Dishforth
	XZ652	WS Lynx AH7 [T]	AAC No 671 Sqn, Middle Wallop
	XZ653	WS Lynx AH7 [UN]	AAC No 664 Sqn, Dishforth
	XZ654	WS Lynx AH7	AAC, stored RNAY Fleetlands
	XZ655	WS Lynx AH7	AAC No 655 Sqn, Aldergrove
	XZ661	WS Lynx AH7	AAC, stored RNAY Fleetlands
	XZ662	WS Lynx AH7	AAC, RNAY Fleetlands
	XZ663	WS Lynx AH7	AAC No 655 Sqn, Aldergrove
	XZ664	WS Lynx AH7	AAC, Wattisham
	XZ665	WS Lynx AH7	AAC 1 Regiment, Gütersloh
	XZ666	WS Lynx AH7	AAC No 661 Sqn, Gütersloh
	XZ667	WS Lynx AH7	AAC No 665 Sqn, Aldergrove
	XZ668	WS Lynx AH7 [T]	*Written off, nr Ploce, Croatia, 18 Aug 1995*
	XZ669	WS Lynx AH7	AAC No 661 Sqn, Gütersloh
	XZ670	WS Lynx AH7 [UN]	AAC No 664 Sqn, Dishforth
	XZ671	WS Lynx AH9 <ff>	AAC, stored RNAY Fleetlands
	XZ672	WS Lynx AH7	AAC No 655 Sqn, Aldergrove
	XZ673	WS Lynx AH7	AAC No 655 Sqn, Aldergrove
	XZ674	WS Lynx AH7	AAC No 659 Sqn, Wattisham
	XZ675	WS Lynx AH7 [E]	AAC No 671 Sqn, Middle Wallop
	XZ676	WS Lynx AH7 [N]	AAC No 671 Sqn, Middle Wallop
	XZ677	WS Lynx AH7 [Y]	AAC No 663 Sqn, Wattisham
	XZ678	WS Lynx AH7 [O]	AAC No 662 Sqn, Wattisham
	XZ679	WS Lynx AH7 [UN]	AAC No 664 Sqn, Dishforth
	XZ680	WS Lynx AH7	AAC No 652 Sqn, Gütersloh
	XZ681	WS Lynx AH1	AAC Middle Wallop, BDRT
	XZ689	WS Lynx HAS3S [403/BX]	RN No 815 Sqn, Portland
	XZ690	WS Lynx HAS3S [462/WM]	RN No 815 Sqn, Portland
	XZ691	WS Lynx HMA8 [300]	RN, stored Fleetlands
	XZ692	WS Lynx HAS3S [301]	RN No 815 Sqn, Portland
	XZ693	WS Lynx HAS3S [632]	RN No 702 Sqn, Portland
	XZ694	WS Lynx HAS3S [307]	RN No 815 Sqn, Portland
	XZ695	WS Lynx HAS3S [372/NL]	RN No 815 Sqn, Portland
	XZ696	WS Lynx HAS3S [479]	RN No 815 Sqn, Portland
	XZ697	WS Lynx HAS3CTS [341]	RNAY Fleetlands
	XZ698	WS Lynx HAS3S [303]	RN No 815 Sqn, Portland
	XZ699	WS Lynx HAS3	RN, stored Fleetlands
	XZ719	WS Lynx HAS3S [644]	RN No 702 Sqn, Portland
	XZ720	WS Lynx HAS3S [332/LP]	RN No 815 Sqn, Portland
	XZ721	WS Lynx HAS3S [360]	RN No 815 Sqn, Portland
	XZ722	WS Lynx HAS3S	RNAY Fleetlands
	XZ723	WS Lynx HAS3S [374/VB]	RN No 815 Sqn, Portland

Serial	Type (other identity) [code]	Owner/operator, location or fate	Notes
XZ724	WS Lynx HAS3S [376/XB]	RN No 815 Sqn, Portland	
XZ725	WS Lynx HAS3S	RN AMG, Portland	
XZ726	WS Lynx HAS3S [302]	RN No 815 Sqn, Portland	
XZ727	WS Lynx HAS3S	RN, stored Fleetlands	
XZ728	WS Lynx HMA8	RNAY Fleetlands (conversion)	
XZ729	WS Lynx HAS3S [632]	RN No 702 Sqn, Portland	
XZ730	WS Lynx HAS3CTS [304]	RN No 815 Sqn, Portland	
XZ731	WS Lynx HAS3S [634]	RN No 702 Sqn, Portland	
XZ732	WS Lynx HMA8 [670]	RN No 815 Sqn OEU, Portland	
XZ733	WS Lynx HAS3S [342/BT]	RN No 815 Sqn, Portland	
XZ735	WS Lynx HAS3S	RN No 815 Sqn, Portland	
XZ736	WS Lynx HAS3S [363/MA]	RN No 815 Sqn, Portland	
XZ918	WS61 Sea King HAS5 [589]	RN, stored Fleetlands	
XZ920	WS61 Sea King HAR5 [822/CU]	RN No 771 Sqn, Culdrose	
XZ921	WS61 Sea King HAS6 [587]	RN No 706 Sqn, Culdrose	
XZ922	WS61 Sea King HAS6 [503/BD]	RN No 810 Sqn, DTEO Boscombe Down	
XZ930	WS Gazelle HT3 [Q]	RAF No 2 FTS, Shawbury	
XZ931	WS Gazelle HT3 [R]	RAF No 2 FTS, Shawbury	
XZ932	WS Gazelle HT3 [S]	RAF No 2 FTS, Shawbury	
XZ933	WS Gazelle HT3 [T]	RAF No 2 FTS, Shawbury	
XZ934	WS Gazelle HT3 [U]	RAF No 2 FTS, Shawbury	
XZ935	WS Gazelle HCC4	RAF No 32(The Royal) Sqn, Northolt	
XZ936	WS Gazelle HT2	MoD(PE)/ETPS, DTEO Boscombe Down	
XZ937	WS Gazelle HT2 [Y]	RAF No 2 FTS, Shawbury	
XZ938	WS Gazelle HT2 [45/CU]	RN No 705 Sqn, Culdrose	
XZ939	WS Gazelle HT2 [Z]	MoD(PE)/ETPS, DTEO Boscombe Down	
XZ940	WS Gazelle HT2 [O]	RAF No 2 FTS, Shawbury	
XZ941	WS Gazelle HT2 [B]	RAF No 2 FTS, Shawbury	
XZ942	WS Gazelle HT2 [42/CU]	RN No 705 Sqn, Culdrose	
XZ964	BAe Harrier GR3 [D]	Royal Engineers Museum, Chatham	
XZ965	BAe Harrier GR3 (9184M) [L]	The Old Flying Machine Company, Duxford	
XZ966	BAe Harrier GR3 (9221M) [G]	Privately owned, Bruntingthorpe	
XZ967	BAe Harrier GR3 (9077M) [F]	Phoenix Aviation, Bruntingthorpe	
XZ968	BAe Harrier GR3 (9222M) [3G]	Muckleborough Collection, Weybourne	
XZ969	BAe Harrier GR3 [D]	SFDO, RNAS Culdrose	
XZ970	BAe Harrier GR3	RAF, stored St Athan	
XZ971	BAe Harrier GR3 (9219M) [G]	RAF Benson, at main gate	
XZ987	BAe Harrier GR3 (9185M) [C]	RAF Stafford, at main gate	
XZ990	BAe Harrier GR3 (wreck)	RAF Wittering, derelict	
XZ991	BAe Harrier GR3 (9162M) [3A]	RAF St Athan, BDRT	
XZ993	BAe Harrier GR3 [M]	RAF St Athan, Fire Section	
XZ994	BAe Harrier GR3 (9170M) [U]	RAF Air Movements School, Brize Norton	
XZ995	BAe Harrier GR3 (9220M) [3G]	RAF St Mawgan, Fire Section	
XZ996	BAe Harrier GR3 [2,3]	SFDO, RNAS Culdrose	
XZ997	BAe Harrier GR3 (9122M) [V]	RAF Museum, Hendon	
XZ998	BAe Harrier GR3 (9161M) [D]	*To RAF Brüggen for BDRT, October 1994*	
ZA101	BAe Hawk 100 (G-HAWK)	BAe, Warton	
ZA105	WS61 Sea King HAR3 [S]	RAF No 78 Sqn, Mount Pleasant, FI	
ZA110	BAe Jetstream T2 (F-BTMI) [573/CU]	RN No 750 Sqn, Culdrose	
ZA111	BAe Jetstream T2 (9Q-CTC) [574/CU]	RN No 750 Sqn, Culdrose	
ZA126	WS61 Sea King HAS6 [509]	RN No 810 Sqn, Culdrose	
ZA127	WS61 Sea King HAS6 [592]	RN No 706 Sqn, Culdrose	
ZA128	WS61 Sea King HAS6 [591/CU]	RN No 706 Sqn, Culdrose	
ZA129	WS61 Sea King HAS6 [502/CU]	RN No 810 Sqn, Culdrose	
ZA130	WS61 Sea King HAS5 [587]	RN, stored Fleetlands	
ZA131	WS61 Sea King HAS6 [011/L]	RN No 820 Sqn, Culdrose	
ZA133	WS61 Sea King HAS6 [013/L]	RN No 820 Sqn, Culdrose	
ZA134	WS61 Sea King HAS5 [598]	RNAY Fleetlands	
ZA135	WS61 Sea King HAS6 [010/L]	RN No 820 Sqn, Culdrose	
ZA136	WS61 Sea King HAS6 [015/L]	RN No 820 Sqn, Culdrose	
ZA137	WS61 Sea King HAS5 [597]	RN No 706 Sqn, Culdrose	
ZA140	BAe VC10 K2 (G-ARVL) [A]	RAF No 101 Sqn, Brize Norton	
ZA141	BAe VC10 K2 (G-ARVG) [B]	RAF No 101 Sqn, Brize Norton	
ZA142	BAe VC10 K2 (G-ARVI) [C]	RAF, stored St Athan	
ZA143	BAe VC10 K2 (G-ARVK) [D]	RAF No 101 Sqn, Brize Norton	
ZA144	BAe VC10 K2 (G-ARVC) [E]	RAF, stored St Athan	
ZA147	BAe VC10 K3 (5H-MMT) [F]	RAF No 101 Sqn, Brize Norton	
ZA148	BAe VC10 K3 (5Y-ADA)	RAF No 101 Sqn, Brize Norton	
ZA149	BAe VC10 K3 (5X-UVJ)	RAF No 101 Sqn, Brize Norton	

ZA150 – ZA446

Notes	Serial	Type (other identity) [code]	Owner/operator, location or fate
	ZA150	BAe VC10 K3 (5H-MOG) [J]	RAF No 101 Sqn, Brize Norton
	ZA166	WS61 Sea King HAS6	RNAY Fleetlands
	ZA167	WS61 Sea King HAR5 [825/CU]	RN No 771 Sqn, Culdrose
	ZA168	WS61 Sea King HAS6 [512]	RN No 810 Sqn, Culdrose
	ZA169	WS61 Sea King HAS6 [266/N]	RN AMG, Culdrose
	ZA170	WS61 Sea King HAS5 [584]	RN, stored Fleetlands
	ZA175	BAe Sea Harrier FA2	MoD(PE)/BAe Dunsfold (conversion)
	ZA176	BAe Sea Harrier FA2 [000]	RN AMG, Yeovilton
	ZA195	BAe Sea Harrier FA2	MoD(PE)/FWTS, DTEO Boscombe Down
	ZA250	BAe Harrier T52 (G-VTOL)	Brooklands Aviation Museum, Weybridge
	ZA254	Panavia Tornado F2	MoD(PE)/BAe Warton
	ZA267	Panavia Tornado F2	MoD(PE)/FWTS, DTEO Boscombe Down
	ZA283	Panavia Tornado F2	MoD(PE)/BAe Warton
	ZA291	WS61 Sea King HC4 [ZX]	RN No 848 Sqn, Yeovilton
	ZA292	WS61 Sea King HC4 [ZR]	RN No 848 Sqn, Yeovilton
	ZA293	WS61 Sea King HC4 [ZT]	RNAY Fleetlands
	ZA295	WS61 Sea King HC4 [VM]	RN No 846 Sqn, Yeovilton
	ZA296	WS61 Sea King HC4 [VO]	RN No 846 Sqn, Yeovilton
	ZA297	WS61 Sea King HC4 [C]	RN No 845 Sqn, Yeovilton
	ZA298	WS61 Sea King HC4 [G]	RN No 845 Sqn, Yeovilton
	ZA299	WS61 Sea King HC4 [ZT]	RN No 848 Sqn, Yeovilton
	ZA310	WS61 Sea King HC4 [ZY]	RN No 848 Sqn, Yeovilton
	ZA312	WS61 Sea King HC4 [ZS]	RN No 848 Sqn, Yeovilton
	ZA313	WS61 Sea King HC4	RNAY Fleetlands
	ZA314	WS61 Sea King HC4 [F]	RN No 845 Sqn, Yeovilton
	ZA319	Panavia Tornado GR1 [B-11]	RAF TTTE, Cottesmore
	ZA320	Panavia Tornado GR1 [B-01]	RAF TTTE, Cottesmore
	ZA321	Panavia Tornado GR1 [B-58]	RAF TTTE, Cottesmore
	ZA322	Panavia Tornado GR1 [B-50]	RAF TTTE, Cottesmore
	ZA323	Panavia Tornado GR1 [B-14]	RAF TTTE, Cottesmore
	ZA324	Panavia Tornado GR1 [B-02]	RAF TTTE, Cottesmore
	ZA325	Panavia Tornado GR1 [B-03]	RAF TTTE, Cottesmore
	ZA326	Panavia Tornado GR1P	MoD(PE)/DRA, DTEO Boscombe Down
	ZA327	Panavia Tornado GR1 [B-51]	RAF TTTE, Cottesmore
	ZA328	Panavia Tornado GR1	MoD(PE)/FWTS, DTEO Boscombe Down
	ZA330	Panavia Tornado GR1 [B-08]	RAF TTTE, Cottesmore
	ZA352	Panavia Tornado GR1 [B-04]	RAF TTTE, Cottesmore
	ZA353	Panavia Tornado GR1 [B-53]	MoD(PE)/FWTS, DTEO Boscombe Down
	ZA354	Panavia Tornado GR1	MoD(PE)/FWTS, DTEO Boscombe Down
	ZA355	Panavia Tornado GR1 [B-54]	RAF TTTE, Cottesmore
	ZA356	Panavia Tornado GR1 [B-07]	RAF TTTE, Cottesmore
	ZA357	Panavia Tornado GR1 [B-05]	RAF TTTE, Cottesmore
	ZA358	Panavia Tornado GR1	MoD(PE)/BAe Warton
	ZA359	Panavia Tornado GR1 [B-55]	RAF TTTE, Cottesmore
	ZA360	Panavia Tornado GR1 [B-56]	RAF TTTE, Cottesmore
	ZA361	Panavia Tornado GR1 [B-57]	RAF TTTE, Cottesmore
	ZA362	Panavia Tornado GR1 [B-09]	RAF TTTE, Cottesmore
	ZA365	Panavia Tornado GR1 [JT]	RAF AMF, Lossiemouth
	ZA367	Panavia Tornado GR1 [II]	RAF No 2 Sqn, Marham
	ZA369	Panavia Tornado GR1A [U]	RAF No 2 Sqn, Marham
	ZA370	Panavia Tornado GR1A [A]	RAF No 2 Sqn, Marham
	ZA371	Panavia Tornado GR1A [C]	RAF No 2 Sqn, Marham
	ZA372	Panavia Tornado GR1A [E]	RAF No 2 Sqn, Marham
	ZA373	Panavia Tornado GR1A [H]	RAF No 2 Sqn, Marham
	ZA374	Panavia Tornado GR1B [AJ-D]	RAF No 617 Sqn, Lossiemouth
	ZA375	Panavia Tornado GR1B [AJ-W]	RAF No 617 Sqn, Lossiemouth
	ZA393	Panavia Tornado GR1 [BE]	RAF No 14 Sqn, Brüggen
	ZA395	Panavia Tornado GR1A [N]	RAF No 2 Sqn, Marham
	ZA398	Panavia Tornado GR1A [S]	RAF No 2 Sqn, Marham
	ZA399	Panavia Tornado GR1B	RAF No 617 Sqn, Lossiemouth
	ZA400	Panavia Tornado GR1A [T]	RAF No 2 Sqn, Marham
	ZA401	Panavia Tornado GR1A [R]	RAF No 2 Sqn, Marham
	ZA402	Panavia Tornado GR1	MoD(PE)/FWTS, DTEO Boscombe Down
	ZA404	Panavia Tornado GR1A [W]	RAF No 2 Sqn, Marham
	ZA405	Panavia Tornado GR1A [Y]	RAF No 2 Sqn, Marham
	ZA406	Panavia Tornado GR1 [CI]	RAF No 17 Sqn, Brüggen
	ZA407	Panavia Tornado GR1B [AJ-G]	RAF No 617 Sqn, Lossiemouth
	ZA409	Panavia Tornado GR1B [FQ]	RAF No 12 Sqn, Lossiemouth
	ZA410	Panavia Tornado GR1 [FZ]	RAF No 12 Sqn, Lossiemouth
	ZA411	Panavia Tornado GR1B [AJ-S]	RAF No 617 Sqn, Lossiemouth
	ZA412	Panavia Tornado GR1 [FX]	RAF, stored St Athan
	ZA446	Panavia Tornado GR1B	RAF AWC/SAOEU, DTEO Boscombe Down

Serial	Type (other identity) [code]	Owner/operator, location or fate	Notes
ZA446	Panavia Tornado GR1 <R> (BAPC 155) [F]	Repainted as ZA468 by July 1995	
ZA447	Panavia Tornado GR1B [FA]	RAF No 12 Sqn, Lossiemouth	
ZA449	Panavia Tornado GR1	MoD(PE)/DRA, DTEO Boscombe Down	
ZA450	Panavia Tornado GR1B [FB]	RAF No 12 Sqn, Lossiemouth	
ZA452	Panavia Tornado GR1B	RAF No 12 Sqn, Lossiemouth	
ZA453	Panavia Tornado GR1B [FD]	RAF No 12 Sqn, Lossiemouth	
ZA455	Panavia Tornado GR1B [FE]	RAF No 12 Sqn, Lossiemouth	
ZA456	Panavia Tornado GR1B [AJ-Q]	RAF No 617 Sqn, Lossiemouth	
ZA457	Panavia Tornado GR1B [AJ-J]	RAF No 617 Sqn, Lossiemouth	
ZA458	Panavia Tornado GR1 [CE]	RAF No 17 Sqn, Brüggen	
ZA459	Panavia Tornado GR1B [AJ-B]	RAF No 617 Sqn, Lossiemouth	
ZA460	Panavia Tornado GR1B [AJ-A]	RAF No 617 Sqn, Lossiemouth	
ZA461	Panavia Tornado GR1B [AJ-M]	RAF No 617 Sqn, Lossiemouth	
ZA462	Panavia Tornado GR1	RAF No 17 Sqn, Brüggen	
ZA463	Panavia Tornado GR1 [CR]	RAF No 17 Sqn, Brüggen	
ZA465	Panavia Tornado GR1B	RAF No 617 Sqn, Lossiemouth	
ZA466	Panavia Tornado GR1 <ff>	RAF St Athan, BDRT	
ZA468	Panavia Tornado GR1 <R> (BAPC 155)	RAF EP&TU, St Athan	
ZA469	Panavia Tornado GR1B [AJ-O]	RAF No 617 Sqn, Lossiemouth	
ZA470	Panavia Tornado GR1 [BQ]	RAF No 14 Sqn, Brüggen	
ZA471	Panavia Tornado GR1B [AJ-K]	RAF No 617 Sqn, Lossiemouth	
ZA472	Panavia Tornado GR1 [CT]	RAF No 17 Sqn, Brüggen	
ZA473	Panavia Tornado GR1B [FG]	RAF No 12 Sqn, Lossiemouth	
ZA474	Panavia Tornado GR1B [FF]	RAF No 12 Sqn, Lossiemouth	
ZA475	Panavia Tornado GR1B [FH]	RAF No 12 Sqn, Lossiemouth	
ZA490	Panavia Tornado GR1B [FJ]	RAF No 12 Sqn, Lossiemouth	
ZA491	Panavia Tornado GR1B [FK]	RAF No 12 Sqn, Lossiemouth	
ZA492	Panavia Tornado GR1B [FL]	RAF No 12 Sqn, Lossiemouth	
ZA541	Panavia Tornado GR1 [TO]	RAF No 15(R) Sqn, Lossiemouth	
ZA542	Panavia Tornado GR1 [JA]	RAF, stored St Athan	
ZA543	Panavia Tornado GR1	RAF, stored St Athan	
ZA544	Panavia Tornado GR1 [TP]	RAF No 15(R) Sqn, Lossiemouth	
ZA546	Panavia Tornado GR1 [AJ-C]	RAF Cottesmore, instructional use	
ZA547	Panavia Tornado GR1 [JC]	RAF, stored St Athan	
ZA548	Panavia Tornado GR1	RAF No 15(R) Sqn, Lossiemouth	
ZA549	Panavia Tornado GR1 [TR]	RAF No 15(R) Sqn, Lossiemouth	
ZA550	Panavia Tornado GR1 [JD]	RAF, stored St Athan	
ZA551	Panavia Tornado GR1 [IV]	RAF No 2 Sqn, Marham	
ZA552	Panavia Tornado GR1 [TS]	RAF No 15(R) Sqn, Lossiemouth	
ZA553	Panavia Tornado GR1 [JE]	RAF, stored St Athan	
ZA554	Panavia Tornado GR1 [DM]	RAF, stored St Athan	
ZA556	Panavia Tornado GR1 [TA]	RAF No 15(R) Sqn, Lossiemouth	
ZA557	Panavia Tornado GR1	RAF, stored St Athan	
ZA559	Panavia Tornado GR1 [F]	RAF No 15(R) Sqn, Lossiemouth	
ZA560	Panavia Tornado GR1	RAF TTTE, Cottesmore	
ZA562	Panavia Tornado GR1 [TT]	RAF No 15(R) Sqn, Lossiemouth	
ZA563	Panavia Tornado GR1 [TC]	RAF No 15(R) Sqn, Lossiemouth	
ZA564	Panavia Tornado GR1 [JK]	RAF, stored St Athan	
ZA585	Panavia Tornado GR1	RAF, stored St Athan	
ZA587	Panavia Tornado GR1 [TD]	RAF No 15(R) Sqn, Lossiemouth	
ZA588	Panavia Tornado GR1 [B-52]	RAF, stored St Athan	
ZA589	Panavia Tornado GR1 [TE]	RAF No 15(R) Sqn, Lossiemouth	
ZA590	Panavia Tornado GR1	RAF, stored St Athan	
ZA591	Panavia Tornado GR1	RAF, stored St Athan	
ZA592	Panavia Tornado GR1 [B]	RAF, stored St Athan	
ZA594	Panavia Tornado GR1 [TU]	RAF No 15(R) Sqn, Lossiemouth	
ZA595	Panavia Tornado GR1 [TV]	RAF No 15(R) Sqn, Lossiemouth	
ZA596	Panavia Tornado GR1	RAF, stored St Athan	
ZA597	Panavia Tornado GR1	RAF, stored St Athan	
ZA598	Panavia Tornado GR1B [AJ-T]	RAF No 617 Sqn, Lossiemouth	
ZA599	Panavia Tornado GR1 [B-16]	RAF TTTE, Cottesmore	
ZA600	Panavia Tornado GR1 [TH]	RAF No 15(R) Sqn, Lossiemouth	
ZA601	Panavia Tornado GR1 [TI]	RAF No 15(R) Sqn, Lossiemouth	
ZA602	Panavia Tornado GR1 [B-17]	RAF TTTE, Cottesmore	
ZA604	Panavia Tornado GR1 [TY]	RAF No 15(R) Sqn, Lossiemouth	
ZA606	Panavia Tornado GR1	RAF, stored St Athan	
ZA607	Panavia Tornado GR1 [TJ]	RAF No 15(R) Sqn, Lossiemouth	
ZA608	Panavia Tornado GR1 [TK]	RAF No 15(R) Sqn, Lossiemouth	
ZA609	Panavia Tornado GR1 [J]	RAF, stored St Athan	
ZA611	Panavia Tornado GR1	RAF, stored St Athan	
ZA612	Panavia Tornado GR1 [TZ]	RAF No 15(R) Sqn, Lossiemouth	

Notes	Serial	Type (other identity) [code]	Owner/operator, location or fate
	ZA613	Panavia Tornado GR1 [TL]	RAF No 15(R) Sqn, Lossiemouth
	ZA614	Panavia Tornado GR1 [TB]	RAF No 15(R) Sqn, Lossiemouth
	ZA634	Slingsby T61F Venture T2 (G-BUHA) [C]	Privately owned, Rufforth
	ZA670	B-V Chinook HC2 [BG]	RAF No 18 Sqn, Laarbruch
	ZA671	B-V Chinook HC2 [BB]	RAF No 18 Sqn, Laarbruch
	ZA673	B-V Chinook HC2 [NX]	RAF No 27(R) Sqn, Odiham
	ZA674	B-V Chinook HC2 [NY]	RAF No 27(R) Sqn, Odiham
	ZA675	B-V Chinook HC2 [EB]	RAF No 7 Sqn, Odiham
	ZA676	B-V Chinook HC1 [FG] (wreck)	RAF, stored Fleetlands
	ZA677	B-V Chinook HC2 [NU]	RAF No 27(R) Sqn, Odiham
	ZA678	B-V Chinook HC1 (9229M) [EZ] (wreck)	RAF Odiham, BDRT
	ZA679	B-V Chinook HC2	RAF No 78 Sqn, Mount Pleasant, FI
	ZA680	B-V Chinook HC2 [BD]	RAF No 18 Sqn, Laarbruch
	ZA681	B-V Chinook HC2 [NS]	RAF No 27(R) Sqn, Odiham
	ZA682	B-V Chinook HC2 [UN]	RAF No 7 Sqn, Odiham
	ZA683	B-V Chinook HC2 [EW]	RAF No 7 Sqn, Odiham
	ZA684	B-V Chinook HC2 [EL]	RAF No 7 Sqn, Odiham
	ZA704	B-V Chinook HC2 [EJ]	RAF No 7 Sqn, Odiham
	ZA705	B-V Chinook HC2 [EO]	RAF No 7 Sqn, Odiham
	ZA707	B-V Chinook HC2 [UN]	RAF No 7 Sqn, Odiham
	ZA708	B-V Chinook HC2 [BC]	RAF No 18 Sqn, Laarbruch
	ZA709	B-V Chinook HC2 [EQ]	RAF No 7 Sqn, Odiham
	ZA710	B-V Chinook HC2 [C]	RAF No 78 Sqn, Mount Pleasant, FI
	ZA711	B-V Chinook HC2 [UN]	RAF No 7 Sqn, Odiham
	ZA712	B-V Chinook HC2 [ER]	RAF No 7 Sqn, Odiham
	ZA713	B-V Chinook HC2 [EM]	RAF No 7 Sqn, Odiham
	ZA714	B-V Chinook HC2 [BA]	RAF No 18 Sqn, Laarbruch
	ZA717	B-V Chinook HC1 (wreck)	RAF St Athan, BDRT
	ZA718	B-V Chinook HC2 [BN]	MoD(PE)/RWTS, DTEO Boscombe Down
	ZA720	B-V Chinook HC2 [EP]	RAF No 7 Sqn, Odiham
	ZA726	WS Gazelle AH1	AAC No 670 Sqn, Middle Wallop
	ZA728	WS Gazelle AH1 [E]	RM No 847 Sqn, Yeovilton
	ZA729	WS Gazelle AH1	AAC No 656 Sqn, Dishforth
	ZA730	WS Gazelle AH1	AAC No 665 Sqn, Aldergrove
	ZA731	WS Gazelle AH1 [A]	AAC No 29 Flt, BATUS, Suffield, Canada
	ZA733	WS Gazelle AH1	AAC No 665 Sqn, Aldergrove
	ZA734	WS Gazelle AH1	AAC, stored Fleetlands
	ZA735	WS Gazelle AH1	AAC No 25 Flt, Belize
	ZA736	WS Gazelle AH1 [S]	AAC No 29 Flt, BATUS, Suffield, Canada
	ZA737	WS Gazelle AH1 [V]	AAC No 670 Sqn, Middle Wallop
	ZA765	WS Gazelle AH1	AAC, RNAY Fleetlands
	ZA766	WS Gazelle AH1	AAC No 651 Sqn, Gütersloh
	ZA767	WS Gazelle AH1	AAC No 25 Flt, Belize
	ZA768	WS Gazelle AH1 [F] (wreck)	AAC, stored Fleetlands
	ZA769	WS Gazelle AH1 [K]	AAC No 670 Sqn, Middle Wallop
	ZA771	WS Gazelle AH1	AAC No 664 Sqn, Dishforth
	ZA772	WS Gazelle AH1 [Q]	AAC No 670 Sqn, Middle Wallop
	ZA773	WS Gazelle AH1	AAC No 665 Sqn, Aldergrove
	ZA774	WS Gazelle AH1	AAC No 665 Sqn, Aldergrove
	ZA775	WS Gazelle AH1 [E1]	AAC, stored Fleetlands
	ZA776	WS Gazelle AH1 [F]	RM No 847 Sqn, Yeovilton
	ZA777	WS Gazelle AH1 [B]	AAC No 670 Sqn, Middle Wallop
	ZA802	WS Gazelle HT3 [W]	RAF No 2 FTS, Shawbury
	ZA803	WS Gazelle HT3 [X]	RAF No 2 FTS, Shawbury
	ZA804	WS Gazelle HT3 [I]	RAF No 2 FTS, Shawbury
	ZA934	WS Puma HC1 [BX]	RAF No 18 Sqn, Laarbruch
	ZA935	WS Puma HC1 [NR]	RAF No 27(R) Sqn, Odiham
	ZA936	WS Puma HC1	RAF No 230 Sqn, Aldergrove
	ZA937	WS Puma HC1	RAF No 230 Sqn, Aldergrove
	ZA938	WS Puma HC1	RAF No 33 Sqn, Odiham
	ZA939	WS Puma HC1 [DN]	RAF No 230 Sqn, Aldergrove
	ZA940	WS Puma HC1	RAF No 230 Sqn, Algergrove
	ZA947	Douglas Dakota C3 [YS-DM]	RAF BBMF, Coningsby
	ZB500	WS Lynx 800 (G-LYNX)	IHM, Weston-super-Mare
	ZB506	WS61 Sea King Mk 4X	MoD(PE)/DRA, DTEO Boscombe Down
	ZB507	WS61 Sea King Mk 4X	MoD(PE)/DRA, DTEO Boscombe Down
	ZB600	BAe Harrier T4 [Z]	BAe Dunsfold for Indian Navy
	ZB601	BAe Harrier T4 (fuselage)	BAe Dunsfold, spares use
	ZB602	BAe Harrier T4 [X]	BAe Dunsfold for Indian Navy
	ZB603	BAe Harrier T4 [718/VL]	RN No 899 Sqn, Yeovilton

Serial	Type (other identity) [code]	Owner/operator, location or fate	Notes
ZB604	BAe Harrier T4N [722]	RN No 899 Sqn, Yeovilton	
ZB605	BAe Harrier T8	RN No 899 Sqn, Yeovilton	
ZB615	SEPECAT Jaguar T2A	MoD(PE)/FWTS, DTEO Boscombe Down	
ZB625	WS Gazelle HT3 [N]	RAF No 2 FTS, Shawbury	
ZB626	WS Gazelle HT3 [L]	RAF No 2 FTS, Shawbury	
ZB627	WS Gazelle HT3 [A]	RAF No 7 Sqn, Odiham	
ZB629	WS Gazelle HCC4	RAF No 32(The Royal) Sqn, Northolt	
ZB646	WS Gazelle HT2 [59/CU]	RN, damaged Jul 95, stored Shawbury	
ZB647	WS Gazelle HT2 [40/CU]	RN No 705 Sqn, Culdrose	
ZB648	WS Gazelle HT2 [40/CU] (wreck)	RN Predannack Fire School	
ZB649	WS Gazelle HT2 [43/CU]	RN No 705 Sqn, Culdrose	
ZB665	WS Gazelle AH1	AAC, stored RNAY Fleetlands	
ZB666	WS Gazelle AH1 [G]	AAC No 670 Sqn, Middle Wallop	
ZB667	WS Gazelle AH1	AAC, UNFICYP, Nicosia	
ZB668	WS Gazelle AH1 [UN]	AAC, stored Fleetlands	
ZB669	WS Gazelle AH1 [O]	AAC No 669 Sqn, Wattisham	
ZB670	WS Gazelle AH1	AAC No 665 Sqn, Aldergrove	
ZB671	WS Gazelle AH1	AAC No 29 Flt, BATUS, Suffield, Canada	
ZB672	WS Gazelle AH1 [V]	AAC No 662 Sqn, Wattisham	
ZB673	WS Gazelle AH1 [P]	AAC No 670 Sqn, Middle Wallop	
ZB674	WS Gazelle AH1	AAC No 665 Sqn, Aldergrove	
ZB676	WS Gazelle AH1 [E1]	AAC, stored Fleetlands	
ZB677	WS Gazelle AH1	AAC No 29 Flt, BATUS, Suffield, Canada	
ZB678	WS Gazelle AH1	AAC No 16 Flt, Dhekelia, Cyprus	
ZB679	WS Gazelle AH1	AAC No 16 Flt, Dhekelia, Cyprus	
ZB682	WS Gazelle AH1	AAC No 665 Sqn, Aldergrove	
ZB683	WS Gazelle AH1	AAC, RNAY Fleetlands	
ZB684	WS Gazelle AH1	AAC No 665 Sqn, Aldergrove	
ZB685	WS Gazelle AH1	AAC No 665 Sqn, Aldergrove	
ZB686	WS Gazelle AH1	AAC No 665 Sqn, Aldergrove	
ZB688	WS Gazelle AH1 [H]	AAC No 670 Sqn, Middle Wallop	
ZB689	WS Gazelle AH1 [W]	AAC No 670 Sqn, Middle Wallop	
ZB690	WS Gazelle AH1	AAC No 16 Flt, Dhekelia, Cyprus	
ZB691	WS Gazelle AH1 [C]	AAC No 664 Sqn, Dishforth	
ZB692	WS Gazelle AH1	AAC No 664 Sqn, Dishforth	
ZB693	WS Gazelle AH1	AAC SEAE, Arborfield	
ZD230	BAC Super VC10 K4 (G-ASGA) [K]	RAF No 101 Sqn, Brize Norton	
ZD232	BAC Super VC10 (G-ASGD/ 8699M)	RAF Brize Norton Fire Section	
ZD234	BAC Super VC10 (G-ASGF/ 8700M)	RAF Brize Norton, tanker simulator	
ZD235	BAC Super VC10 K4 (G-ASGG)	MoD(PE)/BAe Filton	
ZD239	BAC Super VC10 (G-ASGK)	FSCTE, RAF Manston	
ZD240	BAC Super VC10 K4 (G-ASGL) [M]	RAF No 101 Sqn, Brize Norton	
ZD241	BAC Super VC10 K4 (G-ASGM) [N]	RAF No 101 Sqn, Brize Norton	
ZD242	BAC Super VC10 K4 (G-ASGP) [P]	RAF No 101 Sqn, Brize Norton	
ZD243	BAC Super VC10 (G-ASGR)	BAe, Filton (spares use)	
ZD249	WS Lynx HAS3S [642]	RNAY Fleetlands	
ZD250	WS Lynx HAS3S [417/NM]	RN No 815 Sqn, Portland	
ZD251	WS Lynx HAS3S [415/MM]	RN No 815 Sqn, Portland	
ZD252	WS Lynx HAS3S	RNAY Fleetlands	
ZD253	WS Lynx HAS3S [405/LO]	RN No 815 Sqn, Portland	
ZD254	WS Lynx HAS3S [645]	RN No 702 Sqn, Portland	
ZD255	WS Lynx HAS3S	RNAY Fleetlands	
ZD256	WS Lynx HAS3S [328/BA]	RN No 815 Sqn, Portland	
ZD257	WS Lynx HAS3S [334/SN]	RN No 815 Sqn, Portland	
ZD258	WS Lynx HAS3S (XZ258) [633]	RN No 702 Sqn, Portland	
ZD259	WS Lynx HAS3S [336]	RN No 815 Sqn, Portland	
ZD260	WS Lynx HAS3S [335/CF]	RN No 815 Sqn, Portland	
ZD261	WS Lynx HMA8 [672]	RN No 815 Sqn OEU, Portland	
ZD262	WS Lynx HAS3S [641]	RN No 702 Sqn, Portland	
ZD263	WS Lynx HAS3S [636]	RN No 702 Sqn, Portland	
ZD264	WS Lynx HAS3S [420/EX]	RN No 815 Sqn, Portland	
ZD265	WS Lynx HMA8	RNAY Fleetlands (conversion)	
ZD266	WS Lynx HMA8	MoD(PE)/RWTS, DTEO Boscombe Down	
ZD267	WS Lynx HMA8	MoD(PE)/RWTS, DTEO Boscombe Down	
ZD268	WS Lynx HAS3S [344/GW]	RN No 815 Sqn, Portland	
ZD272	WS Lynx AH7 [H]	AAC No 671 Sqn, Middle Wallop	

Notes	Serial	Type (other identity) [code]	Owner/operator, location or fate
	ZD273	WS Lynx AH7	AAC stored, RNAY Fleetlands
	ZD274	WS Lynx AH7 [V]	AAC No 657 Sqn, Dishforth
	ZD276	WS Lynx AH7 [6]	AAC No 656 Sqn, Dishforth
	ZD277	WS Lynx AH7	AAC No 669 Sqn, Wattisham
	ZD278	WS Lynx AH7 [A]	AAC No 671 Sqn, Middle Wallop
	ZD279	WS Lynx AH7 [C]	AAC No 671 Sqn, Middle Wallop
	ZD280	WS Lynx AH7	MoD(PE)/Westland, Yeovil
	ZD281	WS Lynx AH7 [K]	AAC No 671 Sqn, Middle Wallop
	ZD282	WS Lynx AH7 [L]	RM No 847 Sqn, Yeovilton
	ZD283	WS Lynx AH1 [P]	AAC No 671 Sqn, Middle Wallop
	ZD284	WS Lynx AH7 [H]	AAC 1 Regiment, Gütersloh
	ZD285	WS Lynx AH7	MoD(PE)/DRA, DTEO Boscombe Down
	ZD318	BAe Harrier GR7	MoD(PE)/BAe Dunsfold
	ZD319	BAe Harrier GR7	MoD(PE)/BAe Dunsfold
	ZD320	BAe Harrier GR7	MoD(PE)/FWTS, DTEO Boscombe Down
	ZD321	BAe Harrier GR7	MoD(PE)/BAe Dunsfold
	ZD322	BAe Harrier GR7	MoD(PE)/BAe Dunsfold (conversion)
	ZD323	BAe Harrier GR7 [05]	RAF No 1 Sqn, Wittering
	ZD324	BAe Harrier GR7	MoD(PE)/BAe Dunsfold
	ZD326	BAe Harrier GR7 [07]	RAF Laarbruch
	ZD327	BAe Harrier GR7 [08]	RAF No 3 Sqn, Laarbruch
	ZD328	BAe Harrier GR7	MoD(PE)/BAe Dunsfold
	ZD329	BAe Harrier GR7 [H]	RAF HOCU/No 20(R) Sqn, Wittering
	ZD330	BAe Harrier GR7 [11}	RAF No 3 Sqn, Laarbruch
	ZD345	BAe Harrier GR7 [J]	RAF HOCU/No 20(R) Sqn, Wittering
	ZD346	BAe Harrier GR7 [5E]	MoD(PE)/FWTS, DTEO Boscombe Down
	ZD347	BAe Harrier GR7 [11]	RAF No 1 Sqn, Wittering
	ZD348	BAe Harrier GR7 [C]	RAF HOCU/No 20(R) Sqn, Wittering
	ZD350	BAe Harrier GR5 (9189M) [A]	RAF St Athan, BDRT
	ZD351	BAe Harrier GR7	MoD(PE)/BAe Dunsfold
	ZD352	BAe Harrier GR7 [01]	MoD(PE)/BAe Dunsfold
	ZD353	BAe Harrier GR5 (fuselage)	BAe Brough
	ZD354	BAe Harrier GR7 [02]	RAF No 1 Sqn, Wittering
	ZD375	BAe Harrier GR7 [5D]	MoD(PE)/BAe Dunsfold
	ZD376	BAe Harrier GR7 [24]	RAF No 4 Sqn, Laarbruch
	ZD377	BAe Harrier GR7	RAF, stored Shawbury
	ZD378	BAe Harrier GR7 [A]	RAF HOCU/No 20(R) Sqn, Wittering
	ZD379	BAe Harrier GR7 [H]	MoD(PE)/BAe Dunsfold
	ZD380	BAe Harrier GR7 [28]	RAF No 4 Sqn, Laarbruch
	ZD400	BAe Harrier GR7 [02]	MoD(PE)/BAe Dunsfold
	ZD401	BAe Harrier GR7 [D]	RAF HOCU/No 20(R) Sqn, Wittering
	ZD402	BAe Harrier GR7 [E]	RAF HOCU/No 20(R) Sqn, Wittering
	ZD403	BAe Harrier GR7 [G]	RAF HOCU/No 20(R) Sqn, Wittering
	ZD404	BAe Harrier GR7 [H]	RAF HOCU/No 20(R) Sqn, Wittering
	ZD405	BAe Harrier GR7 [34]	RAF No 4 Sqn, Laarbruch
	ZD406	BAe Harrier GR7 [35]	RAF No 4 Sqn, Laarbruch
	ZD407	BAe Harrier GR7 [WM]	RAF No 1 Sqn, Wittering
	ZD408	BAe Harrier GR7 [37]	RAF No 4 Sqn, Laarbruch
	ZD409	BAe Harrier GR7 [B]	RAF HOCU/No 20(R) Sqn, Wittering
	ZD410	BAe Harrier GR7 [39]	RAF No 4 Sqn, Laarbruch
	ZD411	BAe Harrier GR7	MoD(PE)/BAe Dunsfold
	ZD412	BAe Harrier GR5 (wreck)	MoD(PE)/BAe Dunsfold
	ZD431	BAe Harrier GR7 [02]	RAF No 1 Sqn, Wittering
	ZD433	BAe Harrier GR7 [D]	RAF HOCU/No 20(R) Sqn, Wittering
	ZD434	BAe Harrier GR7 [46]	RAF No 4 Sqn, Laarbruch
	ZD435	BAe Harrier GR7 [47]	RAF No 4 Sqn, Laarbruch
	ZD436	BAe Harrier GR7 [F]	RAF HOCU/No 20(R) Sqn, Wittering
	ZD437	BAe Harrier GR7 [04]	RAF No 1 Sqn, Wittering
	ZD438	BAe Harrier GR7 [XX]	RAF HOCU/No 20(R) Sqn, Wittering
	ZD461	BAe Harrier GR7 [WH]	RAF No 1 Sqn, Wittering
	ZD462	BAe Harrier GR7 [07]	RAF No 1 Sqn, Wittering
	ZD463	BAe Harrier GR7 [AL]	RAF No 3 Sqn, Laarbruch
	ZD464	BAe Harrier GR7 [09]	RAF No 1 Sqn, Wittering
	ZD465	BAe Harrier GR7 [06]	RAF No 1 Sqn, Wittering
	ZD466	BAe Harrier GR7 [I]	MoD(PE)/BAe Dunsfold
	ZD467	BAe Harrier GR7	RAF AWC/SAOEU, DTEO Boscombe Down
	ZD468	BAe Harrier GR7 [09]	RAF No 1 Sqn, Wittering
	ZD469	BAe Harrier GR7	RAF HMF, Laarbruch
	ZD470	BAe Harrier GR7 [01]	RAF No 1 Sqn, Wittering
ZD472	BAe Harrier GR5 <R> (BAPC 191) [01]	RAF EP&TU, St Athan
	ZD476	WS61 Sea King HC4 [ZU]	RN No 848 Sqn, Yeovilton

Serial	Type (other identity) [code]	Owner/operator, location or fate	Notes
ZD477	WS61 Sea King HC4 [H]	RN No 845 Sqn, Yeovilton	
ZD478	WS61 Sea King HC4 [VG]	RN No 846 Sqn, Yeovilton	
ZD479	WS61 Sea King HC4 [ZV]	RN No 848 Sqn, Yeovilton	
ZD480	WS61 Sea King HC4 [E]	RN No 845 Sqn, Yeovilton	
ZD559	WS Lynx AH5X	MoD(PE)/DRA, DTEO Boscombe Down	
ZD560	WS Lynx Mk 7	MoD(PE)/ETPS, DTEO Boscombe Down	
ZD565	WS Lynx HAS3S [630]	RN No 702 Sqn, Portland	
ZD566	WS Lynx HAS3S	RNAY Fleetlands	
ZD574	B-V Chinook HC2 [UN]	RAF No 7 Sqn, Odiham	
ZD575	B-V Chinook HC2 [UN]	RAF No 27(R) Sqn, Odiham	
ZD578	BAe Sea Harrier FA2 [000]	RN No 801 Sqn, Yeovilton	
ZD579	BAe Sea Harrier FA2 [002]	RN No 801 Sqn, Yeovilton	
ZD580	BAe Sea Harrier FA2 [710]	RN No 899 Sqn, Yeovilton	
ZD581	BAe Sea Harrier FA2 [124]	MoD(PE)/BAe Dunsfold (conversion)	
ZD582	BAe Sea Harrier FA2 [122]	RN No 800 Sqn, Yeovilton	
ZD607	BAe Sea Harrier FA2	MoD(PE)/BAe Brough (conversion)	
ZD608	BAe Sea Harrier FA2 [717]	RN No 899 Sqn, Yeovilton	
ZD610	BAe Sea Harrier FA2 [129]	MoD(PE)/BAe Brough (conversion)	
ZD611	BAe Sea Harrier FA2 [123]	RN No 800 Sqn, Yeovilton	
ZD612	BAe Sea Harrier FA2 [724/OEU]	RN No 899 Sqn, Yeovilton	
ZD613	BAe Sea Harrier FA2 [005]	RNAS Yeovilton	
ZD614	BAe Sea Harrier FA2 [126]	MoD(PE)/BAe Dunsfold (conversion)	
ZD615	BAe Sea Harrier FA2 [723]	RN No 899 Sqn, Yeovilton	
ZD620	BAe 125 CC3	RAF No 32(The Royal) Sqn, Northolt	
ZD621	BAe 125 CC3	RAF No 32(The Royal) Sqn, Northolt	
ZD625	WS61 Sea King HC4	RNAY Fleetlands	
ZD626	WS61 Sea King HC4 [ZZ]	RN No 848 Sqn, Yeovilton	
ZD627	WS61 Sea King HC4 [VL]	RN No 846 Sqn, Yeovilton	
ZD630	WS61 Sea King HAS6 [271/N]	RN No 814 Sqn, Culdrose	
ZD631	WS61 Sea King HAS6 [66] (fuselage)	RNAS Lee-on-Solent	
ZD633	WS61 Sea King HAS6 [507]	RN No 810 Sqn, Culdrose	
ZD634	WS61 Sea King HAS6 [506/CU]	RN No 810 Sqn, Culdrose	
ZD636	WS61 Sea King AEW7	RN AMG, Culdrose (conversion)	
ZD637	WS61 Sea King HAS6 [700/PW]	RN No 819 Sqn, Prestwick	
ZD657	Schleicher ASW-19B Valiant TX1	RAF No 661 VGS, Kirknewton	
ZD658	Schleicher ASW-19B Valiant TX1	RAF ACCGS, Syerston	
ZD659	Schleicher ASW-19B Valiant TX1	RAF ACCGS, Syerston	
ZD660	Schleicher ASW-19B Valiant TX1	RAF ACCGS, Syerston	
ZD667	BAe Harrier GR3 [3,2]	SFDO, RNAS Culdrose	
ZD668	BAe Harrier GR3 [3E]	Phoenix Aviation, Bruntingthorpe	
ZD670	BAe Harrier GR3 [3A]	Phoenix Aviation, Bruntingthorpe	
ZD703	BAe 125 CC3	RAF No 32(The Royal) Sqn, Northolt	
ZD704	BAe 125 CC3	RAF No 32(The Royal) Sqn, Northolt	
ZD707	Panavia Tornado GR1 [BK]	RAF No 14 Sqn, Brüggen	
ZD708	Panavia Tornado GR4	MoD(PE)/BAe Warton	
ZD709	Panavia Tornado GR1 [DG]	RAF No 31 Sqn, Brüggen	
ZD711	Panavia Tornado GR1 [DY]	RAF No 31 Sqn, Brüggen	
ZD712	Panavia Tornado GR1 [BY]	RAF No 14 Sqn, Brüggen	
ZD713	Panavia Tornado GR1 [TW]	RAF No 15(R) Sqn, Lossiemouth	
ZD714	Panavia Tornado GR1 [AP]	RAF No 9 Sqn, Brüggen	
ZD715	Panavia Tornado GR1 [CC]	RAF No 17 Sqn, Brüggen	
ZD716	Panavia Tornado GR1	RAF AWC/SAOEU, DTEO Boscombe Down	
ZD719	Panavia Tornado GR1	MoD(PE)/DRA, DTEO Boscombe Down	
ZD720	Panavia Tornado GR1 [AG]	RAF No 9 Sqn, Brüggen	
ZD739	Panavia Tornado GR1 [AC]	RAF No 9 Sqn, Brüggen	
ZD740	Panavia Tornado GR1	RAF No 31 Sqn, Brüggen	
ZD741	Panavia Tornado GR1 [DZ]	RAF No 31 Sqn, Brüggen	
ZD742	Panavia Tornado GR1	RAF No 17 Sqn, Brüggen	
ZD743	Panavia Tornado GR1 [CX]	RAF No 17 Sqn, Brüggen	
ZD744	Panavia Tornado GR1	RAF No 14 Sqn, Brüggen	
ZD745	Panavia Tornado GR1 [BM]	RAF No 14 Sqn, Brüggen	
ZD746	Panavia Tornado GR1 [AB]	RAF No 9 Sqn, Brüggen	
ZD747	Panavia Tornado GR1 [AL]	RAF No 9 Sqn, Brüggen	
ZD748	Panavia Tornado GR1 [AK]	RAF No 9 Sqn, Brüggen	
ZD749	Panavia Tornado GR1	RAF AWC/SAOEU, DTEO Boscombe Down	
ZD788	Panavia Tornado GR1 [CB]	RAF No 17 Sqn, Brüggen	
ZD789	Panavia Tornado GR1 [AM]	RAF No 9 Sqn, Brüggen	
ZD790	Panavia Tornado GR1 [BB]	RAF No 14 Sqn, Brüggen	
ZD792	Panavia Tornado GR1 [CF]	RAF No 17 Sqn, Brüggen	
ZD793	Panavia Tornado GR1 [CA]	RAF No 17 Sqn, Brüggen	

Notes	Serial	Type (other identity) [code]	Owner/operator, location or fate
	ZD809	Panavia Tornado GR1 [BA]	RAF No 14 Sqn, Brüggen
	ZD810	Panavia Tornado GR1 [AA]	RAF No 9 Sqn, Brüggen
	ZD811	Panavia Tornado GR1 [DF]	RAF No 31 Sqn, Brüggen
	ZD812	Panavia Tornado GR1 [BW]	RAF No 14 Sqn, Brüggen
	ZD842	Panavia Tornado GR1 [CY]	RAF St Athan
	ZD843	Panavia Tornado GR1 [CJ]	RAF No 17 Sqn, Brüggen
	ZD844	Panavia Tornado GR1 [DE]	RAF TMF, Marham
	ZD845	Panavia Tornado GR1 [AF]	RAF No 9 Sqn, Brüggen
	ZD846	Panavia Tornado GR1 [BL]	*Written off Germany, 11 January 1996*
	ZD847	Panavia Tornado GR1 [CH]	RAF No 17 Sqn, Brüggen
	ZD848	Panavia Tornado GR1 [CD]	RAF No 17 Sqn, Brüggen
	ZD849	Panavia Tornado GR1 [BT]	RAF No 14 Sqn, Brüggen
	ZD850	Panavia Tornado GR1 [DR]	RAF No 31 Sqn, Brüggen
	ZD851	Panavia Tornado GR1 [AJ]	RAF No 9 Sqn, Brüggen
	ZD890	Panavia Tornado GR1 [AE]	RAF No 9 Sqn, Brüggen
	ZD892	Panavia Tornado GR1	RAF No 14 Sqn, Brüggen
	ZD895	Panavia Tornado GR1	RAF No 14 Sqn, Brüggen
	ZD899	Panavia Tornado F2	MoD(PE)/BAe Warton
	ZD900	Panavia Tornado F2	*Fuselage used in rebuild of ZE343, 1996*
	ZD901	Panavia Tornado F2	*Fuselage used in rebuild of ZE154, 1995*
	ZD902	Panavia Tornado F2TIARA	MoD(PE)/DRA, DTEO Boscombe Down
	ZD903	Panavia Tornado F2	*Fuselage used in rebuild of ZE728, 1996*
	ZD904	Panavia Tornado F2	*Fuselage used in rebuild of ZE759, 1996*
	ZD905	Panavia Tornado F2	*Fuselage used in rebuild of ZE258, 1996*
	ZD906	Panavia Tornado F2	*Fuselage used in rebuild of ZE294, 1995*
	ZD932	Panavia Tornado F2	*Fuselage used in rebuild of ZE255, 1995*
	ZD933	Panavia Tornado F2	*Fuselage used in rebuild of ZE729, 1996*
	ZD934	Panavia Tornado F2	*Fuselage used in rebuild of ZE786, 1996*
	ZD935	Panavia Tornado F2	*Fuselage used in rebuild of ZE793, 1996*
	ZD936	Panavia Tornado F2	*Fuselage used in rebuild of ZE251, 1996*
	ZD937	Panavia Tornado F2	*Fuselage used in rebuild of ZE736, 1996*
	ZD938	Panavia Tornado F2	*Fuselage used in rebuild of ZE295, 1996*
	ZD939	Panavia Tornado F2 [AS]	*Fuselage used in rebuild of ZE292, 1996*
	ZD940	Panavia Tornado F2	*Fuselage used in rebuild of ZE288, 1996*
	ZD941	Panavia Tornado F2 [AU]	*Fuselage used in rebuild of ZE254, 1995*
	ZD948	Lockheed Tristar KC1 (G-BFCA)	RAF No 216 Sqn, Brize Norton
	ZD949	Lockheed Tristar K1 (G-BFCB)	RAF No 216 Sqn, Brize Norton
	ZD950	Lockheed Tristar KC1 (G-BFCC)	RAF No 216 Sqn, Brize Norton
	ZD951	Lockheed Tristar K1 (G-BFCD)	RAF No 216 Sqn, Brize Norton
	ZD952	Lockheed Tristar KC1 (G-BFCE)	RAF No 216 Sqn, Brize Norton
	ZD953	Lockheed Tristar KC1 (G-BFCF)	RAF No 216 Sqn, Brize Norton
	ZD974	Schempp-Hirth Kestrel TX1	RAF ACCGS, Syerston
	ZD975	Schempp-Hirth Kestrel TX1	RAF ACCGS, Syerston
	ZD980	B-V Chinook HC2 [UN]	RAF No 7 Sqn, Odiham
	ZD981	B-V Chinook HC2 [NW]	RAF No 27(R) Sqn, Odiham
	ZD982	B-V Chinook HC2 [UN]	RAF No 7 Sqn, Odiham
	ZD983	B-V Chinook HC2 [UN]	RAF No 7 Sqn, Odiham
	ZD984	B-V Chinook HC2 [UN]	RAF No 7 Sqn, Odiham
	ZD990	BAe Harrier T4A [V]	RAF HOCU/No 20(R) Sqn, Wittering
	ZD991	BAe Harrier T4 [V]	RAF Wittering
	ZD992	BAe Harrier T8	MoD(PE)/BAe Dunsfold (conversion)
	ZD993	BAe Harrier T8	RN, St Athan (conversion)
	ZD996	Panavia Tornado GR1A [I]	RAF No 2 Sqn, Marham
	ZE116	Panavia Tornado GR1A [O]	RAF No 2 Sqn, Marham
	ZE154	Panavia Tornado F3 [GI] (comp ZD901)	RAF No 43 Sqn, Leuchars
	ZE155	Panavia Tornado F3	MoD(PE)/BAe Warton
	ZE156	Panavia Tornado F3 [HE]	RAF No 111 Sqn, Leuchars
	ZE157	Panavia Tornado F3 [AI]	RAF F3 OCU/No 56(R) Sqn, Coningsby
	ZE158	Panavia Tornado F3 [DC]	RAF No 11 Sqn, Leeming
	ZE159	Panavia Tornado F3 [DE]	RAF No 11 Sqn, Leeming
	ZE160	Panavia Tornado F3 [DV]	RAF No 11 Sqn, Leeming
	ZE161	Panavia Tornado F3 [FG]	RAF No 25 Sqn, Leeming
	ZE162	Panavia Tornado F3 [FK]	RAF No 25 Sqn, Leeming
	ZE163	Panavia Tornado F3 [AA]	RAF F3 OCU/No 56(R) Sqn, Coningsby
	ZE164	Panavia Tornado F3 [DA]	RAF No 11 Sqn, Leeming
	ZE165	Panavia Tornado F3 [GL]	RAF No 43 Sqn, Leuchars
	ZE166	Panavia Tornado F3 [AF]	*Written off nr Sleaford, 10 January 1996*
	ZE167	Panavia Tornado F3 [HX]	RAF No 111 Sqn, Leuchars
	ZE168	Panavia Tornado F3 [FN]	RAF No 25 Sqn, Leeming
	ZE199	Panavia Tornado F3 [FL]	RAF No 25 Sqn, Leeming
	ZE200	Panavia Tornado F3 [DB]	RAF No 11 Sqn, Leeming

Serial	Type (other identity) [code]	Owner/operator, location or fate	Notes
ZE201	Panavia Tornado F3 [DO]	RAF No 11 Sqn, Leeming	
ZE202	Panavia Tornado F3 [AG]	*Loaned to Italian AF as MM55056, August 1995*	
ZE203	Panavia Tornado F3 [FI]	RAF No 25 Sqn, Leeming	
ZE204	Panavia Tornado F3 [DD]	RAF No 11 Sqn, Leeming	
ZE205	Panavia Tornado F3 [DT]	RAF No 11 Sqn, Leeming	
ZE206	Panavia Tornado F3 [FH]	RAF No 25 Sqn, Leeming	
ZE207	Panavia Tornado F3 [GC]	RAF No 43 Sqn, Leuchars	
ZE208	Panavia Tornado F3 [AN]	RAF F3 OCU/No 56(R) Sqn, Coningsby	
ZE209	Panavia Tornado F3	RAF No 1435 Flt, Mount Pleasant, FI	
ZE210	Panavia Tornado F3 [FB]	RAF, stored Leuchars	
ZE250	Panavia Tornado F3 [HZ]	RAF No 111 Sqn, Leuchars	
ZE251	Panavia Tornado F3 [DE]	RAF St Athan (rebuild using ZD936)	
ZE252	Panavia Tornado F3 [C]	RAF No 1435 Flt, Mount Pleasant, FI	
ZE253	Panavia Tornado F3 [AC]	RAF F3 OCU/No 56(R) Sqn, Coningsby	
ZE254	Panavia Tornado F3 [CA]	RAF St Athan (rebuild using ZD941)	
ZE255	Panavia Tornado F3	RAF St Athan (rebuild using ZD932)	
ZE256	Panavia Tornado F3 [HY]	RAF No 111 Sqn, Leuchars	
ZE257	Panavia Tornado F3 [HN]	RAF No 111 Sqn, Leuchars	
ZE258	Panavia Tornado F3	RAF St Athan (rebuild using ZD905)	
ZE287	Panavia Tornado F3 [AH]	RAF F3 OCU/No 56(R) Sqn, Coningsby	
ZE288	Panavia Tornado F3 [GG]	RAF St Athan (rebuild using ZD940)	
ZE289	Panavia Tornado F3 [HF]	RAF No 111 Sqn, Leuchars	
ZE290	Panavia Tornado F3 [AD]	RAF F3 OCU/No 56(R) Sqn, Coningsby	
ZE291	Panavia Tornado F3 [GQ]	RAF No 43 Sqn, Leuchars	
ZE292	Panavia Tornado F3	RAF St Athan (rebuild using ZD939)	
ZE293	Panavia Tornado F3 [HT]	RAF No 111 Sqn, Leuchars	
ZE294	Panavia Tornado F3 [HM] (comp ZD906)	RAF No 111 Sqn, Leuchars	
ZE295	Panavia Tornado F3 [AW]	RAF St Athan (rebuild using ZD938)	
ZE296	Panavia Tornado F3 [GR]	RAF No 43 Sqn, Leuchars	
ZE338	Panavia Tornado F3 [HG]	RAF No 111 Sqn, Leuchars	
ZE339	Panavia Tornado F3 [AQ]	RAF F3 OCU/No 56(R) Sqn, Coningsby	
ZE340	Panavia Tornado F3 [36-12]	RAF F3 OCU/No 56(R) Sqn, Coningsby	
ZE341	Panavia Tornado F3 [D]	RAF No 1435 Flt, Mount Pleasant, FI	
ZE342	Panavia Tornado F3 [HW]	RAF No 111 Sqn, Leuchars	
ZE343	Panavia Tornado F3 [AI]	RAF St Athan (rebuild using ZD900)	
ZE351	McD Phantom F-4J(UK) (9058M) [I]	*Scrapped November 1995*	
ZE353	McD Phantom F-4J(UK) (9083M) [E]	FSCTE, RAF Manston	
ZE354	McD Phantom F-4J(UK) (9084M) [R]	RAF Coningsby Fire Section	
ZE356	McD Phantom F-4J(UK) (9060M) [Q]	RAF Waddington Fire Section	
ZE359	McD Phantom F-4J(UK) [J]	*Repainted as 155529, 1995*	
ZE360	McD Phantom F-4J(UK) (9059M) [O]	FSCTE, RAF Manston	
ZE361	McD Phantom F-4J(UK) (9057M) [P]	RAF Honington Fire Section	
ZE364	McD Phantom F-4J(UK) (9085M) [Z]	RAF Coltishall Fire Section	
ZE368	WS61 Sea King HAR3	RAF No 202 Sqn, E Flt, Leconfield	
ZE369	WS61 Sea King HAR3	RAF SKTU/No 205(R) Sqn, St Mawgan	
ZE370	WS61 Sea King HAR3	RAF No 202 Sqn, E Flt, Leconfield	
ZE375	WS Lynx AH9 [2]	AAC No 659 Sqn, Wattisham	
ZE376	WS Lynx AH9 [4]	AAC No 659 Sqn, Wattisham	
ZE378	WS Lynx AH7	AAC stored, RNAY Fleetlands	
ZE379	WS Lynx AH7	AAC No 655 Sqn, Aldergrove	
ZE380	WS Lynx AH9 [1]	AAC No 659 Sqn, Wattisham	
ZE381	WS Lynx AH7	AAC, RNAY Fleetlands	
ZE382	WS Lynx AH9 [3]	AAC No 659 Sqn, Wattisham	
ZE395	BAe 125 CC3	RAF No 32(The Royal) Sqn, Northolt	
ZE396	BAe 125 CC3	RAF No 32(The Royal) Sqn, Northolt	
ZE410	Agusta A109A (AE-334)	AAC No 8 Flight, Netheravon	
ZE411	Agusta A109A (AE-331)	AAC No 8 Flight, Netheravon	
ZE412	Agusta A109A	AAC No 8 Flight, Netheravon	
ZE413	Agusta A109A	AAC No 8 Flight, Netheravon	
ZE418	WS61 Sea King AEW7	RN AMG, Culdrose (conversion)	
ZE420	WS61 Sea King AEW7	RN AMG, Culdrose (conversion)	
ZE422	WS61 Sea King HAS6 [588]	RN No 706 Sqn, Culdrose	
ZE425	WS61 Sea King HC4 [J]	RN No 845 Sqn, Yeovilton	
ZE426	WS61 Sea King HC4 [ZW]	RN No 848 Sqn, Yeovilton	

Notes	Serial	Type (other identity) [code]	Owner/operator, location or fate
	ZE427	WS61 Sea King HC4 [B]	RN AMG, Yeovilton
	ZE428	WS61 Sea King HC4 [VK]	RN No 846 Sqn, Yeovilton
	ZE432	BAC 1-11/479FU (DQ-FBV)	MoD(PE)/ETPS, DTEO Boscombe Down
	ZE433	BAC 1-11/479FU (DQ-FBQ)	MoD(PE)/GEC-Ferranti, Edinburgh
	ZE438	BAe Jetstream T3 [576]	RN, stored Shawbury
	ZE439	BAe Jetstream T3 [577]	RN FONA/Heron Flight, Yeovilton
	ZE440	BAe Jetstream T3 [578]	RN FONA/Heron Flight, Yeovilton
	ZE441	BAe Jetstream T3 [579]	RN FONA/Heron Flight, Yeovilton
	ZE449	SA330L Puma HC1 (9017M/PA-12)	MoD(PE)/Westland, Yeovil (under rebuild)
	ZE477	WS Lynx 3	IHM, Weston-super-Mare
	ZE495	Grob G103 Viking T1 (BGA3000)	RAF No 622 VGS, Upavon
	ZE496	Grob G103 Viking T1 (BGA3001)	RAF No 618 VGS, Challock
	ZE497	Grob G103 Viking T1 (BGA3002)	RAFGSA, Syerston
	ZE498	Grob G103 Viking T1 (BGA3003)	RAF No 614 VGS, Wethersfield
	ZE499	Grob G103 Viking T1 (BGA3004)	RAF ACCGS, Syerston
	ZE501	Grob G103 Viking T1 (BGA3006)	RAF ACCGS, Syerston
	ZE502	Grob G103 Viking T1 (BGA3007)	RAF No 645 VGS, Catterick
	ZE503	Grob G103 Viking T1 (BGA3008)	RAF No 645 VGS, Catterick
	ZE504	Grob G103 Viking T1 (BGA3009)	RAF No 645 VGS, Catterick
	ZE520	Grob G103 Viking T1 (BGA3010)	RAF CGMF, Syerston
	ZE521	Grob G103 Viking T1 (BGA3011)	RAF No 626 VGS, Predannack
	ZE522	Grob G103 Viking T1 (BGA3012)	RAF ACCGS, Syerston
	ZE524	Grob G103 Viking T1 (BGA3014)	RAF No 626 VGS, Predannack
	ZE525	Grob G103 Viking T1 (BGA3015)	*To RAFGSA as R70, 1994*
	ZE526	Grob G103 Viking T1 (BGA3016)	RAF No 634 VGS, St Athan
	ZE527	Grob G103 Viking T1 (BGA3017)	RAF No 615 VGS, Kenley
	ZE528	Grob G103 Viking T1 (BGA3018)	RAF No 645 VGS, Catterick
	ZE529	Grob G103 Viking T1 (BGA3019)	RAF No 636 VGS, Swansea
	ZE530	Grob G103 Viking T1 (BGA3020)	RAF No 611 VGS, Wethersfield
	ZE531	Grob G103 Viking T1 (BGA3021)	RAF No 662 VGS, Arbroath
	ZE532	Grob G103 Viking T1 (BGA3022)	RAF No 614 VGS, Wethersfield
	ZE533	Grob G103 Viking T1 (BGA3023)	RAF No 622 VGS, Upavon
	ZE534	Grob G103 Viking T1 (BGA3024)	RAF No 614 VGS, Wethersfield
	ZE550	Grob G103 Viking T1 (BGA3025)	RAF No 622 VGS, Upavon
	ZE551	Grob G103 Viking T1 (BGA3026)	RAF No 614 VGS, Wethersfield
	ZE552	Grob G103 Viking T1 (BGA3027)	RAF ACCGS, Syerston
	ZE553	Grob G103 Viking T1 (BGA3028)	RAF No 611 VGS, Wethersfield
	ZE554	Grob G103 Viking T1 (BGA3029)	RAF No 617 VGS, Manston
	ZE555	Grob G103 Viking T1 (BGA3030)	RAF No 645 VGS, Catterick
	ZE556	Grob G103 Viking T1 (BGA3031)	RAF No 631 VGS, Sealand
	ZE557	Grob G103 Viking T1 (BGA3032)	RAF No 622 VGS, Upavon
	ZE558	Grob G103 Viking T1 (BGA3033)	RAF No 615 VGS, Kenley
	ZE559	Grob G103 Viking T1 (BGA3034)	RAF No 631 VGS, Sealand
	ZE560	Grob G103 Viking T1 (BGA3035)	RAF No 631 VGS, Sealand
	ZE561	Grob G103 Viking T1 (BGA3036)	RAF No 621 VGS, Hullavington
	ZE562	Grob G103 Viking T1 (BGA3037)	RAF No 631 VGS, Sealand
	ZE563	Grob G103 Viking T1 (BGA3038)	RAF ACCGS, Syerston
	ZE564	Grob G103 Viking T1 (BGA3039)	RAF CGMF, Syerston
	ZE584	Grob G103 Viking T1 (BGA3040)	RAF No 661 VGS, Kirknewton
	ZE585	Grob G103 Viking T1 (BGA3041)	RAF No 614 VGS, Wethersfield
	ZE586	Grob G103 Viking T1 (BGA3042)	RAF No 617 VGS, Manston
	ZE587	Grob G103 Viking T1 (BGA3043)	RAF No 611 VGS, Wethersfield
	ZE589	Grob G103 Viking T1 (BGA3045)	RAF
	ZE590	Grob G103 Viking T1 (BGA3046)	RAF No 645 VGS, Catterick
	ZE591	Grob G103 Viking T1 (BGA3047)	RAF No 662 VGS, Arbroath
	ZE592	Grob G103 Viking T1 (BGA3048)	RAF No 661 VGS, Kirknewton
	ZE593	Grob G103 Viking T1 (BGA3049)	RAF No 631 VGS, Sealand
	ZE594	Grob G103 Viking T1 (BGA3050)	RAF ACCGS, Syerston
	ZE595	Grob G103 Viking T1 (BGA3051)	RAF No 622 VGS, Upavon
	ZE600	Grob G103 Viking T1 (BGA3052)	RAF No 622 VGS, Upavon
	ZE601	Grob G103 Viking T1 (BGA3053)	RAF No 615 VGS, Kenley
	ZE602	Grob G103 Viking T1 (BGA3054)	RAF No 634 VGS, St Athan
	ZE603	Grob G103 Viking T1 (BGA3055)	RAF ACCGS, Syerston
	ZE604	Grob G103 Viking T1 (BGA3056)	RAF No 617 VGS, Manston
	ZE605	Grob G103 Viking T1 (BGA3057)	RAF ACCGS, Syerston
	ZE606	Grob G103 Viking T1 (BGA3058)	RAF No 617 VGS, Manston
	ZE607	Grob G103 Viking T1 (BGA3059)	RAF No 625 VGS, Hullavington
	ZE608	Grob G103 Viking T1 (BGA3060)	RAF No 621 VGS, Hullavington
	ZE609	Grob G103 Viking T1 (BGA3061)	RAF No 636 VGS, Swansea
	ZE610	Grob G103 Viking T1 (BGA3062)	RAF No 625 VGS, Hullavington
	ZE611	Grob G103 Viking T1 (BGA3063)	RAF ACCGS, Syerston
	ZE612	Grob G103 Viking T1 (BGA3064)	*To RAFGSA as R71, 1994*
	ZE613	Grob G103 Viking T1 (BGA3065)	RAF ACCGS, Syerston

Serial	Type (other identity) [code]	Owner/operator, location or fate	Notes
ZE614	Grob G103 Viking T1 (BGA3066)	RAF No 661 VGS, Kirknewton	
ZE625	Grob G103 Viking T1 (BGA3067)	RAF No 625 VGS, Hullavington	
ZE626	Grob G103 Viking T1 (BGA3068)	RAF ACCGS, Syerston	
ZE627	Grob G103 Viking T1 (BGA3069)	RAF ACCGS, Syerston	
ZE628	Grob G103 Viking T1 (BGA3070)	RAF No 615 VGS, Kenley	
ZE629	Grob G103 Viking T1 (BGA3071)	RAF No 662 VGS, Arbroath	
ZE630	Grob G103 Viking T1 (BGA3072)	RAF No 662 VGS, Arbroath	
ZE631	Grob G103 Viking T1 (BGA3073)	RAF CGMF, Syerston	
ZE632	Grob G103 Viking T1 (BGA3074)	RAF CGMF, Syerston	
ZE633	Grob G103 Viking T1 (BGA3075)	RAF No 614 VGS, Wethersfield	
ZE634	Grob G103 Viking T1 (BGA3076)	*To Oxford Gliding Club as BGA3076, 1994*	
ZE635	Grob G103 Viking T1 (BGA3077)	RAF ACCGS, Syerston	
ZE636	Grob G103 Viking T1 (BGA3078)	RAF No 636 VGS, Swansea	
ZE637	Grob G103 Viking T1 (BGA3079)	RAF No 622 VGS, Upavon	
ZE650	Grob G103 Viking T1 (BGA3080)	RAF No 617 VGS, Manston	
ZE651	Grob G103 Viking T1 (BGA3081)	RAF No 615 VGS, Kenley	
ZE652	Grob G103 Viking T1 (BGA3082)	RAF ACCGS, Syerston	
ZE653	Grob G103 Viking T1 (BGA3083)	RAF No 631 VGS, Sealand	
ZE654	Grob G103 Viking T1 (BGA3084)	*Written off near RAF Sealand, 5 August 1995*	
ZE655	Grob G103 Viking T1 (BGA3085) (wreck)	RAF CGMF, Syerston	
ZE656	Grob G103 Viking T1 (BGA3086)	RAF No 617 VGS, Manston	
ZE657	Grob G103 Viking T1 (BGA3087)	RAF No 626 VGS, Predannack	
ZE658	Grob G103 Viking T1 (BGA3088)	RAF No 621 VGS, Hullavington	
ZE659	Grob G103 Viking T1 (BGA3089)	RAF No 611 VGS, Wethersfield	
ZE677	Grob G103 Viking T1 (BGA3090)	RAF No 631 VGS Sealand	
ZE678	Grob G103 Viking T1 (BGA3091)	RAF ACCGS, Syerston	
ZE679	Grob G103 Viking T1 (BGA3092)	RAF No 662 VGS, Arbroath	
ZE680	Grob G103 Viking T1 (BGA3093)	RAF No 661 VGS, Kirknewton	
ZE681	Grob G103 Viking T1 (BGA3094)	RAF No 615 VGS, Kenley	
ZE682	Grob G103 Viking T1 (BGA3095)	RAF No 611 VGS, Wethersfield	
ZE683	Grob G103 Viking T1 (BGA3096)	RAF No 645 VGS, Catterick	
ZE684	Grob G103 Viking T1 (BGA3097)	RAF ACCGS, Syerston	
ZE685	Grob G103 Viking T1 (BGA3098)	RAF No 661 VGS, Kirknewton	
ZE686	Grob G103 Viking T1 (BGA3099)	MoD(PE)/Slingsby Kirkbymoorside	
ZE690	BAe Sea Harrier FA2 [003]	RN No 801 Sqn, Yeovilton	
ZE691	BAe Sea Harrier FA2 [712/OEU]	RN No 899 Sqn, Yeovilton	
ZE692	BAe Sea Harrier FA2 [711]	RN No 899 Sqn, Yeovilton	
ZE693	BAe Sea Harrier FA2	MoD(PE)/BAe Dunsfold (conversion)	
ZE694	BAe Sea Harrier FA2	MoD(PE)/BAe Brough (conversion)	
ZE695	BAe Sea Harrier FA2 [124]	RN No 800 Sqn, Yeovilton	
ZE696	BAe Sea Harrier FA2 [125]	RN No 800 Sqn, Yeovilton	
ZE697	BAe Sea Harrier FA2 [004]	RN No 801 Sqn, Yeovilton	
ZE698	BAe Sea Harrier FA2	MoD(PE)/BAe Dunsfold (conversion)	
ZE700	BAe 146 CC2	RAF No 32(The Royal) Sqn, Northolt	
ZE701	BAe 146 CC2	RAF No 32(The Royal) Sqn, Northolt	
ZE702	BAe 146 CC2	RAF No 32(The Royal) Sqn, Northolt	
ZE704	Lockheed Tristar C2 (N508PA)	RAF No 216 Sqn, Brize Norton	
ZE705	Lockheed Tristar C2 (N509PA)	RAF No 216 Sqn, Brize Norton	
ZE706	Lockheed Tristar C2A (N503PA)	RAF No 216 Sqn, Brize Norton	
ZE728	Panavia Tornado F3 [AL]	RAF St Athan (rebuild using ZD903)	
ZE729	Panavia Tornado F3	RAF St Athan (rebuild using ZD933)	
ZE730	Panavia Tornado F3	*Loaned to Italian AF as MM7204, October 1995*	
ZE731	Panavia Tornado F3 [GK]	RAF No 43 Sqn, Leuchars	
ZE732	Panavia Tornado F3 [AS]	RAF F3 OCU/No 56(R) Sqn, Coningsby	
ZE733	Panavia Tornado F3 [GE]	*Written off North Sea, 30 October 1995*	
ZE734	Panavia Tornado F3 [GB]	RAF No 43 Sqn, Leuchars	
ZE735	Panavia Tornado F3 [AL]	RAF F3 OCU/No 56(R) Sqn, Coningsby	
ZE736	Panavia Tornado F3 [HA]	RAF St Athan (rebuild using ZD937)	
ZE737	Panavia Tornado F3 [FF]	RAF No 25 Sqn, Leeming	
ZE755	Panavia Tornado F3 [GJ]	RAF No 43 Sqn, Leuchars	
ZE756	Panavia Tornado F3	RAF F3 OEU, Coningsby	
ZE757	Panavia Tornado F3 [GF]	RAF No 43 Sqn, Leuchars	
ZE758	Panavia Tornado F3	RAF F3 OCU/No 56(R) Sqn, Coningsby	
ZE759	Panavia Tornado F3	RAF St Athan (rebuild using ZD904)	
ZE760	Panavia Tornado F3	*Loaned to Italian AF as MM7206, November 1995*	
ZE761	Panavia Tornado F3	*Loaned to Italian AF as MM7203 August 1995*	
ZE762	Panavia Tornado F3	*Loaned to Italian AF as MM7207, July 1995*	

Notes	Serial	Type (other identity) [code]	Owner/operator, location or fate
	ZE763	Panavia Tornado F3 [DG]	RAF No 11 Sqn, Leeming
	ZE764	Panavia Tornado F3 [DH]	RAF No 11 Sqn, Leeming
	ZE785	Panavia Tornado F3 [AT]	RAF F3 OCU/No 56(R) Sqn, Coningsby
	ZE786	Panavia Tornado F3	RAF St Athan (rebuild using ZD934)
	ZE787	Panavia Tornado F3	*Loaned to Italian AF as MM7205, October 1995*
	ZE788	Panavia Tornado F3 [DF]	RAF No 11 Sqn, Leeming
	ZE789	Panavia Tornado F3	*Written off, North Sea, 10 March 1995*
	ZE790	Panavia Tornado F3 [AO]	RAF F3 OCU/No 56(R) Sqn, Coningsby
	ZE791	Panavia Tornado F3 [FP]	RAF No 25 Sqn, Leeming
	ZE792	Panavia Tornado F3	*Loaned to Italian AF as MM7211, October 1995*
	ZE793	Panavia Tornado F3 (comp ZD935)	RAF, stored St Athan (for rebuild at BAe Warton)
	ZE794	Panavia Tornado F3 [HQ]	RAF No 111 Sqn, Leuchars
	ZE808	Panavia Tornado F3	RAF No 25 Sqn, Leeming
	ZE810	Panavia Tornado F3 [HP]	RAF No 111 Sqn, Leuchars
	ZE811	Panavia Tornado F3 [A8]	*To be loaned to Italian AF as MM7208, 1995*
	ZE812	Panavia Tornado F3	MoD(PE)/BAe Warton
	ZE830	Panavia Tornado F3 [HU]	RAF No 111 Sqn, Leuchars
	ZE831	Panavia Tornado F3 [GG]	RAF No 43 Sqn, Leuchars
	ZE832	Panavia Tornado F3	*Loaned to Italian AF as MM7202, July 1995*
	ZE834	Panavia Tornado F3	RAF No 25 Sqn, Leeming
	ZE835	Panavia Tornado F3	*Loaned to Italian AF as MM7209, October 1995*
	ZE836	Panavia Tornado F3	*Loaned to Italian AF as MM7210, 1995*
	ZE837	Panavia Tornado F3 [GI]	*Loaned to Italian AF as MM55057, October 1995*
	ZE838	Panavia Tornado F3 [GH]	RAF No 43 Sqn, Leuchars
	ZE839	Panavia Tornado F3 [AR]	RAF F3 OCU/No 56(R) Sqn, Coningsby
	ZE862	Panavia Tornado F3 [AB]	*Written off nr Sleaford, 10 January 1996*
	ZE887	Panavia Tornado F3 [DJ]	RAF No 11 Sqn, Leeming
	ZE888	Panavia Tornado F3 [FV]	RAF No 25 Sqn, Leeming
	ZE889	Panavia Tornado F3 [SB]	RAF F3 OEU, Coningsby
	ZE907	Panavia Tornado F3 [FM]	RAF No 25 Sqn, Leeming
	ZE908	Panavia Tornado F3 [FC]	RAF No 25 Sqn, Leeming
	ZE911	Panavia Tornado F3	RAF No 29 Sqn, Coningsby
	ZE934	Panavia Tornado F3 [DX]	RAF No 11 Sqn, Leeming
	ZE936	Panavia Tornado F3 [DL]	RAF No 11 Sqn, Leeming
	ZE941	Panavia Tornado F3 [FE]	RAF No 25 Sqn, Leeming
	ZE942	Panavia Tornado F3 [DK]	RAF No 11 Sqn, Leeming
	ZE961	Panavia Tornado F3 [FD]	RAF No 25 Sqn, Leeming
	ZE962	Panavia Tornado F3 [FJ]	RAF No 25 Sqn, Leeming
	ZE963	Panavia Tornado F3 [FT]	RAF No 25 Sqn, Leeming
	ZE964	Panavia Tornado F3 [DY]	RAF No 11 Sqn, Leeming
	ZE965	Panavia Tornado F3 [DW]	RAF No 11 Sqn, Leeming
	ZE966	Panavia Tornado F3 [DZ]	RAF No 11 Sqn, Leeming
	ZE967	Panavia Tornado F3 [FU]	RAF No 25 Sqn, Leeming
	ZE968	Panavia Tornado F3	RAF F3 OEU, Coningsby
	ZE969	Panavia Tornado F3 [DI]	RAF No 11 Sqn, Leeming
	ZE982	Panavia Tornado F3 [DM]	RAF No 11 Sqn, Leeming
	ZE983	Panavia Tornado F3 [DN]	RAF No 11 Sqn, Leeming
	ZF115	WS61 Sea King HC4	MoD(PE)/RWTS, DTEO Boscombe Down
	ZF116	WS61 Sea King HC4 [K]	RN No 846 Sqn, Yeovilton
	ZF117	WS61 Sea King HC4 [23]	RN AMG, Yeovilton
	ZF118	WS61 Sea King HC4 [VP]	RN No 846 Sqn, Yeovilton
	ZF119	WS61 Sea King HC4 [VH]	RN No 846 Sqn, Yeovilton
	ZF120	WS61 Sea King HC4 [20]	RN AMG, Yeovilton
	ZF121	WS61 Sea King HC4 [VJ]	RN No 846 Sqn, Yeovilton
	ZF122	WS61 Sea King HC4 [VI]	RN No 846 Sqn, Yeovilton
	ZF123	WS61 Sea King HC4 [23]	RN AMG, Yeovilton
	ZF124	WS61 Sea King HC4 [L]	RN No 845 Sqn, Yeovilton
	ZF130	BAe 125-600B (G-BLUW)	MoD(PE)/BAe Dunsfold
	ZF135	Shorts Tucano T1	RAF No 1 FTS, Linton-on-Ouse
	ZF136	Shorts Tucano T1	RAF No 1 FTS, Linton-on-Ouse
	ZF137	Shorts Tucano T1	RAF No 1 FTS, Linton-on-Ouse
	ZF138	Shorts Tucano T1	RAF No 1 FTS, Linton-on-Ouse
	ZF139	Shorts Tucano T1	RAF No 1 FTS, Linton-on-Ouse
	ZF140	Shorts Tucano T1	RAF No 1 FTS, Linton-on-Ouse
	ZF141	Shorts Tucano T1	RAF No 1 FTS, Linton-on-Ouse

Serial	Type (other identity) [code]	Owner/operator, location or fate	Notes
ZF142	Shorts Tucano T1	RAF, stored Shawbury	
ZF143	Shorts Tucano T1	RAF No 1 FTS, Linton-on-Ouse	
ZF144	Shorts Tucano T1	RAF, stored Shawbury	
ZF145	Shorts Tucano T1	RAF, stored Shawbury	
ZF160	Shorts Tucano T1	RAF No 1 FTS, Linton-on-Ouse	
ZF161	Shorts Tucano T1	RAF No 1 FTS, Linton-on-Ouse	
ZF162	Shorts Tucano T1	RAF St Athan (on repair)	
ZF163	Shorts Tucano T1	RAF No 1 FTS, Linton-on-Ouse	
ZF164	Shorts Tucano T1	RAF No 1 FTS, Linton-on-Ouse	
ZF165	Shorts Tucano T1	RAF, stored Shawbury	
ZF166	Shorts Tucano T1	RAF No 1 FTS, Linton-on-Ouse	
ZF167	Shorts Tucano T1	RAF, stored Shawbury	
ZF168	Shorts Tucano T1	RAF No 1 FTS, Linton-on-Ouse	
ZF169	Shorts Tucano T1	RAF No 1 FTS, Linton-on-Ouse	
ZF170	Shorts Tucano T1	RAF, stored Shawbury	
ZF171	Shorts Tucano T1	RAF, stored Shawbury	
ZF172	Shorts Tucano T1	RAF, stored Shawbury	
ZF200	Shorts Tucano T1	RAF No 1 FTS, Linton-on-Ouse	
ZF201	Shorts Tucano T1	RAF CFS, Topcliffe	
ZF202	Shorts Tucano T1	RAF, stored Shawbury	
ZF203	Shorts Tucano T1	RAF No 1 FTS, Linton-on-Ouse	
ZF204	Shorts Tucano T1	RAF, stored Shawbury	
ZF205	Shorts Tucano T1	RAF, stored Shawbury	
ZF206	Shorts Tucano T1	RAF No 1 FTS, Linton-on-Ouse	
ZF207	Shorts Tucano T1	RAF, stored Shawbury	
ZF208	Shorts Tucano T1	RAF, stored Shawbury	
ZF209	Shorts Tucano T1	RAF, stored Shawbury	
ZF210	Shorts Tucano T1	RAF, stored Shawbury	
ZF211	Shorts Tucano T1	RAF No 1 FTS, Linton-on-Ouse	
ZF212	Shorts Tucano T1	RAF No 1 FTS, Linton-on-Ouse	
ZF238	Shorts Tucano T1	RAF CFS, Topcliffe	
ZF239	Shorts Tucano T1	RAF, stored Shawbury	
ZF240	Shorts Tucano T1	RAF, stored Shawbury	
ZF241	Shorts Tucano T1	RAF No 1 FTS, Linton-on-Ouse	
ZF242	Shorts Tucano T1	RAF CFS, Topcliffe	
ZF243	Shorts Tucano T1	RAF, stored Shawbury	
ZF244	Shorts Tucano T1	RAF, stored Shawbury	
ZF245	Shorts Tucano T1	RAF, stored Shawbury	
ZF263	Shorts Tucano T1	RAF No 1 FTS, Linton-on-Ouse	
ZF264	Shorts Tucano T1	RAF, stored Shawbury	
ZF265	Shorts Tucano T1	RAF, stored Shawbury	
ZF266	Shorts Tucano T1	RAF No 1 FTS, Linton-on-Ouse	
ZF267	Shorts Tucano T1	RAF, stored Shawbury	
ZF268	Shorts Tucano T1	RAF No 1 FTS, Linton-on-Ouse	
ZF269	Shorts Tucano T1	RAF, stored Shawbury	
ZF270	Shorts Tucano T1	RAF No 1 FTS, Linton-on-Ouse	
ZF284	Shorts Tucano T1	RAF, stored Shawbury	
ZF285	Shorts Tucano T1	RAF, stored Shawbury	
ZF286	Shorts Tucano T1	RAF CFS, Topcliffe	
ZF287	Shorts Tucano T1	RAF, stored Shawbury	
ZF288	Shorts Tucano T1	RAF No 1 FTS, Linton-on-Ouse	
ZF289	Shorts Tucano T1	RAF, stored Shawbury	
ZF290	Shorts Tucano T1	RAF CFS, Topcliffe	
ZF291	Shorts Tucano T1	RAF, stored Shawbury	
ZF292	Shorts Tucano T1	RAF, stored Shawbury	
ZF293	Shorts Tucano T1	RAF, stored Shawbury	
ZF294	Shorts Tucano T1	RAF, stored Shawbury	
ZF295	Shorts Tucano T1	RAF, stored Shawbury	
ZF315	Shorts Tucano T1	RAF No 1 FTS, Linton-on-Ouse	
ZF317	Shorts Tucano T1	RAF, stored Shawbury	
ZF318	Shorts Tucano T1	RAF No 1 FTS, Linton-on-Ouse	
ZF319	Shorts Tucano T1	RAF, stored Shawbury	
ZF320	Shorts Tucano T1	RAF No 1 FTS, Linton-on-Ouse	
ZF338	Shorts Tucano T1	RAF, stored Shawbury	
ZF339	Shorts Tucano T1	RAF, stored Shawbury	
ZF340	Shorts Tucano T1	RAF, stored Shawbury	
ZF341	Shorts Tucano T1	RAF, stored Shawbury	
ZF342	Shorts Tucano T1	RAF, stored Shawbury	
ZF343	Shorts Tucano T1	RAF No 1 FTS, Linton-on-Ouse	
ZF344	Shorts Tucano T1	RAF, stored Shawbury	
ZF345	Shorts Tucano T1	RAF No 1 FTS, Linton-on-Ouse	
ZF346	Shorts Tucano T1	RAF No 1 FTS, Linton-on-Ouse	
ZF347	Shorts Tucano T1	RAF, stored Shawbury	

ZF348 – ZF586

Notes	Serial	Type (other identity) [code]	Owner/operator, location or fate
	ZF348	Shorts Tucano T1	RAF No 1 FTS, Linton-on-Ouse
	ZF349	Shorts Tucano T1	RAF, stored Shawbury
	ZF350	Shorts Tucano T1	RAF, stored Shawbury
	ZF372	Shorts Tucano T1	RAF No 1 FTS, Linton-on-Ouse
	ZF373	Shorts Tucano T1	RAF No 1 FTS, Linton-on-Ouse
	ZF374	Shorts Tucano T1	RAF, stored Shawbury
	ZF375	Shorts Tucano T1	RAF CFS, Topcliffe
	ZF376	Shorts Tucano T1	RAF No 1 FTS, Linton-on-Ouse
	ZF377	Shorts Tucano T1	RAF, stored Shawbury
	ZF378	Shorts Tucano T1	RAF, stored Shawbury
	ZF379	Shorts Tucano T1	RAF CFS, Topcliffe
	ZF380	Shorts Tucano T1	RAF CFS, Topcliffe
	ZF405	Shorts Tucano T1	RAF No 1 FTS, Linton-on-Ouse
	ZF406	Shorts Tucano T1	RAF No 1 FTS, Linton-on-Ouse
	ZF407	Shorts Tucano T1	RAF, stored Shawbury
	ZF408	Shorts Tucano T1	RAF No 1 FTS, Linton-on-Ouse
	ZF409	Shorts Tucano T1	RAF, stored Shawbury
	ZF410	Shorts Tucano T1	RAF CFS, Topcliffe
	ZF411	Shorts Tucano T1	RAF No 1 FTS, Linton-on-Ouse
	ZF412	Shorts Tucano T1	RAF No 1 FTS, Linton-on-Ouse
	ZF413	Shorts Tucano T1	RAF CFS, Topcliffe
	ZF414	Shorts Tucano T1	RAF No 1 FTS, Linton-on-Ouse
	ZF415	Shorts Tucano T1	RAF CFS, Topcliffe
	ZF416	Shorts Tucano T1	RAF No 1 FTS, Linton-on-Ouse
	ZF417	Shorts Tucano T1	RAF No 1 FTS, Linton-on-Ouse
	ZF418	Shorts Tucano T1	RAF No 1 FTS, Linton-on-Ouse
	ZF445	Shorts Tucano T1	RAF No 1 FTS, Linton-on-Ouse
	ZF446	Shorts Tucano T1	RAF No 1 FTS, Linton-on-Ouse
	ZF447	Shorts Tucano T1	RAF No 1 FTS, Linton-on-Ouse
	ZF448	Shorts Tucano T1	RAF No 1 FTS, Linton-on-Ouse
	ZF449	Shorts Tucano T1	RAF CFS, Topcliffe
	ZF450	Shorts Tucano T1	RAF No 1 FTS, Linton-on-Ouse
	ZF483	Shorts Tucano T1	RAF CFS, Topcliffe
	ZF484	Shorts Tucano T1	RAF No 1 FTS, Linton-on-Ouse
	ZF485	Shorts Tucano T1 (G-BULU)	RAF No 1 FTS, Linton-on-Ouse
	ZF486	Shorts Tucano T1	RAF No 1 FTS, Linton-on-Ouse
	ZF487	Shorts Tucano T1	RAF No 1 FTS, Linton-on-Ouse
	ZF488	Shorts Tucano T1	RAF No 1 FTS, Linton-on-Ouse
	ZF489	Shorts Tucano T1	RAF No 1 FTS, Linton-on-Ouse
	ZF490	Shorts Tucano T1	RAF No 1 FTS, Linton-on-Ouse
	ZF491	Shorts Tucano T1	RAF, stored Shawbury
	ZF492	Shorts Tucano T1	RAF No 1 FTS, Linton-on-Ouse
	ZF510	Shorts Tucano T1	MoD(PE)/ETPS, DTEO Boscombe Down
	ZF511	Shorts Tucano T1	MoD(PE)/ETPS, DTEO Boscombe Down
	ZF512	Shorts Tucano T1	RAF No 1 FTS, Linton-on-Ouse
	ZF513	Shorts Tucano T1	RAF CFS, Topcliffe
	ZF514	Shorts Tucano T1	RAF No 1 FTS, Linton-on-Ouse
	ZF515	Shorts Tucano T1	RAF CFS, Topcliffe
	ZF516	Shorts Tucano T1	RAF No 1 FTS, Linton-on-Ouse
	ZF520	Piper PA-31 Navajo Chieftain 350	MoD(PE)/FWTS, DTEO Boscombe Down
	ZF521	Piper PA-31 Navajo Chieftain 350	MoD(PE), DTEO Llanbedr
	ZF522	Piper PA-31 Navajo Chieftain 350	MoD(PE)/FWTS, DTEO Boscombe Down
	ZF534	BAe EAP	MoD(PE), stored BAe Warton
	ZF537	WS Lynx AH9	AAC stored, RNAY Fleetlands
	ZF538	WS Lynx AH9 [1]	AAC No 653 Sqn, Wattisham
	ZF539	WS Lynx AH9 [5]	AAC No 659 Sqn, Wattisham
	ZF540	WS Lynx AH9 [6]	AAC No 659 Sqn, Wattisham
	ZF557	WS Lynx HMA8 [444/MR]	RN No 815 Sqn, Portland
	ZF558	WS Lynx HMA8 [672]	MoD(PE)/Westland, Yeovil (conversion)
	ZF560	WS Lynx HMA8	RN AMG, Portland
	ZF562	WS Lynx HMA8 [457/LA]	RN No 815 Sqn OEU, Portland
	ZF563	WS Lynx HMA8 [671]	MoD(PE)/Westland, Yeovil (conversion)
	ZF573	PBN 2T Islander CC2A (G-SRAY)	RAF Northolt Station Flight
	ZF577	BAC Lightning F53	Privately owned, stored Warrington
	ZF578	BAC Lightning F53	Wales Aircraft Museum, Cardiff Airport
	ZF579	BAC Lightning F53	Privately owned, stored Warrington
	ZF580	BAC Lightning F53	BAe Samlesbury, at main gate
	ZF581	BAC Lightning F53	Privately owned, stored Warrington
	ZF582	BAC Lightning F53	Privately owned, stored Warrington
	ZF583	BAC Lightning F53	Solway Aviation Society, Carlisle
	ZF584	BAC Lightning F53	Ferranti Ltd, South Gyle, Edinburgh
	ZF585	BAC Lightning F53	Privately owned, stored Warrington
	ZF586	BAC Lightning F53	Privately owned, stored Warrington

Serial	Type (other identity) [code]	Owner/operator, location or fate	Notes
ZF587	BAC Lightning F53	Privately owned, stored Warrington	
ZF588	BAC Lightning F53	East Midlands Airport Aero Park	
ZF589	BAC Lightning F53	Privately owned, stored Warrington	
ZF590	BAC Lightning F53	Privately owned, stored Warrington	
ZF591	BAC Lightning F53	Privately owned, stored Warrington	
ZF592	BAC Lightning F53	Privately owned, stored Warrington	
ZF594	BAC Lightning F53	North-East Aircraft Museum, Usworth	
ZF595	BAC Lightning T55	Privately owned, stored Warrington	
ZF596	BAC Lightning T55	Privately owned, stored Warrington	
ZF597	BAC Lightning T55	Privately owned, stored Warrington	
ZF598	BAC Lightning T55	Midland Air Museum, Coventry	
ZF622	Piper PA-31 Navajo Chieftain 350	MoD(PE), DTEO Boscombe Down	
ZF641	WS/Agusta EH-101 [PP1]	MoD(PE)/Westland, Yeovil	
ZF644	WS/Agusta EH-101 [PP4]	Written off near Chard, Somerset, 7 April 1995	
ZF649	WS/Agusta EH-101 Merlin [PP5]	MoD(PE)/Westland, Yeovil	
ZG101	WS/Agusta EH-101 (mock-up) [GB]	Westland/Agusta, Yeovil	
ZG468	WS70 Blackhawk	Westland Helicopters, Yeovil	
ZG471	BAe Harrier GR7 [AB]	RAF No 4 Sqn, Laarbruch	
ZG472	BAe Harrier GR7	RAF AWC/SAOEU, DTEO Boscombe Down	
ZG474	BAe Harrier GR7 [12]	RAF No 1 Sqn, Wittering	
ZG475	BAe Harrier GR7 [U]	Written off, 1 June 1995, Solway Firth	
ZG476	BAe Harrier GR7 [WT]	RAF No 3 Sqn, Laarbruch	
ZG477	BAe Harrier GR7 [67]	RAF No 3 Sqn, Laarbruch	
ZG478	BAe Harrier GR7 [68]	RAF No 3 Sqn, Laarbruch	
ZG479	BAe Harrier GR7 [69]	RAF No 4 Sqn, Laarbruch	
ZG480	BAe Harrier GR7 [70]	RAF No 3 Sqn, Laarbruch	
ZG500	BAe Harrier GR7 [71]	RAF No 4 Sqn, Laarbruch	
ZG501	BAe Harrier GR7	RAF AWC/SAOEU, DTEO Boscombe Down	
ZG502	BAe Harrier GR7 [73]	RAF No 4 Sqn, Laarbruch	
ZG503	BAe Harrier GR7 [74]	RAF No 3 Sqn, Laarbruch	
ZG504	BAe Harrier GR7 [75]	RAF No 3 Sqn, Laarbruch	
ZG505	BAe Harrier GR7 [WJ]	RAF No 1 Sqn, Wittering	
ZG506	BAe Harrier GR7 [77]	RAF No 3 Sqn, Laarbruch	
ZG507	BAe Harrier GR7 [AC]	RAF No 3 Sqn, Laarbruch	
ZG508	BAe Harrier GR7 [79]	RAF No 3 Sqn, Laarbruch	
ZG509	BAe Harrier GR7 [80]	RAF No 3 Sqn, Laarbruch	
ZG510	BAe Harrier GR7 [81]	RAF No 3 Sqn, Laarbruch	
ZG511	BAe Harrier GR7 [82]	RAF No 4 Sqn, Laarbruch	
ZG512	BAe Harrier GR7 [83]	RAF No 4 Sqn, Laarbruch	
ZG530	BAe Harrier GR7 [84]	RAF No 3 Sqn, Laarbruch	
ZG531	BAe Harrier GR7	RAF St Athan	
ZG532	BAe Harrier GR7 [03]	RAF No 1 Sqn, Wittering	
ZG533	BAe Harrier GR7 [87]	RAF No 3 Sqn, Laarbruch	
ZG705	Panavia Tornado GR1A [J]	RAF No 13 Sqn, Marham	
ZG706	Panavia Tornado GR1A	RAF AWC/SAOEU, DTEO Boscombe Down	
ZG707	Panavia Tornado GR1A [B]	RAF No 13 Sqn, Marham	
ZG709	Panavia Tornado GR1A [V]	RAF No 13 Sqn, Marham	
ZG710	Panavia Tornado GR1A [D]	RAF No 13 Sqn, Marham	
ZG711	Panavia Tornado GR1A [E]	RAF No 13 Sqn, Marham	
ZG712	Panavia Tornado GR1A [F]	RAF No 13 Sqn, Marham	
ZG713	Panavia Tornado GR1A [G]	RAF No 13 Sqn, Marham	
ZG714	Panavia Tornado GR1A [Q]	RAF No 13 Sqn, Marham	
ZG726	Panavia Tornado GR1A [K[	RAF No 13 Sqn, Marham	
ZG727	Panavia Tornado GR1A [L]	RAF No 13 Sqn, Marham	
ZG728	Panavia Tornado F3 [CI]	RAF No 5 Sqn, Coningsby	
ZG729	Panavia Tornado GR1A [M]	RAF No 13 Sqn, Marham	
ZG730	Panavia Tornado F3 [CC]	RAF No 5 Sqn, Coningsby	
ZG731	Panavia Tornado F3 [CG]	RAF No 5 Sqn, Coningsby	
ZG732	Panavia Tornado F3 [BC]	RAF No 29 Sqn, Coningsby	
ZG733	Panavia Tornado F3 [BK]	RAF No 29 Sqn, Coningsby	
ZG734	Panavia Tornado F3 [BA]	RAF No 29 Sqn, Coningsby	
ZG735	Panavia Tornado F3 [AZ]	RAF F3 OCU/No 56(R) Sqn, Coningsby	
ZG750	Panavia Tornado GR1 [III]	RAF No 13 Sqn, Marham	
ZG751	Panavia Tornado F3 [AW]	RAF F3 OCU/No 56(R) Sqn, Coningsby	
ZG752	Panavia Tornado GR1 [XIII]	RAF No 13 Sqn, Marham	
ZG753	Panavia Tornado F3 [AF]	RAF F3 OCU/No 56(R) Sqn, Coningsby	
ZG754	Panavia Tornado GR1	RAF stored, St Athan	
ZG755	Panavia Tornado F3 [AY]	RAF F3 OCU/No 56(R) Sqn, Coningsby	

Notes	Serial	Type (other identity) [code]	Owner/operator, location or fate
	ZG756	Panavia Tornado GR1 [AX]	RAF No 9 Sqn, Brüggen
	ZG757	Panavia Tornado F3 [CA]	RAF No 5 Sqn, Coningsby
	ZG768	Panavia Tornado F3 [AX]	RAF F3 OCU/No 56(R) Sqn, Coningsby
	ZG769	Panavia Tornado GR1 [AY]	RAF No 9 Sqn, Brüggen
	ZG770	Panavia Tornado F3 [BD]	RAF No 29 Sqn, Coningsby
	ZG771	Panavia Tornado GR1 [DW]	RAF No 31 Sqn, Brüggen
	ZG772	Panavia Tornado F3 [CO]	RAF No 5 Sqn, Coningsby
	ZG773	Panavia Tornado GR4	MoD(PE)/BAe Warton (conversion)
	ZG774	Panavia Tornado F3 [BE]	RAF No 29 Sqn, Coningsby
	ZG775	Panavia Tornado GR1 [DN]	RAF No 31 Sqn, Brüggen
	ZG776	Panavia Tornado F3	RAF Coningsby
	ZG777	Panavia Tornado GR1 [DP]	RAF No 31 Sqn, Brüggen
	ZG778	Panavia Tornado F3 [BG]	RAF No 29 Sqn, Coningsby
	ZG779	Panavia Tornado GR1 [DK]	RAF No 31 Sqn, Brüggen
	ZG780	Panavia Tornado F3 [BH]	RAF No 29 Sqn, Coningsby
	ZG791	Panavia Tornado GR1 [DC]	RAF No 31 Sqn, Brüggen
	ZG792	Panavia Tornado GR1 [DD]	RAF No 31 Sqn, Brüggen
	ZG793	Panavia Tornado F3 [CY]	RAF No 5 Sqn, Coningsby
	ZG794	Panavia Tornado GR1 [DJ]	RAF No 31 Sqn, Brüggen
	ZG795	Panavia Tornado F3 [CB]	RAF No 5 Sqn, Coningsby
	ZG796	Panavia Tornado F3 [CE]	RAF No 5 Sqn, Coningsby
	ZG797	Panavia Tornado F3 [BF]	RAF No 29 Sqn, Coningsby
	ZG798	Panavia Tornado F3 [CD]	RAF No 5 Sqn, Coningsby
	ZG799	Panavia Tornado F3 [BB]	RAF No 29 Sqn, Coningsby
	ZG816	WS61 Sea King HAS6 [701/PW]	RN No 819 Sqn, Prestwick
	ZG817	WS61 Sea King HAS6 [504]	RN No 810 Sqn, Culdrose
	ZG818	WS61 Sea King HAS6 [707]	RN No 819 Sqn, Prestwick
	ZG819	WS61 Sea King HAS6 [270/N]	RN No 814 Sqn, Culdrose
	ZG820	WS61 Sea King HC4 [A]	RN No 845 Sqn, Yeovilton
	ZG821	WS61 Sea King HC4 [D]	RN No 845 Sqn, Yeovilton
	ZG822	WS61 Sea King HC4 [VN]	RN No 846 Sqn, Yeovilton
	ZG844	PBN 2T Islander AL1 (G-BLNE)	AAC No 1 Flt, Aldergrove
	ZG845	PBN 2T Islander AL1 (G-BLNT)	AAC Islander Training Flt, Middle Wallop
	ZG846	PBN 2T Islander AL1 (G-BLNU)	AAC No 1 Flt, Aldergrove
	ZG847	PBN 2T Islander AL1 (G-BLNV)	AAC No 1 Flt, Aldergrove
	ZG848	PBN 2T Islander AL1 (G-BLNY)	AAC No 1 Flt, Aldergrove
	ZG856	BAe Harrier GR7 [88]	RAF No 4 Sqn, Laarbruch
	ZG857	BAe Harrier GR7 [89]	RAF No 3 Sqn, Laarbruch
	ZG858	BAe Harrier GR7 [90]	RAF No 3 Sqn, Laarbruch
	ZG859	BAe Harrier GR7 [91]	RAF No 4 Sqn, Laarbruch
	ZG860	BAe Harrier GR7 [08]	RAF No 1 Sqn, Wittering
	ZG861	BAe Harrier GR7 [93]	RAF No 3 Sqn, Laarbruch
	ZG862	BAe Harrier GR7 [94]	RAF No 3 Sqn, Laarbruch
	ZG875	WS61 Sea King HAS6 [702/PW]	RN No 819 Sqn, Prestwick
	ZG879	Powerchute Raider Mk 1	MoD(PE)/Powerchute, Hereford
	ZG884	WS Lynx AH9	MoD(PE)/Westland, Yeovil
	ZG885	WS Lynx AH9 [2]	AAC No 659 Sqn, Wattisham
	ZG886	WS Lynx AH9 [3]	AAC No 653 Sqn, Wattisham
	ZG887	WS Lynx AH9 [4]	AAC No 653 Sqn, Wattisham
	ZG888	WS Lynx AH9	AAC, RNAY Fleetlands
	ZG889	WS Lynx AH9 [6]	AAC No 653 Sqn, Wattisham
	ZG914	WS Lynx AH9 [G]	AAC No 653 Sqn, Wattisham
	ZG915	WS Lynx AH9 [7]	AAC No 653 Sqn, Wattisham
	ZG916	WS Lynx AH9 [8]	AAC No 659 Sqn, Wattisham
	ZG917	WS Lynx AH9 [9]	AAC No 659 Sqn, Wattisham
	ZG918	WS Lynx AH9 [10]	AAC No 659 Sqn, Wattisham
	ZG919	WS Lynx AH9 [7]	AAC No 653 Sqn, Wattisham
	ZG920	WS Lynx AH9 [8]	AAC No 653 Sqn, Wattisham
	ZG921	WS Lynx AH9 [11]	AAC No 659 Sqn, Wattisham
	ZG922	WS Lynx AH9 [9]	AAC No 653 Sqn, Wattisham
	ZG923	WS Lynx AH9 [10]	AAC No 653 Sqn, Wattisham
	ZG969	Pilatus PC-9 (HB-HQE)	BAe Warton
	ZG989	PBN 2T Islander Astor (G-DLRA)	MoD(PE)/PBN, Bembridge
	ZG993	PBN 2T Islander AL1 (G-BOMD)	AAC Islander Flight, Middle Wallop
	ZG994	PBN 2T Islander AL1 (G-BPLN)	AAC No 1 Flight, Aldergrove
	ZH101	Boeing E-3D Sentry AEW1	RAF No 8 Sqn, Waddington
	ZH102	Boeing E-3D Sentry AEW1	RAF No 8 Sqn, Waddington
	ZH103	Boeing E-3D Sentry AEW1	RAF No 8 Sqn, Waddington
	ZH104	Boeing E-3D Sentry AEW1	RAF No 8 Sqn, Waddington
	ZH105	Boeing E-3D Sentry AEW1	RAF No 8 Sqn, Waddington
	ZH106	Boeing E-3D Sentry AEW1	RAF No 8 Sqn, Waddington
	ZH107	Boeing E-3D Sentry AEW1	RAF No 8 Sqn, Waddington

Serial	Type (other identity) [code]	Owner/operator, location or fate	Notes
ZH115	Grob G109B Vigilant T1	RAF ACCGS, Syerston	
ZH116	Grob G109B Vigilant T1	RAF No 632 VGS, Ternhill	
ZH117	Grob G109B Vigilant T1	RAF ACCGS, Syerston	
ZH118	Grob G109B Vigilant T1	RAF No 624 VGS, Chivenor	
ZH119	Grob G109B Vigilant T1	RAF CGMF, Syerston	
ZH120	Grob G109B Vigilant T1	RAF ACCGS, Syerston	
ZH121	Grob G109B Vigilant T1	RAF No 612 VGS, Abingdon	
ZH122	Grob G109B Vigilant T1	RAF No 616 VGS, Henlow	
ZH123	Grob G109B Vigilant T1	RAF ACCGS, Syerston	
ZH124	Grob G109B Vigilant T1	RAF No 637 VGS, Little Rissington	
ZH125	Grob G109B Vigilant T1	RAF No 633 VGS, Cosford	
ZH126	Grob G109B Vigilant T1	RAF No 616 VGS, Henlow	
ZH127	Grob G109B Vigilant T1	RAF ACCGS, Syerston	
ZH128	Grob G109B Vigilant T1	RAF No 624 VGS, Chivenor	
ZH129	Grob G109B Vigilant T1	RAF ACCGS, Syerston	
ZH144	Grob G109B Vigilant T1	RAF No 616 VGS, Henlow	
ZH145	Grob G109B Vigilant T1	RAF ACCGS, Syerston	
ZH146	Grob G109B Vigilant T1	RAF No 637 VGS, Little Rissington	
ZH147	Grob G109B Vigilant T1	RAF No 637 VGS, Little Rissington	
ZH148	Grob G109B Vigilant T1	RAF No 637 VGS, Little Rissington	
ZH184	Grob G109B Vigilant T1	RAF No 624 VGS, Chivenor	
ZH185	Grob G109B Vigilant T1	RAF No 632 VGS, Ternhill	
ZH186	Grob G109B Vigilant T1	RAF No 633 VGS, Cosford	
ZH187	Grob G109B Vigilant T1	RAF ACCGS, Syerston	
ZH188	Grob G109B Vigilant T1	RAF ACCGS, Syerston	
ZH189	Grob G109B Vigilant T1	RAF No 635 VGS, Samlesbury	
ZH190	Grob G109B Vigilant T1	RAF ACCGS, Syerston	
ZH191	Grob G109B Vigilant T1	RAF No 612 VGS, Abingdon	
ZH192	Grob G109B Vigilant T1	RAF No 663 VGS, Kinloss	
ZH193	Grob G109B Vigilant T1	RAF ACCGS, Syerston	
ZH194	Grob G109B Vigilant T1	RAF No 612 VGS, Abingdon	
ZH195	Grob G109B Vigilant T1	RAF No 663 VGS, Kinloss	
ZH196	Grob G109B Vigilant T1	RAF No 633 VGS, Cosford	
ZH197	Grob G109B Vigilant T1	RAF No 642 VGS, Church Fenton	
ZH200	BAe Hawk 200	MoD(PE), stored BAe Warton	
ZH205	Grob G109B Vigilant T1	RAF No 624 VGS, Chivenor	
ZH206	Grob G109B Vigilant T1	RAF No 642 VGS, Church Fenton	
ZH207	Grob G109B Vigilant T1	RAF No 632 VGS, Ternhill	
ZH208	Grob G109B Vigilant T1	RAF No 612 VGS, Abingdon	
ZH209	Grob G109B Vigilant T1	RAF No 613 VGS, Halton	
ZH210	Grob G109B Vigilant T1 (wreck)	Sold to Germany	
ZH211	Grob G109B Vigilant T1	RAF No 663 VGS, Kinloss	
ZH247	Grob G109B Vigilant T1	RAF No 613 VGS, Halton	
ZH248	Grob G109B Vigilant T1	RAF No 642 VGS, Church Fenton	
ZH249	Grob G109B Vigilant T1	RAF No 616 VGS, Henlow	
ZH263	Grob G109B Vigilant T1	RAF No 635 VGS, Samlesbury	
ZH264	Grob G109B Vigilant T1	RAF No 642 VGS, Church Fenton	
ZH265	Grob G109B Vigilant T1	RAF No 633 VGS, Cosford	
7H266	Grob G109B Vigilant T1	RAF No 633 VGS, Cosford	
ZH267	Grob G109B Vigilant T1	RAF No 635 VGS, Samlesbury	
ZH268	Grob G109B Vigilant T1	RAF ACCGS, Syerston	
ZH269	Grob G109B Vigilant T1	RAF No 613 VGS, Halton	
ZH270	Grob G109B Vigilant T1	RAF No 632 VGS, Ternhill	
ZH271	Grob G109B Vigilant T1	RAF ACCGS, Syerston	
ZH506	Shorts Tucano T52 (KAF 101)	To Kuwait AF as KAF 101, 18 May 1995	
ZH507	Shorts Tucano T52 (KAF 102)	To Kuwait AF as KAF 102, 18 May 1995	
ZH508	Shorts Tucano T52 (KAF 103)	To Kuwait AF as KAF 103, 11 May 1995	
ZH509	Shorts Tucano T52 (KAF 104)	To Kuwait AF as KAF 104, 18 May 1995	
ZH510	Shorts Tucano T52 (KAF 105)	To Kuwait AF as KAF 105, 18 May 1995	
ZH511	Shorts Tucano T52 (KAF 106)	To Kuwait AF as KAF 106, 27 April 1995	
ZH512	Shorts Tucano T52 (KAF 107)	To Kuwait AF as KAF 107, 27 April 1995	
ZH513	Shorts Tucano T52 (KAF 108)	To Kuwait AF as KAF 108, 18 May 1995	
ZH526	Shorts Tucano T52 (KAF 109)	To Kuwait AF as KAF 109, 11 May 1995	
ZH527	Shorts Tucano T52 (KAF 110)	To Kuwait AF as KAF 110, 4 May 1995	
ZH528	Shorts Tucano T52 (KAF 111)	To Kuwait AF as KAF 111, 27 April 1995	
ZH529	Shorts Tucano T52 (KAF 112)	To Kuwait AF as KAF 112, 4 May 1995	
ZH530	Shorts Tucano T52 (KΛF 113)	To Kuwait AF as KAF 113, 11 May 1995	
ZH531	Shorts Tucano T52 (KAF 114)	To Kuwait AF as KAF 114, 4 May 1995	
ZH532	Shorts Tucano T52 (KAF 115)	To Kuwait AF as KAF 115, 4 May 1995	
ZH533	Shorts Tucano T52 (KAF 116)	To Kuwait AF as KAF 116, 4 May 1995	
ZH536	PBN 2T Islander CC2 (G-BSAH)	RAF Northolt Station Flight	
ZH540	WS61 Sea King HAR3A	MoD(PE)/RWTS, DTEO Boscombe Down	
ZH541	WS61 Sea King HAR3A	RAF No 22 Sqn, St Mawgan	

Notes	Serial	Type (other identity) [code]	Owner/operator, location or fate
	ZH542	WS61 Sea King HAR3A	RAF No 22 Sqn, St Mawgan
	ZH543	WS61 Sea King HAR3A	RAF No 22 Sqn, St Mawgan
	ZH544	WS61 Sea King HAR3A	RAF No 22 Sqn, St Mawgan
	ZH545	WS61 Sea King HAR3A	RAF No 22 Sqn, St Mawgan
	ZH552	Panavia Tornado F3	RAF F3 OEU, Coningsby
	ZH553	Panavia Tornado F3 [BY]	RAF No 29 Sqn, Coningsby
	ZH554	Panavia Tornado F3 [BZ]	RAF No 29 Sqn, Coningsby
	ZH555	Panavia Tornado F3 [CV]	RAF No 5 Sqn, Coningsby
	ZH556	Panavia Tornado F3 [AK]	RAF F3 OCU/No 56(R) Sqn, Coningsby
	ZH557	Panavia Tornado F3 [CT]	RAF No 5 Sqn, Coningsby
	ZH559	Panavia Tornado F3 [AJ]	RAF F3 OCU/No 56(R) Sqn, Coningsby
	ZH582	WS Lynx Mk 95	*To Portuguese Navy as 9203, 1994*
	ZH586	Eurofighter 2000 (DA1/98+29)	*Serial not used*
	ZH588	Eurofighter 2000 (DA2)	MoD(PE)/BAe Warton
	ZH590	Eurofighter 2000(T) (DA4)	MoD(PE)/BAe Warton
	ZH629	BAe Hawk 102	For Abu Dhabi AF as 1059
	ZH634	BAe Hawk 102	For Abu Dhabi AF as 1060
	ZH635	BAe Hawk 102	For Abu Dhabi AF as 1061
	ZH636	BAe Hawk 102	For Abu Dhabi AF as 1062
	ZH637	BAe Hawk 102	For Abu Dhabi AF as 1063
	ZH638	BAe Hawk 102	For Abu Dhabi AF as 1064
	ZH639	BAe Hawk 102	For Abu Dhabi AF as 1065
	ZH640	BAe Hawk 102	For Abu Dhabi AF as 1066
	ZH641	BAe Hawk 102	For Abu Dhabi AF as 1067
	ZH642	BAe Hawk 102	For Abu Dhabi AF as 1068
	ZH647	WS/Agusta EH-101 (G-EHIL)	MoD(PE)/Westland, Yeovil
	ZH653	BAe Harrier T10	MoD(PE)/FWTS, DTEO Boscombe Down
	ZH654	BAe Harrier T10	MoD(PE)/FWTS, DTEO Boscombe Down
	ZH655	BAe Harrier T10 [Q]	RAF, stored Wittering (damaged)
	ZH656	BAe Harrier T10 [104]	RAF HOCU/No 20(R) Sqn, Wittering
	ZH657	BAe Harrier T10 [M]	RAF HOCU/No 20(R) Sqn, Wittering
	ZH658	BAe Harrier T10 [N]	RAF HOCU/No 20(R) Sqn, Wittering
	ZH659	BAe Harrier T10 [O]	RAF HOCU/No 20(R) Sqn, Wittering
	ZH660	BAe Harrier T10 [P]	RAF HOCU/No 20(R) Sqn, Wittering
	ZH661	BAe Harrier T10 [10]	RAF No 1 Sqn, Wittering
	ZH662	BAe Harrier T10 [R]	RAF HOCU/No 20(R) Sqn, Wittering
	ZH663	BAe Harrier T10 [Q]	RAF HOCU/No 20(R) Sqn, Wittering
	ZH664	BAe Harrier T10	RAF No 4 Sqn, Laarbruch
	ZH665	BAe Harrier T10	RAF No 3 Sqn, Laarbruch
	ZH670	BAe Hawk 103	*To RAF of Oman as 102, 14 February 1995*
	ZH700	BAe Hawk 51A	*To Finnish AF as HW-353 by June 1995*
	ZH702	BAe Hawk 51A	*To Finnish AF as HW-355*
	ZH703	BAe Hawk 51A	*To Finnish AF as HW-356*
	ZH704	BAe Hawk 51A	*To Finnish AF as HW-357 by June 1995*
	ZH710	BAe Hawk 203	*To RAF of Oman as 121*
	ZH711	BAe Hawk 203	*To RAF of Oman as 122*
	ZH712	BAe Hawk 203	*To RAF of Oman as 123, 16 December 1994*
	ZH714	BAe Hawk 203	*To RAF of Oman as 125*
	ZH715	BAe Hawk 203	*To RAF of Oman as 126*
	ZH720	BAe Hawk 203	*To RAF of Oman as 127*
	ZH721	BAe Hawk 203	*To RAF of Oman as 128, 14 February 1995*
	ZH722	BAe Hawk 203	*To RAF of Oman as 129*
	ZH729	BAe Hawk 203	*To RAF of Oman as 130*
	ZH730	BAe Hawk 203	*To RAF of Oman as 131*
	ZH731	BAe Hawk 203	*To RAF of Oman as 132*
	ZH752	BAe Hawk 108	*To R Malaysian AF as M40-07 3 July 1995*
	ZH762	Westinghouse Skyship 500 (G-SKSC)	*Written off at Boscombe Down, 9 May 1995*
	ZH763	BAC 1-11/539GL (G-BGKE)	MoD(PE)/DRA, DTEO Boscombe Down
	ZH775	B-V Chinook HC2	Boeing, Philadelphia, for RAF
	ZH776	B-V Chinook HC2	Boeing, Philadelphia, for RAF
	ZH777	B-V Chinook HC2	Boeing, Philadelphia, for RAF
	ZH781	BAe Hawk 208	*To R Malaysian AF as M40-24, 24 September 1994*
	ZH782	BAe Hawk 208	*To R Malaysian AF as M40-25, 24 September 1994*
	ZH783	BAe Hawk 208	*To R Malaysian AF as M40-26, 24 September 1994*
	ZH785	BAe Hawk 208	*To R Malaysian AF as M40-28*

Serial	Type (other identity) [code]	Owner/operator, location or fate	Notes
ZH786	BAe Hawk 208	To R Malaysian AF as M40-29, 15 November 1994	
ZH787	BAe Hawk 208	To R Malaysian AF as M40-30	
ZH788	BAe Hawk 208	To R Malaysian AF as M40-31, 15 November 1994	
ZH789	BAe Hawk 208	To R Malaysian AF as M40-32, 13 March 1995	
ZH790	BAe Hawk 208	To R Malaysian AF as M40-33, 12 December 1994	
ZH791	BAe Hawk 208	To R Malaysian AF as M40-34, 6 January 1995	
ZH792	BAe Hawk 208	To R Malaysian AF as M40-35, 6 January 1995	
ZH793	BAe Hawk 208	To R Malaysian AF as M40-36, 13 March 1995	
ZH794	BAe Hawk 208	To R Malaysian AF as M40-37, 3 July 1995	
ZH795	BAe Hawk 208	To R Malaysian AF as M40-38, 13 March 1995	
ZH796	BAe Sea Harrier FA2 [716]	RN No 899 Sqn, Yeovilton	
ZH797	BAe Sea Harrier FA2	RN	
ZH798	BAe Sea Harrier FA2	BAe, for RN	
ZH799	BAe Sea Harrier FA2	BAe, for RN	
ZH800	BAe Sea Harrier FA2	BAe, for RN	
ZH801	BAe Sea Harrier FA2	BAe, for RN	
ZH802	BAe Sea Harrier FA2	BAe, for RN	
ZH803	BAe Sea Harrier FA2	BAe, for RN	
ZH804	BAe Sea Harrier FA2	BAe, for RN	
ZH805	BAe Sea Harrier FA2	BAe, for RN	
ZH806	BAe Sea Harrier FA2	BAe, for RN	
ZH807	BAe Sea Harrier FA2	BAe, for RN	
ZH808	BAe Sea Harrier FA2	BAe, for RN	
ZH809	BAe Sea Harrier FA2	BAe, for RN	
ZH810	BAe Sea Harrier FA2	BAe, for RN	
ZH811	BAe Sea Harrier FA2	BAe, for RN	
ZH812	BAe Sea Harrier FA2	BAe, for RN	
ZH813	BAe Sea Harrier FA2	BAe, for RN	
ZH814	Bell 212 (G-BGMH)	AAC No 7 Flt, Brunei	
ZH815	Bell 212 (G-BGCZ)	AAC No 7 Flt, Brunei	
ZH816	Bell 212 (G-BGMG)	AAC No 7 Flt, Brunei	
ZH817	BAe Hawk T63C	To UAE AF as 1017, 21 February 1995	
ZH818	BAe Hawk T63C	To UAE AF as 1018, 21 February 1995	
ZH819	BAe Hawk T63C	To UAE AF as 1019, 23 March 1995	
ZH820	BAe Hawk T63C	To UAE AF as 1020, 23 March 1995	
ZH821	WS/Agusta EH-101 Merlin HAS1	Westland, for RN	
ZH822	WS/Agusta EH-101 Merlin HAS1	Westland, for RN	
ZH823	WS/Agusta EH-101 Merlin HAS1	Westland, for RN	
ZH824	WS/Agusta EH-101 Merlin HAS1	Westland, for RN	
ZH825	WS/Agusta EH-101 Merlin HAS1	Westland, for RN	
ZH826	WS/Agusta EH-101 Merlin HAS1	Westland, for RN	
ZH827	WS/Agusta EH-101 Merlin HAS1	Westland, for RN	
ZH828	WS/Agusta EH-101 Merlin HAS1	Westland, for RN	
ZH829	WS/Agusta EH-101 Merlin HAS1	Westland, for RN	
ZH830	WS/Agusta EH-101 Merlin HAS1	Westland, for RN	
ZH831	WS/Agusta EH-101 Merlin HAS1	Westland, for RN	
ZH832	WS/Agusta EH-101 Merlin HAS1	Westland, for RN	
ZH833	WS/Agusta EH-101 Merlin HAS1	Westland, for RN	
ZH834	WS/Agusta EH-101 Merlin HAS1	Westland, for RN	
ZH835	WS/Agusta EH-101 Merlin HAS1	Westland, for RN	
ZH836	WS/Agusta EH-101 Merlin HAS1	Westland, for RN	
ZH837	WS/Agusta EH-101 Merlin HAS1	Westland, for RN	
ZH838	WS/Agusta EH-101 Merlin HAS1	Westland, for RN	
ZH839	WS/Agusta EH-101 Merlin HAS1	Westland, for RN	
ZH840	WS/Agusta EH-101 Merlin HAS1	Westland, for RN	
ZH841	WS/Agusta EH-101 Merlin HAS1	Westland, for RN	
ZH842	WS/Agusta EH-101 Merlin HAS1	Westland, for RN	
ZH843	WS/Agusta EH-101 Merlin HAS1	Westland, for RN	
ZH844	WS/Agusta EH-101 Merlin HAS1	Westland, for RN	
ZH845	WS/Agusta EH-101 Merlin HAS1	Westland, for RN	
ZH846	WS/Agusta EH-101 Merlin HAS1	Westland, for RN	
ZH847	WS/Agusta EH-101 Merlin HAS1	Westland, for RN	
ZH848	WS/Agusta EH-101 Merlin HAS1	Westland, for RN	
ZH849	WS/Agusta EH-101 Merlin HAS1	Westland, for RN	

ZH850 – ZJ201

Notes	Serial	Type (other identity) [code]	Owner/operator, location or fate
	ZH850	WS/Agusta EH-101 Merlin HAS1	Westland, for RN
	ZH851	WS/Agusta EH-101 Merlin HAS1	Westland, for RN
	ZH852	WS/Agusta EH-101 Merlin HAS1	Westland, for RN
	ZH853	WS/Agusta EH-101 Merlin HAS1	Westland, for RN
	ZH854	WS/Agusta EH-101 Merlin HAS1	Westland, for RN
	ZH855	WS/Agusta EH-101 Merlin HAS1	Westland, for RN
	ZH856	WS/Agusta EH-101 Merlin HAS1	Westland, for RN
	ZH857	WS/Agusta EH-101 Merlin HAS1	Westland, for RN
	ZH858	WS/Agusta EH-101 Merlin HAS1	Westland, for RN
	ZH859	WS/Agusta EH-101 Merlin HAS1	Westland, for RN
	ZH860	WS/Agusta EH-101 Merlin HAS1	Westland, for RN
	ZH861	WS/Agusta EH-101 Merlin HAS1	Westland, for RN
	ZH862	WS/Agusta EH-101 Merlin HAS1	Westland, for RN
	ZH863	WS/Agusta EH-101 Merlin HAS1	Westland, for RN
	ZH864	WS/Agusta EH-101 Merlin HAS1	Westland, for RN
	ZH865	Lockheed C-130J-30 Hercules C4 (N130JA)	Lockheed-Martin, Marietta
	ZH866	Lockheed C-130J-30 Hercules C4 (N130JE)	Lockheed-Martin, for RAF
	ZH867	Lockheed C-130J-30 Hercules C4 (N130JJ)	Lockheed-Martin, for RAF
	ZH868	Lockheed C-130J-30 Hercules C4	Lockheed-Martin, for RAF
	ZH869	Lockheed C-130J-30 Hercules C4	Lockheed-Martin, for RAF
	ZH870	Lockheed C-130J-30 Hercules C4	Lockheed-Martin, for RAF
	ZH871	Lockheed C-130J-30 Hercules C4	Lockheed-Martin, for RAF
	ZH872	Lockheed C-130J-30 Hercules C4	Lockheed-Martin, for RAF
	ZH873	Lockheed C-130J-30 Hercules C4	Lockheed-Martin, for RAF
	ZH874	Lockheed C-130J-30 Hercules C4	Lockheed-Martin, for RAF
	ZH875	Lockheed C-130J-30 Hercules C4	Lockheed-Martin, for RAF
	ZH876	Lockheed C-130J-30 Hercules C4	Lockheed-Martin, for RAF
	ZH877	Lockheed C-130J-30 Hercules C4	Lockheed-Martin, for RAF
	ZH878	Lockheed C-130J-30 Hercules C4	Lockheed-Martin, for RAF
	ZH879	Lockheed C-130J-30 Hercules C4	Lockheed-Martin, for RAF
	ZH880	Lockheed C-130J Hercules C5	Lockheed-Martin, for RAF
	ZH881	Lockheed C-130J Hercules C5	Lockheed-Martin, for RAF
	ZH882	Lockheed C-130J Hercules C5	Lockheed-Martin, for RAF
	ZH883	Lockheed C-130J Hercules C5	Lockheed-Martin, for RAF
	ZH884	Lockheed C-130J Hercules C5	Lockheed-Martin, for RAF
	ZH885	Lockheed C-130J Hercules C5	Lockheed-Martin, for RAF
	ZH886	Lockheed C-130J Hercules C5	Lockheed-Martin, for RAF
	ZH887	Lockheed C-130J Hercules C5	Lockheed-Martin, for RAF
	ZH888	Lockheed C-130J Hercules C5	Lockheed-Martin, for RAF
	ZH889	Lockheed C-130J Hercules C5	Lockheed-Martin, for RAF
	ZH890	Grob G109B Vigilant T1	RAF ACCGS, Syerston
	ZH891	B-V Chinook HC2	Boeing, Philadelphia, for RAF
	ZH892	B-V Chinook HC2	Boeing, Philadelphia, for RAF
	ZH893	B-V Chinook HC2	Boeing, Philadelphia, for RAF
	ZH894	B-V Chinook HC2	Boeing, Philadelphia, for RAF
	ZH895	B-V Chinook HC2	Boeing, Philadelphia, for RAF
	ZH896	B-V Chinook HC2	Boeing, Philadelphia, for RAF
	ZH897	B-V Chinook HC3	Boeing, Philadelphia, for RAF
	ZH898	B-V Chinook HC3	Boeing, Philadelphia, for RAF
	ZH899	B-V Chinook HC3	Boeing, Philadelphia, for RAF
	ZH900	B-V Chinook HC3	Boeing, Philadelphia, for RAF
	ZH901	B-V Chinook HC3	Boeing, Philadelphia, for RAF
	ZH902	B-V Chinook HC3	Boeing, Philadelphia, for RAF
	ZH903	B-V Chinook HC3	Boeing, Philadelphia, for RAF
	ZH904	B-V Chinook HC3	Boeing, Philadelphia, for RAF
	ZH953	BAe Hawk 109	For Indonesian Air Force
	ZH954	BAe Hawk 109	For Indonesian Air Force
	ZH955	BAe Hawk 109	For Indonesian Air Force
	ZH956	BAe Hawk 109	For Indonesian Air Force
	ZH957	BAe Hawk 109	For Indonesian Air Force
	ZH958	BAe Hawk 109	For Indonesian Air Force
	ZH959	BAe Hawk 109	For Indonesian Air Force
	ZH960	BAe Hawk 109	For Indonesian Air Force
	ZH975	Pilatus PC-9 (HB-HQP)	*To R Saudi AF as 901, 4 December 1995*
	ZH976	Pilatus PC-9 (HB-HQQ)	*To R Saudi AF as 902, 4 December 1995*
	ZH977	Pilatus PC-9 (HB-HQV)	*To R Saudi AF as 903, 10 January 1996*
	ZH978	Pilatus PC-9 (HB-HQW)	*To R Saudi AF as 904, 10 January 1996*
	ZJ100	BAe Hawk 102D	BAe Warton
	ZJ201	BAe Hawk 200RDA	BAe Warton

Harvard T2B KF183 is operated at Boscombe Down by the Fixed Wing Trials Squadron. *Daniel March*

Spitfire LF IXE TE566 landing at Duxford. *PRM*

B2(mod)/TT18 WH734 is one of the last Canberras to be retained for trials flying. *Daniel March*

Privately owned Hunter T7 XL573 is based at Exeter. *PRM*

Black-painted display Jaguar GR1A XX116 of No 16(R) Squadron. *PRM*

Army Air Corps Lynx AH7 XZ674 based at Wattisham. *PRM*

Harrier GR7 ZD431 of No 1 Sqn at RAF Wittering. *Daniel March*

Tornado F3s ZE156 of No 111 Sqn and ZG774 of No 29 Sqn. *PRM*

1764M/K4972	7525M/WT619	7816M/WG763	7983M/XD506
2015M/K5600	7530M/WT648	7817M/TX214	7984M/XN597
2292M/K8203	7532M/WT651	7825M/WK991	7986M/WG777
2361M/K6035	7533M/WT680	7829M/XH992	7988M/XL149
3118M/H5199/BK892	7544M/WN904	7839M/WV781	7990M/XD452
3858M/X7688	7548M/PS915	7840M/XK482	7997M/XG452
4354M/BL614	7554M/FS890	7841M/WV783	7998M/*XM515*/(XD515)
5377M/EP120	7555M/AR614	7851M/WZ706	8001M/WV395
5378M/AR614	7556M/WK584	7852M/XG506	8005M/WG768
5405M/LF738	7564M/XE982	7854M/XM191	8009M/XG518
5466M/*BN230*/(LF751)	7570M/XD674	7855M/XK416	8010M/XG547
5690M/MK356	7582M/*WP180*/(WP190)	7859M/XP283	8012M/VS562
5718M/BM597	7583M/WP185	7860M/XL738	8016M/XT677
5758M/DG202	7602M/WE600	7862M/XR246	8017M/XL762
6457M/ML427	7605M/WS692	7863M/*XP248*	8018M/XN344
6490M/LA255	7606M/WV562	7864M/XP244	8019M/WZ869
6850M/TE184	7607M/TJ138	7865M/TX226	8021M/XL824
6946M/RW388	7615M/WV679	7866M/XH278	8022M/XN341
6948M/DE673	7616M/WW388	7867M/XH980	8023M/XD463
6960M/MT847	7618M/WW442	7868M/WZ736	8027M/XM555
7008M/EE549	7622M/WV606	7869M/WK935	8032M/XH837
7014M/N6720	7625M/WD356	7872M/*WZ826*/(XD826)	8033M/XD382
7015M/NL985	7631M/VX185	7881M/WD413	8034M/XL703
7035M/*K2567*/(DE306)	7641M/XA634	7882M/XD525	8041M/XF690
7060M/VF301	7645M/WD293	7883M/XT150	8043M/XF836
7090M/EE531	7646M/VX461	7886M/XR985	8046M/XL770
7118M/LA198	7648M/XF785	7887M/XD375	8049M/WE168
7119M/LA226	7663M/XA571	7890M/XD453	8050M/XG329
7150M/PK683	7673M/WV332	7891M/XM693	8051M/XN929
7154M/WB188	7688M/WW421	7894M/XD818	8052M/WH166
7174M/VX272	7693M/WV483	7895M/WF784	8054AM/XM410
7175M/VV106	7696M/WV493	7898M/XP854	8054BM/XM417
7200M/VT812	7698M/WV499	7899M/XG540	8055AM/XM402
7241M/*X4474*(TE311)	7703M/WG725	7900M/WA576	8055BM/XM404
7243M/TE462	7704M/TW536	7902M/WZ550	8056M/XG337
7244M/*MK673*(TB382)	7705M/WL505	7906M/WH132	8057M/XR243
7246M/TD248	7706M/WB584	7917M/WA591	8063M/WT536
7256M/TB752	7709M/WT933	7920M/WL360	8070M/EP120
7257M/TB252	7711M/PS915	7923M/XT133	8072M/PK624
7279M/TB752	7712M/WK281	7925M/WV666	8073M/TB252
7281M/TB252	7715M/XK724	7928M/XE849	8077M/XN594
7288M/PK724	7716M/WS776	7930M/WH301	8078M/XM351
7293M/RW393	7718M/WA577	7931M/RD253	8079M/XN492
7323M/VV217	7719M/WK277	7932M/WZ744	8080M/XM480
7325M/R5868	7722M/XA571	7933M/XR220	8081M/XM468
7326M/VN485	7728M/WZ458	7937M/WS843	8082M/XM409
7362M/475081/(VP546)	7729M/WB758	7938M/XH903	8085M/XM467
7416M/WN907	7734M/XD536	7939M/XD596	8086M/TB752
7421M/WT660	7736M/WZ559	7940M/XL764	8088M/XN602
/422M/WT684	7737M/XD602	7955M/XH767	8092M/WK654
7428M/WK198	7739M/XA801	7957M/XF545	8094M/WT520
7432M/WZ724	7741M/VZ477	7959M/WS774	8101M/WH984
7438M/WP905	7750M/*WK864*/(WL168)	7960M/WS726	8103M/WR985
7443M/WX853	7751M/WL131	7961M/WS739	8106M/WR982
7451M/TE476	7755M/WG760	7964M/WS760	8108M/WV703
7458M/WX905	7758M/PM651	7965M/WS792	8113M/WV753
7464M/XA564	7759M/PK664	7967M/WS788	8117M/WR974
7467M/WP978	7761M/XH318	7970M/WP907	8118M/WZ549
7470M/XA553	7762M/XE670	7971M/XK699	8119M/WR971
7473M/XE946	7770M/WT746	7973M/WS807	8121M/XM474
7491M/WT569	7793M/XG523	7976M/XK418	8124M/XD614
7496M/WT612	7796M/WJ676	7979M/XM529	8128M/WH775
7499M/WT555	7806M/TA639	7980M/XM561	8131M/WT507
7510M/WT694	7809M/XA699	7982M/XH892	8140M/XJ571

RAF Maintenance cross-reference

8141M/XN688	8366M/XG454	8479M/730301	8638M/XS101
8142M/XJ560	8367M/XG474	8481M/191614	8640M/XR977
8143M/XN691	8368M/XF926	8482M/112372/(VK893)	8642M/XR537
8147M/XR526	8369M/WE139	8483M/420430	8645M/XD163
8151M/WV795	8370M/N1671	8484M/5439	8648M/XK526
8153M/WV903	8371M/XA847	8485M/997	8653M/XS120
8154M/WV908	8372M/K8042	8486M/BAPC 99	8655M/XN126
8155M/WV797	8373M/P2617	8487M/J-1172	8656M/XP405
8156M/XE339	8375M/NX611	8488M/WL627	8657M/VZ634
8158M/XE369	8376M/RF398	8491M/WJ880	8661M/XJ727
8159M/XD528	8377M/R9125	8492M/WJ872	8662M/XR458
8160M/XD622	8378M/*T9707*	8493M/XR571	8664M/WJ603
8161M/XE993	8379M/DG590	8494M/XP557	8666M/XE793
8162M/WM913	8380M/Z7197	8495M/XR672	8667M/WP972
8163M/XP919	8382M/VR930	8498M/XR670	8668M/WJ821
8164M/*WN105*/(WF299)	8383M/K9942	8501M/XP640	8671M/XJ435
8165M/WH791	8384M/X4590	8502M/XP686	8672M/XP351
8169M/WH364	8385M/N5912	8503M/XS451	8673M/XD165
8171M/XJ607	8386M/NV778	8507M/XS215	8674M/XP395
8173M/XN685	8387M/T6296	8508M/XS218	8676M/XL577
8176M/WH791	8388M/XL993	8509M/XT141	8677M/*XF519*/(XJ695)
8177M/*WM311*/(WM224)	8389M/VX573	8513M/XN724	8678M/XE656
8179M/XN928	8392M/SL674	8514M/XS176	8679M/XF526
8180M/XN930	8393M/XK987	8535M/XN776	8680M/XF527
8182M/XN953	8394M/WG422	8538M/XN781	8681M/XG164
8183M/*XN972*/(XN962)	8395M/WF408	8546M/XN728	8682M/XP404
8184M/WT520	8396M/XK740	8548M/WT507	8684M/XJ634
8185M/WH946	8399M/WR539	8549M/WT534	8687M/XJ639
8186M/WR977	8401M/XP686	8551M/XN774	8689M/WK144
8187M/WH791	8402M/XN769	8554M/TG511	8693M/WH863
8189M/WD646	8406M/XP831	8560M/XR569	8696M/WH773
8190M/XJ918	8407M/XP585	8565M/*WT720*/(E-408)	8699M/ZD232
8192M/XR658	8408M/XS186	8566M/XV279	8700M/ZD234
8196M/XE920	8409M/XS209	8568M/XP503	8702M/XG196
8198M/WT339	8410M/XR662	8569M/XR535	8703M/VW453
8203M/XD377	8413M/XM192	8570M/XR954	8704M/XN643
8205M/XN819	8414M/XM173	8573M/XM708	8706M/XF383
8206M/WG419	8417M/XM144	8575M/XP542	8708M/XF509
8207M/WD318	8422M/XM169	8576M/XP502	8709M/XG209
8208M/WG303	8427M/XM172	8578M/XR534	8710M/XG274
8209M/WG418	8429M/XH592	8581M/WJ775	8711M/XG290
8210M/WG471	8431M/XR651	8582M/XE874	8713M/XG225
8211M/WK570	8435M/XN512	8583M/BAPC 94	8714M/XK149
8213M/WK626	8436M/XN554	8584M/WH903	8718M/XX396
8214M/WP864	8437M/WG362	8585M/XE670	8719M/XT257
8215M/WP869	8439M/WZ846	8586M/XE643	8720M/XP353
8216M/WP927	8440M/WD935	8587M/XP677	8721M/XP354
8217M/WZ866	8442M/XP411	8588M/XR681	8723M/XL567
8229M/XM355	8445M/XK968	8589M/XR700	8724M/XW923
8230M/XM362	8447M/XP359	8590M/XM191	8726M/XP299
8231M/XM375	8453M/XP745	8591M/XA813	8727M/XR486
8232M/XM381	8457M/XS871	8595M/XH278	8728M/WT532
8234M/XN458	8458M/XP672	8596M/LH208	8729M/WJ815
8235M/XN549	8459M/XR650	8598M/WP270	8730M/XD186
8236M/XP573	8460M/XP680	8600M/XX761	8731M/XP361
8237M/XS179	8462M/XX477	8602M/*PF179*/(XR541)	8732M/XJ729
8238M/XS180	8463M/XP355	8606M/XP530	8733M/XL318
8333M/XM408	8464M/XJ758	8608M/XP540	8736M/XF375
8344M/WH960	8465M/W1048	8609M/XR953	8739M/XH170
8345M/XG540	8466M/L-866	8610M/XL502	8740M/WE173
8350M/WH840	8467M/WP912	8611M/WF128	8741M/XW329
8352M/XN632	8468M/MM5701/(BT474)	8617M/XM709	8743M/WD790
8355M/*KG374*/(KN645)	8470M/584219	8618M/*XM693*/(XP504)	8746M/XH171
8357M/WK576	8471M/701152	8620M/XP534	8749M/XH537
8359M/WF825	8472M/120227/(VN679)	8621M/XA538	8751M/XT255
8360M/WP863	8473M/WP180/(WP190)	8624M/*XR991*/(XS102)	8753M/WL795
8361M/WB670	8474M/494083	8627M/XP558	8755M/*WH699*/(WJ637)
8362M/WG477	8475M/360043/(PJ876)	8628M/XJ380	8757M/XM656
8363M/WG463	8476M/24	8630M/WG362	8762M/WH740
8364M/WG464	8477M/4101/(DG200)	8631M/XR574	8763M/WH665
8365M/XK421	8478M/10639	8634M/WP314	8764M/XP344

RAF Maintenance cross-reference

8767M/XX635
8768M/A-522
8769M/A-528
8770M/XL623
8771M/XM602
8772M/WR960
8774M/XV338
8777M/XX914
8778M/XM598
8779M/XM607
8780M/WK102
8781M/WE982
8782M/XH136
8783M/XW272
8785M/XS642
8786M/XN495
8791M/XP329
8792M/XP345
8793M/XP346
8794M/XP398
8796M/XK943
8797M/XX947
8799M/WV787
8800M/XG226
8805M/XT772
8806M/XP140
8807M/XL587
8810M/XJ825
8813M/VT260
8814M/XM927
8818M/XK527
8819M/XS479
8820M/VP952
8821M/XX115
8822M/VP957
8824M/VP971
8828M/XS587
8829M/XE653
8830M/XF515
8831M/XG160
8832M/XG172
8833M/XL569
8834M/XL572
8836M/XL592
8838M/*34037*/(429356)
8839M/XG194
8840M/XG252
8844M/XJ676
8845M/XS572
8847M/XX344
8848M/XZ135
8851M/XT595
8852M/XV337
8853M/XT277
8855M/XT284
8857M/XW544
8860M/XW549
8861M/XW528
8862M/XN473
8863M/XG154
8865M/XN641
8867M/XK532
8868M/WH775
8869M/WH957
8870M/WH964
8871M/WJ565
8873M/XR453
8874M/XE597
8875M/XE624
8876M/*VM791*/(XA312)
8877M/XP159

8879M/XX948
8880M/XF435
8881M/XG254
8883M/XX946
8884M/VX275
8886M/XA243
8888M/XA231
8889M/XN239
8890M/WT532
8892M/XL618
8894M/XT669
8895M/XX746
8896M/XX821
8897M/XX969
8898M/XX119
8899M/XX756
8900M/XZ368
8901M/XZ383
8902M/XX739
8903M/XX747
8904M/XX966
8905M/XX975
8906M/XX976
8907M/XZ371
8908M/XZ382
8909M/XV784
8910M/XL160
8911M/XH673
8915M/XH132
8916M/XL163
8917M/XM372
8918M/XX109
8919M/XT486
8920M/XT469
8921M/XT466
8923M/XX819
8924M/XP701
8925M/XP706
8931M/XV779
8932M/XR718
8933M/XX297
8934M/XR749
8935M/XR713
8937M/XX751
8938M/WV746
8939M/XP741
8941M/XT456
8943M/XE799
8944M/WZ791
8945M/XX818
8946M/XZ389
8947M/XX726
8948M/XX757
8949M/XX743
8950M/XX956
8951M/XX727
8952M/XX730
8953M/XX959
8954M/XZ384
8955M/XX110
8956M/XN577
8957M/XN582
8958M/XN501
8959M/XN472
8960M/XM455
0961M/XS925
8967M/XV263
8968M/XM471
8969M/XR753
8972M/XR754
8973M/XS922

8974M/XM473
8978M/XX837
8979M/XV747
8981M/XW764
8983M/XM478
8984M/XN551
8985M/WK127
8986M/XV261
8987M/XM358
8988M/XN593
8990M/XM419
8991M/XR679
8992M/XP547
8995M/XM425
8996M/XM414
8997M/XX669
8998M/XT864
9002M/XW763
9003M/XZ390
9004M/XZ370
9005M/XZ374
9006M/XX967
9007M/XX968
9008M/XX140
9009M/XX763
9010M/XX764
9011M/XM412
9012M/XN494
9014M/XN584
9015M/XW320
9017M/ZE449
9018M/XW365
9019M/XX824
9020M/XX825
9021M/XX826
9022M/XX958
9023M/XX844
9026M/XP629
9027M/XP556
9028M/XP563
9029M/XS217
9030M/XR674
9031M/XP688
9032M/XR673
9033M/XS181
9034M/XP638
9036M/XM350
9037M/XN302
9038M/XV810
9039M/XN586
9040M/XZ138
9041M/XW763
9042M/XL954
9044M/XS177
9045M/XN636
9046M/XM349
9047M/XW409
9048M/XM403
9049M/XW404
9050M/XG577
9052M/WJ717
9053M/XT755
9054M/XT766
9055M/XT770
9056M/XS488
9057M/ZE361
9058M/ZE351
9059M/ZE360
9060M/ZE356
9061M/XW335
9062M/XW351

9064M/XT867
9065M/XV577
9066M/XV582
9067M/XV586
9070M/XV581
9072M/XW768
9073M/XW924
9074M/XV738
9075M/XV753
9076M/XV808
9077M/XZ967
9078M/XV752
9079M/XZ130
9083M/ZE353
9084M/ZE354
9085M/ZE364
9087M/XV753
9090M/XW353
9091M/XW434
9092M/XH669
9093M/WK124
9095M/XW547
9096M/WV322
9097M/XW366
9098M/XV406
9099M/XT900
9100M/XL188
9101M/WL756
9103M/XV411
9107M/XV482
9108M/XT475
9109M/XW312
9110M/XX736
9111M/XW421
9112M/XM475
9113M/XV500
9115M/XV663
9119M/XW303
9120M/XW419
9122M/XZ997
9123M/XT773
9124M/XW427
9125M/XW410
9126M/XW413
9127M/XW432
9128M/XW292
9129M/XW294
9130M/XW327
9131M/*DD931*
9132M/XX977
9133M/*413573*
9134M/XT288
9136M/XT891
9137M/XN579
9139M/XV863
9140M/XZ287
9141M/XV118
9143M/XN589
9144M/XV353
9145M/XV863
9146M/XW299
9147M/XW301
9148M/XW436
9149M/XW375
9150M/*FX760*
9151M/XT907
9152M/XV424
9153M/XW360
9154M/XW321
9155M/WL679
9157M/XV422

RAF Maintenance cross-reference

9158M/XV467	9181M/XW358	9201M	9222M/XZ968
9159M/XV468	9182M	9202M/*433*	9223M/XL616
9162M/XZ991	9183M/*XF519*	9203M/*3066*	9224M/XL568
9163M/XV415	9184M/XZ965	9205M/*E449*	9225M/XX885
9165M/XV408	9185M/XZ987	9206M/F6314	9226M/XV865
9166M/XW323	9186M/XF967	9207M/8417/18	9227M/XB812
9167M/XV744	9187M/XW405	9208M/F938	9228M
9168M/XZ132	9188M/XW364	9209M/164	9229M/ZA678
9169M/XW547	9189M/ZD350	9210M/MF628	9230M
9170M/XZ994	9190M/XW318	9211M/733682	9231M
9171M/XT895	9191M/XW416	9212M/*KL216*(45-49295)	9232M
9172M/XW304	9192M/XW361	9213M/N5182	9233M
9173M/XW418	9193M/XW367	9214M/XL161	9234M
9174M/XZ131	9194M/XW420	9215M/XL164	9235M
9175M/P1344	9195M/XW330	9216M/XL190	9236M
9176M/XW430	9196M/XW370	9217M	9237M/XF995
9177M/XW328	9197M	9218M/XL563	9238M
9178M/XS793	9198M/XS641	9219M/XZ971	9239M
9179M/XW309	9199M/XW290	9220M/XZ995	9240M
9180M/XW311	9200M/XW425	9221M/XZ966	9241M

RN Landing Platform and Shore Station Code-letters

Code	Deck Letters	Vessel Name & Pennant No	Vessel Type & Unit
—	AS	RFA *Argus* (A135)	Aviation Training ship
365/6	AY	HMS *Argyll* (F232)	Type 23 (815 Sqn)
328/9	BA	HMS *Brave* (F94)	Type 22 (815 Sqn)
503/514	BD	DTEO Boscombe Down	(RN 810 Sqn)
—	BE	RFA *Blue Rover* (A270)	Fleet tanker
333	BM	HMS *Birmingham* (D86)	Type 42 (815 Sqn)
342/3	BT	HMS *Brilliant* (F90)	Type 22 (815 Sqn)
—	BV	HMS *Black Rover* (A273)	Fleet tanker
402/3	BX	HMS *Battleaxe* (F89)	Type 22 (815 Sqn)
330/1	BZ	HMS *Brazen* (F91)	Type 22 (815 Sqn)
335	CF	HMS *Cardiff* (D108)	Type 42 (815 Sqn)
350/1	CL	HMS *Cumberland* (F85)	Type 22 (815 Sqn)
515	CM	HMS *Chatham* (F87)	Type 22 (810 Sqn)
338/9	CT	HMS *Campbeltown* (F86)	Type 22 (815 Sqn)
—	CU	RNAS Culdrose (HMS *Seahawk*)	
336/7	CV	HMS *Coventry* (F98)	Type 22 (815 Sqn)
412/3	CW	HMS *Cornwall* (F99)	Type 22 (815 Sqn)
—	DC	HMS *Dumbarton Castle* (P268)	Fishery protection
—	DG	RFA *Diligence* (A132)	Maintenance
411	EB	HMS *Edinburgh* (D97)	Type 42 (815 Sqn)
434/5	ED	HMS *Endurance* (A176)	Ice Patrol (815 Sqn)
420	EX	HMS *Exeter* (D89)	Type 42 (815 Sqn)
—	FA	RFA *Fort Austin* (A386)	Support ship
—	FG	RFA *Fort Grange* (A385)	Support ship
—	FL	RNAY Fleetlands	
—	FS	HMS *Fearless* (L10)	Assault
410	GC	HMS *Gloucester* (D96)	Type 42 (815 Sqn)
—	GD	RFA *Sir Galahad* (L3005)	Landing ship
—	GN	RFA *Green Rover* (A268)	Fleet tanker
—	GR	RFA *Sir Geraint* (L3027)	Landing ship
437	GT	HMS *Grafton* (F241)	Type 23
—	GV	RFA *Gold Rover* (A271)	Fleet tanker
344	GW	HMS *Glasgow* (D88)	Type 42 (815 Sqn)
—	GY	RFA *Grey Rover* (A269)	Fleet tanker
—	HC	HMS *Hecla* (A133)	Survey ship
—	HR	HMS *Herald*	Survey ship
—	ID	HMS *Intrepid* (L11)	Assault
404	IR	HMS *Iron Duke* (F234)	Type 23 (815 Sqn)
—	L	HMS *Illustrious* (R06)	Carrier
457	LA	HMS *Lancaster* (F229)	Type 23 (815 Sqn)
—	LC	HMS *Leeds Castle* (P258)	Fishery protection
405/6	LO	HMS *London* (F95)	Type 22 (815 Sqn)
332	LP	HMS *Liverpool* (D92)	Type 42 (815 Sqn)
363/4	MA	HMS *Marlborough* (F233)	Type 23 (815 Sqn)
360	MC	HMS *Manchester* (D95)	Type 42 (815 Sqn)
415	MM	HMS *Monmouth* (F235)	Type 23 (815 Sqn)
444	MR	HMS *Montrose* (F236)	Type 23 (815 Sqn)
—	N	HMS *Invincible* (R05)	Carrier
345	NC	HMS *Newcastle* (D87)	Type 42 (815 Sqn)
361/2	NF	HMS *Norfolk* (F230)	Type 23 (815 Sqn)
372	NL	HMS *Northumberland* (F238)	Type 23 (815 Sqn)
417	NM	HMS *Nottingham* (D91)	Type 42 (815 Sqn)
—	OD	RFA *Olmeda* (A124)	Fleet tanker
—	ON	RFA *Olna* (A123)	Fleet tanker
—	OW	RFA *Olwen* (A122)	Fleet tanker
—	PO	RNAS Portland (HMS *Osprey*)	
—	PV	RFA *Sir Percival* (L3036)	Landing ship
—	PW	Prestwick Airport (HMS *Gannet*)	
—	R	HMS *Ark Royal* (R09)	Carrier
—	RG	RFA *Regent* (A486)	Support ship
474	RM	HMS *Richmond* (F239)	Type 23 (815 Sqn)

RN Landing Platforms

Code	Deck Letters	Vessel Name & Pennant No	Vessel Type & Unit
—	RS	RFA *Resource* (A480)	Support ship
352/3	SD	HMS *Sheffield* (F96)	Type 23 (815 Sqn)
355	SM	HMS *Somerset* (F240)	Type 23 (815 Sqn)
334	SN	HMS *Southampton* (D90)	Type 42 (815 Sqn)
422	SU	HMS *Sutherland* (F242)	Type 23
—	TM	RFA *Sir Tristram* (L3505)	Landing ship
374/5	VB	HMS *Beaver* (F93)	Type 22 (815 Sqn)
—	VL	RNAS Yeovilton (HMS *Heron*)	
462	WM	HMS *Westminster* (F237)	Type 23 (815 Sqn)
376	XB	HMS *Boxer* (F92)	Type 22 (815 Sqn)
407	YK	HMS *York* (D98)	Type 42 (815 Sqn)
—	—	RFA *Fort Victoria* (A387)	Auxiliary Oiler
—	—	RFA *Fort George* (A388)	Auxiliary Oiler

"See foregoing separate ships' Deck Letter Analysis

Note that only the 'last two' digits of the Code are worn by some aircraft types, especially helicopters.

Sea King HC4 ZE426 of 848 Sqn flying from RNAS Yeovilton. *PRM*

Ships' Numeric Code – Deck Letters Analysis

	0	1	2	3	4	5	6	7	8	9
32				AB					BA	BA
33	BZ	BZ	LP	BM	SN	CF	CV	CV	CT	CT
34			BT	BT	GW	NC				
35	CL	CL	SD	SD		SM				
36	MC	NF	NF	MA	MA	AY	AY			
37			NL		VB	VB	XB			
40			BX	BX	IR	LO	LO	YK		
41	GC	EB	CW	CW		MM		NM		
42	EX		SU							
43					ED	ED		GT		
44					MR					
45								LA		
46			WM							
47			AM		RM					

RN Code – Squadron – Base – Aircraft Cross-Check

Deck/Base Code Numbers	Letters	Unit	Location	Aircraft Type(s)
000 — 005	R	801 Sqn	Yeovilton	Sea Harrier FA2
010 — 020	L/R	820 Sqn	Culdrose	Sea King HAS6
122 — 129	N	800 Sqn	Yeovilton	Sea Harrier FA2
180 — 187	L/R	849 Sqn	Culdrose	Sea King AEW2A
264 — 274	N	814 Sqn	Culdrose	Sea King HAS6
300 — 308	PO	815 Sqn	Portland	Lynx HAS3
320 — 479	*	815 Sqn	Portland	Lynx HAS3
500 — 515	CU	810 Sqn	Culdrose	Sea King HAS6
538 — 559	CU	705 Sqn	Culdrose	Gazelle HT2
560 — 575	CU	750 Sqn	Culdrose	Jetstream T2
576 — 579	—	FONA	Yeovilton	Jetstream T3
580 — 599	—	706 Sqn	Culdrose	Sea King HAS6
630 — 638	PO	702 Sqn	Portland	Lynx HAS3
640 — 648	PO	702 Sqn	Portland	Lynx HAS3
670 — 672	PO	815 Sqn OEU	Portland	Lynx HMA8
699 — 709	PW	819 Sqn	Prestwick	Sea King HAS6
710 — 717	VL	899 Sqn	Yeovilton	Sea Harrier FA2
718 — 722	VL	899 Sqn	Yeovilton	Harrier T4/T4N/T8
820 — 826	CU	771 Sqn	Culdrose	Sea King HAR5

*See foregoing separate ships' Deck Letter Analysis
Note that only the 'last two' digits of the Code are worn by some aircraft types, especially helicopters.

Replica Fokker Dr.1 Dreidekker 450/17 is operated from Middle Wallop. *PRM*

This Hawker Fury FB10 wears R Netherlands Air Force markings. *PRM*

British-based Historic Aircraft in Overseas Markings

Some *historic, classic and warbird* aircraft carry the markings of overseas air arms and can be seen in the UK, mainly preserved in museums and collections or taking part in air shows.

Notes	Serial	Type (other identity)	Owner/operator, location
	Argentina		
	0729	Beech T-34C Turbo Mentor	FAA Museum, stored Wroughton
	0767	Aermacchi MB339AA	Rolls-Royce, Filton
	A-515	FMA IA58 Pucara (ZD485)	RAF Cosford Aerospace Museum
	A-517	FMA IA58 Pucara (G-BLRP)	Privately owned, Channel Islands
	A-522	FMA IA58 Pucara (8768M)	North-East Aircraft Museum, Usworth
	A-528	FMA IA58 Pucara (8769M)	Norfolk & Suffolk Aviation Museum, Flixton
	A-533	FMA IA58 Pucara (ZD486)	Museum of Army Flying, Middle Wallop
	A-549	FMA IA58 Pucara (ZD487)	Imperial War Museum, Duxford
	AE-406	Bell UH-1H Iroquois	Museum of Army Flying, Middle Wallop
	AE-409	Bell UH-1H Iroquois [656]	Museum of Army Flying, Middle Wallop
	AE-422	Bell UH-1H Iroquois	FAA Museum, RNAS Yeovilton
	Australia		
	A2-4	Supermarine Seagull V (VH-ALB)	RAF Museum, Hendon
	A8-324	Bristol 156 Beaufighter X	The Fighter Collection, Duxford
	A16-199	Lockheed Hudson IIIA (G-BEOX) [SF-R]	RAF Museum, Hendon
	A17-48	DH82A Tiger Moth (G-BPHR)	Privately owned, Swindon
	A19-144	Bristol 156 Beaufighter XIC (JM135)	The Fighter Collection, Duxford
	A68-192	CAC-18 Mustang 23 (G-HAEC)	The Old Flying Machine Company, Duxford
	A92-480	GAF Jindivik 4A	DTEO Llanbedr, on display
	A92-664	GAF Jindivik 4A	Maes Artro Craft Village, Llanbedr
	Belgium		
	FT-36	Lockheed T-33A	Dumfries & Galloway Av'n Mus, Tinwald Downs
	HD-75	Hanriot HD1 (G-AFDX)	RAF Museum, Hendon
	MT-11	Fouga CM-170R Magister (G-BRFU)	Privately owned, North Weald
	SG-3	VS379 Spitfire FR XIV (SG-31/ G-BSKP)	Privately owned, Duxford
	Brazil		
	1317	Embraer T-27 Tucano	Shorts, Belfast (engine test bed)
	Canada		
	622	Piasecki HUP-3 Retriever (116622/N6699D)	IHM, Weston-super-Mare
	920	VS Stranraer (CF-BXO) [Q-N]	RAF Museum, Hendon
	9059	Bristol 149 Bolingbroke IVT	Privately owned, Portsmouth
	9754	Consolidated PBY-5A Catalina (VR-BPS) [P]	Plane Sailing Ltd, Duxford
	9893	Bristol 149 Bolingbroke IVT	Imperial War Museum store, Duxford
	9940	Bristol 149 Bolingbroke IVT	Royal Scottish Mus'm of Flight, E Fortune
	16693	Auster J/1N Alpha (G-BLPG) [693]	Privately owned, Headcorn
	18013	DHC1 Chipmunk 22 (G-TRIC) [013]	Privately owned, North Weald
	18393	Avro Canada CF-100 (G-BCYK) [671]	Imperial War Museum, Duxford
	18671	DHC1 Chipmunk 22 (G-BNZC)	Privately owned, Wombleton
	20310	CCF T-6J Harvard IV (G-BSBG)	Privately owned, Liverpool
	20385	CCF T-6J Harvard IV (G-BGPB)	The Aircraft Restoration Co, Duxford
	21417	Canadair CT-133 Silver Star	Yorkshire Air Museum, Elvington
	23140	Canadair CL-13 Sabre [AX] (fuselage)	Midland Air Museum, Coventry

Serial	Type (other identity)	Owner/operator, location	Notes
China			
1532008	Nanchang CJ-6A (G-BVFX) [08]	Privately owned, Slinfold	
Croatia			
5	Nord 1203 (G-BEDB)	Privately owned, Chirk	
Czech Republic			
3309	Mikoyan MiG-15	Royal Scottish Museum of Flight, E Fortune	
3794	Letov S-102 (MiG-15) (623794)	Imperial War Museum, Duxford	
9147	Mil Mi-4	IHM, Weston-super-Mare	
Denmark			
A-011	SAAB A-35XD Draken	NATO Aircraft Museum, New Waltham, Humberside	
AR-107	SAAB S-35XD Draken	Newark Air Museum, Winthorpe	
E-402	Hawker Hunter F51	Privately owned, Staverton	
E-409	Hawker Hunter F51 (*XF383*)	City of Norwich Aviation Museum	
E-419	Hawker Hunter F51	North-East Aircraft Museum, Usworth	
E-420	Hawker Hunter F51 (G-9-442)	Privately owned, Marlow	
E-421	Hawker Hunter F51	Brooklands Museum, Weybridge	
E-423	Hawker Hunter F51 (G-9-444)	SWWAPS, Lasham	
E-424	Hawker Hunter F51 (G-9-445)	South Yorkshire Air Museum, Firbeck	
E-425	Hawker Hunter F51	Midland Air Museum, Coventry	
E-430	Hawker Hunter F51	Privately owned, Charlwood, Surrey	
ET-273	Hawker Hunter T7 <ff>	Jet Heritage Ltd, Bournemouth	
L-866	Consolidated PBY-6A Catalina (8466M)	RAF Cosford Aerospace Museum	
R-756	Lockheed F-104G Starfighter	Midland Air Museum, Coventry	
S-881	Sikorsky S-55C	IHM, Weston-super-Mare	
S-882	Sikorsky S-55C	IHM, Weston-super-Mare	
S-885	Sikorsky S-55C	Privately owned,	
S-886	Sikorsky S-55C	IHM, Weston-super-Mare	
S-887	Sikorsky S-55C	IHM, Weston-super-Mare	
Egypt			
0446	Mikoyan MiG-21UM <ff>	The Air Defence Collection, Salisbury	
2684	Mikoyan MiG-19	DERA Farnborough Fire Section	
7907	Sukhoi Su-7 <ff>	Robertsbridge Aviation Society, Headcorn	
France			
37	Nord 3400 (G-ZARA) [MAB]	Privately owned, Boston	
57	Dassault Mystère IVA [8-MT]	Imperial War Museum, Duxford	
59	Dassault Mystère IVA [2-SF]	Wales Aircraft Museum, Cardiff	
68	Nord 3400 [MHA]	Privately owned, Coventry	
70	Dassault Mystère IVA	Midland Air Museum, Coventry	
79	Dassault Mystère IVA [8-NB]	Norfolk & Suffolk Aviation Museum, Flixton	
83	Dassault Mystère IVA [8-MS]	Newark Air Museum, Winthorpe	
84	Dassault Mystère IVA [8-NF]	Robertsbridge Aviation Society, Headcorn	
85	Dassault Mystère IVA [8-MV]	Privately owned, Bruntingthorpe	
101	Dassault Mystère IVA [8-MN]	Bomber County Aviation Museum, Hemswell	
FR108	SO1221 Djinn [CDL]	IHM, Weston-super-Mare	
120	SNCAN Stampe SV4C (G-AZGC)	Privately owned, Reading	
121	Dassault Mystère IVA	City of Norwich Aviation Museum	
143	Morane-Saulnier MS733 Alcyon (G-MSAL)	Privately owned, Booker	
FR145	SO1221 Djinn [CDL]	Privately owned, Luton Airport	
146	Dassault Mystère IVA [8-MC]	North-East Aircraft Museum, Usworth	
157	Morane MS230 (G-AVEB) [01/M573]	Privately owned, Booker	
192	MH1521M Broussard (G-BKPT) [44-GI]	Privately owned, Rednal	
318	Dassault Mystère IVA [8-NY]	Dumfries & Galloway Av'n Mus, Tinwald Downs	
319	Dassault Mystère IVA [8-ND]	Rebel Air Museum, Andrewsfield	
538	Dassault Mirage IIIE	Yorkshire Air Museum, Elvington	
14286	Lockheed T-33A [WK]	Imperial War Museum, Duxford	
42204	NA F-100D Super Sabre [11-MQ]	RAF Alconbury	
63938	NA F-100F Super Sabre [11-MU]	Lashenden Air Warfare Museum, Headcorn	

Historic Aircraft

Notes	Serial	Type (other identity)	Owner/operator, location
	18-1528	PA-18 Cub 95 (F-MBCH)	Privately owned, stored Southampton
	MS824	Morane-Saulnier Type N <R> (G-AWBU)	Privately owned, Booker
	S3398	Spad X.III <R> (G-BFYO) [2]	FAA Museum, RNAS Yeovilton
	S4523	Spad S.VII (N4727V) [1]	Imperial War Museum, Duxford
	Germany		
	C850	Albatros D.V <R>	Macclesfield Hist Av'n Society
	D5397/17	Albatros D.VA <R> (G-BFXL)	FAA Museum, RNAS Yeovilton
	1Z+NK	Amiot AAC1 (Port.AF 6316)	Imperial War Museum, Duxford
	LG+01	Bucker Bu.133C Jungmeister (G-AYSJ)	The Fighter Collection, Duxford
	LG+03	Bucker Bu.133C Jungmeister (G-AEZX)	Privately owned, Milden
	BU+CC	CASA 1.131E Jungmann (G-BUCC)	Privately owned, Goodwood
	BU+CK	CASA 1.131E Jungmann (G-BUCK)	Privately owned, White Waltham
	S5+B06	CASA 1.131E Jungmann 2000 (G-BSFB)	Privately owned, Stretton
	6J+PR	CASA 2.111D (G-AWHB)	Aces High Ltd, North Weald
	14	Fiat G.46-3B (G-BBII)	Privately owned, stored Rendcomb
	—	Fieseler Fi103 (V-1) (BAPC 36)	Kent Battle of Britain Mus'm, Hawkinge
	—	Fieseler Fi103 (V-1) (BAPC 91)	Lashenden Air Warfare Museum, Headcorn
	—	Fieseler Fi103 (V-1) (BAPC 92)	RAF Museum, Hendon
	—	Fieseler Fi103 (V-1) (BAPC 93)	Imperial War Museum, Duxford
	—	Fieseler Fi103 (V-1) (8583M/BAPC 94)	RAF Cosford Aerospace Museum
	—	Fieseler Fi103 (V-1) (BAPC 158)	Defence School, Chattenden
	477663	Fieseler Fi103 (V-1) (BAPC 198)	Imperial War Museum, Lambeth
	442795	Fieseler Fi103 (V-1) (BAPC 199)	Science Museum, South Kensington
	475081	Fieseler Fi156C-7 Storch (7362M) [GM+AK]	RAF Cosford Aerospace Museum
	28368	Flettner Fl282/B-V20 Kolibri (frame only)	Midland Air Museum, Coventry
	100143	Focke-Achgelis Fa330A	Imperial War Museum, Duxford
	100502	Focke-Achgelis Fa330A	The Real Aeroplane Company, Breighton
	100509	Focke-Achgelis Fa330A	Science Museum, stored South Kensington
	100545	Focke-Achgelis Fa330A	Fleet Air Arm Museum stored, Wroughton
	100549	Focke-Achgelis Fa330A	Lashenden Air Warfare Museum, Headcorn
	112100	Focke Wulf Fw189A-1 [V7+1H]	Privately owned, Lancing
	2+1	Focke Wulf Fw190 <R> (G-SYFW) [7334]	Privately owned, Guernsey, CI
	4	Focke Wulf Fw190 <R> (G-BSLX)	Privately owned, Shoreham
	+8	Focke Wulf Fw190 <R> (G-WULF)	Privately owned, Breighton
	5415	Focke Wulf Fw190A-4	The Old Flying Machine Company, USA
	733682	Focke Wulf Fw190A-8/R7 (9211M)	Imperial War Museum, Lambeth
	584219	Focke Wulf Fw190F-8/U1 (8470M) [38]	RAF Museum, Hendon
	4253/18	Fokker D.VII <R> (G-BFPL)	Privately owned, North Weald
	626/18	Fokker D.VII <R> (N6268)	Blue Max Movie Aircraft Museum, Booker
	8417/18	Fokker D.VII (9207M)	RAF Museum Restoration Centre, Cardington
	102/17	Fokker Dr.1 Dreidekker <R> (BAPC 88)	FAA Museum, RNAS Yeovilton
	152/17	Fokker Dr.1 Dreidekker <R> (G-ATJM)	The Old Flying Machine Company
	425/17	Fokker Dr.1 Dreidekker <R> (BAPC 133)	Newark Air Museum, Winthorpe
	450/17	Fokker Dr.1 Dreidekker <R> (G-BVGZ)	Museum of Army Flying, Middle Wallop
	210/16	Fokker EIII (BAPC 56)	Science Museum, South Kensington
	422/15	Fokker EIII <R> (G-AVJO)	Privately owned, Booker

Serial	Type (other identity)	Owner/operator, location	Notes
701152	Heinkel He111H-23 (8471M) [NT+SL]	RAF Museum, Hendon	
120227	Heinkel He162A-2 Salamander (8472M) [2]	RAF Museum, Hendon	
120235	Heinkel He162A Salamander	Imperial War Museum, Lambeth	
166238	Hispano HA 1.112MIL Buchon (G-BOML) [3]	The Old Flying Machine Company, Duxford	
494083	Junkers Ju87G-2 (8474M) [RI+JK]	RAF Museum, Hendon	
5858	Junkers Ju87R-4 [L1+BL]	Privately owned, Milden	
360043	Junkers Ju88R-1 (8475M) [D5+EV]	RAF Museum, Hendon	
22+35	Lockheed F-104G Starfighter	SWWAPS, Lasham	
22+57	Lockheed F-104G Starfighter	NATO Aircraft Museum, New Waltham, Humberside	
7198/18	LVG C.VI (G-AANJ)	The Shuttleworth Collection, Old Warden	
14	Messerschmitt Bf109 <R> (BAPC 67)	Kent Battle of Britain Museum, Hawkinge	
1480	Messerschmitt Bf109 <R> (BAPC 66) [6]	Kent Battle of Britain Museum, Hawkinge	
6357	Messerschmitt Bf109 <R> (BAPC 74) [6]	Kent Battle of Britain Museum, Hawkinge	
1190	Messerschmitt Bf109E-3	Privately owned, Bournemouth	
1342	Messerschmitt Bf109E	Privately owned, Colchester	
3579	Messerschmitt Bf109E-1	Privately owned, Colchester	
4101	Messerschmitt Bf109E-3 (8477M) [12]	RAF Museum, Hendon	
8147	Messerschmitt Bf109F-4	Privately owned, Colchester	
10132	Messerschmitt Bf109F-4	Privately owned, Milden	
10639	Messerschmitt Bf109G-2/Trop (8478M/G-USTV) [6]	Imperial War Museum, Duxford	
151591	Messerschmitt Bf109G-10 (D-FEHD) [2]	Privately owned, Duxford	
3235	Messerschmitt Bf110C-4 [LN+ER]	Privately owned, Lancing	
4502	Messerschmitt Bf110E-2 [M8+ZE]	Privately owned, Lancing	
5052	Messerschmitt Bf110F-2	Privately owned, Lancing	
730301	Messerschmitt Bf110G-4 (8479M) [D5+RL]	RAF Museum, Hendon	
191316	Messerschmitt Me163B Komet	Science Museum, South Kensington	
191614	Messerschmitt Me163B Komet (8481M)	RAF Cosford Aerospace Museum	
191659	Messerschmitt Me163B Komet (8480M) [15]	Royal Scottish Mus'm of Flight, E Fortune	
191660	Messerschmitt Me163B Komet [3]	Imperial War Museum, Duxford	
112372	Messerschmitt Me262A-2a (8482M) [9K-XK]	RAF Cosford Aerospace Museum	
420430	Messerschmitt Me410A-1/U2 (8483M) [3U+CC]	RAF Cosford Aerospace Museum	
959	Mikoyan MiG-21SPS	The Old Flying Machine Company, Duxford	
20+48	Mikoyan MiG-23BN [702]	DTEO Boscombe Down	
96+26	Mil Mi-24D	IHM, Weston-super-Mare	
7A+WN	Morane-Saulnier MS500 (G-AZMH)	The Old Flying Machine Company, Duxford	
CF+HF	Morane-Saulnier MS502 (EI-AUY)	Imperial War Museum, Duxford	
FI+S	Morane-Saulnier MS505 (G-BIRW)	Royal Scottish Mus'm of Flight, E Fortune	
TA+RC	Morane-Saulnier MS505 (G-BPHZ)	The Aircraft Restoration Co, Duxford	
NJ+C11	Nord 1002 (G-ATBG)	Privately owned, Duxford	
14	Pilatus P-2 (G-BJAX)	Privately owned, stored Duxford	
CC+43	Pilatus P-2 (G-CJCI)	Privately owned, Norwich	
97+04	Putzer Elster B (G-APVF)	Privately owned, Tadlow	
14	SNCAN 1101 Noralpha (G-BSMD)	Privately owned, Breighton	
D-692	Staaken Z-1 Flitzer (G-BVAW)	Privately owned, Aberdare	
AM+YA	Zlin Z.381 Bestmann (G-AMYA)	Privately owned, Wombleton, N. Yorks	
Ghana			
G-102	SA122 Bulldog	Privately owned, Henstridge	
G 103	SA122 Bulldog (G-BWIB)	Privately owned, Henstridge	
G-105	SA122 Bulldog	Privately owned, Henstridge	
G-107	SA122 Bulldog (G-BCUO)	Privately owned, Henstridge	
G-108	SA122 Bulldog (G-BCUP)	Privately owned, Henstridge	
G-111	SA122 Bulldog (G-BCUU)	Privately owned, Henstridge	
G-112	SA122 Bulldog (G-BCUV)	Privately owned, Henstridge	

Historic Aircraft

Notes	Serial	Type (other identity)	Owner/operator, location
	G-350	PBN 2A Islander 9 (G-BAZW) [A]	Privately owned, Pontypridd
	G-351	PBN 2A Islander 9 (G-BAZZ) [B]	Privately owned, Pontypridd
	G-352	PBN 2A Islander 9 (G-BBAL) [C]	Privately owned, Pontypridd
	G-353	PBN 2A Islander 9 (G-BBAM) [D]	Privately owned, Pontypridd
	G-354	PBN 2A Islander 9 (G-BBAN) [E]	Privately owned, Pontypridd
	G-355	PBN 2A Islander 9 (G-BBAO) [F]	Privately owned, Pontypridd
	G-356	PBN 2A Islander 9 (G-BBDW) [G]	Privately owned, Pontypridd
	G-357	PBN 2A Islander 9 (G-BBDX) [H]	Privately owned, Pontypridd
	Greece		
	52-6541	Republic F-84F Thunderflash	North-East Aircraft Museum, Usworth
	51-6151	NA F-86D Sabre (51-6171)	North-East Aircraft Museum, Usworth
	Hungary		
	501	Mikoyan MiG-21PF	Privately owned, St Athan
	503	Mikoyan MiG-21SMT (G-BRAM)	Aces High, North Weald
	India		
	Q497	EE Canberra T4 (fuselage)	BAe Warton Fire Service
	Iraq		
	243	Hawker Fury FB10 (G-BTTA)	The Old Flying Machine Company, Duxford
	333	DH115 Vampire T55	Military Aircraft Pres'n Grp, Barton
	26186	Bell 214ST (tail only)	Museum of Army Flying, Middle Wallop
	Israel		
	41	NA P-51D Mustang	Privately owned, Teesside Airport
	Italy		
	MM5701	Fiat CR42 (8468M) [13-95]	RAF Museum, Hendon
	MM53211	Fiat G.46-4 (BAPC 79) [ZI-4]	The Aircraft Restoration Co., stored Duxford
	MM53432	NA T-6D Texan [RM-11]	Privately owned, South Wales
	MM53692	CCF T-6G Texan	RAeS Medway Branch, Rochester
	MM54099	NA T-6G Texan (G-BRBC) [RR-56]	Privately owned, Chigwell
	MM542372	PA-18 Super Cub 95	Privately owned, Kesgrave
	W7	Avia FL.3 (G-AGFT)	Privately owned, Leicester
	Japan		
	24	Kawasaki Ki100-1B (8476M/ BAPC 83)	RAF Cosford Aerospace Museum
	5439	Mitsubishi Ki46-III (8484M/ BAPC 84)	RAF Cosford Aerospace Museum
	15-1585	Yokosuka MXY 7 Ohka II (BAPC 58)	FAA Museum, RNAS Yeovilton
	997	Yokosuka MXY 7 Ohka II (8485M/ BAPC 98)	Gr Manchester Mus'm of Science & Industry
	I-13	Yokosuka MXY 7 Ohka II (8486M/ BAPC 99)	RAF Cosford Aerospace Museum
	—	Yokosuka MXY 7 Ohka II (BAPC 159)	Defence School, Chattenden
	Jordan		
	109	DH100 Vampire FB6 (G-BVPO/ J-1106)	RJAF Historic Flight, Bournemouth
	209	DH115 Vampire T55 (G-BVLM/ ZH563)	RJAF Historic Flight, Bournemouth
	800	Hawker Hunter T7 (G-BOOM) [F]	RJAF Historic Flight, Bournemouth
	Netherlands		
	204	Lockheed SP-2H Neptune [V]	RAF Cosford Aerospace Museum
	361	Hawker Fury FB10 (N36SF)	Privately owned, Bournemouth
	B-168	Noorduyn AT-16 Harvard IIB	British Aerial Museum, Duxford (spares use)
	E-15	Fokker S-11 Instructor (G-BIYU)	Privately owned, White Waltham
	E-31	Fokker S-11 Instructor (G-BEPV)	Privately owned, Elstree
	N-202	Hawker Hunter F6 [10] <ff>	Privately owned, Eaglescott
	N-250	Hawker Hunter F6 <ff>	Science Museum, Wroughton
	N-268	Hawker Hunter F6 (Qatar QA-10)	Yorkshire Air Museum, Elvington
	N-315	Hawker Hunter T7	Jet Aviation Preservation Group, Long Marston

Serial	Type (other identity)	Owner/operator, location	Notes
R-163	Piper L-21B Super Cub (54-2453/G-BIRH)	Privately owned, Lee-on-Solent	
R-167	Piper L-21B Super Cub (54-2457/G-LION)	Privately owned, Bishops Stortford	

New Zealand

NZ233	Vickers Varsity T1 (WJ944)	Wales Aircraft Museum, Cardiff	
NZ5648	Goodyear FG-1D Corsair (NX55JP) [1]	Old Flying Machine Co, Duxford	

Norway

56321	Saab S91B Safir (G-BKPY) [U-AB]	Newark Air Museum, Winthorpe	

Poland

05	WSK SM-2 (Mi-2) (1005)	IHM, Weston-super-Mare	
07	WSK SM-1 (Mi-1) (2007)	IHM, Weston-super-Mare	
1120	WSK Lim-2 (MiG-15bis)	RAF Museum, Hendon	
1211	WSK Lim-5 (MiG-17F)	The Old Flying Machine Company, Duxford	
09008	WSK SBLim-2A (MiG-15UTI)	Privately owned, Bruntingthorpe	

Portugal

1662	NA AT-6D Harvard III (EZ341/ G-ELMH)	Privately owned, Sudbury	
1741	CCF Harvard IV (G-HRVD)	Privately owned, Wellesbourne	

Qatar

QA12	Hawker Hunter FGA 78	Lovaux Ltd., Bournemouth (dismantled)	
QP30	WS Lynx Mk 28	RN, stored RNAS Lee-on-Solent	
QP31	WS Lynx Mk 28	RNAY Fleetlands Apprentice School	
QP32	WS Lynx Mk 28	RN, stored RNAY Fleetlands	

Russia (& former Soviet Union)

2	Yakovlev Yak-52 (9311708/G-YAKS)	Privately owned, North Weald	
03	Mil Mi-24D (3532461715415)	Privately owned, Hawarden	
04	Mikoyan MiG-23ML (024003607)	Privately owned, Hawarden	
05	Yakovlev Yak-50 (832507/YL-YAK)	Privately owned, Strathallan	
06	Let L-29 Delfin (591636)	Privately owned, Cumbernauld	
06	Mil Mi-24D (3532464505029)	Privately owned, Hawarden	
07	Yakovlev Yak-18M (G-BMJY)	Privately owned, North Weald	
09	Let L-29 Delfin (591378)	Privately owned, Cumbernauld	
15	Yakovlev Yak-52 (844605/ RA-01361)	Privately owned, Wellesbourne Mountford	
18	Let L-29 Delfin (591771)	Privately owned, Hawarden	
19	Yakovlev Yak-52 (811202/YL-CBI)	Privately owned, Strathallan	
20	Lavochkin La-11	The Fighter Collection, Duxford	
20	Yakovlev Yak-52 (790404/YL-CBJ)	Privately owned, Strathallan	
23	Mikoyan MiG-27D (83712515040)	Privately owned, Hawarden	
26	Yakovlev Yak-52 (9111306/ G-BVXK)	Privately owned, White Waltham	
27	SPP Yak C-11 (G-OYAK)	Privately owned, North Weald	
35	Sukhoi Su-17M-3 (25102)	Privately owned, Hawarden	
36	Let/Yak C-11 (G-KYAK)	The Fighter Collection, Duxford	
37	Let L-29 Delfin (491119)	Privately owned, Cumbernauld	
40	Let L-29 Delfin (491165)	Privately owned, Cumbernauld	
42	Yakovlev Yak-52 (LY-AMU)	Privately owned, North Weald	
50	Mikoyan MiG-23MF (023003508)	Privately owned, Hawarden	
51	Let L-29 Delfin (491273)	Privately owned, Hawarden	
51	Yakovlev Yak-50 (RA-01386)	Privately owned, Swanton Morley	
52	Yakovlev Yak-52 (878202/ LY-AKQ)	Privately owned, Denham	
53	Curtiss P-40C Warhawk (41-13390)	The Fighter Collection, Duxford	
54	Sukhoi Su-17M (69004)	Privately owned, Hawarden	
55	Yakovlev Yak-52 (9111505/ G-BVOK)	Intrepid Aviation, North Weald	
56	Yakovlev Yak-52 (811504/ LY-AKW)	Privately owned, Strathallan	
69	Yakovlev Yak-50 (G-BTZB)	The Fighter Collection, Duxford	
69	Yakovlev Yak-52 (855509/LY-ALS)	Privately owned, North Weald	
71	Mikoyan MiG-27K (61912507006)	Privately owned, Hawarden	

Historic Aircraft

Notes	Serial	Type (other identity)	Owner/operator, location
	72	Yakovlev Yak-52 (9111608/ RA-01325)	Privately owned, Newcastle
	73	Yakovlev Yak-52 (G-YAKK)	Privately owned, Wellesbourne Mountford
	74	Yakovlev Yak-52 (888802/LY-ALG)	Privately owned, Wellesbourne Mountford
	100	Yakovlev Yak-52 (866904/G-YAKI)	Privately owned, Popham
	112	Yakovlev Yak-52 (822610/LY-AFB)	Privately owned, Little Gransden
	1342	Yakovlev Yak-1 (G-BTZD)	Privately owned, Audley End
6247	WSK SBLim-2A (MiG-15UTI) (622047/G-OMIG)	The Old Flying Machine Company, Duxford
165221	WSK-Mielec An-2T (G-BTCU) [77]	Privately owned, Henstridge
	822303	Yakovlev Yak-50 (G-YAKA)	Privately owned, Warminster, Dorset
	899404	Yakovlev Yak-52 (G-CCCP)	Privately owned, Little Gransden
1-12	Yakovlev Yak-52 (9011013/ RA-02293)	Privately owned, Halfpenny Green
	(RK858)	VS361 Spitfire LF IX	The Fighter Collection, Duxford

Singapore

Notes	Serial	Type (other identity)	Owner/operator, location
	311	BAC Strikemaster 84 (N2146S/ G-SARK)	Classic Jets Flying Museum, Biggin Hill

Slovakia

Notes	Serial	Type (other identity)	Owner/operator, location
	7708	Mikoyan MiG-21MF	RAF Benevolent Fund, DTEO Boscombe Down

South Africa

Notes	Serial	Type (other identity)	Owner/operator, location
	6130	Lockheed Ventura II	RAF Cosford Aerospace Museum (stored)

Spain

Notes	Serial	Type (other identity)	Owner/operator, location
	B21-103	CASA 2.111B (He111H-16)	The Old Flying Machine Company, Spain
	C4E-88	Messerschmitt Bf109E	Privately owned, Hungerford
	E3B-153	CASA 1.131E Jungmann (G-BPTS) [781-75]	The Old Flying Machine Company, Duxford
	E3B-369	CASA 1.131E Jungmann (G-BPDM) [781-32]	Privately owned, Shoreham
	E3B-540	CASA 1.131E Jungmann (G-BRSH) [781-25]	Privately owned, Breighton
EM-01	DH60G Moth (G-AAOR) [30-76]	Privately owned, Shoreham
	ES.1-9	CASA 1.133L Jungmeister (G-BVXJ)	Privately owned, Breighton
	ES.1-16	CASA 1.133L Jungmeister	Privately owned, Stretton, Cheshire

Sweden

Notes	Serial	Type (other identity)	Owner/operator, location
	05108	DH60 Moth	Privately owned, Langham
	29640	SAAB J-29F [20-08]	Midland Air Museum, Coventry
	32028	SAAB 32A Lansen (G-BMSG)	Privately owned, Cranfield
	35075	SAAB J-35J Draken [40]	Imperial War Museum, Duxford

Switzerland

Notes	Serial	Type (other identity)	Owner/operator, location
A-10	CASA 1.131E Jungmann (G-BECW)	Privately owned, Headcorn
A-57	CASA 1.131E Jungmann (G-BECT)	Privately owned, Shoreham
	A-806	Pilatus P3-03 (G-BTLL)	Privately owned, Headcorn
	C-558	EKW C-3605	Privately owned, stored Gransden
	J-1008	DH100 Vampire FB6	Mosquito Aircraft Museum, London Colney
	J-1121	DH100 Vampire FB6 <ff>	Jet Heritage, Bournemouth
	J-1149	DH100 Vampire FB6 (G-SWIS)	Jet Heritage, Bournemouth
	J-1172	DH100 Vampire FB6 (8487M)	Gtr Manchester Mus'm of Science & Industry
	J-1539	DH112 Venom FB50	Source Classic Jet Flight, Bournemouth
	J-1573	DH112 Venom FB50 (G-VICI)	Source Classic Jet Flight, Bournemouth
	J-1605	DH112 Venom FB50 (G-BLID)	Privately owned, Charlwood, Surrey
	J-1611	DH112 Venom FB50	Source Classic Jet Flight, Bournemouth
	J-1614	DH112 Venom FB50 (G-BLIE)	Privately owned, Ipswich
	J-1632	DH112 Venom FB50 (G-VNOM)	Privately owned, Cranfield
	J-1704	DH112 Venom FB54	RAF Cosford Aerospace Museum
	J-1758	DH112 Venom FB54 (N203DM)	Aces High Ltd, North Weald
	J-4021	Hawker Hunter F58 (G-BWIU)	Historic Flying Ltd, North Weald

Historic Aircraft

Serial	Type (other identity)	Owner/operator, location	Notes
J-4025	Hawker Hunter F58 (G-BWKC)	RJAF Historic Flight, Bournemouth	
J-4031	Hawker Hunter F58 (G-BWFR)	The Old Flying Machine Company, Duxford	
J-4058	Hawker Hunter F58 (G-BWFS)	The Old Flying Machine Company, Duxford	
J-4075	Hawker Hunter F58 (G-BWKA)	RJAF Historic Flight, Bournemouth	
J-4076	Hawker Hunter F58 (G-HONE)	Privately owned, North Weald	
J-4081	Hawker Hunter F58 (G-BWKB)	RJAF Historic Flight, Bournemouth	
J-4083	Hawker Hunter F58 (G-EGHH)	Jet Heritage, Bournemouth	
J-4087	Hawker Hunter F58 (G-HTWO)	Privately owned, North Weald	
J-4090	Hawker Hunter F58 (G-SIAL)	Privately owned, Exeter	
J-4091	Hawker Hunter F58	British Aviation Heritage, Bruntingthorpe	
U-80	Bucker Bu.133D Jungmeister (G-BUKK)	Privately owned, White Waltham	
U-110	Pilatus P-2 (G-PTWO)	Privately owned, Earls Colne	
U-142	Pilatus P-2 (G-BONE)	Privately owned, Goudhurst	
U-1214	DH115 Vampire T55 (G-DHVV)	Source Classic Jet Flight, Bournemouth	
U-1230	DH115 Vampire T55 (G-DHZZ)	Source Classic Jet Flight, Bournemouth	
U-1234	DH115 Vampire T55 (G-DHAV)	Privately owned, Bridgend	
V-54	SE.3130 Alouette II (G-BVSD)	Privately owned, Shoreham	
USA			
2	Boeing-Stearman N2S-5 Kaydet (G-AZLE)	Privately owned, Denham	
5	Boeing P-26A Peashooter <R> (G-BEEW)	Privately owned, Barton	
23	Fairchild PT-23 (N49272)	Privately owned, Halfpenny Green	
26	Boeing-Stearman A75N-1 Kaydet (G-BAVO)	Privately owned, Streethay, Lichfield	
27	NA SNJ-7 Texan (G-BRVG)	Intrepid Aviation Co, North Weald	
28	Boeing-Stearman PT-13D Kaydet (N8162G)	Privately owned, Swanton Morley	
33	Boeing-Stearman N2S-5 Kaydet (G-THEA)	Privately owned, Sutton Bridge	
41	NA T-6G Texan (G-DDMV) [BA]	Privately owned, Sywell	
44	PA-18 Super Cub 95 (G-BJLH) [33-K]	Privately owned, Felthorpe	
57	WS55 Whirlwind HAS7 (XG592)	Task Force Adventure Park, Cowbridge, S Glam.	
85	WAR P-47 Thunderbolt <R> (G-BTBI)	Privately owned, Manchester	
88	NA P-51D Mustang <R>	The Old Flying Machine Company, stored Duxford	
112	Boeing-Stearman PT-13D Kaydet (G-BSWC)	Privately owned, Old Sarum	
118	Boeing-Stearman PT-13A Kaydet (G-BSDS)	Privately owned, Swanton Morley	
205	Boeing-Stearman A.75N-1 Kaydet (G-BRUJ)	Privately owned, Rendcomb	
208	Boeing-Stearman N2S-5 Kaydet (N75664)	Privately owned, Spanhoe Lodge, Northants	
243	Boeing-Stearman A.75N-1 Kaydet (G-BUKE)	Privately owned, Goodwood	
295	Ryan PT-22 (N56028)	Privately owned, Oaksey Park, Wilts	
379	Boeing-Stearman PT-13D Kaydet (G-BUKE)	Privately owned, Compton Abbas	
441	Boeing-Stearman N2S-4 Kaydet (G-BTFG)	Privately owned, Bryngwyn Bach, Clwyd	
442	Boeing-Stearman PT-17 Kaydet (G-BTFG)	Privately owned, Paddock Wood	
494	Republic F-105G Thunderchief (24434)[LN]	RAF Lakenheath, BDRT	
540	Piper L-4H Cub (G-BCNX)	Privately owned, Monewden	
796	Boeing-Stearman PT-13D Kaydet (N43SV)	Privately owned, Rendcomb	
854	Ryan PT-22 (G-BTBH)	Privately owned, Wellesbourne Mountford	
855	Ryan PT-22 (N56421)	Privately owned, Halfpenny Green	
897	Aeronca 11AC Chief (G-BJEV)	Privately owned, English Bicknor	
1164	Beech D.18S (G-BKGL)	Classic Wings, Duxford	
1180	Boeing-Stearman N2S-3 Kaydet (G-BRSK)	Privately owned, Swanton Morley	
1411	Grumman G.44A Widgeon (N444M)	Privately owned, Biggin Hill	

Historic Aircraft

Notes	Serial	Type (other identity)	Owner/operator, location
	2807	NA T-6G Texan (G-BHTH) [V-103]	Privately owned, Thruxton
	5547	Lockheed T-33A (19036)	Newark Air Museum, Winthorpe
	6771	Republic F-84F Thunderstreak (BAF FU-6)	Cosford Aerospace Museum, store
	7797	Aeronca L-16A (G-BFAF)	Privately owned, Finmere
	8178	NA F-86A Sabre (48-0178/ G-SABR) [FU-178]	Golden Apple Operations/OFMC, Duxford
	01532	Northrop F-5E Tiger II <R>	RAF Alconbury on display
	14419	Lockheed T-33A	Midland Air Museum, Coventry
	14863	NA AT-6D Harvard III (G-BGOR)	Privately owned, Goudhurst, Kent
	15195	Fairchild PT-19A Cornell	RAF Museum, stored Cardington
	16443	Hughes OH-6A Cayuse (FY67)	IHM, Weston-super-Mare
	16579	Bell UH-1H Iroquois (FY66)	IHM, Weston-super-Mare
	16718	Lockheed T-33A	City of Norwich Aviation Museum
	17473	Lockheed T-33A	Midland Air Museum, Coventry
	17657	Douglas A-26K Invader <ff>	Booker Aircraft Museum
	O-17899	Convair VT-29B	Imperial War Museum, Duxford
	19252	Lockheed T-33A	Tangmere Military Aviation Museum
	24518	Kaman HH-43F Huskie (24535)	Midland Air Museum, Coventry
	28521	CCF Harvard IV (G-TVIJ) [TA-521]	Privately owned, Shoreham
	29963	Lockheed T-33A	Wales Aircraft Museum, Cardiff
	30861	NA TB-25J Mitchell (N9089Z)	Privately owned, North Weald
	31952	Aeronca O-58B Defender (G-BRPR)	Privately owned, Earls Colne
	32947	Piper L-4H Cub (G-BGXA/329471) [44-F]	Privately owned, Martley, Worcs
	34037	NA TB-25N Mitchell (N9115Z/ 8838M)	RAF Museum, Hendon
	37414	McD F-4C Phantom (FY63)	Midland Air Museum, Coventry
	37699	McD F-4C Phantom (FY63)	Midland Air Museum, Coventry
	38674	Thomas-Morse S4 Scout <R> (G-MTKM)	Privately owned, Rugby
	39624	Wag Aero Sport Trainer (G-BVMH) [39-D]	Privately owned, Lincoln
	40467	Grumman F6F-5K Hellcat (G-BTCC) [19]	The Fighter Collection, Duxford
	40707	McD F-4C Phantom (FY64)	RAF Lakenheath, BDRT
	41386	Thomas-Morse S4 Scout <R> (G-MJTD)	Privately owned, Hitchin
	42157	NA F-100D Super Sabre	North-East Aviation Museum, Usworth
	42163	NA F-100D Super Sabre [HE]	Dumfries & Galloway Av'n Mus, Tinwald Downs
	42165	NA F-100D Super Sabre [VM]	Imperial War Museum, Duxford
	42174	NA F-100D Super Sabre [UH]	Midland Air Museum, Coventry
	42196	NA F-100D Super Sabre [LT]	Norfolk & Suffolk Aviation Museum, Flixton
	42223	NA F-100D Super Sabre	Newark Air Museum, Winthorpe
	53319	Grumman TBM-3R Avenger (G-BTDP) [319-RB]	Privately owned, North Weald
	54137	CCF Harvard IV (G-CTKL) [69]	Privately owned, Duxford
	54433	Lockheed T-33A	Norfolk & Suffolk Av'n Museum, Flixton
	54439	Lockheed T-33A	North-East Aircraft Museum, Usworth
	60312	McDonnell F-101F Voodoo [AR]	Midland Air Museum, Coventry
	60689	Boeing B-52D Stratofortress	Imperial War Museum, Duxford
	63000	NA F-100D Super Sabre (42160) [FW-000]	Wales Aircraft Museum, Cardiff
	63000	NA F-100D Super Sabre (42212) [FW-000]	USAF Croughton, Oxon, at gate
	63319	NA F-100D Super Sabre (42269) [FW-319]	RAF Lakenheath, on display
	63428	Republic F-105G Thunderchief (24428)	USAF Croughton, Oxon, at gate
	66692	Lockheed U-2CT	Imperial War Museum, Duxford
	70270	McDonnell F-101B Voodoo (fuse)	Midland Air Museum, Coventry
	80260	McDonnell F-101B Voodoo	Midland Air Museum, Coventry
	82062	DHC U-6A Beaver	Midland Air Museum, Coventry
	88297	Goodyear FG-1D Corsair (G-FGID) [29]	The Fighter Collection, Duxford
	91007	Lockheed T-33A (G-NASA) [TR-007]	Privately owned, Bruntingthorpe
	93542	CCF Harvard IV (G-BRLV) [LTA-542]	Privately owned, White Waltham

118

Serial	Type (other identity)	Owner/operator, location	Notes
111836	NA AT-6C Harvard IIA (G-TSIX) [JZ-6]	Privately owned, Breighton	
111989	Cessna L-19A Bird Dog (N33600)	Museum of Army Flying, Middle Wallop	
115042	NA T-6G Texan (G-BGHU) [TA-042]	Privately owned, Headcorn	
115302	Piper L-18C Super Cub (G-BJTP)	Privately owned, Winterbourne, Bristol	
115684	Piper L-21A Super Cub (G-BKVM) [D-C]	Privately owned, Woodhall Spa	
121714	Grumman F8F-2P Bearcat (NX700HL) [100-S]	The Fighter Collection, Duxford	
121752	Grumman F8F-2P Bearcat (N800H) [106-A]	The Fighter Collection, Duxford	
122351	Beech C-45G (G-BKRG)	Aces High, North Weald	
124485	Boeing B-17G Fortress (G-BEDF) [DF-A]	B-17 Preservation Ltd., Duxford	
126922	Douglas AD-4NA Skyraider (G-RAID) [402-AK]	The Fighter Collection, Duxford	
140547	NA T-28C Trojan (N2800Q)	Privately owned	
146289	NA T-28C Trojan (N99153) [2W]	Norfolk & Suffolk Aviation Museum, Flixton	
150225	WS58 Wessex 60 (G-AWOX) [123]	IHM, Weston-super-Mare	
151632	NA TB-25N Mitchell (G-BWGR)	Aces High Ltd, North Weald	
153008	McD F-4N Phantom	RAF Alconbury, BDRT	
155529	McD F-4S Phantom (ZE359) [AJ-114]	Imperial War Museum, Duxford	
155848	McD F-4S Phantom [WT-11]	FAA Museum stored, RNAS Yeovilton	
159233	McD AV-8A Harrier [CG-33]	FAA Museum, RNAS Yeovilton	
160810	Bell AH-1T Sea Cobra <ff>	GEC, Rochester	
211072	Boeing-Stearman PT-17 Kaydet (N50755)	Privately owned, Swanton Morley	
217786	Boeing-Stearman PT-13D Kaydet (G-BRTK) [177]	Privately owned, Swanton Morley	
219993	Bell P-39Q Airacobra (N319DP)	The Fighter Collection, Duxford	
224211	Douglas C-47A Dakota (G-BPMP) [M2-Z]	Privately owned, Coventry	
226671	Republic P-47M Thunderbolt (NX47DD)[MX-X]	The Fighter Collection, Duxford	
231983	Boeing B-17G Fortress (F-BDRS) [IY-G]	Imperial War Museum, Duxford	
236800	Piper L-4A Cub (G-BHPK) [44-A]	Privately owned, Tibenham	
243809	Waco CG-4A Hadrian (BAPC 185)	Museum of Army Flying, Middle Wallop	
267543	Lockheed P-38J Lightning (NX3145X) [KI-S]	The Fighter Collection, Duxford	
269097	Bell P-63A Kingcobra (G-BTWR)	The Fighter Collection, Duxford	
314887	Fairchild Argus III (G-AJPI)	Privately owned, Swanton Morley	
315509	Douglas C-47A (G-BHUB) [W7-S]	Imperial War Museum, Duxford	
329405	Piper L-4H Cub (G-BCOB) [23-A]	Privately owned, South Walsham	
329417	Piper L-4A Cub (G-BDHK)	Privately owned, Coleford	
329601	Piper L-4H Cub (G-AXHR) [44-D]	Privately owned, Nayland	
329854	Piper L-4H Cub (G-BMKC) [44-R]	Privately owned, St Just	
329934	Piper L-4H Cub (G-BCPH) [72-B]	Privately owned, White Waltham	
330238	Piper L-4H Cub (G-LIVH) [24-A]	Privately owned, Barton	
330485	Piper L-4H Cub (G-AJES) [44-C]	Privately owned, Saltash	
343251	Boeing-Stearman N2S-5 Kaydet (G-NZSS)	Privately owned, Cumbernauld	
413573	NA P-51D Mustang (9133M/ N6526D) [B6-V]	RAF Museum, Hendon	
431171	NA B-25J Mitchell (N7614C)	Imperial War Museum, Duxford	
436021	Piper J-3C Cub 65 (G-BWEZ)	Privately owned, Cumbernauld	
454467	Piper L-4J Cub (G-BILI) [44-J]	Privately owned, White Waltham	
454537	Piper L-4J Cub (G-BFDL) [04-J]	Privately owned, Pontefract	
461748	Boeing B-29A Superfortress (G-BHDK) [Y]	Imperial War Museum, Duxford	
463221	NA P-51D Mustang (G-BTCD) [G4-S]	The Fighter Collection, Duxford	
472216	NA P-51D Mustang (G-BIXL) [AJ L]	Privately owned, North Weald	
472258	NA P-51D Mustang (473979) [WZ-I]	Imperial War Museum, Lambeth	
472773	NA P-51D Mustang (G-SUSY) [AJ-C]	Privately owned, Sywell	
474008	NA P-51D Mustang (N51RR) [VF-R]	Intrepid Aviation Co, North Weald	

Historic Aircraft

Notes	Serial	Type (other identity)	Owner/operator, location
	479744	Piper L-4H Cub (G-BGPD) [49-M]	Privately owned, Enstone
	479766	Piper L-4H Cub (G-BKHG) [63-D]	Privately owned, Goldcliff, Gwent
	480015	Piper L-4H Cub (G-AKIB)	Privately owned, Bodmin
	480133	Piper L-4J Cub (G-BDCD) [44-B]	Privately owned, Slinfold
	480321	Piper L-4J Cub (G-FRAN) [44-H]	Privately owned, Rayne, Essex
	480480	Piper L-4J Cub (G-BECN) [44-E]	Privately owned, Kersey, Suffolk
	480636	Piper L-4J Cub (G-AXHP) [58-A]	Privately owned, Southend
	480752	Piper L-4J Cub (G-BCXJ) [39-E]	Privately owned, Old Sarum
	483868	Boeing B-17G Fortress (N5237V) [A-N]	RAF Museum, Hendon
	511701A	Beech C-45H (G-BSZC) [AF258]	Privately owned, Bryngwyn Bach
	607327	PA-18 Super Cub 95 (G-ARAO) [09-L]	Privately owned, Lambley
	2-134	NA T-6G Texan (114700)	Aces High Ltd, North Weald
	3-1923	Aeronca O-58B Defender (G-BRHP)	Privately owned, Chiseldon
	18-2001	Piper L-18C Super Cub (G-BIZV)	Privately owned, Oxenhope
	40-1766	Boeing-Stearman PT-17 Kaydet	Privately owned, Swanton Morley
	41-33275	NA AT-6C Texan (G-BICE) [CE]	Privately owned, Ipswich
	42-12417	NA AT-16 Harvard IIB	Thameside Aviation Museum, East Tilbury
	42-58678	Taylorcraft DF-65 (G-BRIY) [IY]	Privately owned, North Weald
	42-78044	Aeronca 11AC Chief (G-BRXL)	Privately owned, High Cross, Herts
	42-93510	Douglas C-47A Skytrain [CM] <ff>	Museum of Army Flying, Middle Wallop
	44-14574	NA P-51D Mustang (fuselage)	East Essex Aviation Museum, Clacton
	44-79609	Piper L-4H Cub (G-BHXY) [PR]	Privately owned, Aldergrove
	44-80594	Piper L-4J Cub (G-BEDJ)	Privately owned, Overton
	45-49192	Republic P-47D Thunderbolt (N47DD)	Imperial War Museum, Duxford
	51-14526	NA T-6G Texan (G-BRWB)	Privately owned, Duxford
	51-15227	NA T-6G Texan (G-BKRA) [10]	Privately owned, Shoreham
	51-15673	Piper L-18C Super Cub (G-CUBI)	Privately owned, Felixkirk
	52-8543	CCF Harvard IV (G-BUKY) [66]	Privately owned, Rochester
	54-2447	Piper L-21B Super Cub (G-SCUB)	Privately owned, Anwick
	54-2474	Piper L-21B Super Cub (G-PCUB)	Privately owned, Headcorn
	54-21261	Lockheed T-33A (N33VC)	The Old Flying Machine Company, Duxford
	61-2414	B-V CH-47A Chinook	RAF Odiham, instructional use
	63-471	McD F-4C Phantom (37471)	RAF Lakenheath, BDRT
	63-610	McD F-4C Phantom (37610)	RAF Lakenheath, BDRT
	65-777	McD F-4C Phantom (37419) [LN]	RAF Lakenheath, on display
	67-120	GD F-111E (70120) [UH]	Imperial War Museum, Duxford
	68-060	GD F-111E (80060) <ff>	Dumfries & Galloway Av'n Mus, Tinwald Downs
	72-448	GD F-111E (80011) [LN]	RAF Lakenheath, on display
	73-091	McD F-15A Eagle (30091)	RAF Lakenheath, BDRT
	76-029	McD F-15A Eagle (60029)	RAF Lakenheath, BDRT
	76-124	McD F-15B Eagle (60124) [LN, 48 LSS]	RAF Lakenheath
	77-259	Fairchild A-10A Thunderbolt (70259) [AR]	Imperial War Museum, Duxford
	80-219	Fairchild GA-10A Thunderbolt (00219) [AR]	RAF Alconbury, on display
	92-048	McD F-15A Eagle (40131) [LN]	RAF Lakenheath, on display
	146-11042	Wolf WII <R> (G-BMZX) [7]	Privately owned, Haverfordwest
	146-11083	Wolf WII <R> (G-BNAI) [5]	Privately owned, Haverfordwest
	H-57	Piper J-3C Cub (G-AKAZ)	Privately owned, Duxford
	I-492	Ryan PT-22 (G-BPUD)	Privately owned, Swanton Morley

Yugoslavia

| | 30149 | Soko P-2 Kraguj (G-SOKO) [149] | Privately owned, Liverpool |

Irish Air Corps Military Aircraft Markings

Serial	Type (other identity)	Owner/operator, location	Notes
34	Miles M14A Magister	Irish Aviation Museum Store, Dublin	
141	Avro 652A Anson C19	Irish Aviation Museum Store, Dublin	
157	VS358 Seafire L III	Privately owned, Battle, East Sussex	
164	DHC1 Chipmunk T20	Engineering Wing stored, Baldonnel	
168	DHC1 Chipmunk T20	No 2 Support Wing, Gormanston	
172	DHC1 Chipmunk T20	Training Wing stored, Gormanston	
173	DHC1 Chipmunk T20	South East Aviation Enthusiasts, Waterford	
176	DH104 Dove 4 (VP-YKF)	South East Aviation Enthusiasts, Waterford	
177	Percival P56 Provost T51 (G-BLIW)	Privately owned, Shoreham	
181	Percival P56 Provost T51	Privately owned, Thatcham	
183	Percival P56 Provost T51	Irish Aviation Museum Store, Dublin	
184	Percival P56 Provost T51	South East Aviation Enthusiasts, Waterford	
187	DH115 Vampire T55	Av'n Society of Ireland, stored, Waterford	
189	Percival P56 Provost T51	Baldonnel, Fire Section	
191	DH115 Vampire T55	Irish Aviation Museum Store, Dublin	
192	DH115 Vampire T55	South East Aviation Enthusiasts, Waterford	
193	DH115 Vampire T55 <ff>	Baldonnel Fire Section	
195	Sud Alouette III	No 3 Support Wing, Baldonnel	
196	Sud Alouette III	No 3 Support Wing, Baldonnel	
197	Sud Alouette III	No 3 Support Wing, Baldonnel	
198	DH115 Vampire T11	Engineering Wing, Baldonnel	
199	DHC1 Chipmunk T22	Training Wing store, Gormanston (spares)	
203	Reims-Cessna FR172H	No 2 Support Wing, Gormanston	
205	Reims-Cessna FR172H	No 2 Support Wing, Gormanston	
206	Reims-Cessna FR172H	No 1 Support Wing, Baldonnel, on rebuild	
207	Reims-Cessna FR172H	No 2 Support Wing, Gormanston	
208	Reims-Cessna FR172H	No 2 Support Wing, Gormanston	
209	Reims-Cessna FR172H	No 2 Support Wing, Gormanston	
210	Reims-Cessna FR172H	No 2 Support Wing, Gormanston	
211	Sud SA316 Alouette III	No 3 Support Wing, Baldonnel	
212	Sud SA316 Alouette III	No 3 Support Wing, Baldonnel	
213	Sud SA316 Alouette III	No 3 Support Wing, Baldonnel	
214	Sud SA316 Alouette III	No 3 Support Wing, Baldonnel	
215	Fouga CM170 Super Magister	No 1 Support Wing, Baldonnel	
216	Fouga CM170 Super Magister	No 1 Support Wing, Baldonnel	
217	Fouga CM170 Super Magister	No 1 Support Wing, Baldonnel	
218	Fouga CM170 Super Magister	No 1 Support Wing, Baldonnel	
219	Fouga CM170 Super Magister	No 1 Support Wing, Baldonnel	
220	Fouga CM170 Super Magister	No 1 Support Wing, Baldonnel	
221	Fouga CM170 Super Magister [79/3-KE]	Engineering Wing, Baldonnel	
222	SIAI SF-260WE Warrior	Training Wing, Baldonnel	
225	SIAI SF-260WE Warrior	Training Wing, Baldonnel	
226	SIAI SF-260WE Warrior	Training Wing, Baldonnel	
227	SIAI SF-260WE Warrior	Training Wing, Baldonnel	
229	SIAI SF-260WE Warrior	Training Wing, Baldonnel	
230	SIAI SF-260WE Warrior	Training Wing, Baldonnel	
231	SIAI SF-260WE Warrior	Training Wing, Baldonnel	
233	SIAI SF-260MC	Engineering Wing stored, Baldonnel	
237	Aérospatiale SA341F Gazelle	Advanced FTS, Baldonnel	
240	Beech Super King Air 200	Transport & Training Squadron, Baldonnel	
241	Aérospatiale SA341F Gazelle	Advanced FTS, Baldonnel	
243	Reims-Cessna FR172K	No 2 Support Wing, Gormanston	
244	Aérospatiale SA365F Dauphin II	No 3 Support Wing, Baldonnel	
245	Aérospatiale SA365F Dauphin II	No 3 Support Wing, Baldonnel	
246	Aérospatiale SA365F Dauphin II	No 3 Support Wing, Baldonnel	
247	Aérospatiale SA365F Dauphin II	No 3 Support Wing, Baldonnel	
248	Aérospatiale SA365F Dauphin II	No 3 Support Wing, Baldonnel	
251	Grumman G1159C Gulfstream IV	Transport & Training Squadron, Baldonnel	
252	Airtech CN.235 MPA Persuader	Transport & Training Squadron, Baldonnel	
253	Airtech CN.235 MPA Persuader	Transport & Training Squadron, Baldonnel	

Belgian Air Force F-16A has the insignia of 1Sm of 2 Wg at Florennes. *PRM*

French Air Force C-160NG Transall operates from Evreux. *Daniel March*

Italian Air Force leased Tornado F3 36-12/MM7202. *BSS*

124

Overseas Military Aircraft Markings

Aircraft included in this section are a selection of those likely to be seen visiting UK civil and military airfields on transport flights, exchange visits, exercises and for air shows. It is not a comprehensive list of *all* aircraft operated by the air arms concerned.

ALGERIA
Force Aérienne Algerienne
 Lockheed C-130H
 Hercules
 4911 (7T-WHT)
 4912 (7T-WHS)
 4913 (7T-WHY)
 4914 (7T-WHZ)
 4924 (7T-WHR)
 4926 (7T-WHQ)
 4928 (7T-WHJ)
 4930 (7T-WHI)
 4934 (7T-WHF)
 4935 (7T-WHE)

 Lockheed C-130H-30
 Hercules
 4984 (7T-WHN)
 4987 (7T-WHO)
 4989 (7T-WHL)
 4997 (7T-WHA)
 5224 (7T-WHB)

AUSTRALIA
Royal Australian Air Force
 Boeing 707-338C/368C*
 33 Sqn, Amberley
 A20-261*
 A20-623
 A20-624
 A20-627
 A20-629

 Lockheed
 C-130H Hercules
 36 Sqn, Richmond, NSW
 A97-001
 A97-002
 A97-003
 A97-004
 A97-005
 A97-006
 A97-007
 A97-008
 A97-009
 A97-010
 A97-011
 A97-012

 Lockheed
 C-130E Hercules
 37 Sqn, Richmond, NSW
 A97-159
 A97-160
 A97-167
 A97-168
 A97-171
 A97-172
 A97-177
 A97-178
 A97-180

A97-181
A97-189
A97-190

 Lockheed
 P-3C Orion
 10/11 Sqns, Edinburgh, NSW
 A9-654   11 Sqn
 A9-657   11 Sqn
 A9-658   11 Sqn
 A9-659   11 Sqn
 A9-660   11 Sqn
 A9-661   11 Sqn
 A9-662   11 Sqn
 A9-663   11 Sqn
 A9-664   11 Sqn
 A9-665   11 Sqn
 A9-751   10 Sqn
 A9-752   10 Sqn
 A9-753   10 Sqn
 A9-755   10 Sqn
 A9-756   10 Sqn
 A9-757   10 Sqn
 A9-758   10 Sqn
 A9-759   10 Sqn
 A9-760   10 Sqn

AUSTRIA
Oesterreichische
 Luftstreitkrafte
 SAAB 105ÖE
 Fliegerregiment III
  1 Staffel/JbG, Linz
 (yellow)
 1102/B
 1104/D
 1105/E
 1106/F
 1107/G
 1108/H
 1109/I
 1110/J
 (green)
 1111/A
 1112/B
 1114/D
 1116/F
 1117/G
 1119/I
 1120/J
 (red)
 1122/B
 1123/C
 1124/D
 1125/E
 1126/F
 1127/G
 1128/H
 1129/I
 1130/J

 (blue)
 1131/A
 1132/B
 1133/C
 1134/D
 1135/E
 1136/F
 1137/G
 1139/I
 1140/J

 Short SC7
 Skyvan 3M
 Fliegerregiment I
  Flachenstaffel, Tulln
 5S-TA
 5S-TB

BELGIUM
Force Aérienne Belge/
 Belgische Luchtmacht
 D-BD Alpha Jet E
 7/11 Smaldeel
 Brustem (9Wg)
 AT01
 AT02
 AT03
 AT05
 AT06
 AT08
 AT09
 AT10
 AT11
 AT12
 AT13
 AT14
 AT15
 AT16
 AT17
 AT18
 AT19
 AT20
 AT21
 AT22
 AT23
 AT24
 AT25
 AT26
 AT27
 AT28
 AT29
 AT30
 AT31
 AT32
 AT33

 Boeing 727-29C
 21 Smaldeel, Melsbroek
 CB01
 CB02

Belgium

Dassault
Falcon 900B
21 Smaldeel, Melsbroek
CD01

Swearingen
Merlin IIIA
21 Smaldeel, Melsbroek
CF01
CF02
CF04
CF05
CF06

Lockheed
C-130H Hercules
20 Smaldeel, Melsbroek
CH01
CH02
CH03
CH04
CH05
CH06
CH07
CH08
CH09
CH10
CH11
CH12

Dassault
Falcon 20E
21 Smaldeel, Melsbroek
CM01
CM02

Hawker-Siddeley
HS748 Srs 2A
21 Smaldeel, Melsbroek
CS01
CS02
CS03

General Dynamics
F-16A/F-16B*
349 Sm, 350 Sm, OCU,
 Bevekom (1Wg);
1,2 Smaldeel, Florennes
 (2 Wg);
23,31 Smaldeel,
 Kleine-Brogel (10 Wg)

FA39	23 Sm
FA46	349 Sm
FA47	349 Sm
FA48	350 Sm
FA49	350 Sm
FA50	350 Sm
FA53	349 Sm
FA55	349 Sm
FA56	23 Sm
FA57	23 Sm
FA58	23 Sm
FA60	31 Sm
FA61	349 Sm
FA65	23 Sm
FA66	31 Sm
FA67	23 Sm
FA68	2 Sm
FA69	23 Sm
FA70	70 Sm
FA71	23 Sm
FA72	31 Sm
FA73	23 Sm
FA74	31 Sm

FA75	349 Sm
FA76	350 Sm
FA77	1 Sm
FA78	31 Sm
FA80	31 Sm
FA81	31 Sm
FA82	31 Sm
FA83	349 Sm
FA84	31 Sm
FA86	31 Sm
FA87	23 Sm
FA88	349 Sm
FA89	23 Sm
FA90	31 Sm
FA91	349 Sm
FA92	31 Sm
FA93	23 Sm
FA94	31 Sm
FA95	349 Sm
FA96	350 Sm
FA97	349 Sm
FA98	2 Sm
FA99	349 Sm
FA100	350 Sm
FA101	1 Sm
FA102	2 Sm
FA103	1 Sm
FA104	2 Sm
FA106	350 Sm
FA107	1 Sm
FA108	2 Sm
FA109	1 Sm
FA110	349 Sm
FA111	1 Sm
FA112	2 Sm
FA114	350 Sm
FA115	23 Sm
FA116	350 Sm
FA117	349 Sm
FA118	2 Sm
FA119	349 Sm
FA120	31 Sm
FA121	1 Sm
FA122	2 Sm
FA123	349 Sm
FA124	23 Sm
FA125	350 Sm
FA126	23 Sm
FA127	1 Sm
FA128	2 Sm
FA129	1 Sm
FA130	2 Sm
FA131	1 Sm
FA132	2 Sm
FA133	349 Sm
FA134	2 Sm
FA135	1 Sm
FA136	2 Sm
FB01*	OCU
FB02*	OCU
FB04*	OCU
FB05*	OCU
FB07*	349 Sm
FB08*	350 Sm
FB09*	OCU
FB10*	OCU
FB12*	2 Sm
FB14*	1 Sm
FB15*	2 Wg
FB17*	23 Sm
FB18*	10 Wg
FB19*	350 Sm
FB20*	31 Sm
FB21*	OCU

FB22*	10 Wg
FB23*	1 Sm
FB24*	2 Sm

Fouga CM170R Magister
33 Sm (9 Wg), Brustem
MT04
MT13
MT14
MT26
MT34
MT35
MT36
MT37
MT40
MT44
MT48

Westland Sea
King Mk48/48A*
40 Smaldeel, Koksijde
RS01
RS02
RS03*
RS04
RS05

SIAI Marchetti
SF.260MB/SF.260D*
Ecole de Pilotage
 Elementaire (5 Sm),
 Gossoncourt
ST02
ST03
ST04
ST06
ST09
ST12
ST15
ST16
ST17
ST18
ST19
ST20
ST21
ST22
ST23
ST24
ST25
ST26
ST27
ST30
ST31
ST32
ST33
ST34
ST35
ST36
ST40*
ST41*
ST42*
ST43*
ST44*
ST45*
ST46*
ST47*
ST48*

Belgische Landmacht
Sud Alouette II
16 Batallion, Bierset;
17 Battalion, Bierset;
SLV, Brasschaat
A22   16 Batt

A38	16 Batt
A40	SLV
A41	17 Batt
A42	16 Batt
A44	16 Batt
A46	16 Batt
A47	16 Batt
A49	SLV
A50	17 Batt
A53	16 Batt
A54	SLV
A55	SLV
A57	SLV
A59	16 Batt
A61	SLV
A62	16 Batt
A64	17 Batt
A65	SLV
A66	SLV
A68	16 Batt
A70	SLV
A73	17 Batt
A75	16 Batt
A77	16 Batt
A78	16 Batt
A79	SLV
A80	16 Batt
A81	17 Batt

Britten-Norman BN-2A/BN-2B-21* Islander
16 Batallion, Bierset; SLV, Brasschaat

B01/LA	SLV
B02/LB	SLV
B03/LC	SLV
B04/LD	SLV
B07/LG	16 Batt
B08/LH	16 Batt
B09/LI*	16 Batt
B10/LJ	16 Batt
B11/LK	SLV
B12/LL	SLV

Agusta A109HA/HO*
17 Battalion, Bierset; 18 Battalion, Bierset; SLV, Brasschaat

H01*	18 Batt
H02*	SLV
H03*	SLV
H04*	18 Batt
H05*	18 Batt
H06*	18 Batt
H07*	18 Batt
H08*	17 Batt
H09*	18 Batt
H10*	18 Batt
H11*	SLV
H12*	SLV
H13*	SLV
H14*	SLV
H15*	SLV
H16*	17 Batt
H17*	17 Batt
H18*	18 Batt
H19	17 Ratt
H20	18 Batt
H21	18 Batt
H22	17 Batt
H23	17 Batt
H24	17 Batt
H25	17 Batt
H26	18 Batt
H27	18 Batt
H28	17 Batt
H29	17 Batt
H30	18 Batt
H31	17 Batt
H32	17 Batt
H33	17 Batt
H34	17 Batt
H35	17 Batt
H36	18 Batt
H37	17 Batt
H38	18 Batt
H39	18 Batt
H40	18 Batt
H41	17 Batt
H42	18 Batt
H43	17 Batt
H44	17 Batt
H45	17 Batt
H46	17 Batt

Force Navale Belge/Belgische Zeemacht
SA316B Alouette III
Koksijde Heli Flight

M1	(OT-ZPA)
M2	(OT-ZPB)
M3	(OT-ZPC)

Gendarmerie
Britten-Norman PBN-2T Islander
Base: Melsbroek

G05	(OT-GLA)

Cessna 182 Skylane
Base: Melsbroek

G01	C.182Q
G04	C.182R

Sud Alouette II
Base: Melsbroek
G90
G92
G93
G94
G95

BRAZIL
Forca Aerea Brazileira
Boeing KC-137
2° GT 2° Esq, Galeão
2401
2402
2403
2404

Lockheed C-130E Hercules
1° GT 1° Esq, Galeão;
1° GTT 1° Esq, Afonsos

2451	C-130E	1° GTT
2453	C-130E	1° GTT
2454	C-130E	1° GTT
2455	C-130E	1° GTT
2456	C-130E	1° GTT
2458	SC-130E	1° GT
2459	SC-130E	1° GT
2461	KC-130H	1° GT
2462	KC-130H	1° GT
2463	C-130H	1° GT
2464	C-130H	1° GT
2465	C-130H	1° GT
2466	C-130H	1° GT
2467	C-130H	1° GT

CANADA
Canadian Forces
Lockheed CC-130E/CC-130E(SAR)* Hercules
413 Sqn, Greenwood (SAR) (14 Wing);
418 Sqn, Edmonton (SAR) (18 Wing)
424 Sqn, Trenton (SAR) (8 Wing);
426 Sqn, Trenton (8 Wing);
429 Sqn, Trenton (8 Wing);
435 Sqn, Edmonton (18 Wing);
436 Sqn, Trenton (8 Wing)

130305*	8 Wing
130306*	8 Wing
130307*	8 Wing
130308	8 Wing
130310*	8 Wing
130311	8 Wing
130313	8 Wing
130314*	8 Wing
130315	8 Wing
130316	18 Wing
130317	8 Wing
130319	18 Wing
130320	8 Wing
130323	8 Wing
130324	18 Wing
130325	8 Wing
130326	8 Wing
130327	18 Wing
130328	8 Wing

Lockheed CC-130H/CC-130H(T)* Hercules

130332	8 Wing
130333	8 Wing
130334	8 Wing
130335	
130336	8 Wing
130337	8 Wing
130338*	18 Wing
130339*	18 Wing
130340*	18 Wing
130341*	18 Wing
130342*	18 Wing

Boeing CC-137 (B.707-374C)
437 Sqn, Trenton (8 Wing)
13703
13704
13705

Lockheed CP-140 Aurora
404/405/415 Sqns, Greenwood (14 Wing);
407 Sqn, Comox (19 Wing)

140101	14 Wing
140102	14 Wing
140103	14 Wing
140104	14 Wing
140105	407 Sqn
140106	14 Wing
140107	407 Sqn
140108	14 Wing
140109	14 Wing

140110 407 Sqn
140111 14 Wing
140112 407 Sqn
140113
140114 14 Wing
140115 14 Wing
140116 407 Sqn
140117 14 Wing
140118 14 Wing

**Lockheed
CP-140A Arcturus**
140119 14 Wing
140120 14 Wing
140121 14 Wing

**Canadair CC-144A/
CC-144B/CE-144A
Challenger**
412 Sqn, Ottawa-Uplands
  (7 Wing);
434 Sqn, Shearwater
  (12 Wing)
144601 CC-144A 434 Sqn
144602 CC-144A 434 Sqn
144603 CE-144A 434 Sqn
144604 CC-144A 434 Sqn
144605 CC-144A 434 Sqn
144606 CE-144A 434 Sqn
144607 CC-144A 434 Sqn
144608 CE-144A 434 Sqn
144609 CC-144A 434 Sqn
144610 CC-144A 434 Sqn
144611 CE-144A 434 Sqn
144614 CC-144B 412 Sqn
144615 CC-144B 412 Sqn
144616 CC-144B 412 Sqn

**Airbus CC-150 Polaris
(A310-304)**
437 Sqn, Trenton (8 Wing)
15001
15002
15003
15004
15005

CHILE
**Fuerza Aérea de Chile
Boeing 707-321B/330/351C**
902 351C
903 330B
905 385C

Extra EA-300
Los Halcones
021 [1]
022 [2]
023 [3]
024 [6]
025 [5]
027 [4]

**Lockheed
C-130B/H Hercules**
Grupo 10, Santiago
993 C-130B
994 C-130H
995 C-130H
996 C-130H
997 C-130B
998 C-130B
999 C-130B

**CZECH REPUBLIC
Ceske Vojenske Letectvo
Aero L.39 Albatros**
41, 42 & 43 slt/4 zSL,Cáslav;
322 tlt/32 zTL, Náměšt;
341 vlt/34 zSL, Pardubice;
LZú, Praha/Kbely
0001 L.39MS LZú
0004 L.39MS 341 vlt/34 zSL
0005 L.39MS 341 vlt/34 zSL
0006 L.39MS 341 vlt/34 zSL
0103 L.39C   341 vlt/34 zSL
0105 L.39C   341 vlt/34 zSL
0106 L.39C   341 vlt/34 zSL
0107 L.39C   341 vlt/34 zSL
0113 L.39C   341 vlt/34 ZSL
0115 L.39C   341 vlt/34 ZSL
0440 L.39C   341 vlt/34 zSL
0441 L.39C   341 vlt/34 zSL
0444 L.39C   341 vlt/34 zSL
2341 L.39ZA 4 zSL
2344 L.39ZA 4 zSL
2347 L.39ZA 4 zSL
2350 L.39ZA 4 zSL
2415 L.39ZA 4 zSL
2418 L.39ZA 4 zSL
2421 L.39ZA 4 zSL
2427 L.39ZA 4 zSL
2430 L.39ZA 4 zSL
2433 L.39ZA 4 zSL
2436 L.39ZA 4 zSL
3903 L.39ZA 4 zSL
4605 L.39C   341 vlt/34 ZSL
4606 L.39C   341 vlt/34 ZSL
4607 L.39C   341 vlt/34 ZSL
5013 L.39ZA LZú
5015 L.39ZA 322 tlt/32 zTL
5017 L.39ZA 322 tlt/32 zTL
5019 L.39ZA 322 tlt/32 zTL

Antonov An-24V
61 dlt/6 zDL, Praha/Kbely
2904
5803
7109
7110

Antonov An-26
344 pzdlt/34 zSL, Pardubice;
61 dlt/6 zDL, Praha/Kbely;
LZú, Praha/Kbely
2408 61 dlt/6 zDL
2409 344 pzdlt/34 zSL
2507 61 dlt/6 zDL
3209 344 pzdlt/34 zSL

Antonov An-30FG
344 pzdlt/34 zSL, Pardubice
1107

Let 410 Turbolet
61 dlt/6 zDL, Praha/Kbely;
344 pzdlt/34 zSL, Pardubice
0402 L.410M   344 pzdlt/
                      34 zSL
0403 L.410M   344 pzdlt/
                      34 zSL
0501 L.410M   61 dlt/6 zDL
0503 L.410M   344 pzdlt/
                      34zSL
0712 L.410UVP 61dlt/6 zDL
0731 L.410UVP 61 dlt/6 zDL
0926 L.410T   61 dlt/6 zDL
0928 L.410T   61 dlt/6 zDL

0929 L.410T   61 dlt/6 zDL
1132 L.410T   61 dlt/6 zDL
1134 L.410T   344 pzdlt/
                      34 zSL
1504 L.410UVP 344 pzdlt/
                      34 zSL
1522 L.410FG 344 pzdlt/
                      34 zSL
1523 L.410FG 344 pzdlt/
                      34 zSL
1524 L.410FG 344 pzdlt/
                      34 zSL
1525 L.410FG 344 pzdlt/
                      34 zSL
1526 L.410FG 344 pzdlt/
                      34 zSL
2312 L.410UVP 61 dlt/
                      6 zDL

Let 610M
61 dlt/6 zDL, Praha/Kbely;
LZú, Praha/Kbely
0003 61 dlt/6 zDL
0005 LZú

**Sukhoi
Su-22M-4K/Su-22UM-3K***
321 tpzlt/32 zTL, Náměšt
2619 34 NA-2D
2620 35 NA-2D
3313 24 NA-2A
3315 39 NA-2B
3403 08 NA-1B
3405
3406
3701 02 NA-1A
3703 43 NA-1D
3704 44 NA-1D
3706 52 NA-1E
3802 26 NA-2B
3803 27 NA-2B
4005 30 NA-2C
4006 31 NA-2C
4007 32 NA-2C
4008 29 NA-2B
4010 28 NA-2B
4011 22 NA-2A
4208 53 NA-1E
4209 54 NA-1E
7103 03 NA-1A*
7104 40 NA-2C*
7309 41 NA-2D*
7310 25 NA-2A*

Sukhoi Su-25K/Su-25UBK*
322 tlt/32 zTL, Náměšt
1002
1003
1005
3348*
5003
5006
5007
5008
5039
5040
6020
8072
8076
8077
8078
8079
8080
8081

9013
9014
9093
9094
9098
9099

Tupolev Tu-134A
61 dlt/6 zDL, Praha/Kbely
1407

Tupolev Tu-154B-2
61 dlt/6 zDL, Praha/Kbely
0601

DENMARK
Kongelige Danske
Flyvevaabnet
Lockheed
C-130H Hercules
Eskadrille 721, Vaerløse
B-678
B-679
B-680

General Dynamics
F-16A/F-16B*
Eskadrille 723, Aalborg;
Eskadrille 726, Aalborg;
Eskadrille 727, Skrydstrup;
Eskadrille 730, Skrydstrup

E-004	Esk 726
E-005	Esk 726
E-006	Esk 726
E-007	Esk 726
E-008	Esk 726
E-016	Esk 726
E-017	Esk 726
E-018	Esk 726
E-024	
E-075	
E-107	
E-174	Esk 727
E-176	Esk 723
E-177	Esk 723
E-178	Esk 723
E-180	Esk 726
E-181	Esk 727
E-182	Esk 730
E-183	Esk 723
E-184	Esk 723
E-187	Esk 727
E-188	Esk 723
E-189	Esk 723
E-190	Esk 723
E-191	Esk 730
E-192	Esk 730
E-193	Esk 727
E-194	Esk 730
E-195	Esk 723
E-196	Esk 723
E-197	Esk 723
E-198	Esk 730
E-199	Esk 727
E-200	Esk 723
E-202	Esk 730
E-203	Esk 723
E-596	Esk 726
E-597	Esk 730
E-598	Esk 730
E-599	Esk 730
E-600	Esk 727
E-601	Esk 727
E-602	Esk 730

E-603	Esk 727
E-604	Esk 726
E-605	Esk 730
E-606	Esk 730
E-607	Esk 723
E-608	Esk 723
E-609	Esk 727
E-610	Esk 727
E-611	Esk 727
ET-022*	Esk 726
ET-197*	Esk 726
ET-198*	Esk 726
ET-199*	Esk 726
ET-204*	Esk 727
ET-205*	Esk 730
ET-206*	Esk 730
ET-207*	Esk 727
ET-208*	Esk 730
ET-210*	Esk 726
ET-612*	Esk 727
ET-613*	Esk 727
ET-614*	Esk 723
ET-615*	Esk 727

Grumman
Gulfstream III
Eskadrille 721, Vaerløse
F-249
F-313
F-330

SAAB T-17
Supporter
Flyveskolen, Avnø (FLSK);
Haerens Flyvetjaeneste
  (Danish Army), Vandel;
Eskadrille 721, Vaerløse

T-401	Karup Stn Flt
T-402	Skrydstrup Stn Flt
T-403	Karup Stn Flt
T-404	Karup Stn Flt
T-405	Karup Stn Flt
T-407	Esk 721
T-408	Esk 721
T-409	FLSK
T-410	Karup Stn Flt
T-411	FLSK
T-413	FLSK
T-414	Army
T-415	FLSK
T-417	Army
T-418	FLSK
T-419	FLSK
T-420	FLSK
T-421	FLSK
T-423	FLSK
T-425	Aalborg Stn Flt
T-426	FLSK
T-427	FLSK
T-428	FLSK
T-429	FLSK
T-430	FLSK
T-431	FLSK
T-432	FLSK

Sikorsky S-61A Sea King
Eskadrille 722, Vaerløse
Detachments at:
Aalborg, Ronne, Skrydstrup
U-240
U-275
U-276
U-277
U-278

U-279
U-280
U-481

Sovaernets
Flyvetjaeneste (Navy)
Westland Lynx Mk 80/90*
Eskadrille 722, Vaerløse
S-035
S-134
S-142
S-170
S-175
S-181
S-191
S-249*
S-256*

Haerens
Flyvetjaeneste (Army)
Hughes 500M
Vandel
H-201
H-202
H-203
H-205
H-206
H-207
H-209
H-210
H-211
H-213
H-244
H-245
H-246

Aérospatiale AS550C-2
Fennec
P-090
P-234
P-254
P-275
P-276
P-287
P-288
P-319
P-320
P-352
P-369

ECUADOR
Fuerza Aérea Ecuatoriana
Lockheed
C-130H Hercules
FAE-812
FAE-893

EGYPT
Al Quwwat al-Jawwiya
  Ilmisriya
  Lockheed
  C-130H/C-130H-30*
  Hercules
  16 Sqn, Cairo West
  1271/SU-BAB
  1272/SU-BAC
  1273/SU-BAD
  1274/SU-BAE
  1275/SU-BAF
  1277/SU-BAI
  1278/SU-BAJ
  1279/SU-BAK
  1280/SU-BAL

Egypt – France

1281/SU-BAM
1282/SU-BAN
1283/SU-BAP
1284/SU-BAQ
1285/SU-BAR
1286/SU-BAS
1287/SU-BAT
1288/SU-BAU
1289/SU-BAV
1290/SU-BEW
1291/SU-BEX
1292/SU-BEY
1293/SU-BKS*
1294/SU-BKT*
1295/SU-BKU*

FRANCE
Armée de l'Air
Aérospatiale SN601 Corvette
CEV, Bretigny

1	MV
2	MW
10	MX

Aérospatiale TB-30 Epsilon
GI 312, Salon de Provence;
EPE 315, Cognac

1	315-UA	EPE 315
2	315-UB	EPE 315
3	FZ	
4	312-YE	GI 312
5	315-UD	EPE 315
6	315-UE	EPE 315
7	315-UF	EPE 315
8	315-UG	EPE 315
9	315-UH	EPE 315
10	315-UI	EPE 315
11	315-UJ	EPE 315
12	315-UK	EPE 315
13	315-UL	EPE 315
14	315-UM	EPE 315
15	315-UN	EPE 315
16	312-YF	GI 312
17	315-UP	EPE 315
18	315-UQ	EPE 315
19	312-YG	GI 312
20	315-US	EPE 315
21	312-YH	GI 312
23	312-YW	GI 312
24	315-UW	EPE 315
25	315-UX	EPE 315
26	315-UY	EPE 315
27	312-VI	GI 312
28	315-VA	EPE 315
29	312-YV	GI 312
30	312-YX	GI 312
31	315-VD	EPE 315
32	315-VE	EPE 315
33	315-VF	EPE 315
34	315-VG	EPE 315
35	315-VH	EPE 315
36	315-VI	EPE 315
37	315-VJ	EPE 315
38	315-VK	EPE 315
39	315-VL	EPE 315
40	315-VM	EPE 315
41	312-YI	GI 312
42	315-VO	EPE 315
43	315-VP	EPE 315
44	315-VQ	EPE 315
45	312-YJ	GI 312
46	312-YY	GI 312
47	315-VT	EPE 315
48	315-VU	EPE 315
49	312-YZ	GI 312
50	315-VW	EPE 315
51	2-BD	
52	315-VX	EPE 315
53	315-VY	EPE 315
54	315-VZ	EPE 315
56	312-YK	GI 312
57	F-ZVLB	
58	312-YU	GI 312
60	315-WC	EPE 315
61	315-WD	EPE 315
62	315-WE	EPE 315
63	315-WF	EPE 315
64	315-WG	EPE 315
65	315-WH	EPE 315
66	315-WI	EPE 315
67	315-WJ	EPE 315
68	315-WK	EPE 315
69	315-WL	EPE 315
70	315-WM	EPE 315
71	315-WN	EPE 315
72	315-WO	EPE 315
73	315-WP	EPE 315
74	315-WQ	EPE 315
75	312-VF	GI 312
76	315-WS	EPE 315
77	315-WT	EPE 315
78	315-WU	EPE 315
79	312-YT	GI 312
80	315-WW	EPE 315
81	315-WX	EPE 315
82	315-WY	EPE 315
83	315-WZ	EPE 315
84	315-XA	EPE 315
85	315-XB	EPE 315
86	315-XC	EPE 315
87	315-XD	EPE 315
88	315-XE	EPE 315
89	315-XF	EPE 315
90	315-XG	EPE 315
91	315-XH	EPE 315
92	F-SEXI	EPE 315 [1]
93	315-XJ	EPE 315
94	315-XK	EPE 315
95	315-XL	EPE 315
96	315-XM	EPE 315
97	312-VJ	GI 312
98	315-XO	EPE 315
99	315-XP	EPE 315
100	F-SEXQ	EPE 315 [2]
101	315-XR	EPE 315
102	315-XS	EPE 315
103	315-XT	EPE 315
104	312-VH	GI 312
105	F-SEXV	EPE 315 [3]
106	315-XW	EPE 315
107	315-XX	EPE 315
108	315-XY	EPE 315
109	315-XZ	EPE 315
110	315-YA	EPE 315
111	315-YB	EPE 315
112	315-YC	EPE 315
113	315-YD	EPE 315
114	315-YE	EPE 315
115	315-YF	EPE 315
116	315-YG	EPE 315
117	F-SEYH	EPE 315 [4]
118	315-YI	EPE 315
119	315-YJ	EPE 315
120	315-YK	EPE 315
121	315-YL	EPE 315
122	315-YM	EPE 315
123	315-YN	EPE 315
124	315-YO	EPE 315
125	312-YL	GI 312
126	315-YQ	EPE 315
127	315-YR	EPE 315
128	315-YS	EPE 315
129	315-YT	EPE 315
130	315-YU	EPE 315
131	315-YV	EPE 315
132	315-YW	EPE 315
133	315-YX	EPE 315
134	315-YY	EPE 315
135	315-YZ	EPE 315
136	315-ZA	EPE 315
137	315-ZB	EPE 315
138	312-VX	GI 312
139	315-ZD	EPE 315
140	315-ZE	EPE 315
141	315-ZF	EPE 315
142	315-ZG	EPE 315
143	315-ZH	EPE 315
144	315-ZI	EPE 315
145	315-ZJ	EPE 315
146	315-ZK	EPE 315
148	315-ZL	EPE 315
149	315-ZM	EPE 315
150	315-ZN	EPE 315
152	315-ZO	EPE 315
153	315-ZP	EPE 315
154	315-ZQ	EPE 315
155	315-ZR	EPE 315
158	315-ZS	EPE 315
159	315-ZT	EPE 315

Airbus A.300B2-103
CEV, Bretigny
03

Airbus A.310-304
ET 03.060 'Esterel',
Paris/Charles de Gaulle

421	F-RADA
422	F-RADB

Airtech CN-235M-100
ETL 01.062 'Vercours', Creil

043	62-IA
045	62-IB
065	62-IC
066	62-ID
071	62-IE
072	62-IF

Boeing C-135FR Stratotanker
ERV 01.093 'Aunis' &
ERV 03.093 'Landes', Istres

470	93-CA
471	93-CB
472	93-CC
474	93-CE
475	93-CF
735	93-CG
736	93-CH
737	93-CI
738	93-CJ
739	93-CK
740	93-CL

Boeing KC-135R Stratotanker
ERV 093, Istres
23516
38033

Boeing E-3F Sentry
EDCA 00.036, Avord

201	36-CA
202	36-CB
203	36-CC
204	36-CD

CASA 212-300 Aviocar
CEV, Bretigny

377	MO
378	MP
386	MQ
387	MR
388	MS

Cessna 310
CEV, Bretigny & Melun

046	310L	AV
185	310N	AU
187	310N	BJ
188	310N	BK
190	310N	BL
192	310N	BM
193	310N	BG
194	310N	BH
242	310K	AW
244	310K	AX
513	310	BE
693	310N	BI
820	310Q	CL
981	310	BF

D-BD Alpha Jet
Patrouille de France (PDF),
Salon de Provence;
ETO 01.008 'Saintonge' &
ETO 02.008 'Nice' Cazaux;
EAC 314, Tours;
CEAM (330), Mont-de-Marsan;
AMD-BA, Istres;
CEV, Bretigny

01	F-ZJTS	CEV
02	F-ZWRU	AMD-BA
E1		CEV
E3	8-NC	02.008
E4		CEV
E5	8-NS	02.008
E7		
E8		CEV
E9	8-MJ	01.008
E10	8-NM	02.008
E11	8-MW	01.008
E12		CEV
E13	314-TK	
E14	314-LE	
E15		
E17	8-NK	02.008
E18	8-MD	01.008
E19	314-TS	
E20	8-ML	01.008
E21	314-UO	
E22	314-TG	
E23	F-TERO	PDF [9]
E24	8-NO	02.008
E25	314-LL	
E26		
E27		
E28	8-MI	01.008
E29	314-TM	
E30	8-NR	02.008
E31	314-UA	
E32	8-NQ	02.008
E33	8-NN	02.008
E34	314-TC	
E35	314-UF	
E36	314-TT	
E37	F-TERI	PDF
E38		
E40		
E41	314-LC	
E42		
E43	314-TZ	
E44		CEV
E45	330-AK	CEAM
E46		CEV
E47	314-LO	
E48	8-MO	01.008
E49		
E51	314-UB	
E52		
E53	314-LV	
E55	314-UN	
E58	314-TD	
E59		
E60		CEV
E61	314-LJ	
E63	314-TA	
E64	314-TJ	
E65	8-MU	01.008
E66	8-ME	01.008
E67	314-TB	
E68		
E69	8-NX	02.008
E70		
E72	F-TERG	PDF [8]
E73	314-TV	
E74		
E75	314-TU	
E76	314-TH	
E79	314-LN	
E80		CEV
E81	314-LR	
E82	8-MM	01.008
E83	8-NG	02.008
E84	8-MH	01.008
E85	330-AL	CEAM
E86		
E87	314-LU	
E88	314-TF	
E89		
E90	314-LF	
E91	8-NL	02.008
E92	314-UE	
E93	314-LD	
E94		
E95		
E96	8-MT	01.008
E97	F-TERL	PDF [2]
E98	314-LT	
E99	314-LW	
E100		CEV
E101	314-LX	
E102	8-MC	01.008
E103		
E104	F-TERB	PDF
E105	F-TERF	PDF [3]
E106	F-TERJ	PDF [4]
E107		CEV
E108	8-NJ	02.008
E109	8-NI	02.008
E110	8-ND	02.008
E111	314-LH	
E112	314-LH	
E113	314-LK	
E114	314-UC	
E115	8-MS	01.008
E116	8-NB	02.008
E117	314-UL	
E118		
E119	314-LZ	
E120	314-LM	
E121		
E122	8-MN	01.008
E123	8-MQ	01.008
E124		
E125	F-TERH	PDF [5]
E126	314-LI	
E127		
E128	314-LS	
E129	314-TO	
E130	314-LQ	
E131	314-TQ	
E132	F-TERN	PDF [7]
E133	314-TE	
E134	8-MB	01.008
E135	314-LP	
E136	314-LY	
E137	314-LB	
E138	314-UK	
E139	330-AH	CEAM
E140	F-TERD	PDF [6]
E141	F-TERA	PDF
E142	MB	CEAM
E143	314-UJ	
E144	8-NU	02.008
E145		
E146	314-TX	
E147	8-NP	02.008
E148		
E149		
E150	8-NF	02.008
E151	314-TR	
E152		
E153	8-NA	02.008
E154	314-TE	
E155	314-LA	
E156	314-TI	
E157	314-LG	
E158	8-NT	02.008
E159		
E160		
E161		
E162		
E163		
E164		
E165	314-TP	
E166		
E167	8-MV	01.008
E168	314-TN	
E169		
E170		
E171		
E173	F-TERP	PDF [0]
E174		
E175		
E176		

Dassault
Falcon 20
CEV, Bretigny[1], Cazaux[2], Istres[3] & Melun[4];
ETEC 02.065, Villacoublay;
SIET 98.120, Cazaux;
CITac 00.339, Luxeuil

22	CS	CEV[3]
49	120-FA	
79	CT	CEV[1]
86	CG	CEV[2]
93	F-RAED	02.065
96	CB	CEV[1]
104	CW	CEV[1]
115	339-JG	

France

<table>
<tr><td>124</td><td>CC</td><td>CEV[1]</td></tr>
<tr><td>131</td><td>CD</td><td>CEV[1]</td></tr>
<tr><td>138</td><td>CR</td><td>CEV[2]</td></tr>
<tr><td>145</td><td>CU</td><td>CEV[1]</td></tr>
<tr><td>167</td><td>F-RAEB</td><td>02.065</td></tr>
<tr><td>182</td><td>339-JA</td><td></td></tr>
<tr><td>186</td><td>339-JE</td><td></td></tr>
<tr><td>188</td><td>CX</td><td>CEV[4]</td></tr>
<tr><td>238</td><td>F-RAEE</td><td>02.065</td></tr>
<tr><td>252</td><td>CA</td><td>CEV[1]</td></tr>
<tr><td>260</td><td>(F-RAEA)</td><td>02.065</td></tr>
<tr><td>263</td><td>CY</td><td>CEV[1]</td></tr>
<tr><td>268</td><td>(F-RAEF)</td><td>02.065</td></tr>
<tr><td>288</td><td>CV</td><td>CEV[1]</td></tr>
<tr><td>291</td><td>(F-RAEG)</td><td>02.065</td></tr>
<tr><td>342</td><td>(F-RAEC)</td><td>02.065</td></tr>
<tr><td>375</td><td>CZ</td><td>CEV[1]</td></tr>
<tr><td>422</td><td>65-EH</td><td>02.065</td></tr>
<tr><td>451</td><td>339-JC</td><td></td></tr>
<tr><td>483</td><td>339-JI</td><td></td></tr>
</table>

Dassault Falcon 50
ET 01.060, Villacoublay

5	(F-RAFI)
27	(F-RAFK)
034	(F-RAFL)
78	(F-RAFJ)

Dassault Falcon 900
ET 01.060, Villacoublay

| 2 | (F-RAFP) |
| 4 | (F-RAFQ) |

Dassault Mirage IVP
EB 01.091 'Gascogne', Mont-de-Marsan;
EB 02.091 'Bretagne', Cazaux

8/01	AG	
11	AJ	01.091
13	AL	
23	AV	01.091
25	AX	02.091
26	AY	01.091
31	BD	01.091
48	BU	01.091
49	BV	01.091
52	BY	02.091
54	CA	02.091
55	CB	01.091
56	CC	01.091
57	CD	01.091
59	CF	01.091
61	CH	02.091
62	CI	01.091

Dassault Mirage F.1C/F.1CT*
GC 02.030 'Normandie Niemen'&
GC 03.030 'Alsace', Colmar;
EC 03.033 'Lorraine', Reims;
EC 04.033 'Vexin', Djibouti;
CEAM (330), Mont-de-Marsan;
CEV, Bretigny & Istres

2		
3		
4	12-YE	CEV
5		
6		
9		
10		

<table>
<tr><td>14</td><td></td><td></td></tr>
<tr><td>15</td><td>33-FD</td><td>03.033</td></tr>
<tr><td>16</td><td></td><td></td></tr>
<tr><td>17</td><td></td><td></td></tr>
<tr><td>18</td><td></td><td></td></tr>
<tr><td>19</td><td></td><td></td></tr>
<tr><td>20</td><td></td><td></td></tr>
<tr><td>21</td><td></td><td></td></tr>
<tr><td>22</td><td></td><td></td></tr>
<tr><td>23</td><td></td><td></td></tr>
<tr><td>24</td><td>33-FS</td><td>03.033</td></tr>
<tr><td>25</td><td></td><td></td></tr>
<tr><td>26</td><td></td><td></td></tr>
<tr><td>27</td><td></td><td></td></tr>
<tr><td>29</td><td></td><td></td></tr>
<tr><td>30</td><td></td><td></td></tr>
<tr><td>31</td><td>330-AC</td><td>CEAM</td></tr>
<tr><td>32</td><td>33-FW</td><td>03.033</td></tr>
<tr><td>33</td><td></td><td></td></tr>
<tr><td>35</td><td></td><td></td></tr>
<tr><td>36</td><td></td><td></td></tr>
<tr><td>38</td><td></td><td></td></tr>
<tr><td>39</td><td></td><td></td></tr>
<tr><td>40</td><td></td><td></td></tr>
<tr><td>41</td><td></td><td></td></tr>
<tr><td>42</td><td></td><td></td></tr>
<tr><td>43</td><td></td><td></td></tr>
<tr><td>44</td><td></td><td></td></tr>
<tr><td>47</td><td></td><td></td></tr>
<tr><td>49</td><td></td><td></td></tr>
<tr><td>50</td><td></td><td></td></tr>
<tr><td>52</td><td>33-LP</td><td>04.033</td></tr>
<tr><td>55</td><td></td><td></td></tr>
<tr><td>60</td><td></td><td></td></tr>
<tr><td>62</td><td></td><td></td></tr>
<tr><td>63</td><td></td><td></td></tr>
<tr><td>64</td><td>33-FC</td><td>03.033</td></tr>
<tr><td>68</td><td></td><td></td></tr>
<tr><td>69</td><td></td><td></td></tr>
<tr><td>70</td><td></td><td></td></tr>
<tr><td>72</td><td>330-AG</td><td>CEAM</td></tr>
<tr><td>74</td><td>33-FO</td><td>03.033</td></tr>
<tr><td>75</td><td></td><td></td></tr>
<tr><td>76</td><td>33-FQ</td><td>03.033</td></tr>
<tr><td>77</td><td></td><td></td></tr>
<tr><td>80</td><td>33-FK</td><td>03.033</td></tr>
<tr><td>81</td><td></td><td></td></tr>
<tr><td>82</td><td>33-LK</td><td>04.033</td></tr>
<tr><td>83</td><td>33-LB</td><td>04.033</td></tr>
<tr><td>84</td><td></td><td></td></tr>
<tr><td>85</td><td></td><td></td></tr>
<tr><td>87</td><td>33-FR</td><td>03.033</td></tr>
<tr><td>90</td><td>33-L.</td><td>04.033</td></tr>
<tr><td>100</td><td>33-LA</td><td>04.033</td></tr>
<tr><td>103</td><td>33-L.</td><td>04.033</td></tr>
<tr><td>201</td><td>33-FI</td><td>03.033</td></tr>
<tr><td>202</td><td>33-LG</td><td>04.033</td></tr>
<tr><td>203</td><td></td><td></td></tr>
<tr><td>205</td><td>33-FX</td><td>03.033</td></tr>
<tr><td>206</td><td></td><td></td></tr>
<tr><td>207*</td><td>330-AO</td><td>CEAM</td></tr>
<tr><td>210</td><td></td><td></td></tr>
<tr><td>211</td><td></td><td></td></tr>
<tr><td>213</td><td></td><td></td></tr>
<tr><td>214</td><td>33-LH</td><td>04.033</td></tr>
<tr><td>216</td><td></td><td></td></tr>
<tr><td>218</td><td>33-LD</td><td>04.033</td></tr>
<tr><td>219*</td><td>30-SF</td><td>03.030</td></tr>
<tr><td>220*</td><td>30-ST</td><td>03.030</td></tr>
<tr><td>221*</td><td>30-QR</td><td>02.030</td></tr>
<tr><td>223*</td><td>30-QT</td><td>02.030</td></tr>
<tr><td>224</td><td>33-LE</td><td>04.033</td></tr>
<tr><td>225*</td><td>30-QC</td><td>02.030</td></tr>
<tr><td>226*</td><td>30-QO</td><td>02.030</td></tr>
</table>

<table>
<tr><td>227*</td><td>330-AP</td><td>CEAM</td></tr>
<tr><td>228*</td><td>30-SN</td><td>03.030</td></tr>
<tr><td>229*</td><td>30-QF</td><td>02.030</td></tr>
<tr><td>230*</td><td>30-QM</td><td>02.030</td></tr>
<tr><td>231</td><td></td><td></td></tr>
<tr><td>232*</td><td>30-SP</td><td>03.030</td></tr>
<tr><td>233*</td><td>30-QG</td><td>02.030</td></tr>
<tr><td>234*</td><td>30-QL</td><td>02.030</td></tr>
<tr><td>235*</td><td>30-QS</td><td>02.030</td></tr>
<tr><td>236*</td><td>30-SW</td><td>03.030</td></tr>
<tr><td>237*</td><td>30-SE</td><td>03.030</td></tr>
<tr><td>238*</td><td>30-SB</td><td>03.030</td></tr>
<tr><td>239*</td><td>30-QD</td><td>02.030</td></tr>
<tr><td>241*</td><td>30-SI</td><td>03.030</td></tr>
<tr><td>242*</td><td>30-SG</td><td>03.030</td></tr>
<tr><td>243*</td><td>30-QN</td><td>02.030</td></tr>
<tr><td>244*</td><td></td><td></td></tr>
<tr><td>245*</td><td>30-SA</td><td>03.030</td></tr>
<tr><td>246*</td><td>30-QJ</td><td>02.030</td></tr>
<tr><td>247*</td><td>30-QP</td><td>02.030</td></tr>
<tr><td>248*</td><td>30-QQ</td><td>02.030</td></tr>
<tr><td>249*</td><td></td><td></td></tr>
<tr><td>251*</td><td>330-AY</td><td>CEAM</td></tr>
<tr><td>252*</td><td>30-SK</td><td>03.030</td></tr>
<tr><td>253*</td><td></td><td></td></tr>
<tr><td>254*</td><td>330-AJ</td><td>CEAM</td></tr>
<tr><td>255*</td><td>30-QK</td><td>02.030</td></tr>
<tr><td>256*</td><td>30-SL</td><td>03.030</td></tr>
<tr><td>257*</td><td>30-SD</td><td>03.030</td></tr>
<tr><td>258*</td><td>30-SM</td><td>03.030</td></tr>
<tr><td>259</td><td></td><td></td></tr>
<tr><td>260*</td><td>30-SO</td><td>03.030</td></tr>
<tr><td>261*</td><td>30-SV</td><td>03.030</td></tr>
<tr><td>262*</td><td></td><td></td></tr>
<tr><td>264*</td><td>30-QH</td><td>02.030</td></tr>
<tr><td>265*</td><td>30-SR</td><td>03.030</td></tr>
<tr><td>267*</td><td>30-QB</td><td>02.030</td></tr>
<tr><td>268</td><td>33-LI</td><td>04.033</td></tr>
<tr><td>271</td><td></td><td></td></tr>
<tr><td>272*</td><td>30-SQ</td><td>03.030</td></tr>
<tr><td>273*</td><td>30-SJ</td><td>03.030</td></tr>
<tr><td>274*</td><td></td><td></td></tr>
<tr><td>275</td><td></td><td></td></tr>
<tr><td>277</td><td></td><td></td></tr>
<tr><td>278*</td><td>30-QA</td><td>02.030</td></tr>
<tr><td>279*</td><td>30-SC</td><td>03.030</td></tr>
<tr><td>280*</td><td>30-QE</td><td>02.030</td></tr>
<tr><td>281*</td><td>30-QI</td><td>02.030</td></tr>
<tr><td>283*</td><td>30-SH</td><td>03.030</td></tr>
</table>

Dassault Mirage F.1CR
ER 01.033 'Belfort' &
ER 02.033 'Savoie', Reims;
CEAM (330), Mont-de-Marsan;
CEV, Istres

<table>
<tr><td>601</td><td></td><td>CEV</td></tr>
<tr><td>602</td><td></td><td>CEV</td></tr>
<tr><td>603</td><td>33-CB</td><td>01.033</td></tr>
<tr><td>604</td><td>33-CE</td><td>01.033</td></tr>
<tr><td>605</td><td>33-NF</td><td>02.033</td></tr>
<tr><td>606</td><td>33-NP</td><td>02.033</td></tr>
<tr><td>607</td><td>330-AB</td><td>CEAM</td></tr>
<tr><td>608</td><td>33-NG</td><td>02.033</td></tr>
<tr><td>610</td><td>33-NQ</td><td>02.033</td></tr>
<tr><td>611</td><td>33-CO</td><td>01.033</td></tr>
<tr><td>612</td><td>33-NJ</td><td>02.033</td></tr>
<tr><td>613</td><td>33-NK</td><td>02.033</td></tr>
<tr><td>614</td><td>33-CN</td><td>01.033</td></tr>
<tr><td>615</td><td>33-CU</td><td>01.033</td></tr>
<tr><td>616</td><td>33-CY</td><td>01.033</td></tr>
<tr><td>617</td><td>33-CI</td><td>01.033</td></tr>
<tr><td>620</td><td>33-CT</td><td>01.033</td></tr>
<tr><td>622</td><td>33-CR</td><td>01.033</td></tr>
</table>

623	33-CM	01.033
624	33-NY	02.033
627	33-NI	02.033
628	33-NN	02.033
629	33-CG	01.033
630	33-NL	02.033
631	33-CD	01.033
632	33-NE	02.033
634	33-CK	01.033
635	33-NS	02.033
636	33-CS	01.033
637	33-CP	01.033
638	33-NU	02.033
640	33-NV	02.033
641	33-NT	02.033
642	33-NC	02.033
643	330-AF	CEAM
645	33-NO	02.033
646	33-NW	02.033
647	33-NX	02.033
648	33-CF	01.033
649	33-NZ	02.033
650	33-CJ	01.033
651	33-NB	02.033
653	33-CQ	01.033
654	33-CL	01.033
655	33-NR	02.033
656	33-NH	02.033
657	33-CV	01.033
658	33-CW	01.033
659		
660	33-ND	02.033
661	33-CX	01.033
662	33-NA	02.033

Dassault Mirage 2000-5
AMD-BA, Istres

01	
BX1	
BY1	

Dassault Mirage 2000B
CEV, Bretigny
EC 02.002 'Côte d'Or', Dijon;
EC 01.005 'Vendée',
EC 02.005 'Ile de France' &
EC 03.005
'Comtat-Venaissin',
Orange;
EC 01.012 'Cambrésis' &
EC 02.012 'Picardie',
Cambrai

B01		CEV
502	2-FA	02.002
504		CEV
505	2-FB	02.002
506	2-FC	02.002
507	2-FD	02.002
508	2-FE	02.002
509	2-FF	02.002
510	2-FG	02.002
511	2-FH	02.002
512	2-FI	02.002
513	2-FJ	02.002
514	2-FK	02.002
515	2-FT	02.002
516	2-FM	02.002
518	2-FU	02.002
519	2-FV	02.002
520	2-FW	02.002
521	2-FX	02.002
522	2-FY	02.002
523	5-OJ	02.005
524	330-AZ	CEAM
525	12-KN	02.012
526	12-KM	02.012
527	5-NO	01.005
528	330-AN	CEAM
529	5-AA	03.005
530	12-YA	01.012

Dassault Mirage 2000C
CEAM (330), Mont-de-Marsan;
CEV, Istres;
EC 01.002 'Cicogne' &
EC 02.002 'Côte d'Or', Dijon;
EC 01.005 'Vendée',
EC 02.005 'Ile de France' &
EC 03.005
'Comtat-Venaissin',
Orange;
EC 01.012 'Cambrésis' &
EC 02.012 'Picardie',
Cambrai

04		
1	2-EP	CEV
2		CEV
3	2-FP	02.002
4	2-FR	02.002
5	2-FQ	02.002
8	2-EC	01.002
9	2-EB	01.002
11	2-EF	01.002
12	2-FS	02.002
13	2-EI	01.002
14	2-FO	02.002
15	2-EK	01.002
16	2-EL	01.002
17	2-EM	01.002
18	2-FL	02.002
19	2-EA	01.002
20	2-EQ	01.002
21	2-EG	01.002
22	2-EH	01.002
25	2-EJ	01.002
27	2-EO	01.002
28	2-ER	01.002
29	2-ED	01.002
30	2-EV	01.002
32	2-EP	01.002
33	2-ES	01.002
34	2-ET	01.002
35	2-EE	01.002
36	2-EN	01.002
37	2-EU	01.002
38	5-ND	01.005
39	5-OF	02.005
40	5-NJ	01.005
41	5-NL	01.005
42	5-AB	03.005
43	5-AE	03.005
44	5-AQ	03.005
45	5-OM	02.005
46	5-AG	03.005
47	5-ON	02.005
48	5-AF	03.005
49	5-AL	03.005
51	5-OG	02.005
52	5-OC	02.005
53	5-AJ	03.005
54	5-AR	03.005
55	5-OH	02.005
56	5-OA	02.005
57	5-OL	02.005
58	5-AM	03.005
59	5-OB	02.005
61	5-OD	02.005
62	5-AC	03.005
63	5-OK	02.005
64	330-AQ	CEAM
65	5-OO	02.005
66	5-AN	03.005
67	5-OQ	02.005
68	5-AI	03.005
69	5-OR	02.005
70	5-AO	03.005
71	5-AD	02.005
72	5-OE	02.005
73	5-AK	03.005
74	5-OP	02.005
76	5-NP	01.005
77	12-KB	02.012
78	5-NE	01.005
79		
80	330-AC	CEAM
81	330-AS	CEAM
82	5-NM	01.005
83	5-NG	01.005
84	5-NH	01.005
85	5-NI	01.005
86	5-NR	01.005
87	5-NK	01.005
88		
89	12-YB	01.012
90	12-KO	02.012
91	12-YO	01.012
92	330-AW	CEAM
93	330-AR	CEAM
94	12-KA	02.012
95		
96	12-KK	02.012
97	12-KP	02.012
98	12-YJ	01.012
99	12-YP	01.012
100	5-NQ	01.005
101	12-KJ	02.012
102	12-YE	01.012
103	12-YN	01.012
104	12-YK	01.012
105	12-YL	01.012
106	12-KL	02.012
107	12-YR	01.012
108	330-AT	CEAM
109	12-YI	01.012
111	12-KI	02.012
112	5-NB	01.005
113	5-NC	01.005
114	12-YG	01.012
115	12-KC	02.012
116	12-KG	02.012
117	12-YD	01.012
118	12-KH	02.012
119	12-KD	02.012
120	12-YM	01.012
121	12-KF	02.012
122	12-YC	01.012
123	12-KR	02.012
124	5-NF	01.005

Dassault Mirage 2000D
EC 01.003 'Navarre' &
EC 03.003 'Ardennes',
Nancy;
CEAM (330), Mont-de-Marsan;
AMD-BA, Istres

D01	AMD-BA	
601	3-IA	01.003
602		
603	3-IC	01.003
604		

605	3-IE	01.003
606	3-XM	03.003
607		
608	3-XB	03.003
609	3-XD	03.003
610	3-II	01.003
611	330-AM	CEAM
612	330-AX	CEAM
613	330-AE	CEAM
614	3-IJ	01.003
615	3-XE	01.003
616	3-IL	01.003
617	3-XA	03.003
618	3-IG	01.003
619	3-ID	01.003
620	3-IM	03.003
621	3-XC	03.003
622	3-IH	01.003
623	3-IB	01.003
624	3-XF	03.003
625	3-IK	01.003
626	3-XH	03.003
627	3-IN	01.003
628	3-XI	01.003
629	3-XJ	03.003
630	3-IO	01.003
631	3-IF	01.003
632	3-XL	03.003
633		
634		
635		
636		
637		
638		
639		
640		

Dassault Mirage 2000N
EC 02.003
'Champagne', Nancy;
EC 01.004 'Dauphiné' &
EC 02.004 'Lafayette',
Luxeuil;
EC 03.004 'Limousin', Istres;
CEAM (330), Mont-de-Marsan;

301		
302	4-CA	03.004
303		
304	3-CB	03.004
305	4-BF	02.004
306	4-CC	03.004
307	4-BC	02.004
308	4-CD	03.004
309	4-BA	02.004
310	4-CE	03.004
311	4-BD	02.004
312	4-CF	03.004
313	4-BE	02.004
314	4-CG	03.004
315	4-BG	02.004
316	4-CH	03.004
317	4-BH	02.004
318	4-CI	03.004
319	4-BI	02.004
320		
322	4-BK	02.004
323	4-CJ	03.004
324	4-CL	03.004
325	4-BL	02.004
326	4-CM	03.004
327	4-BM	03.004
329	4-CN	03.004
330	4-CO	03.004

331	4-CP	03.004
332	4-BN	02.004
333	4-AB	01.004
334	330-AV	CEAM
335	4-BJ	02.004
336	4-BP	02.004
337	3-JT	02.003
338	4-AC	01.004
339	4-AD	01.004
340	4-AA	01.004
341	4-AF	01.004
342	4-AG	01.004
343	4-AH	01.004
344	4-AJ	01.004
345	4-AK	01.004
347	4-BT	02.004
348	3-JA	02.003
349	4-AO	01.004
350	3-JR	02.003
351	4-AQ	01.004
353	3-JS	02.003
354	3-JC	02.003
355	4-AL	01.004
356	3-JE	02.003
357	3-JF	02.003
358	3-JG	02.003
359	3-JH	02.003
360	3-JI	02.003
361	3-JJ	02.003
362	3-JK	02.003
363	3-JL	02.003
364	3-JM	02.003
365	3-JN	02.003
366	4-BO	02.004
367	3-JP	02.003
368	4-AR	01.004
369	3-JU	02.003
370	4-AT	01.004
371	4-AV	01.004
372	4-BR	02.004
373	3-JV	02.003
374	4-BS	02.004
375	3-JB	02.003

Dassault Rafale-B
AMD-BA, Istres
B01 AMD-BA

Dassault Rafale-C
C01 CEV

DHC 6 Twin Otter 200/300*
GAM 00.056 'Vaucluse',
Evreux;
EdC 00.070, Chateaudun;
ETL 01.062 'Vercours', Creil;
CEAM, Mont-de-Marsan

292	CC	00.056
298	CD	00.056
300	CE	00.056
603*	MB	00.070
730*	CA	01.062
742*	IA	CEAM
743*	MA	00.070
745*	IB	CEAM
786*	CT	01.062
790*	CW	01.062

Douglas DC-8-53¹/55F²/72CF³
EE 00.051 'Aubrac', Evreux;
ET 03.060 'Esterel',
Paris/Charles de Gaulle

45570¹	F-RAFE	00.051
45819²	F-RAFC	03.060
46013³	F-RAFG	03.060
46043³	F-RAFD	03.060
46130³	F-RAFF	03.060

Embraer EMB.121 Xingu
ETE 00.043
Médoc', Bordeaux;
ETE 00.044 'Mistral',
Aix-en-Provence;
EAT 319, Avord;
CEAM, Mont-de-Marsan;
CITac 00.339, Luxeuil;

054	YX	EAT 319
064	YY	EAT 319
072	YA	EAT 319
073	YB	EAT 319
075	YC	EAT 319
076	YD	EAT 319
078	YE	EAT 319
080	YF	EAT 319
082	YG	EAT 319
084	YH	EAT 319
086	YI	EAT 319
089	YJ	EAT 319
091	YK	EAT 319
092	YL	EAT 319
095	YM	EAT 319
096	YN	EAT 319
098	YO	EAT 319
099	YP	EAT 319
101	YR	EAT 319
102	YS	EAT 319
103	YT	EAT 319
105	YU	EAT 319
107	YV	EAT 319
108	YW	EAT 319
111	YQ	EAT 319

Embraer EMB.312F Tucano
GI 312, Salon de Provence;
CEAM (330), Mont-de-Marsan

438	312-DJ
439	330-DM
456	312-JA
457	312-JB
458	312-JC
459	312-JD
460	312-JE
461	312-JF
462	312-JG
463	312-JH
464	312-JI
465	312-JJ
466	312-JK
467	312-JL
468	312-JM
469	312-JN
470	312-JO
471	312-JP
472	312-JQ
473	312-JR
474	312-JS
475	312-JT
477	312-JU
478	312-JV
479	312-JW
480	312-JX
481	312-JY
482	312-JZ

Lockheed C-130H/C-130H-30* Hercules

ET 02.061 'Franche-Comté', Orléans

5114	61-PA
5116	61-PB
5119	61-PC
5140	61-PD
5142*	61-PE
5144*	61-PF
5150*	61-PG
5151*	61-PH
5152*	61-PI
5153*	61-PJ
5226*	61-PK
5227*	61-PL

Morane Saulnier 760 Paris

CEAM (330), Mont-de-Marsan;
CEV, Bretigny & Istres;
EAC 314, Tours;
ENOSA 316, Toulouse;
ETE 00.041 'Verdun', Metz;
ETEC 01.065, Villacoublay;
GI 312, Salon de Provence;
SALE 09.112, Reims;
SALE 09.115, Orange;
SALE 09.116, Luxeuil;
SALE 09.121, Nancy;
SALE 09.126, Solenzara;
SALE 09.132, Colmar

1	330-DA	CEAM
19	3-KB	09.121
23	3-KA	09.121
24	330-DB	CEAM
25	41-AP	00.041
26	330-DR	CEAM
27	41-AR	00.041
29	314-DE	EAC 314
30		09.116
34		
35	33-QG	09.112
36	316-DH	ENOSA
38	41-AS	00.041
44		
45	316-DI	ENOSA
53	316-DK	ENOSA
54	330-DQ	CEAM
56	DJ	ENOSA
57	4-WD	09.116
58	312-DG	GI 312
59		
60	312-DE	GI 312
61	312-DF	GI 312
68	NB	CEV
70	65-LF	01.065
71	41-AC	00.041
73	330-DF	CEAM
75	316-DK	ENOSA
78	5-ME	09.115
83	NC	CEV
91	316-DM	ENOSA
92	316-DL	ENOSA
93	30-TB	09.132
94	5-MF	09.115
100	NG	CEV
113	NI	CEV
114	NJ	CEV
115	OV	CEV
116	ON	CEV
118	NQ	CEV
119	NL	CEV

Nord 262 Frégate

CEV, Istres;
ETE 00.041 'Verdun', Metz;
ETE 00.043 'Médoc', Bordeaux;
ETE 00.044 'Mistral', Aix-en-Provence;
ETEC 01.065, Villacoublay;
EdC 00.070, Chateaudun;
ENOSA 316, Toulouse;
CIEH 341, Toulouse;
CEAM (330), Mont-de-Marsan

01		CEV
3	OH	CEV
55	MH	CEV
58	MJ	CEV
64	AA	CIEH 341
66	AB	01.065
67	MI	CEV
68	AC	01.065
76	DA	ENOSA
77	AK	01.065
78	AF	01.065
80	AW	00.041
81	AH	01.065
83	DB	ENOSA
86	DD	ENOSA
87	DC	ENOSA
88	AL	00.044
89	AZ	01.065
91	AT	00.043
92	DE	ENOSA
93	AP	CIEH 341
94	AU	00.044
95	AR	00.041
105	AE	00.041
106	AY	01.065
107	AX	00.043
108	AG	CIEH 341
109	AM	00.043
110	AS	00.041

SEPECAT Jaguar A

CEV, Bretigny & Istres;
EC 01.007 'Provence',
EC 02.007 'Argonne' &
EC 03.007 'Languedoc', St Dizier;
EC 02.011 'Vosges' &
EC 03.011 'Corse', Toul;
CEAM (330), Mont-de-Marsan;
CITac 00.339, Luxeuil

A1	7-IA	03.007
A2	7-PW	02.007
A3		CEV
A5		
A7		
A9		
A11		
A13	7-HR	01.007
A14	7-PO	02.007
A15	7-HG	01.007
A16		
A17	7-PJ	02.007
A19		
A23	7-HH	01.007
A24		
A25	7-PU	02.007
A26	11-MH	02.011
A27		
A28	7-HB	01.007

A29	7-IK	03.007
A32		
A33		
A34	7-ID	03.007
A35	7-PN	02.007
A36		
A37		
A38	7-PV	02.007
A39	7-HI	01.007
A40	7-IQ	03.007
A41	7-HE	01.007
A43		
A44	11-MC	02.011
A46	7-HP	01.007
A47	7-IG	03.007
A48		
A49	11-RD	03.011
A50	7-IE	03.007
A53	7-IP	03.007
A54	11-MN	02.011
A55	7-PA	02.007
A58	7-HL	01.007
A59	7-IH	03.007
A60		
A61	11-RG	03.011
A64	7-IS	03.007
A65		
A66	7-IB	03.007
A70	11-RL	03.011
A72		
A73		
A74		
A75	7-IJ	03.007
A76		
A79	7-IM	03.007
A80		
A82	7-HM	01.007
A84	7-IO	03.007
A86	11-MS	02.011
A87	7-IN	03.007
A88	7-II	03.007
A89	11-RE	03.011
A90	11-MI	02.011
A92	7-PC	02.007
A93		
A94		
A96		
A97	11-RU	03.011
A98	7-HJ	01.007
A99	11-MQ	02.011
A100	7-HQ	01.007
A101		
A103	11-RI	03.011
A104	7-IL	03.007
A107		
A108	11-RF	03.011
A112	11-MA	02.011
A113	11-RB	03.011
A115	7-HF	01.007
A117	7-HO	01.007
A118		
A119		
A120	11-MR	02.011
A121		
A122	11-ME	02.011
A123	11-RQ	03.011
A124	7-HN	01.007
A126		
A127	7-HA	01.007
Λ128		
A129	11-MP	02.011
A130	11-RN	03.011
A131		
A133		

France

A135	11-RR	03.011
A137	11-MM	02.011
A138		
A139	11-RC	03.011
A140	11-MV	02.011
A141	11-MK	02.011
A142		
A144	11-MG	02.011
A145	11-MO	02.011
A148	11-MZ	02.011
A149	11-RK	03.011
A150	11-MF	02.011
A151	11-ML	02.011
A152		
A153	11-RO	03.011
A154	11-RP	03.011
A157	11-MW	02.011
A158	11-RM	03.011
A159	11-RV	03.011
A160	11-RT	03.011

SEPECAT Jaguar E

E1	CEV	
E2	11-RA	03.011
E3	7-IC	03.007
E4	7-PG	02.007
E5	11-RY	03.011
E6	7-PD	02.007
E7		
E8	339-WG	00.339
E9	7-PQ	02.007
E10	339-WF	00.339
E11	7-PE	02.007
E12		
E13	11-RX	03.011
E15		
E18	11-MD	02.011
E19	11-MJ	02.011
E20	7-PR	02.007
E21	7-PP	02.007
E22	7-PI	02.007
E23	7-PB	02.007
E24	7-PL	02.007
E25	7-PK	02.007
E27		
E28	7-PF	02.007
E29	339-WJ	00.339
E30		
E32		
E33		
E35	7-PM	02.007
E36		
E37		
E39	7-PH	02.007
E40		

SOCATA TBM 700

ETE 00.041 'Verdun', Metz;
ETE 00.043 Médoc',
  Bordeaux;
ETE 00.044 'Mistral',
  Aix-en-Provence;
ETEC 02.065, Villacoublay;
CEAM (330), Mont-de-
  Marsan;

33	65-XA	02.065
35	43-XB	00.043
70	43-XC	00.043
77	65-XD	02.065
78	65-XE	02.065
80	65-XF	02.065
93	330-IC	CEAM
94	44-XG	00.044
95	65-XH	02.065
103	41-XI	00.041
104	41-XJ	00.041
105	65-XK	02.065
106	MN	CEV

Transall C-160/C-160H[1]/C-1 60NG[2]/C-160NG GABRIEL[3]/C-160R[4]

CEV, Bretigny;
EET 01.054 'Dunkerque',
  Metz;
ETOM 00.055 'Ouessant',
  Dakar;
EA 01.059 'Bigorre',
  Evreux;
ET 01.061 'Touraine' &
ET 03.061 'Poitou' Orléans;
ET 01.064 'Bearn' &
ET 02.064 'Anjou', Evreux;
CEAM (330), Mont-de-
  Marsan

R02[4]	61-MI	01.061
R06[4]	61-ZB	03.061
R1[4]	61-MA	01.061
A04	61-BI	CEV
F2	61-MB	01.061
R3[4]	61-MC	01.061
R4[4]	61-MD	01.061
R5[4]		01.061
R11[4]	61-MF	01.061
F12	61-MG	01.061
F13	61-MH	01.061
R15[4]	61-MJ	01.061
F16	61-MK	01.061
R18[4]	61-MM	01.061
F42	61-MN	01.061
F43	61-MO	01.061
F44	61-MP	01.061
F45	61-MQ	01.061
F46	61-MR	01.061
F48	61-MT	01.061
F49	61-MU	01.061
F51	61-MW	01.061
F52	61-MX	01.061
F53	61-MY	01.061
F54	61-MZ	01.061
F55	61-ZC	03.061
F86	61-ZD	03.061
F87	61-ZE	03.061
F88	61-ZF	03.061
F89	61-ZG	03.061
F90	61-ZH	03.061
F91	61-ZI	03.061
R92[4]	61-ZJ	03.061
F93	61-ZK	03.061
F94	61-ZL	03.061
F95	61-ZM	03.061
F96	61-ZN	03.061
R97[4]	61-ZA	03.061
F98	61-ZP	03.061
R99[4]	61-ZQ	03.061
F100	61-ZR	03.061
F153	61-ZS	03.061
F154	61-ZT	03.061
F155	61-ZU	03.061
F157	61-ZW	03.061
F158	61-ZX	03.061
F159	61-ZY	03.061
F160	61-ZZ	03.061
F201[2]	64-GA	01.064
F202[2]	64-GB	02.064
R203[4]	330-IS	CEAM
F204[2]	64-GD	02.064
F205[2]	64-GE	01.064
F206[2]	64-GF	02.064
F207[2]	64-GG	01.064
F208[2]	64-GH	02.064
F210[2]	64-GJ	02.064
F211[2]	64-GK	02.064
F212[2]	64-GL	02.064
F213[2]	64-GM	01.064
F214[2]	64-GN	02.064
F215[2]	64-GO	01.064
F216[3]	54-GT	01.054
F217[2]	64-GQ	01.064
F218[2]	64-GR	01.054
F221[3]	54-GS	01.054
F223[2]	64-GW	01.064
F224[2]	64-GX	02.064
F225[2]	64-GY	01.064
F226[2]	64-GZ	02.064
H01[1]	59-BA	01.059
H02[1]	59-BB	01.059
H03[1]	59-BC	01.059
H04[1]	59-BD	01.059

Aéronavale/Marine

Aérospatiale SA.321G Super Frelon

32 Flotille, Lanvéoc;
33 Flotille, San Mandrier

101	32F
102	33F
106	32F
118	32F
120	32F
122	32F
134	32F
137	33F
141	32F
144	33F
148	33F
149	32F
160	33F
162	32F
163	33F
164	32F
165	33F

Breguet Br.1050M Alizé

4 Flotille, Lann Bihoué;
6 Flotille, Nimes-Garons;
ES 59, Hyères

11	6F
12	4F
17	4F
22	6F
24	6F
25	6F
26	6F
30	6F
31	4F
33	6F
36	6F
41	4F
43	4F
47	4F
48	6F
49	6F
50	4F
51	6F
52	4F
53	6F
55	4F
56	4F

59	6F
60	6F
64	6F
65	4F
67	59S
73	6F
76	6F

Breguet Br 1150 Atlantic/Atlantique 2*
21 Flotille/22 Flotille, Nimes-Garons;
23 Flotille/24 Flotille, Lann Bihoué;
CEV, Bretigny

03	21F/22F
04	21F/22F
2	21F/22F
11	21F/22F
21	21F/22F
24	23F/24F
25	21F/22F
31	21F/22F
45	21F/22F
51	21F/22F
52	21F/22F
53	21F/22F
54	21F/22F
55	23F/24F
56	21F/22F
57	21F/22F
61	21F/22F
65	23F/24F
66	21F/22F
67	21F/22F
68	21F/22F
02*	21F/22F
03*	CEV
04*	21F/22F
1*	21F/22F
2*	23F/24F
3*	23F/24F
4*	23F/24F
5*	23F/24F
6*	23F/24F
7*	23F/24F
8*	21F/22F
9*	23F/24F
10*	21F/22F
11*	23F/24F
12*	21F/22F
13*	21F/22F
14*	21F/22F
15*	21F/22F
16*	23F/24F
17*	23F/24F
18*	21F/22F
19*	21F/22F
20*	23F/24F
21*	
22*	21F/22F
23*	
24*	
25*	
26*	
27*	
28*	
29*	
30*	

Dassault Etendard IVMP
16 Flotille, Landivisiau
101
107

109	
114	
115	
118	
120	
153	
162	
163	

Dassault Super Etendard
11 Flotille, Landivisiau;
17 Flotille, Landivisiau;
CEV, Bretigny & Istres;
ES 59, Hyères

1	11F
2	59S
3	11F
4	11F
6	59S
8	11F
10	11F
12	11F
13	11F
14	11F
15	59S
16	11F
17	17F
18	59S
19	59S
23	17F
24	17F
25	59S
26	11F
28	59S
29	
30	11F
31	11F
32	11F
33	17F
34	11F
35	17F
37	59S
38	11F
39	
41	11F
42	
43	11F
44	11F
45	11F
46	17F
47	17F
48	11F
49	59S
50	17F
51	
52	11F
53	
55	17F
57	11F
59	17F
61	11F
62	11F
63	11F
64	11F
65	17F
66	11F
68	CEV
69	11F
71	11F

Dassault Falcon 10(MER)
ES 3, Hyères;
ES 57, Landivisiau

32	3S
101	57S
129	57S
133	57S
143	57S
185	57S

Dassault Falcon Guardian
ES 9 Noumea;
ES 12 Papeete;
CEPA, Istres

48	12S
65	9S
72	12S
77	9S
80	CEPA

Dassault Rafale-M

M01	AMD-BA
M02	AMD-BA

Embraer EMB.121 Xingu
ERCS, Cuers;
ES 2, Lann Bihoué;
ES 3, Hyères;
ES 11, Le Bourget;
ES 52, Lann Bihoué;
ES 57, Landivisiau

30	11S
47	11S
55	11S
65	11S
66	2S
67	2S
68	57S
69	2S
70	11S
71	57S
74	11S
77	3S
79	52S
81	ERCS
83	52S
85	52S
87	52S
90	52S

LTV F-8P Crusader
12 Flotille, Landivisiau
3
4
5
7
8
10
11
17
19
22
23
29
32
34
35
37
39

Morane Saulnier 760 Paris
ES 57, Landivisiau
32
33

France – Germany

40	
41	
42	
46	
85	
87	
88	

Nord 262 Frégate
ERCS, Cuers;
ES 2, Lann Bihoué;
ES 3, Hyères;
ES 11, Le Bourget;
ES 56, Nimes-Garons;
ES 57, Landivisiau

1	ERCS
16	3S
28	2S
43	ERCS
45	2S
46	56S
51	56S
52	56S
53	56S
59	3S
60	2S
61	2S
62	2S
63	3S
65	2S
69	56S
70	2S
71	2S
72	56S
73	56S
75	56S
79	56S
100	56S
102	11S
104	11S

Piper Navajo
ES 3, Hyeres

227
925
931

**Westland Lynx
HAS2 (FN);
HAS4 (FN)***
31 Flotile, San Mandrier;
34 Flotile, Lanvéoc;
ES 20, St Raphael

260	20S
262	35F
263	34F
264	31F
265	34F
266	34F
267	
268	
269	34F
270	31F
271	34F
272	34F
273	34F
274	34F
275	34F
276	31F
278	34F
620	31F
621	34F
622	34F
623	34F
624	31F

625	34F
627	31F
801*	31F
802*	34F
803*	31F
804*	31F
806*	34F
807*	31F
808*	34F
809*	31F
810*	31F
811*	34F
812*	31F
813*	31F
814*	34F

**Aviation Legére de
l'Armée de Terre
(ALAT)
Cessna F.406 Caravan II**
EMAT, Rennes

0008	ABM
0010	ABN

SOCATA TBM 700
EMAT, Rennes

99	ABO
100	ABP

GERMANY
**Luftwaffe, Marineflieger
Boeing 707-307C**
1/FBS, Köln-Bonn

10+01
10+02
10+03
10+04

Airbus A310-304
1/FBS, Köln-Bonn

10+21
10+22
10+23

Tupolev Tu-154M
1/FBS, Köln-Bonn

11+01
11+02

**Canadair CL601-1A
Challenger**
1/FBS, Köln-Bonn

12+01
12+02
12+03
12+04
12+05
12+06
12+07

VFW-Fokker 614-100
1/FBS, Köln-Bonn

17+01
17+02
17+03

Mikoyan MiG-29
JG-73, Laage;
WTD-61, Ingolstadt
MiG-29A

29+01	JG-73
29+02	JG-73
29+03	JG-73
29+04	JG-73

29+05	JG-73
29+07	JG-73
29+08	JG-73
29+09	JG-73
29+10	JG-73
29+11	JG-73
29+12	JG-73
29+14	JG-73
29+15	JG-73
29+16	JG-73
29+17	JG-73
29+18	JG-73
29+20	JG-73
98+06	WTD-61
98+08	WTD-61

MiG-29UB

29+22	JG-73
29+23	JG-73
29+24	JG-73
29+25	JG-73

McD F-4F Phantom
JG-71, Wittmundhaven;
JG-72, Hopsten;
JG-73, Pferdsfeld;
JG-74, Neuburg/Donau;
TsLw-1, Kaufbeuren;
WTD-61, Ingolstadt

37+01	JG-72
37+03	JG-71
37+04	TsLw-1
37+05	JG-72
37+06	JG-72
37+07	JG-72
37+08	JG-74
37+09	JG-73
37+10	JG-73
37+11	JG-74
37+12	JG-73
37+13	JG-74
37+14	TsLw-1
37+15	WTD-61
37+16	WTD-61
37+17	JG-72
37+18	JG-72
37+19	JG-72
37+20	JG-73
37+21	JG-73
37+22	JG-72
37+23	JG-72
37+24	JG-72
37+25	JG-73
37+26	JG-72
37+28	JG-71
37+29	JG-73
37+30	JG-73
37+31	JG-74
37+32	JG-74
37+33	JG-73
37+34	JG-73
37+35	JG-73
37+36	JG-73
37+37	JG-72
37+38	JG-71
37+39	JG-71
37+40	JG-73
37+41	JG-73
37+42	JG-73
37+43	JG-73
37+44	JG-73
37+45	JG-73
37+47	JG-73
37+48	JG-74
37+49	JG-74

37+50	JG-73		38+42	JG-72		41+42	FLG FFB	
37+52	JG-73		38+43	JG-72		41+45	FLG FFB	
37+53	JG-74		38+44	JG-71		41+49	FLG FFB	
37+54	JG-74		38+45	JG-72		41+53	FLG FFB	
37+55	JG-74		38+46	JG-74		41+55	FLG FFB	
37+57	JG-73		38+47	JG-72		41+56	FLG FFB	
37+58	JG-73		38+48	JG-71		41+57	WTD-61	
37+60	JG-74		38+49	JG-72		41+58	FLG FFB	
37+61	JG-74		38+50	JG-72		41+59	FLG FFB	
37+63	JG-74		38+51	JG-73		41+61	FLG FFB	
37+64	JG-74		38+53	JG-72		41+62	FLG FFB	
37+65	JG-71		38+54	JG-72		41+63	FLG FFB	
37+66	JG-74		38+55	JG-71		41+64	FLG FFB	
37+67	JG-74		38+56	JG-72		41+66	FLG FFB	
37+69	JG-73		38+57	JG-72		41+67	FLG FFB	
37+70	JG-74		38+58	JG-72		41+68	FLG FFB	
37+71	JG-74		38+59	JG-72		41+71	FLG FFB	
37+73	JG-74		38+60	JG-72		41+72	FLG FFB	
37+75	JG-72		38+61	JG-72		41+73	FLG FFB	
37+76	JG-74		38+62	JG-71		41+74	FLG FFB	
37+77	JG-74		38+63	JG-72		41+75	FLG FFB	
37+78	JG-71		38+64	JG-72				
37+79	JG-74		38+66	JG-72				
37+81	JG-74		38+67	JG-72		**Panavia Tornado**		
37+82	JG-71		38+68	JG-72		**Strike/Trainer[1]/ECR[2]**		
37+83	JG-74		38+69	JG-72		TTTE, RAF Cottesmore;		
37+84	JG-74		38+70	JG-72		AkG-51, Schleswig/Jagel;		
37+85	JG-71		38+72	JG-73		JbG-31, Nörvenich;		
37+86	JG-71		38+73	JG-72		JbG-32, Lechfeld;		
37+88	JG-71		38+74	JG-72		JbG-33, Böchel;		
37+89	JG-74		38+75	JG-72		JbG-34, Memmingen;		
37+90	JG-71		99+91	WTD-61		JbG-38, Jever;		
37+92	JG-74					MFG-2, Eggebek;		
37+93	JG-72		**D-BD Alpha Jet A**			TsLw-1, Kaufbeuren;		
37+94	JG-71		FLG FFB, Fürstenfeldbruck;			WTD-61, Ingolstadt		
37+96	JG-74		WTD-61, Ingolstadt			43+01[1]	[G-20]	TTTE
37+97	JG-74		40+01	WTD-61		43+02[1]	[G-21]	TTTE
37+98	JG-71		40+02	WTD-61		43+03[1]	[G-22]	TTTE
38+00	JG-74		40+03	FLG FFB		43+04[1]	JbG-31	
38+01	JG-72		40+05	FLG FFB		43+05[1]	[G-24]	TTTE
38+02	JG-71		40+09	FLG FFB		43+06[1]	[G-25]	TTTE
38+03	JG-72		40+11	FLG FFB		43+07[1]	[G-26]	TTTE
38+04	JG-71		40+12	FLG FFB		43+08[1]	JbG-34	
38+05	JG-74		40+15	WTD-61		43+09[1]	[G-28]	TTTE
38+06	JG-71		40+18	FLG FFB		43+10[1]	[G-29]	TTTE
38+07	JG-71		40+22	FLG FFB		43+11[1]	[G-30]	TTTE
38+08	JG-74		40+26	FLG FFB		43+12[1]	AkG-51	
38+09	JG-71		40+27	FLG FFB		43+13	[G-71]	TTTE
38+10	JG-71		40+40	FLG FFB		43+14	[G-72]	TTTE
38+11	JG-71		40+44	FLG FFB		43+15[1]	[G-31]	TTTE
38+12	JG-71		40+49	FLG FFB		43+16[1]	[G-32]	TTTE
38+13	WTD-61		40+56	WTD-61		43+17[1]	[G-33]	TTTE
38+14	JG-71		40+59	TsLw-3		43+18	JbG-34	
38+16	JG-74		40+61	FLG FFB		43+19	JbG-31	
38+17	JG-71		40+65	WTD-61		43+20	JbG-38	
38+18	JG-71		40+76	FLG FFB		43+22[1]	JbG-38	
38+20	JG-72		40+78	TsLw-3		43+23[1]	JbG-38	
38+21	JG-72		40+85	FLG FFB		43+25	[G-75]	TTTE
38+24	JG-72		40+93	FLG FFB		43+26	JbG-38	
38+25	JG-71		40+94	FLG FFB		43+27	AkG-51	
38+26	JG-71		41+02	FLG FFB		43+28	JbG-38	
38+27	JG-71		41+04	FLG FFB		43+29[1]	JbG-31	
38+28	JG-71		41+09	FLG FFB		43+30	JbG-38	
38+29	JG-72		41+14	FLG FFB		43+31[1]	JbG-31	
38+30	JG-71		41+25	FLG FFB		43+32	[G-73]	TTTE
38+31	JG-72		41+26	FLG FFB		43+33[1]	JbG-38	
38+32	JG-71		41+29	FLG FFB		43+34	TsLw-1	
38+33	JG-74		41+30	WTD-61		43+35[1]	JbG-38	
38+34	JG-72		41+34	FLG FFB		43+36	JbG-34	
38+36	JG-72		41+35	FLG FFB		43+37[1]	JbG-38	
38+37	JG-72		41+36	FLG FFB		43+38	JbG-34	
38+38	JG-72		41+37	FLG FFB		43+40	JbG-38	
38+39	JG-72		41+38	FLG FFB		43+41	JbG-31	
38+40	JG-71		41+39	WTD-61		43+42[1]	[G-39]	TTTE
						43+43[1]	AkG-51	

Germany

43+44[1]	AkG-51		44+28	JbG-31	45+08	JbG-33
43+45[1]	AkG-51		44+29	JbG-31	45+09	JbG-31
43+46	AkG-51		44+30	JbG-31	45+10	JbG-33
43+47	AkG-51		44+31	JbG-31	45+11	JbG-33
43+48	AkG-51		44+32	JbG-38	45+12[1]	MFG-2
43+50	AkG-51		44+33	JbG-31	45+13[1]	MFG-2
43+52	AkG-51		44+34	JbG-38	45+14[1]	MFG-2
43+53	AkG-51		44+35	JbG-31	45+15[1]	MFG-2
43+54	AkG-51		44+36[1]	JbG-38	45+16[1]	MFG-2
43+55	MFG-2		44+37[1]	JbG-38	45+17	JbG-33
43+57	AkG-51		44+38[1]	JbG-38	45+18	JbG-38
43+58	AkG-51		44+39[1]	JbG-33	45+19	JbG-33
43+59	MFG-2		44+40	JbG-33	45+20	AkG-51
43+60	AkG-51		44+41	JbG-31	45+21	JbG-33
43+61	JbG-32		44+42	AkG-51	45+22	JbG-33
43+62	AkG-51		44+43	JbG-34	45+23	JbG-33
43+63	AkG-51		44+44	JbG-31	45+24	JbG-33
43+64	AkG-51		44+46	JbG-34	45+25	JbG-33
43+65	AkG-51		44+48	JbG-31	45+26	MFG-2
43+67	AkG-51		44+50	JbG-38	45+27	AkG-51
43+68	JbG-34		44+51	JbG-38	45+28	MFG-2
43+69	MFG-2		44+52	JbG-31	45+29	WTD-61
43+70	AkG-51		44+53	JbG-38	45+30	MFG-2
43+71	AkG-51		44+54	JbG-33	45+31	MFG-2
43+72	AkG-51		44+55	JbG-38	45+32	MFG-2
43+73	TsLw-1		44+56	JbG-34	45+33	MFG-2
43+75	[G-77]	TTTE	44+57	JbG-31	45+34	MFG-2
43+76	JbG-38		44+58	JbG-38	45+35	MFG-2
43+77	AkG-51		44+59	JbG-31	45+36	MFG-2
43+78	JbG-34		44+60	JbG-31	45+37	MFG-2
43+79	[G-76]	TTTE	44+61	JbG-34	45+38	MFG-2
43+80	AkG-51		44+62	JbG-33	45+39	MFG-2
43+81	AkG-51		44+63	JbG-33	45+40	MFG-2
43+82	AkG-51		44+64	AkG-51	45+41	MFG-2
43+83	AkG-51		44+65	JbG-34	45+42	MFG-2
43+85	JbG-38		44+66	JbG-31	45+43	MFG-2
43+86	AkG-51		44+67	JbG-33	45+44	MFG-2
43+87	MFG-2		44+68	AkG-51	45+45	MFG-2
43+88	JbG-34		44+69	JbG-38	45+46	MFG-2
43+90[1]	JbG-38		44+70	JbG-38	45+47	MFG-2
43+91[1]	JbG-32		44+71	JbG-31	45+48	MFG-2
43+92[1]	JbG-31		44+72[1]	JbG-33	45+49	MFG-2
43+94[1]	JbG-31		44+73[1]	JbG-33	45+50	MFG-2
43+96	AkG-51		44+75[1]	JbG-33	45+51	MFG-2
43+97[1]	JbG-31		44+76	JbG-34	45+52	MFG-2
43+98	AkG-51		44+77	JbG-31	45+53	MFG-2
43+99	JbG-31		44+78	JbG-31	45+54	MFG-2
44+00	JbG-31		44+79	JbG-33	45+55	MFG-2
44+01[1]	JbG-32		44+80	JbG-33	45+56	MFG-2
44+02	JbG-31		44+81	JbG-34	45+57	MFG-2
44+03	JbG-31		44+82	JbG-31	45+59	MFG-2
44+04	AkG-51		44+83	JbG-33	45+60[1]	JbG-38
44+05[1]	JbG-38		44+84	JbG-33	45+61[1]	JbG-34
44+06	AkG-51		44+85	JbG-38	45+62[1]	JbG-38
44+07	JbG-31		44+86	JbG-38	45+64	TsLw-1
44+08	JbG-38		44+87	AkG-51	45+65	MFG-2
44+09	JbG-31		44+88	JbG-33	45+66	MFG-2
44+10[1]	JbG-38		44+89	JbG-33	45+67	MFG-2
44+11	JbG-34		44+90	JbG-33	45+68	MFG-2
44+12	JbG-38		44+91	JbG-33	45+69	MFG-2
44+13	TsLw-1		44+92	JbG-33	45+70[1]	JbG-33
44+14	JbG-34		44+94	JbG-33	45+71	MFG-2
44+15[1]	JbG-38		44+95	JbG-33	45+72	MFG-2
44+16	JbG-31		44+96	JbG-32	45+73[1]	JbG-31
44+17	AkG-51		44+97	JbG-33	45+74	MFG-2
44+19	JbG-31		44+98	JbG-33	45+76	JbG-38
44+20[1]	JbG-32		45+00	JbG-33	45+77[1]	JbG-38
44+21	JbG-31		45+01	JbG-33	45+78	JbG-34
44+22	JbG-31		45+02	JbG-33	45+79	JbG-31
44+23	JbG-31		45+03	JbG-33	45+81	JbG-34
44+24	AkG-51		45+04	JbG-33	45+82	JbG-34
44+25[1]	JbG-38		45+05	JbG-33	45+83	JbG-34
44+26	JbG-31		45+06	JbG-33	45+84	AkG-51
44+27	JbG-31		45+07	JbG-33	45+85	AkG-51

45+86	JbG-34
45+87	JbG-34
45+88	JbG-34
45+89	JbG-34
45+90	JbG-34
45+91	JbG-34
45+92	JbG-34
45+93	JbG-34
45+94	JbG-34
45+95	JbG-34
45+96	JbG-34
45+98	JbG-34
45+99[1]	AkG-51
46+00	JbG-38
46+01	JbG-34
46+02	JbG-34
46+03	JbG-34
46+04[1]	MFG-2
46+05[1]	MFG-2
46+06[1]	JbG-32
46+07	JbG-34
46+08	JbG-34
46+09	JbG-34
46+10	WTD-61
46+11	MFG-2
46+12	MFG-2
46+13	MFG-2
46+14	MFG-2
46+15	MFG-2
46+18	MFG-2
46+19	MFG-2
46+20	MFG-2
46+21	MFG-2
46+22	MFG-2
46+23[2]	JbG-32
46+24[2]	JbG-32
46+25[2]	JbG-32
46+26[2]	JbG-32
46+27[2]	JbG-32
46+28[2]	JbG-32
46+29[2]	JbG-32
46+30[2]	JbG-32
46+31[2]	JbG-32
46+32[2]	JbG-32
46+33[2]	JbG-32
46+34[2]	JbG-32
46+35[2]	JbG-32
46+36[2]	JbG-32
46+37[2]	JbG-32
46+38[2]	JbG-32
46+39[2]	JbG-32
46+40[2]	JbG-32
46+41[2]	JbG-32
46+42[2]	JbG-32
46+43[2]	JbG-32
46+44[2]	JbG-32
46+45[2]	JbG-32
46+46[2]	JbG-32
46+47[2]	JbG-32
46+48[2]	JbG-32
46+49[2]	JbG-32
46+50[2]	JbG-32
46+51[2]	JbG-32
46+52[2]	JbG-32
46+53[2]	JbG-32
46+54[2]	JbG-32
46+55[2]	JbG-32
46+56[2]	JbG-32
46+57[2]	JbG-32
98+02	WTD-61
98+03[2]	WTD-61
98+59	WTD-61
98+60	WTD-61

98+79[2]	WTD-61
98+97[2]	WTD-61

Transall C-160D
LTG-61, Landsberg;
LTG-62, Wunstorf;
LTG-63, Hohn;
WTD-61, Ingolstadt

50+06	LTG-63
50+07	LTG-61
50+08	LTG-61
50+09	LTG-62
50+10	LTG-62
50+17	LTG-62
50+29	LTG-62
50+33	LTG-61
50+34	LTG-63
50+35	LTG-62
50+36	LTG-62
50+37	LTG-62
50+38	LTG-62
50+40	LTG-61
50+41	LTG-63
50+42	LTG-63
50+44	LTG-61
50+45	LTG-63
50+46	LTG-62
50+47	LTG-61
50+48	LTG-61
50+49	LTG-61
50+50	LTG-63
50+51	LTG-63
50+52	LTG-62
50+53	LTG-62
50+54	LTG-61
50+55	LTG-62
50+56	LTG-63
50+57	LTG-61
50+58	LTG-63
50+59	LTG-63
50+60	LTG-62
50+61	LTG-63
50+62	LTG-61
50+64	LTG-63
50+65	LTG-62
50+66	LTG-61
50+67	LTG-63
50+68	LTG-61
50+69	LTG-61
50+70	WTD-61
50+71	LTG-63
50+72	LTG-61
50+73	LTG-62
50+74	LTG-61
50+75	WTD-61
50+76	LTG-63
50+77	LTG-63
50+78	LTG-62
50+79	LTG-63
50+81	LTG-62
50+82	LTG-63
50+83	LTG-62
50+84	LTG-61
50+85	LTG-63
50+86	LTG-62
50+87	LTG-63
50+88	LTG-61
50+89	LTG-63
50+90	LTG-62
50+91	LTG-62
50+92	LTG-61
50+93	LTG-61
50+94	LTG-63
50+95	LTG-63

50+96	LTG-61
50+97	LTG-62
50+98	LTG-61
50+99	LTG-61
51+00	LTG-62
51+01	LTG-62
51+02	LTG-63
51+03	LTG-63
51+04	LTG-61
51+05	LTG-62
51+06	LTG-63
51+07	LTG-62
51+08	LTG-63
51+09	LTG-63
51+10	LTG-61
51+11	LTG-62
51+12	LTG-63
51+13	LTG-61
51+14	LTG-63
51+15	LTG-61

LET L.410UVP-T/UVP-S*
3/FBS, Berlin-Tegel
53+08
53+09*
53+10*
53+11*
53+12*

Dornier Do.228
WTD-61, Ingolstadt;
MFG-3, Nordholz
57+01 MFG-3
98+78 WTD-61

Breguet Br1151 Atlantic
Elint
MFG-3, Nordholz
61+01
61+02*
61+03*
61+04
61+05
61+06*
61+08
61+09
61+10
61+11
61+12
61+13
61+14
61+15
61+16
61+17
61+18
61+19*
61+20*

Westland
Lynx Mk88
MFG-3, Nordholz
83+02
83+03
83+04
83+05
83+06
83+07
83+08
83+09
83+10
83+11
83+12
83+13
83+14

83+15
83+17
83+18
83+19

**Westland Sea
King HAS41**
MFG-5, Kiel-Holtenau
89+50
89+51
89+52
89+53
89+54
89+55
89+56
89+57
89+58
89+59
89+60
89+61
89+62
89+63
89+64
89+65
89+66
89+67
89+68
89+69
89+70
89+71

Eurofighter EF2000
98+29 WTD-61 (ZH586)

**English Electric
Canberra B2**
WTD-61, Ingolstadt
99+34

**Heeresfliegertruppe
Sikorsky/VFW CH-53G**
HFlgRgt-15, Rheine-
  Bentlage;
HFlgRgt-25, Laupheim;
HFlgRgt-35, Mendig;
HFWS, Bückeburg;
Tslw-3, Fassberg;
WTD-61, Ingolstadt
84+01 WTD-61
84+02 WTD-61
84+03 HFR-15
84+04 Tslw-3
84+05 HFR-35
84+06 HFR-35
84+07 HFWS
84+08 HFR-35
84+09 HFR-25
84+10 HFWS
84+11 HFWS
84+12 HFR-15
84+13 HFWS
84+14 HFWS
84+15 HFR-25
84+16 HFWS
84+17 HFR-25
84+18 HFWS
84+19 HFWS
84+20 HFR-35
84+21 HFWS
84+22 HFR-35
84+23 HFR-25
84+24 HFR-35
84+25 HFR-35
84+26 HFR-35
84+27 HFR-35

84+28 HFR-35
84+29 HFR-35
84+30 HFR-35
84+31 HFR-35
84+32 HFR-35
84+33 HFR-35
84+34 HFR-35
84+35 HFR-35
84+36 HFR-35
84+37 HFR-35
84+38 HFR-35
84+39 HFR-35
84+40 HFR-25
84+41 HFWS
84+42 HFR-25
84+43 HFR-25
84+44 HFR-25
84+45 HFR-25
84+46 HFR-25
84+47 HFR-25
84+48 HFR-25
84+49 HFWS
84+50 HFR-25
84+51 HFR-25
84+52 HFR-25
84+53 HFR-25
84+54 HFR-25
84+55 HFR-25
84+56 HFR-25
84+57 HFR-25
84+58 HFR-25
84+59 HFR-25
84+60 HFR-25
84+62 HFR-25
84+63 HFR-25
84+64 HFR-25
84+65 HFR-35
84+66 HFR-35
84+67 HFR-35
84+68 HFR-15
84+69 HFR-15
84+70 HFR-15
84+71 HFR-15
84+72 HFR-15
84+73 HFR-15
84+74 HFR-15
84+75 HFR-15
84+76 HFR-15
84+77 HFR-15
84+78 HFR-15
84+79 HFR-15
84+80 HFR-15
84+82 HFR-15
84+83 HFR-15
84+84 HFR-15
84+85 HFR-15
84+86 HFR-15
84+87 HFR-15
84+88 HFR-15
84+89 HFR-15
84+90 HFR-15
84+91 HFR-15
84+92 HFR-35
84+93 HFR-35
84+94 HFR-35
84+95 HFR-25
84+96 HFR-25
84+97 HFR-25
84+98 HFR-15
84+99 HFR-15
85+00 HFR-15
85+01 HFR-35
85+02 HFR-35
85+03 HFR-35

85+04 HFR-25
85+05 HFR-25
85+06 HFR-25
85+07 HFR-15
85+08 HFR-15
85+09 HFR-25
85+10 HFR-35
85+11 HFR-25
85+12 HFR-15

**GREECE
Helliniki Aeroporia**
  **Lockheed C-130H
  Hercules**
  356 Mira, Elefsis
  741
  742
  743
  744
  745
  746
  747
  749
  750
  751
  752

**HUNGARY
Magyar Honvédseg Repülö
Csapatai**
  Antonov An-26
  Szolnok Mixed Air Carrier
    Regiment
  202 (02202)
  203 (02203)
  204 (02204)
  208 (02208)
  209 (02209)
  405 (03405)
  406 (03406)
  407 (03407)
  603 (03603)

**ISRAEL
Heyl Ha'Avir**
  Lockheed C-130 Hercules
  103 Sqn, 131 Sqn, Lod
  C-130E
  208
  301
  304/4X-FBE
  305
  307
  310
  311/4X-FBD
  313
  314
  316
  318

  C-130H
  102/4X-FBA
  106
  309
  420
  427
  428
  435/4X-FBT
  436/4X-FBW
  448/4X-FBU

  KC-130H
  545
  622

ITALY
Aeronautica Militare Italiano
  Aeritalia G222
    46ª Brigata Aerea, Pisa;
    14° Stormo, Pratica di Mare;
    RSV, Pratica di Mare

MM62101	RS-45
MM62102	46-20
MM62104	46-91
MM62105	46-82
MM62108	46-30
MM62109	46-96
MM62110	46-81
MM62111	46-83
MM62112	46-85
MM62114	46-80
MM62115	46-22
MM62117	46-25
MM62118	46-24
MM62119	46-21
MM62120	46-90
MM62121	46-86
MM62122	46-23
MM62123	46-28
MM62124	46-88
MM62125	46-87
MM62126	46-26
MM62127	46-27
MM62130	RS-51
MM62132	46-32
MM62133	46-93
MM62134	46-33
MM62143	46-36
MM62144	46-98
MM62145	46-50
MM62146	46-51
MM62147	46-52

Aeritalia G222TCM

MM62103	RS-14
MM62135	46-94
MM62136	46-97
MM62137	46-95
MM62152	46-38
MM62153	46-99
MM62154	
MM62155	

Aeritalia G222RM

MM62107	
MM62138	
MM62139	14-20
MM62140	14-21
MM62141	14-22
MM62142	(14° Stormo)

Aeritalia-EMB AMX/AMX-T*
  2° Stormo, Rivolto;
  3° Stormo, Villafranca;
  32° Stormo, Amendola;
  51° Stormo, Istrana;
  RSV, Pratica di Mare

MMX595	Aeritalia
MMX596	Alenia
MMX597	Alenia
MMX599	Alenia
MM7089	
MM7090	RS-12
MM7091	32-64
MM7092	RS-14
MM7093	
MM7094	3-37
MM7095	(51)
MM7096	32-03
MM7097	3-36
MM7098	3-35
MM7099	2-02
MM7100	3-44
MM7101	(51)
MM7102	2-03
MM7103	
MM7104	(51)
MM7105	32-13
MM7106	(51)
MM7107	
MM7110	2-14
MM7111	3-16
MM7112	32-01
MM7114	2-07
MM7115	2-12
MM7116	
MM7117	3-34
MM7118	2-11
MM7119	
MM7120	3-10
MM7121	3-31
MM7122	3-32
MM7123	3-13
MM7124	
MM7125	3-15
MM7126	
MM7127	3-12
MM7128	
MM7129	3-30
MM7130	(51)
MM7131	RS-13
MM7132	(51)
MM7133	(51)
MM7134	(51)
MM7135	(51)
MM7138	(51)
MM7139	(51)
MM7140	(51)
MM7141	(51)
MM7142	(51)
MM7143	(51)
MM7144	3-03
MM7145	3-06
MM7146	(51)
MM7147	2-20
MM7148	(51)
MM7149	3-11
MM7150	(51)
MM7151	(51)
MM7152	(51)
MM7153	3-45
MM7154	(51)
MM7155	32-05
MM7156	2-22
MM7157	(51)
MM7158	
MM7159	3-33
MM7160	(51)
MM7161	3-51
MM7162	(51)
MM7163	3-22
MM7164	(51)
MM7165	
MM7166	3-24
MM7167	
MM7168	2-24
MM7169	2-01
MM7170	
MM7171	2 15
MM7172	3-53
MM7173	2-16
MM7174	3-25
MM7175	3-01
MM7176	
MM7177	
MM7178	
MM7179	
MM7180	
MM55024*	Aeritalia
MM55025*	(RSV)
MM55026*	Aeritalia
MM55027*	(51)
MM55028*	2-10
MM55029*	3-55
MM55030*	32-41
MM55031*	32-40
MM55032*	
MM55033*	
MM55034*	
MM55035*	
MM55036*	
MM55037*	
MM55038*	
MM55039*	
MM55040*	
MM55041*	
MM55042*	
MM55043*	

Aermacchi MB339A
Frecce Tricolori
(MB339PAN)
  (313 Gruppo), Rivolto;
  61ª Brigata Aerea, Lecce;
  14° Stormo, Pratica di Mare;
  RSV, Pratica di Mare

MM54438	61-93
MM54439	6*
MM54440	61-00
MM54442	61-95
MM54443	61-50
MM54445	8*
MM54446	61-01
MM54447	61-02
MM54448	61-03
MM54449	61-04
MM54450	61-94
MM54451	61-86
MM54452	61-41
MM54453	61-05
MM54454	61-06
MM54455	61-07
MM54456	RS-10
MM54457	61-11
MM54458	61-12
MM54459	61-13
MM54460	61-14
MM54461	(RSV)
MM54462	61-16
MM54463	61-17
MM54464	
MM54467	61-23
MM54468	61-24
MM54471	61-27
MM54472	61-30
MM54473	4*
MM54475	1*
MM54476	
MM54477	9*
MM54478	7*
MM54479	11*
MM54480	0*
MM54482	5*
MM54483	13*
MM54484	3*
MM54485	
MM54486	2*

MM54487	61-31
MM54488	61-32
MM54489	61-33
MM54490	61-34
MM54491	61-35
MM54492	61-36
MM54493	61-37
MM54494	61-40
MM54496	61-42
MM54497	61-43
MM54498	61-44
MM54499	61-45
MM54500	*
MM54503	61-51
MM54504	61-52
MM54505	61-53
MM54506	61-54
MM54507	61-55
MM54508	61-56
MM54509	61-57
MM54510	61-60
MM54511	(RSV)
MM54512	61-62
MM54513	61-63
MM54514	61-64
MM54515	61-65
MM54516	61-66
MM54517	*
MM54518	61-70
MM54532	61-71
MM54533	61-72
MM54534	61-73
MM54535	61-74
MM54536	10*
MM54537	
MM54538	61-75
MM54539	61-76
MM54540	61-77
MM54541	61-80
MM54542	61-81
MM54543	61-82
MM54544	61-83
MM54545	61-84
MM54546	61-85
MM54547	61-87
MM54548	61-90
MM54549	61-91
MM54550	61-92
MM54551	
MM55052	61-96
MM55053	61-97
MM55054	
MM55055	61-20
MM55054	
MM55054	

Boeing 707-328B/-3F5C*
14º Stormo, Pratica di Mare;
31º Stormo, Roma-Ciampino

MM62148	14-01
MM62149	(14)
MM62150*	(31)
MM62151*	14-02

Breguet Br 1150 Atlantic
30º Stormo, Cagliari;
41º Stormo, Catania

MM40108	41-70
MM40109	30-71
MM40110	41-72
MM40111	41-73
MM40112	30-74
MM40113	30-75
MM40114	41-76
MM40115	41-77
MM40116	30-01
MM40117	41-02
MM40118	30-03
MM40119	30-04
MM40120	41-05
MM40121	41-06
MM40122	30-07
MM40123	30-10
MM40124	41-11
MM40125	30-12

Dassault Falcon 50
31º Stormo, Roma-Ciampino

MM62020	
MM62021	
MM62026	
MM62029	

Eurofighter EF2000
Aeritalia, Torino/Caselle

MMX602	

Grumman Gulfstream III
31º Stormo, Roma-Ciampino

MM62022	
MM62025	

Lockheed F-104 Starfighter
4º Stormo, Grosseto;
5º Stormo, Cervia
9º Stormo, Grazzanise;
36º Stormo, Gioia del Colle;
37º Stormo, Trapani;
51º Stormo, Istrana;
53º Stormo, Cameri
F-104S

MM6701	
MM6703	51-23
MM6704	
MM6705	
MM6710	
MM6713	
MM6714	
MM6716	53-21
MM6717	9-32
MM6719	51-06
MM6720	9-40
MM6721	9-42
MM6722	5-45
MM6726	4-21
MM6727	9-45
MM6730	9-33
MM6731	4-10
MM6732	4-5
MM6733	4-44
MM6734	9-43
MM6735	51-22
MM6736	
MM6737	5-43
MM6739	51-01
MM6740	9-35
MM6741	37-21
MM6742	4-52
MM6744	5-07
MM6747	37-24
MM6748	
MM6749	9-41
MM6750	37-04
MM6756	37-10
MM6758	
MM6759	37-26
MM6760	4-50
MM6761	4-3
MM6762	5-37
MM6763	53-12
MM6764	51-03
MM6767	
MM6768	
MM6769	
MM6770	5-30
MM6771	5-31
MM6772	9-52
MM6773	
MM6774	36-21
MM6775	9-50
MM6776	
MM6778	4-4
MM6780	
MM6781	51-14
MM6782	37-15
MM6784	37-27
MM6785	5-25
MM6786	5-32
MM6787	4-7
MM6788	5-01
MM6789	37-02
MM6791	
MM6792	5-21
MM6794	37-20
MM6795	5-46
MM6796	53-06
MM6797	
MM6798	37-01
MM6800	53-03
MM6802	4-1
MM6804	51-07
MM6805	
MM6807	
MM6808	9-30
MM6809	
MM6810	5-41
MM6812	
MM6814	53-16
MM6815	53-05
MM6816	
MM6817	51-02
MM6818	36-22
MM6819	9-31
MM6821	5-16
MM6822	53-11
MM6823	
MM6824	53-02
MM6825	
MM6826	53-03
MM6827	53-20
MM6828	4-55
MM6830	5-27
MM6831	4-22
MM6833	5-22
MM6835	
MM6836	5-10
MM6838	
MM6839	4-6
MM6840	37-25
MM6841	
MM6842	
MM6843	
MM6844	37-23
MM6845	5-11
MM6847	37-11
MM6848	53-04
MM6849	5-33
MM6850	51-12
MM6870	51-04
MM6872	53-15
MM6873	5

MM6875	
MM6876	5-40
MM6879	
MM6880	4-12
MM6881	5-42
MM6886	5-02
MM6887	9-51
MM6890	4-11
MM6908	
MM6909	
MM6910	37-12
MM6912	4-20
MM6913	51-10
MM6914	5-13
MM6915	5-15
MM6916	37-03
MM6918	37-22
MM6920	5-35
MM6921	
MM6922	5-04
MM6923	
MM6924	
MM6925	53-01
MM6926	53-14
MM6929	51-11
MM6930	
MM6932	51-05
MM6934	
MM6935	
MM6936	5-36
MM6937	51-16
MM6938	4-16
MM6939	
MM6940	
MM6941	51-20
MM6942	53-13
MM6943	
MM6944	5-44
MM6946	37-06

TF-104G

MM54226	4-23
MM54228	4-26
MM54232	4-29
MM54233	4-30
MM54237	4-32
MM54250	4-33
MM54251	4-34
MM54253	4-35
MM54254	4-36
MM54255	4-37
MM54256	4-38
MM54257	4-39
MM54258	4-40
MM54260	4-41
MM54261	4-42
MM54552	
MM54553	
MM54554	4-48
MM54555	4-45
MM54556	4-47
MM54557	
MM54558	4-46

**Lockheed
C-130H Hercules**
46ª Brigata Aerea, Pisa

MM61988	46-02
MM61989	46-03
MM61990	46-04
MM61991	46-05
MM61992	46-06
MM61993	46-07
MM61994	46-08
MM61995	46-09
MM61997	46-11
MM61998	46-12
MM61999	46-13
MM62001	46-15

**McDonnell Douglas
DC-9-32**
31° Stormo, Roma-Ciampino

MM62012	
MM62013	

**Panavia Tornado
ADV/Trainer[1]**
36° Stormo, Gioia del Colle

MM7202	36-12	(ZE832)
MM7203	36-02	(ZE761)
MM7204	36-05	(ZE730)
MM7205	36-06	(ZE787)
MM7206	36-07	(ZE761)
MM7207	36-10	(ZE762)
MM7208	36-11	(ZE811)
MM7209	36-13	(ZE835)
MM7210	36-14	(ZE836)
MM7211	36-16	(ZE792)
MM55056[1]	36-01	(ZE202)
MM55057[1]	36-03	(ZE837)

**Panavia Tornado Strike/
Trainer[1]/ECR[2]**
TTTE, RAF Cottesmore;
6° Stormo, Ghedi;
36° Stormo, Gioia del Colle;
50° Stormo, Piacenza;
RSV, Pratica di Mare

MM586		
MM7002	I-92	TTTE
MM7003	I-93	TTTE
MM7004	36-37	
MM7005	6-05	
MM7006	6-06	
MM7007	50-07	
MM7008	50-03	
MM7009	50-45	
MM7010	6-33	
MM7011	6-11	
MM7013	6-13	
MM7014	50-43	
MM7015	50-05	
MM7016	6-16	
MM7017	50-34	
MM7018	6-18	
MM7019	19	
MM7020	50-12	
MM7021	6-21	
MM7022	6-02	
MM7023	36-31	
MM7024	6-24	
MM7025	6-30	
MM7026	50-06	
MM7027	6-47	
MM7028	50-40	
MM7029		
MM7030	6-14	
MM7031	50-01	
MM7033	6-03	
MM7034	6-04	
MM7035		
MM7036	6-43	
MM7037	6-37	
MM7038	36-33	
MM7039	50-47	
MM7040	36-35	
MM7041	36-44	
MM7042	6-22	
MM7043	43	
MM7044	36-44	
MM7046	50-46	
MM7047	36-36	
MM7048	36-54	(Alenia)
MM7049	50-44	
MM7050	50	
MM7051	36-32	
MM7052	6-32	
MM7053	53	
MM7054	6-54	
MM7055	6-55	
MM7056	6-46	
MM7057	36-54	
MM7058	36-57	
MM7059	36-50	
MM7060	6-34	
MM7061	36-41	
MM7062	36-53	
MM7063	36-43	
MM7064	6-26	
MM7065	6-05	
MM7066	6-44	
MM7067	50-37	
MM7068		
MM7070	6-07	
MM7071	6-42	
MM7072	6-36	
MM7073		
MM7075	6-12	
MM7078	50-02	
MM7079[2]	(Alenia)	
MM7080		
MM7081	81	
MM7082	RS-02	
MM7083	36-30	
MM7084	36-42	
MM7085	36-50	(Alenia)
MM7086	86	
MM7087		
MM7088	6-27	
MM55000[1]	I-42	TTTE
MM55001[1]	I-40	TTTE
MM55002[1]	I-41	TTTE
MM55003[1]	I-43	TTTE
MM55004[1]	6-15	
MM55005[1]	I-45	TTTE
MM55006[1]		
MM55007[1]	50-51	
MM55008[1]		
MM55009[1]		
MM55010[1]	50-50	
MM55011[1]	36-55	

Piaggio RP-180 Avanti
31° Stormo, Roma-
    Ciampino;
RSV, Pratica di Mare

MM62159		RSV
MM62160	54	RSV
MM62161		RSV
MM62162		(31)
MM62163		
MM62164		RSV

**Piaggio-Douglas PD-808/
[1]PD-808-GE/[2]PD-808-RM/
[3]PD-808-TA**
14° Stormo, Pratica di Mare;
31° Stormo, Roma-
    Ciampino;
RSV, Pratica di Mare

MM577[3]	RS-48
MM578[3]	RS-49

Italy – Netherlands

MM61948	(14)
MM61949	(14)
MM61950	(14)
MM61951	(31)
MM61952[1]	(14)
MM61953[3]	(14)
MM61954[3]	(31)
MM61955[1]	(14)
MM61956[2]	(14)
MM61957[3]	(14)
MM61958[1]	(14)
MM61959[1]	(14)
MM61960[1]	(14)
MM61961[1]	(14)
MM61962[1]	(14)
MM62014[2]	(14)
MM62015[2]	(14)
MM62016[2]	(14)
MM62017[2]	(14)

Marina Militare Italiano
McDonnell AV-8B/TAV-8B
Harrier II+
Gruppo Aerei Imbarcarti,
  Taranto/Grottaglie
AV-8B

MM7199	1-03
MM7200	1-04
MM7201	1-05
MM7212	1-06
MM7213	1-07
MM7214	1-08
MM7215	1-09
MM7216	1-10
MM7217	1-11
MM7218	1-12
MM7219	1-13
MM7220	1-14
MM7221	1-15
MM7222	1-16
MM7223	1-17
MM7224	1-18

TAV-8B

MM55032	1-01
MM55033	1-02

JORDAN
Al Quwwat al-Jawwiya
  al Malakiya al-Urduniya
  Lockheed C-130H
  Hercules
3 Sqn, Amman
344
345
346
347

KUWAIT
Kuwait Air Force
  McDonnell Douglas
  DC9-32
42 Sqn, Ali Al Salem
KAF 321

  McDonnell Douglas
  DC9-83
42 Sqn, Ali Al Salem
KAF 26

Lockheed
L100-30 Hercules
41 Sqn, Kuwait International
KAF 323
KAF 324
KAF 325

LUXEMBOURG
NATO
  Boeing E-3A
  NAEWF, Geilenkirchen
LX-N90442
LX-N90443
LX-N90444
LX-N90445
LX-N90446
LX-N90447
LX-N90448
LX-N90449
LX-N90450
LX-N90451
LX-N90452
LX-N90453
LX-N90454
LX-N90455
LX-N90456
LX-N90457
LX-N90458
LX-N90459

  Boeing 707-329C
  NAEWF,
  Geilenkirchen
LX-N19996
LX-N20198
LX-N20199

MOROCCO
Force Aerienne Royaume
  Marocaine
  CAP-230
  Marche Verte
04 CN-ABD
05 CN-ABF
06 CN-ABI
07 CN-ABJ
08 CN-ABK
09 CN-ABL
22 CN-ABM
23 CN-ABN
24 CN-ABO

  Lockheed C-130H
  Hercules
4535 CN-AOA
4551 CN-AOC
4575 CN-AOD
4581 CN-AOE
4583 CN-AOF
4713 CN-AOG
4717 CN-AOH
4733 CN-AOI
4738 CN-AOJ
4739 CN-AOK
4742 CN-AOL
4875 CN-AOM
4876 CN-AON
4877 CN-AOO
4888 CN-AOP
4892 CN-AOQ
4907 CN-AOR
4909 CN-AOS
4940 CN-AOT

NETHERLANDS
Koninklijke Luchtmacht
  Aerospatiale AS.532U2
  Cougar
300 Sqn, Soesterberg
S-400
S-401
S-402

Agusta-Bell AB.412SP
SAR Flight, Leeuwarden
R-01
R-02
R-03

Boeing-Vertol
CH-47D Chinook
298 Sqn, Soesterberg
D-661
D-662
D-663
D-664
D-665
D-666
D-667

Fokker F-27-100
Friendship
334 Sqn, Eindhoven
C-1
C-2
C-3

Fokker F-27-300M
Troopship
334 Sqn, Eindhoven
C-4
C-5
C-6
C-7
C-8
C-9
C-11

Fokker 60
334 Sqn, Eindhoven
U-01
U-02
U-03
U-04

General Dynamics
F-16A/F-16B*
TGp/306/311/312 Sqns,
Volkel;
313/315 Sqns, Twente;
322/323 Sqns, Leeuwarden

J-001	306 Sqn
J-002	313 Sqn
J-003	312 Sqn
J-004	311 Sqn
J-005	315 Sqn
J-006	315 Sqn
J-008	315 Sqn
J-009	315 Sqn
J-010	312 Sqn
J-011	315 Sqn
J-012	315 Sqn
J-013	311 Sqn
J-014	315 Sqn
J-015	312 Sqn
J-016	311 Sqn
J-017	315 Sqn
J-018	315 Sqn
J-019	311 Sqn
J-020	315 Sqn
J-021	312 Sqn
J-055	315 Sqn
J-057	315 Sqn
J-058	311 Sqn
J-059	311 Sqn
J-060	311 Sqn
J-061	312 Sqn

J-062	311 Sqn	J-267*	315 Sqn		
J-063	312 Sqn	J-269*	313 Sqn	**Grumman G-1159C**	
J-064*	312 Sqn	J-270*	313 Sqn	**Gulfstream IV**	
J-065*	311 Sqn	J-360	313 Sqn	334 Sqn, Eindhoven	
J-066*	311 Sqn	J-361	323 Sqn	V-11	
J-067*	312 Sqn	J-362	323 Sqn		
J-068*	312 Sqn	J-363	323 Sqn	**Lockheed C-130H-30**	
J-135	315 Sqn	J-364		**Hercules**	
J-136	322 Sqn	J-365	322 Sqn	334 Sqn, Eindhoven	
J-137	311 Sqn	J-366	322 Sqn	G-273	
J-138	323 Sqn	J-367		G-275	
J-139	323 Sqn	J-368*	315 Sqn		
J-140	322 Sqn	J-369*	323 Sqn	**MBB Bo.105CB/**	
J-141	322 Sqn	J-508	306 Sqn	**Bo.105DB[1]**	
J-142	322 Sqn	J-509	315 Sqn	299 Sqn, Deelen	
J-143	323 Sqn	J-510	315 Sqn	B-37	
J-144	323 Sqn	J-511	311 Sqn	B-38	
J-145		J-512	312 Sqn	B-39	
J-146	312 Sqn	J-513	312 Sqn	B-40	
J-192	322 Sqn	J-514	315 Sqn	B-41	
J-193	322 Sqn	J-515	315 Sqn	B-42	
J-194	322 Sqn	J-516	315 Sqn	B-43	
J-196	322 Sqn	J-616	323 Sqn	B-44	
J-197	306 Sqn	J-617	323 Sqn	B-47	
J-198	322 Sqn	J-619	322 Sqn	B-48	
J-199	322 Sqn	J-620	322 Sqn	B-63	
J-201	312 Sqn	J-622	311 Sqn	B-64	
J-202	322 Sqn	J-623	322 Sqn	B-66	
J-203	322 Sqn	J-624	322 Sqn	B-67	
J-204	322 Sqn	J-627	306 Sqn	B-68	
J-205	322 Sqn	J-628	306 Sqn	B-69	
J-206	322 Sqn	J-630	306 Sqn	B-70	
J-207	322 Sqn	J-631	306 Sqn	B-71	
J-208*	322 Sqn	J-632	306 Sqn	B-72	
J-209*	322 Sqn	J-633	306 Sqn	B-74	
J-210*	313 Sqn	J-635	306 Sqn	B-75	
J-211*	322 Sqn	J-636	306 Sqn	B-76	
J-212	311 Sqn	J-637	306 Sqn	B-77	
J-213	312 Sqn	J-638	306 Sqn	B-78	
J-214	312 Sqn	J-640	306 Sqn	B-79	
J-215	312 Sqn	J-641	306 Sqn	B-80	
J-218	313 Sqn	J-642	306 Sqn	B-83[1]	
J-220	312 Sqn	J-643	306 Sqn		
J-221	315 Sqn	J-644	306 Sqn	**McDonnell-Douglas**	
J-223	311 Sqn	J-646	306 Sqn	**KDC-10**	
J-226		J-647	306 Sqn	334 Sqn, Eindhoven	
J-228	312 Sqn	J-648	306 Sqn	T-235	
J-230	313 Sqn	J-649*	306 Sqn	T-264	
J-231	312 Sqn	J-650*	Lockheed		
J-232	315 Sqn	J-651*	306 Sqn	**Pilatus PC-7**	
J-234	315 Sqn	J-652*	313 Sqn	EMVO, Woensdrecht	
J-235	311 Sqn	J-653*	TGp	L-01	
J-236	312 Sqn	J-654*	323 Sqn	L-02	
J-239	313 Sqn	J-655*	306 Sqn	L-03	
J-240	311 Sqn	J-656*	323 Sqn	L-04	
J-241	311 Sqn	J-657*	323 Sqn	L-05	
J-243	313 Sqn	J-864	306 Sqn	L-06	
J-245	323 Sqn	J-866	306 Sqn	L-07	
J-246	313 Sqn	J-867	306 Sqn	L-08	
J-248	312 Sqn	J-868	323 Sqn	L-09	
J-249	311 Sqn	J-869	323 Sqn	L-10	
J-250	311 Sqn	J-871	323 Sqn		
J-251	315 Sqn	J-872	323 Sqn	**Sud Alouette III**	
J-253	313 Sqn	J-873	323 Sqn	298 Sqn, Soesterberg;	
J-254	312 Sqn	J-874	323 Sqn	300 Sqn, Deelen;	
J-255		J-875	306 Sqn	302 Sqn, Gilze-Rijen	
J-256	311 Sqn	J-876	323 Sqn	A-177	302 Sqn
J-257	313 Sqn	J-877	323 Sqn	A-208	298 Sqn
J-259*	315 Sqn	J-878	323 Sqn	A-209	300 Sqn
J-261*	313 Sqn	J-879	323 Sqn	A-217	300 Sqn
J-262*	313 Sqn	J-881	312 Sqn	A-218	302 Sqn
J-264*	313 Sqn	J-882*	323 Sqn	A-227	300 Sqn
J-265*	313 Sqn	J-884*	315 Sqn	A-235	298 Sqn
J-266*	313 Sqn	J-885*	311 Sqn	A-246	302 Sqn
				A-247	302 Sqn

Netherlands – Norway

A-253	302 Sqn
A-260	302 Sqn
A-261	302 Sqn
A-275	302 Sqn
A-292	302 Sqn
A-301	302 Sqn
A-307	302 Sqn
A-343	302 Sqn
A-374	302 Sqn
A-390	302 Sqn
A-398	302 Sqn
A-399	302 Sqn
A-407	298 Sqn
A-451	300 Sqn
A-452	302 Sqn
A-453	302 Sqn
A-464	302 Sqn
A-471	302 Sqn
A-482	300 Sqn
A-483	302 Sqn
A-488	302 Sqn
A-489	300 Sqn
A-494	302 Sqn
A-495	302 Sqn
A-499	302 Sqn
A-500	298 Sqn
A-514	302 Sqn
A-515	302 Sqn
A-521	302 Sqn
A-522	300 Sqn
A-528	302 Sqn
A-529	302 Sqn
A-535	300 Sqn
A-536	302 Sqn
A-542	302 Sqn
A-549	298 Sqn
A-550	302 Sqn

Marine Luchtvaart Dienst
Fokker F-27-200MPA
336 Sqn, Hato, Antilles
M-1
M-2

Lockheed
P-3C Orion
MARPAT, Valkenburg,
Sigonella and Keflavik
300
301
302
303
304
305
306
307
308
309
310
311
312

Westland SH-14D Lynx
7 Sqn & 860 Sqn, De Kooij
(7 Sqn operate 860 Sqn
 aircraft on loan)
260
261
262
264
265
266
267
268

269
270
271
272
273
274
276
277
278
279
280
281
282
283

NEW ZEALAND
Royal New Zealand Air Force
 Boeing 727-22C
 40 Sqn, Whenuapai
 NZ7271
 NZ7272

Lockheed
C-130H Hercules
 40 Sqn, Whenuapai
 NZ7001
 NZ7002
 NZ7003
 NZ7004
 NZ7005

Lockheed
P-3K Orion
 5 Sqn, Whenuapai
 NZ4201
 NZ4202
 NZ4203
 NZ4204
 NZ4205
 NZ4206

NIGERIA
Federal Nigerian Air Force
 Lockheed
 C-130H Hercules
 Lagos
 NAF-910
 NAF-912
 NAF-913
 NAF-914
 NAF-915
 NAF-917
 NAF-918
 NAF-918 (NAF 916)

NORWAY
Kongelige Norske
 Luftforsvaret
 Dassault
 Falcon 20 ECM
 717 Skv, Gardermoen
 041
 053
 0125

DHC-6 Twin Otter
 719 Skv, Bødø
 057
 184
 7062

General Dynamics
F-16A/*F-16B
 331 Skv, Bodø (*r/w/bl*);

332	Skv, Rygge (*y/bk*);
334	Skv, Bodø (*r/w*);
338	Skv, Ørland
272	332 Skv
273	332 Skv
274	332 Skv
275	332 Skv
276	332 Skv
277	332 Skv
279	332 Skv
281	332 Skv
282	332 Skv
284	332 Skv
285	332 Skv
288	338 Skv
289	338 Skv
291	338 Skv
292	338 Skv
293	338 Skv
295	338 Skv
297	338 Skv
298	338 Skv
299	338 Skv
302*	332 Skv
304*	332 Skv
305*	332 Skv
306*	332 Skv
658	334 Skv
659	334 Skv
660	334 Skv
661	334 Skv
662	334 Skv
663	334 Skv
664	334 Skv
665	334 Skv
666	334 Skv
667	334 Skv
668	334 Skv
669	334 Skv
670	334 Skv
671	338 Skv
672	331 Skv
673	331 Skv
674	331 Skv
675	331 Skv
677	331 Skv
678	331 Skv
680	331 Skv
681	331 Skv
682	331 Skv
683	331 Skv
686	331 Skv
687	331 Skv
688	331 Skv
689*	338 Skv
690*	338 Skv
691*	334 Skv
692*	334 Skv
693*	338 Skv
711*	331 Skv
712*	331 Skv

Lockheed
C-130H Hercules
335 Skv, Gardermoen
952
953
954
955
956
957

Lockheed P-3C Orion
333 Skv, Andøya
3296
3297
3298
3299

Lockheed P-3N Orion
333 Skv Andøya
4576
6603

Northrop F-5A
336 Skv, Rygge
128
130
131
132
133
134
208
210
215
896
898
902

Northrop F-5B
336 Skv, Rygge
136
241
243
244
387
594
595
906
907
908
909

**Westland Sea King Mk43/
Mk43A^A/Mk43B^B**
330 Skv, Bodø
060^A
062
066^A
069^A
070^A
071^B
072^A
073^A
074^A
189
322^B

Kystvakt (Coast Guard)
Westland Lynx Mk86
337 Skv, Bardufoss
207
216
228
232
237
350

OMAN
Royal Air Force of Oman
  BAC 1-11/485GD
4 Sqn, Seeb
551
552
553

**Lockheed
C-130H Hercules**
4 Sqn, Seeb
501
502
503

Short Skyvan 3M
2 Sqn, Seeb
901
902
903
904
905
906
907
908
910
911
912
913
914
915
916

PAKISTAN
Pakistan Fiza'ya
  Boeing 707-340C
68-19866   12 Sqn
69-19635   12 Sqn

PORTUGAL
Forca Aerea Portuguesa
  CASA 212A/212ECM*
    Aviocar
401 Esq, Sintra;
502 Esq, Sintra;
503 Esq, Lajes
16501   502 Esq
16502* 401 Esq
16503   502 Esq
16504   502 Esq
16505   502 Esq
16506   502 Esq
16507   502 Esq
16508   502 Esq
16509   502 Esq
16510   401 Esq
16511   502 Esq
16512   401 Esq
16513   503 Esq
16514   503 Esq
16515   503 Esq
16517   503 Esq
16519   401 Esq
16520   503 Esq
16521* 401 Esq
16522* 401 Esq
16523* 401 Esq
16524* 401 Esq

  CASA 212-300 Aviocar
401 Esq, Sintra
17201
17202

  D-BD Alpha Jet
103 Esq, Beja;
301 Esq, Beja
15201
15208
15209
15210
15211

15213
15214
15217
15218
15220
15221
15222
15223
15224
15225
15226
15227
15228
15229
15230
15231
15232
15233
15234
15235
15236
15237
15238
15239
15240
15241
15242
15243
15244
15245
15246
15247
15248
15249
15250

**Dassault
Falcon 20C**
504 Esq, Lisbon/Montijo
17103

**Dassault
Falcon 50**
504 Esq, Lisbon/Montijo
17401
17402
17403

**Lockheed
C-130H/C-130H-30***
    Hercules
501 Esq, Lisbon/Montijo
16801*
16802*
16803
16804
16805
16806*

**Lockheed (GD)
F-16A/F-16B***
201 Esq, Monte Real
15101
15102
15103
15104
15105
15106
15107
15108
15109
15110
15111
15112

15113	
15114	
15115	
15116	
15117	
15118*	
15119*	
15120*	

Lockheed P-3P Orion
601 Esq, Lisbon/Montijo
14801
14802
14803
14804
14805
14806

LTV A-7P/TA-7P* Corsair II
302 Esq, Monte Real;
304 Esq, Monte Real
15502
15503
15504
15506
15507
15508
15509
15511
15512
15513
15514
15515
15516
15517
15519
15521
15522
15524
15526
15527
15528
15529
15531
15532
15534
15536
15537
15538
15539
15544
15545*
15546*
15547*
15549*
15550*

RUSSIA
Voenno-Vozdushniye Sily
Rossioki Federatsii (Russian Air Force)
Sukhoi Su-27
TsAGI, Gromov Flight
Institute Zhukhovsky

595	(27595)	Su-27P
597	(27597)	Su-30
598	(27598)	Su-27P

SAUDI ARABIA
Al Quwwat al-Jawwiya as Sa' udiya
Boeing E-3A/KE3A* Sentry
18 Sqn, Riyadh
1801

1802	
1803	
1804	
1805	
1811*	
1812*	
1813*	
1814*	
1815*	
1816*	
1817*	
1818*	

Lockheed C-130 Hercules
1 Sqn, Riyadh;
4 Sqn, Jeddah;
16 Sqn, Jeddah

112	VC-130H	1 Sqn
451	C-130E	4 Sqn
452	C-130E	4 Sqn
455	C-130E	4 Sqn
461	C-130H	4 Sqn
462	C-130H	4 Sqn
463	C-130H	4 Sqn
464	C-130H	4 Sqn
465	C-130H	4 Sqn
466	C-130H	4 Sqn
467	C-130H	4 Sqn
468	C-130H	4 Sqn
470	C-130H	4 Sqn
471	C-130H-30	4 Sqn
472	C-130H	4 Sqn
473	C-130H	4 Sqn
474	C-130H	4 Sqn
475	C-130H	4 Sqn
1601	C-130H	16 Sqn
1602	C-130H	16 Sqn
1603	C-130H	16 Sqn
1604	C-130H	16 Sqn
1605	C-130H	16 Sqn
1606	C-130E	16 Sqn
1607	C-130E	16 Sqn
1608	C-130E	16 Sqn
1609	C-130E	16 Sqn
1610	C-130E	16 Sqn
1611	C-130E	16 Sqn
1612	C-130H	16 Sqn
1613	C-130H	16 Sqn
1614	C-130H	16 Sqn
1615	C-130H	16 Sqn
1616	KC-130H	16 Sqn
1617	KC-130H	16 Sqn
1618	C-130H	16 Sqn
1619	C-130H	16 Sqn
1620	KC-130H	16 Sqn
1621	KC-130H	16 Sqn
1622	C-130H-30	16 Sqn
1623	C-130H-30	16 Sqn
1624	C-130H	16 Sqn
1625	C-130H	16 Sqn
1626	C-130H	16 Sqn
1627	C-130H	16 Sqn
1628	C-130H	16 Sqn
3201	KC-130H	32 Sqn
3202	KC-130H	32 Sqn
3203	KC-130H	32 Sqn
3204	KC-130H	32 Sqn

SINGAPORE
Republic of Singapore Air Force
Lockheed C-130 Hercules
122 Sqn, Paya Labar

720	KC-130B
721	C-130B
724	KC-130B
725	KC-130B
730	C-130H
731	C-130H
732	C-130H
733	C-130H
734	KC-130H
735	KC-130H

SLOVAKIA
Slovacke Vojenske Letectvo
Aero L.39/L.59 (L.39MS) Albatros
31 SLK/3 Letka, Sliač;
33 SBoLK/2 Letka, Malacky;
VSL, Košice;
White Albatroses, Košice (WA)

0002	L.39MS	VSL
0003	L.39MS	VSL
0101	L.39C	WA [4]
0102	L.39C	WA [6]
0103	L.39C	VSL
0111	L.39C	WA [5]
0112	L.39C	WA [1]
0442	L.39C	WA [0]
0443	L.39C	WA [7]
0730	L.39V	VSL
0745	L.39V	VSL
1725	L.39ZA	33 SBoLK
1730	L.39ZA	33 SBoLK
3905	L.39ZA	33 SBoLK
4355	L.39C	WA [3]
4357	L.39C	WA [2]
4701	L.39ZA	31 SLK
4703	L.39ZA	31 SLK
4705	L.39ZA	31 SLK
4707	L.39ZA	31 SLK
4711	L.39ZA	31 SLK

Antonov An-12BP
32 ZmDK/1 Letka, Piešťany
2209

Antonov An-24V
32 ZmDK/1 Letka, Piešťany
2903
5605

Antonov An-26
32 ZmDK/1 Letka, Piešťany
2506
3208

Let 410
VSL, Košice;
32 ZmDK/1 Letka, Piešťany

0404	L.410M	32 ZmDK
0405	L.410M	32 ZmDK
0730	L.410UVP	32 ZmDK
0927	L.410T	VSL
0930	L.410T	VSL
1133	L.410T	VSL
1203	L.410FG	32 ZmDK
1504	L.410UVP	
1511	L.410UVP	32 ZmDK
1521	L.410FG	32 ZmDK
1810	L.410UVP-E	32 ZmDK
2006	L.410UVP-E	32 ZmDK
2311	L.410UVP	32 ZmDK

Mikoyan MiG-29A/UB*
31 SLK/1 Letka, Sliač;
0619
0820
0921
1303*
2022
2123
3709
3911
4401*
5113
5515
5817
7501
8003
8605
9207
9308

Sukhoi Su-25K/BK*
33 SBoLK/2 Letka, Malacky
1006
1007
1008
1027
3237*
5033
5036
6017
6018
8073
8074
8075

Tupolev Tu-154B-2
32 ZmDK/1 Letka, Bratislava
0420

SPAIN
Ejercito del Aire
 Airtech CN.235M-10 (T.19A)/
 CN.235M-100 (T.19B)
 Ala 35, Getafe
 T.19A-1   35-60
 T.19A-02   35-61
 T.19B-03   35-21
 T.19B-04   35-22
 T.19B-05   35-23
 T.19B-06   35-24
 T.19B-07   35-25
 T.19B-08   35-26
 T.19B-09   35-27
 T.19B-10   35-28
 T.19B-11   35-29
 T.19B-12   35-30
 T.19B-13   35-31
 T.19B-14   35-32
 T.19B-15   35-33
 T.19B-16   35-34
 T.19B-17   35-35
 T.19B-18   35-36
 T.19B-19   35-37
 T.19B-20   35-38

 Boeing 707-381B/368C*
 Grupo 45, Torrejon
 T.17-1   45-10
 TK.17-2   45-11
 T.17-3*   45-12

 CASA 101 Aviojet
 Grupo 21, Moron;
 Grupo 54, Torrejon;

Grupo de Escuelas de
   Matacan (74);
AGA, San Javier (79);
Patrulla Aguila, San Javier*
E.25-01   79-01   [6]*
E.25-02   793-02
E.25-03   79-03
E.25-04   79-04
E.25-05   79-05
E.25-06   79-06   [8]*
E.25-07   79-07   [4]*
E.25-08   79-08   [1]*
E.25-09   79-09
E.25-10   79-10
E.25-11   79-11
E.25-12   79-12
E.25-13   79-13   [3]*
E.25-14   79-14   [4]*
E.25-15   79-15
E.25-16   79-16
E.25-17   21-01
E.25-18   21-02
E.25-19   79-19
E.25-20   79-20
E.25-21   79-21   [9]*
E.25-22   79-22   [7]*
E.25-23   79-23   [4]*
E.25-24   79-24
E.25-25   79-25   [5]*
E.25-26   79-26   [2]*
E.25-27   79-27   [6]*
E.25-28   79-28   [2]*
E.25-29   79-29
E.25-30   79-30
E.25-31   79-31
E.25-33   74-02
E.25-34   21-04
E.25-35   21-05
E.25-36   79-36
E.25-37   21-06
E.25-38   79-38
E.25-40   79-40   [2]*
E.25-41   21-07
E.25-42   793-32
E.25-43   21-08
E.25-44   79-44
E.25-45   79-45
E.25-46   79-46
E.25-47   79-47
E.25-48   79-48
E.25-49   79-49
E.25-50   79-33
E.25-51   74-07
E.25-52   74-08
E.25-53   411-07
E.25-54   79-35
E.25-55   44-05
E.25-56   21-09
E.25-57   74-12
E.25-59   21-10
E.25-61   21-11
E.25-62   74-16
E.25-63   74-17
E.25-64   74-18
E.25-65   74-19
E.25-66   21-12
E.25-67   21-13
E.25-68   79-95
E.25-69   79-97
E.25-71   21-14
E.25-72   74-26
E.25-73   79-98
E.25-74   74-28
E.25-75   21-16

E.25-76   21-17
E.25-78   79-02
E.25-79   74-32
E.25-80   74-33
E.25-81   74-34
E.25-83   21-18
E.25-84   79-04
E.25-86   74-37
E.25-87   74-38
E.25-88   74-39

CASA 212 Aviocar
212 (XT.12)/212A (T.12B)/
212B (TR.12A)/212D
  (TE.12B)/212DE
(TM.12D)/212E
  (T.12C)/212S
(D.3A)/212S1 (D.3B)
Ala 22, Moron;
Ala 37, Villanubla;
Ala 46, Gando, Las Palmas;
CLAEX, Torrejon (54);
Grupo 72, Alcantarilla;
Grupo Esc, Matacan (74);
AGA (Ala 79), San Javier;
403 Esc, Getafe;
408 Esc, Torrejon;
721 Esc, Alcantarilla;
801 Esc, Palma/San Juan;
803 Esc, Cuatro Vientos
D.3A-01   801 Esc
D.3A-02   803-11
D.3B-03   803 Esc
D.3B-04   801 Esc
D.3B-05   801 Esc
D.3B-06   803-12
D.3B-07   803-13
D.3B-08   22-92
D.3B-09   803-14
XT.12A-1   54-10
XT.12A-2   54-12
TR.12A-3   403-01
TR.12A-4   403-02
TR.12A-5   403-03
TR.12A-6   403-04
TR.12A-7   403-05
TR.12A-8   403-06
TE.12B-9   74-83
TE.12B-10   79-92
T.12B-12   74-82
T.12B-13   74-70
T.12B-14   37-01
T.12B-15   37-02
T.12B-16   74-71
T.12B-17   37-03
T.12B-18   46-31
T.12B-19   46-32
T.12B-20   37-04
T.12B-21   37-05
T.12B-22   37-06
T.12B-23   72-01
T.12B-24   37-07
T.12B-25   74-72
T.12B-26   72-02
T.12B-27   46-33
T.12B-28   72-03
T.12B-29   37-08
T.12B-30   74-73
T.12B-31   46-34
T.12B-33   72-04
T.12B-34   74-74
T.12B-35   37-09
T.12B-36   37-10
T.12B-37   72-05

Spain – Sweden

T.12B-38	35-10
T.12B-39	74-75
TE.12B-40	79-93
TE.12B-41	79-94
TE.12B-42	744-42
T.12C-43	46-50
T.12C-44	37-50
T.12B-46	74-76
T.12B-47	72-06
T.12B-48	37-11
T.12B-49	46-36
T.12B-50	74-77
T.12B-51	74-78
T.12B-52	72-07
T.12B-53	46-37
T.12B-54	37-54
T.12B-55	46-38
T.12B-56	74-79
T.12B-57	72-08
T.12B-58	46-39
T.12C-59	37-51
T.12C-60	37-52
T.12C-61	37-53
T.12B-63	37-14
T.12B-64	46-40
T.12B-65	74-80
T.12B-66	72-09
T.12B-67	74-81
T.12B-68	37-15
T.12B-69	37-16
T.12B-70	37-17
T.12B-71	37-18
TM.12D-72	408-01
TM.12D-73	408-02
TM.12D-74	408-03

Cessna 560 Citation VI
403 Esc, Getafe

TR.20-02	403-12

Dassault Falcon 20
Grupo 45, Torrejon;
408 Esc, Torrejon

T.11-1	45-02
TM.11-2	45-03
TM.11-3	408-11
TM.11-4	408-12
T.11-5	45-05

Dassault Falcon 50
Grupo 45, Torrejon

T.16-1	45-20

Dassault Falcon 900
Grupo 45, Torrejon

T.18-1	45-40
T.18-2	45-41

**Fokker F.27M
Friendship 400MPA**
802 Esc, Gando

D.2-01	802-10
D.2-02	802-11
D.2-03	802-12

**Lockheed P-3A/
P-3B* Orion**
Grupo 22, Moron

P.3-01	22-21
P.3-03	22-22
P.3-08	22-31*
P.3-09	22-32*
P.3-10	22-33*
P.3-11	22-34*
P.3-12	22-35*

**Lockheed Hercules
C-130H/C-130H-30[1]**
311/312 Esc (Ala 31),
Zaragoza

TL.10-01	31-01[1]
T.10-02	31-02
T.10-03	31-03
T.10-04	31-04
T.10-08	31-05
T.10-09	31-06
T.10-10	31-07

KC-130H
312 Esc (Ala 31), Zaragosa

TK.10-05	31-50
TK.10-06	31-51
TK.10-07	31-52
TK.10-11	31-53
TK.10-12	31-54

**McDonnell Douglas
EF-18A/EF-18B* Hornet**
Ala 12, Torrejon;
Grupo 15, Zaragoza

CE.15-1	15-70*
CE.15-2	15-71*
CE.15-3	15-72*
CE.15-4	15-73*
CE.15-5	15-74*
CE.15-6	15-75*
CE.15-7	12-70*
CE.15-8	12-71*
CE.15-9	12-72*
CE.15-10	12-73*
CE.15-11	12-74*
CE.15-12	12-75*
C.15-13	12-01
C.15-14	15-01
C.15-15	15-02
C.15-16	15-03
C.15-18	15-05
C.15-20	15-07
C.15-21	15-08
C.15-22	15-09
C.15-23	15-10
C.15-24	15-11
C.15-25	15-12
C.15-26	15-13
C.15-27	15-14
C.15-28	15-15
C.15-29	15-16
C.15-30	15-17
C.15-31	15-18
C.15-32	15-19
C.15-33	15-20
C.15-34	15-21
C.15-35	15-22
C.15-36	15-23
C.15-37	15-24
C.15-38	15-25
C.15-39	15-26
C.15-40	15-27
C.15-41	15-28
C.15-42	15-29
C.15-43	15-30
C.15-44	12-02
C.15-45	12-03
C.15-46	12-04
C.15-47	12-05
C.15-48	12-06
C.15-49	12-07
C.15-50	12-08
C.15-51	12-09
C.15-52	12-10
C.15-53	12-11
C.15-54	12-12

C.15-55	12-13
C.15-56	12-14
C.15-57	12-15
C.15-58	12-16
C.15-59	12-17
C.15-60	12-18
C.15-61	12-19
C.15-62	12-20
C.15-63	12-21
C.15-64	12-22
C.15-65	12-23
C.15-66	12-24
C.15-67	12-25
C.15-68	12-26
C.15-69	12-27
C.15-70	12-28
C.15-72	12-30

**Arma Aérea de
l'Armada Espanola
BAe/McDonnell-Douglas
EAV-8B Harrier II**
Esc 009, Rota

VA.2-1	01-901
VA.2-2	01-902
VA.2-3	01-903
VA.2-4	01-904
VA.2-5	01-905
VA.2-6	01-906
VA.2-7	01-907
VA.2-8	01-908
VA.2-9	01-909
VA.2-10	01-910
VA.2-11	01-911
VA.2-12	01-912

TAV-8S Matador
Esc 008, Rota

VAE.1-1	01-807
VAE.1-2	01-808

Cessna 550 Citation 2
Esc 004, Rota

U.20-1	01-405
U.20-2	01-406
U.20-3	01-407

**SUDAN
Silakh Al Jawwiya as Sudaniya
Lockheed
C-130H Hercules**

1100
1101
1102
1103
1104
1105

**SWEDEN
Kungliga Svenska Flygvapnet
Aerospatiale AS.332M-1
Super Puma (Hkp.10)**
Flottiljer 7, Såtenäs;
Flottiljer 15, Söderhamn;
Flottiljer 17, Ronneby/
Kallinge;
Flottiljer 21, Luleå/Kallax

10401	91	F7
10402	92	F7
10403	93	F21
10404	94	F21
10405	95	F15
10406	96	F17
10407	97	F17

10408	98	F15
10409	99	F17
10410	90	F17
10411	88	F21
10412	89	F7

Beechcraft Super King Air (Tp.101)
Flottiljer 7, Satenäs;
Flottiljer 17, Ronneby;
Flottiljer 21, Lulea

101002	012	F21
101003	013	F17
101004	014	F7

Grumman G.1159C
Gulfstream IV
(Tp.102/S.102B*)
Flottiljer 16, Uppsala

102001	021
102002*	022
102003*	023

Lockheed
C-130E Hercules (Tp.84)
Flottiljer 7, Satenäs

84001	841
84002	842

Lockheed
C-130H Hercules (Tp.84)
Flottiljer 7, Satenäs

84003	843
84004	844
84005	845
84006	846
84007	847
84008	848

SAAB SF.340B (Tp.100)/
SF.340AEW&C (S.100B)*
Flottiljer 16, Uppsala

100001	001	F16
100002*	002	

Swearingen
Metro III (Tp.88)
Flottiljer 16, Uppsala
88003   883

Marine Flygtjanst
Vertol 107-II-5 (Hkp.4C)
1 Hkp Div, Berga

04061	61
04063	63
04064	64

Kawasaki-Vertol
KV.107-II (Hkp.4C)
1 Hkp Div, Berga;
2 Hkp Div, Säve;
3 Hkp Div, Ronneby;
FC, Malmslatt

04065	65	2 Hkp Div
04067	67	2 Hkp Div
04068	68	2 Hkp Div
04069	69	1 Hkp Div
04070	70	1 Hkp Div
04071	71	2 Hkp Div
04072	72	FC
04073	73	1 Hkp Div
04074	74	3 Hkp Div
04075	75	3 Hkp Div

Armen
MBB Bo.105CB (Hkp.9B)
Armeflyget 1 (AF1),
  Boden;
Armeflyget 2 (AF2),
  Malmslatt;
FC, Malmslatt (Air Force)

09201	01	AF2
09202	02	AF1
09203	03	AF2
09204	04	AF2
09205	05	AF1
09206	06	AF1
09207	07	AF1
09208	08	AF1
09209	09	AF2
09210	10	AF1
09211	11	AF1
09212	12	AF2
09214	14	AF2
09215	15	AF2
09216	16	AF2
09217	17	AF2
09218	18	
09219	19	AF1
09220	20	AF2
09221	90	FC

SWITZERLAND
Schweizerische Flugwaffe
Aérospatiale AS.532
Super Puma
Leichte Fliegerstaffeln 5
  (LtSt St), Mollis;
Leichte Fliegerstaffeln 6
  (LtSt 6), Mollis;
Leichte Fliegerstaffeln 8
  (LtSt 8), Mollis
Detachments at Interlaken,
Meiringen, Payerne & Sion
T-311
T-312
T-313
T-314
T-315
T-316
T-317
T-318
T-319
T-320
T-321
T-322
T-323
T-324
T-325

Dassault Mirage III
Flieger Staffel 10 (FlSt 10),
  Payerne;
Flieger Staffel 16 (FlSt 16),
  Stans;
Flieger Staffel 17 (FlSt 17),
  Meiringen;
Gruppe fur Rustungdienste
  (GRD), Emmen;
Instrumentation Flieger
Staffel 14 (InstruFlSt 14),
  Dübendorf;

Mirage IIIDS
J-2001   InstruFlSt 14

Mirage IIIUDS
J-2011   InstruFlSt 14
J-2012   InstruFlSt 14

Mirage IIIS

J-2301	
J-2302	GRD
J-2303	GRD
J-2304	FlSt 10
J-2305	FlSt 10
J-2306	FlSt 16/17
J-2308	FlSt 16/17
J-2309	FlSt 16
J-2311	FlSt 10
J-2312	
J-2313	FlSt 10
J-2314	FlSt 16
J-2315	
J-2317	
J-2318	FlSt 16
J-2319	FlSt 16/17
J-2321	FlSt 16/17
J-2322	
J-2324	FlSt 10
J-2325	
J-2326	FlSt 16
J-2327	FlSt 16
J-2329	FlSt 16
J-2330	FlSt 16/17
J-2331	FlSt 16/17
J-2332	FlSt 10
J-2333	FlSt 16/17
J-2334	FlSt 16
J-2335	FlSt 16/17

Mirage IIIRS

R-2101	FlSt 10
R-2102	FlSt 10
R-2103	FlSt 10
R-2104	FlSt 10
R-2105	FlSt 10
R-2106	FlSt 10
R-2107	FlSt 10
R-2108	FlSt 10
R-2109	FlSt 10
R-2110	FlSt 10
R-2112	FlSt 10
R-2113	FlSt 10
R-2114	FlSt 10
R-2115	FlSt 10
R-2116	FlSt 10
R-2117	FlSt 10
R-2118	FlSt 10

Mirage IIIBS
U-2004   InstruFlSt 14

Gates Learjet 35A
Swiss Air Force, Dubendorf
T-781
T-782

Northrop F-5 Tiger II
Flieger Staffel 1 (FlSt 1),
  Turtman;
Flieger Staffel 6 (FlSt 6),
  Sion;
Flieger Staffel 8 (FlSt 8),
  Meiringen;
Flieger Staffel 11 (FlSt 11),
  Alpnach;
Flieger Staffel 13 (FlSt 13),
  Meiringen;
Flieger Staffel 18 (FlSt 18),
  Payerne;
Flieger Staffel 19 (FlSt 19),
  Alpnach;

Switzerland – Turkey

Gruppe fur Rustunggdienste (GRD),
Emmen;Instrumentation
Fliege
  Staffel 14 (InstruFlSt 14),
  Dübendorf;
Patrouille Suisse, Emmen
(P. Suisse)

F-5E

J-3001	GRD
J-3002	FlSt 11
J-3003	FlSt 11
J-3004	FlSt 11
J-3005	FlSt 18
J-3006	FlSt 11
J-3007	FlSt 11
J-3008	InstruFlSt 14
J-3009	FlSt 11
J-3010	FlSt 18
J-3011	FlSt 13
J-3012	FlSt 11
J-3014	FlSt 11
J-3015	FlSt 11
J-3016	FlSt 11
J-3019	FlSt 11
J-3020	FlSt 18
J-3021	FlSt 18
J-3022	FlSt 19
J-3023	FlSt 13
J-3023	FlSt 13
J-3025	FlSt 13
J-3026	FlSt 18
J-3027	FlSt 18
J-3028	FlSt 13
J-3029	FlSt 19
J-3030	FlSt 6
J-3031	FlSt 13
J-3032	FlSt 13
J-3033	FlSt 19
J-3034	FlSt 13
J-3035	FlSt 19
J-3036	FlSt 13
J-3037	FlSt 13
J-3038	FlSt 18
J-3039	FlSt 13
J-3040	
J-3041	FlSt 19
J-3043	FlSt 13
J-3044	FlSt 1
J-3045	FlSt 19
J-3046	FlSt 18
J-3047	FlSt 13
J-3049	FlSt 1
J-3050	FlSt 19
J-3051	FlSt 1
J-3052	FlSt 13
J-3053	FlSt 13
J-3054	FlSt 18
J-3055	FlSt 18
J-3056	FlSt 1
J-3057	
J-3058	FlSt 13
J-3060	FlSt 1
J-3061	FlSt 13
J-3062	FlSt 18
J-3063	FlSt 18

J-3064	FlSt 13
J-3065	FlSt 13
J-3066	
J-3067	FlSt 1
J-3068	FlSt 13
J-3069	FlSt 13
J-3070	FlSt 8
J-3072	FlSt 13
J-3073	FlSt 13
J-3074	FlSt 13
J-3075	FlSt 13
J-3076	FlSt 13
J-3077	FlSt 8
J-3079	FlSt 1
J-3080	P. Suisse
J-3081	P. Suisse
J-3082	FlSt 1
J-3083	FlSt 13
J-3084	FlSt 11
J-3085	P. Suisse
J-3086	P. Suisse
J-3087	P. Suisse
J-3088	P. Suisse
J-3089	P. Suisse
J-3090	
J-3091	P. Suisse
J-3092	FlSt 13
J-3093	FlSt 18
J-3094	FlSt 1
J-3095	
J-3096	FlSt 18
J-3097	GRD
J-3098	FlSt 19

F-5F

J-3201	FlSt 1
J-3202	FlSt 1
J-3203	FlSt 18
J-3204	GRD
J-3205	FlSt 13
J-3206	
J-3207	FlSt 13
J-3208	FlSt 11
J-3209	FlSt 13
J-3210	FlSt 1
J-3211	
J-3212	

TURKEY
Turk Hava Kuvvetleri
  Boeing KC-135R
  Stratotanker
  Tanker Squadron, Incirlik

23512
23568
72591
72592

Cessna 650 Citation VII
224 Filo, Etimesgut
93-7024 ETI-024
93-7026 ETI-026

Grumman G.1159C
Gulstream IV
224 Filo, Etimesgut
003

Transall C-160D
221 Filo, Erkilet

019	
020	12-020
021	
022	12-022
023	12-023
024	12-024
025	12-025
026	12-026
027	12-027
028	12-028
029	
030	12-030
031	12-031
032	12-032
033	12-033
034	12-034
035	12-035
036	12-036
037	12-037
038	12-038
039	12-039
040	12-040

Lockheed
C-130B Hercules
222 Filo, Erkilet
10960
10963
23496
70527
80736
91527

Lockheed
C-130E Hercules
222 Filo, Erkilet

00991	12-991
01468	12-468
01947	12-947
13186	12-186
13187	12-187
13188	12-188
13189	12-189
17949	12-949

UNITED ARAB EMIRATES
United Arab Emirates Air Force
Abu Dhabi
Lockheed
C-130H Hercules
1211
1212
1213
1214

Dubai
Lockheed
L.100-30 Hercules
311
312

US Military Aircraft Markings

All USAF aircraft have been allocated a fiscal year (FY) number since 1921. Individual aircraft are given a serial according to the fiscal year in which they are ordered. The numbers commence at 0001 and are prefixed with the year of allocation. For example F-15C Eagle 40001 (84-001) was the first aircraft ordered in 1984. The fiscal year (FY) serial is carried on the technical data block which is usually stencilled on the left-hand side of the aircraft just below the cockpit. The number displayed on the fin is a corruption of the FY serial. Most tactical aircraft carry the fiscal year in small figures followed by the last three or four digits of the serial in large figures. For example Lakenheath-based F-15E Eagle 10311 carries 91-0311/LN on its tail. Large transport and tanker aircraft such as C-130s and KC-135s sometimes display a five-figure number commencing with the last digit of the appropriate fiscal year and four figures of the production number. An example of this is KC-135R 58-0128 which displays 80128 on its fin.

USN serials follow a straightforward numerical sequence which commenced, for the present series, with the allocation of 00001 to an SB2C Helldiver by the Bureau of Aeronautics in 1940. Numbers in the 165000 series are presently being issued. They are usually carried in full on the aircraft's rear fuselage .

UK based USAF Aircraft

The following aircraft are normally based in the UK. They are listed in numerical order of type with individual aircraft in serial number order, as depicted on the aircraft. The number in brackets is either the alternative presentation of the five-figure number commencing with the last digit of the fiscal year, or the fiscal year where a five-figure serial is presented on the aircraft. Where it is possible to identify the allocation of aircraft to individual squadrons by means of colours carried on fin or cockpit edge, this is also provided.

McDonnell Douglas F-15C Eagle/F-15D Eagle/ F-15E Strike Eagle 48 FW, RAF Lakenheath [LN] 492 FS *blue*/white 493 FS black/yellow 494 FS *red*/white		
86-0147 (60147) F-15C *y*	86-0182 (60182) F-15D *y*	91-0315 (10315) F-15E *r*
86-0154 (60154) F-15C *y*	90-0248 (00248) F-15E [48 FW]	91-0316 (10316) F-15E *r*
86-0156 (60156) F-15C *y*	90-0251 (00251) F-15E *bl*	91-0317 (10317) F-15E *r*
86-0159 (60159) F-15C *y*	[492 FS]	91-0318 (10318) F-15E *r*
86-0160 (60160) F-15C *y*	90-0255 (00255) F-15E *bl*	91-0319 (10319) F-15E *r*
86-0163 (60163) F-15C *y*	90-0256 (00256) F-15E *bl*	91-0320 (10320) F-15E *r*
86-0164 (60164) F-15C *y*	90-0257 (00257) F-15E *bl*	91-0321 (10321) F-15E *r*
[493 FS]	90-0258 (00258) F-15E *bl*	91-0322 (10322) F-15E *r*
86-0165 (60165) F-15C *y*	90-0259 (00259) F-15E *bl*	91-0323 (10323) F-15E *r*
86-0166 (60166) F-15C [48 OG]	90-0260 (00260) F-15E *bl*	91-0324 (10324) F-15E *r*
86-0167 (60167) F-15C *y*	90-0261 (00261) F-15E *bl*	91-0325 (10325) F-15E *bl*
86-0169 (60169) F-15C *y*	90-0262 (00262) F-15E *bl*	91-0326 (10326) F-15E *bl*
86-0171 (60171) F-15C *y*	91-0300 (10300) F-15E *bl*	91-0327 (10327) F-15E *r*
86-0172 (60172) F-15C *y*	91-0301 (10301) F-15E *bl*	91-0328 (10328) F-15E *r*
86-0173 (60173) F-15C *y*	91-0302 (10302) F-15E *bl*	91-0329 (10329) F-15E *bl*
86-0174 (60174) F-15C *y*	91-0303 (10303) F-15E *bl*	91-0330 (10330) F-15E *r*
86-0175 (60175) F-15C *y*	91-0304 (10304) F-15E *bl*	91-0331 (10331) F-15E *r*
86-0176 (60176) F-15C *y*	91-0305 (10305) F-15E *bl*	91-0332 (10332) F-15E *bl*
86-0178 (60178) F-15C *y*	91-0306 (10306) F-15E *r*	91-0333 (10333) F-15E *r*
86-0180 (60180) F-15C *y*	91-0307 (10307) F-15E *bl*	91-0334 (10334) F-15E *r*
	91-0308 (10308) F-15E *bl*	91-0335 (10335) F-15E *r*
	91-0309 (10309) F-15E *bl*	91-0601 (10601) F-15E *r*
	91-0310 (10310) F-15E *bl*	91-0602 (10602) F-15E *r*
	91-0311 (10311) F-15E *bl*	91-0603 (10603) F-15E *r*
	91-0312 (10312) F-15E *bl*	91-0604 (10604) F-15E *r*
	91-0313 (10313) F-15E [3rd AF]	91-0605 (10605) F-15E *r*
	91-0314 (10314) F-15E [494 FS]	92-0364 (20364) F-15E *r*

USAF/USN UK

Sikorsky MH-53J
21 SOS, 352 SOG
RAF Mildenhall
01625 (FY70)
01626 (FY70)
10924 (FY68)
10930 (FY68)
31648 (FY73)
95784 (FY69)
95794 (FY69)
95795 (FY69)

Lockheed C-130 Hercules
7 SOS* & 67 SOS, 352 SOG
RAF Mildenhall
37814 (FY63) C-130E
40476 (FY84) MC-130H*
60223 (FY66) HC-130P
61699 (FY86) MC-130H*
70023 (FY87) MC-130H*
80193 (FY88) MC-130H*
80194 (FY88) MC-130H*
95820 (FY69) HC-130N
95823 (FY69) HC-130N
95826 (FY69) HC-130N
95831 (FY69) HC-130N

Boeing KC-135R
Stratotanker
351 ARS, 100 ARW [D]
RAF Mildenhall (*r/w/bl*)
23541 (FY62)
38008 (FY63)
38023 (FY63)
38877 (FY63)
71439 (FY57)
71456 (FY57)
71486 (FY57)
71499 (FY57)
71506 (FY57)

F-15E Strike Eagle 90-0248 is based at Lakenheath with the 48th FW. *Daniel March*

UK based US Navy Aircraft

Beech UC-12M
Super King Air
Naval Air Facility, Mildenhall [8G]
3837 (163837)
3840 (163840)
3843 (163843)

These aircraft are normally based in Western Europe with the USAFE. They are shown in numerical order of type designation, with individual aircraft in serial number order as carried on the aircraft. An alternative five-figure presentation of the serial is shown in brackets where appropriate. Fiscal year (FY) details are also provided if necessary. The unit allocation and operating bases are given for most aircraft.

McDonnell Douglas
C-9A Nightingale
75 AAS, 86 AW Ramstein,
Germany
SHAPE, Chievres, Belgium[1]
FY71
10876[1] (VIP)
10879
10880
10881
10882

Fairchild A-10A/OA-10A*
Thunderbolt II
SP: 52 FW Spangdahlem,
Germany
81 FS *black*
81-951   (10951)   *bk*
81-952   (10952)*   *m* [52 FW]
81-954   (10954)*   *bk*
81-956   (10956)*   *bk*
81-962   (10962)   *bk*
81-963   (10963)   *bk*
81-966   (10966)   *bk*
81-976   (10976)   *bk*
81-978   (10978)*   *bk*
81-980   (10980)   *bk* [81 FS]
81-983   (10983)   *bk*
81-984   (10984)   *bk*
81-985   (10985)*   *bk*
81-988   (10988)   *bk*
81-991   (10991)*   *bk*
81-992   (10992)   *bk*
82-649   (20649)*   *bk*
82-650   (20650)   *bk*
82-654   (20654)   *bk*
82-655   (20655)   *bk*
82-656   (20656)   *bk*

Beech C-12C/C-12D*
[1]JUSMG, Ankara, Turkey
[2]US Embassy Flight, Athens
[3]US Embassy Flight, Budapest
30495*   (FY83)[3]
31216   (FY73)[1]
31218   (FY73)[2]
60173   (FY76)[1]

McDonnell Douglas
F-15C/F-15D* Eagle
SP: 52
FW Spangdahlem, Germany
53 FS *yellow/black*
78-514   (80514)   *y*
79-012   (90012)*   *y*
79-025   (90025)   *y*
79-057   (90057)   *y*
79-064   (90064)   *y*
80-004   (00004)   *y*
80-012   (00012)   *y*
80-052   (00052)   *m* [52 FW]

84-001   (40001)   *y* [53 FS]
84-003   (40003)   *y*
84-005   (40005)   *y*
84-008   (40008)   *y*
84-009   (40009)   *y*
84-010   (40010)   *y*
84-014   (40014)   *y*
84-015   (40015)   *y*
84-019   (40019)   *y*
84-023   (40023)   *y*
84-024   (40024)   *y*
84-025   (40025)   *y*
84-027   (40027)   *y* [53 FS]
84-044   (40044)*   *y*

Lockheed (GD)
F-16C/F-16D*
AV: 31 FW Aviano, Italy
510 FS *purple/white*
555 FS *blue/yellow*
SP: 52 FW Spangdahlem,
Germany
22 FS *red/white*
23 FS *blue/white*
87-350   (70350)   AV *pr*
87-351   (70351)   AV *bl*
87-355   (70355)   AV *pr*
87-359   (70359)   AV *bl*
88-413   (80413)   AV *pr*
                               [510 FS]
88-425   (80425)   AV *bl*
88-435   (80435)   AV *bl*
88-443   (80443)   AV *pr*
88-444   (80444)   AV *pr*
88-446   (80446)   AV *pr*
88-491   (80491)   AV *pr*
88-525   (80525)   AV *pr*
88-526   (80526)   AV *bl*
88-529   (80529)   AV *pr*
88-532   (80532)   AV *bl*
88-535   (80535)   AV *bl*
88-541   (80541)   AV *pr*
88-550   (80550)   AV *bl*
                               [555 FS]
89-001   (92001)   AV *bl* [31 FW]
89-009   (92009)   AV *bl*
89-011   (92011)   AV *pr*
89-016   (92016)   AV *bl*
89-023   (92023)   AV *bl*
89-024   (92024)   AV *bl*
89-026   (92026)   AV *pr*
89-029   (92029)   AV *bl*
89-030   (92030)   AV *bl*
89-035   (92035)   AV *bl*
89-038   (92038)   AV *bl*
89-039   (92039)   AV *bl*
89-044   (92044)   AV *pr*
89-046   (92046)   AV *pr*
89-047   (92047)   AV *pr*
89-049   (92049)   AV *bl*
89-050   (92050)   AV *pr*

89-057   (92057)   AV *bl*
89-137   (92137)   AV *bl*
89-178   (92178)*   AV *pr*
90-709   (00709)   AV *pr*
90-795   (00795)*   AV *bl*
90-796   (00796)*   AV *pr*
90-800   (00800)*   AV *bl*
90-813   (00813)   SP *r*
90-818   (00818)   SP *r*
90-827   (00827)   SP *r*
90-828   (00828)   SP *r*
90-829   (00829)   SP *r*
90-831   (00831)   SP *r*
90-833   (00833)   SP *r*
90-843   (00843)*   SP *r*
90-846   (00846)*   SP *r*
91-336   (10336)   SP *r* [22 FS]
91-337   (10337)   SP *m*
                               [52 FW]
91-338   (10338)   SP *r*
91-339   (10339)   SP *r*
91-340   (10340)   SP *r*
91-341   (10341)   SP *r*
91-342   (10342)   SP *r*
91-343   (10343)   SP *r*
91-344   (10344)   SP *r*
91-351   (10351)   SP *r*
91-352   (10352)   SP *m*
                               [52 FW]
91-402   (10402)   SP *bl*
91-403   (10403)   SP *bl* [23 FS]
91-405   (10405)   SP *bl*
91-406   (10406)   SP *bl* [23 FS]
91-407   (10407)   SP *bl*
91-408   (10408)   SP *bl*
91-409   (10409)   SP *bl*
91-410   (10410)   SP *bl*
91-412   (10412)   SP *m*
                               [52 FW]
91-414   (10414)   SP *bl*
91-415   (10415)   SP *bl*
91-416   (10416)   SP *bl*
91-417   (10417)   SP *bl*
91-418   (10418)   SP *bl*
91-419   (10419)   SP *bl*
91-420   (10420)   SP *bl*
91-421   (10421)   SP *bl*
91-464   (10464)*   SP *r*
91-472   (10472)*   SP *bl*
91-474   (10474)*   SP *bl*
92-915   (29315)   SP *bl*
92-918   (29318)   SP *bl*

Grumman C-20A
Gulfstream III
76 AS, 86
AW Ramstein, Germany
FY83
30500
30501
30502

USAF/USN Europe

Gates C-21A
Learjet
76 AS, 86
AW Ramstein, Germany
*7005 ABS/HQ USEUCOM,
Stuttgart, Germany
FY84
40068*
40081*
40082*
40083*
40084
40085
40086
40087
40108
40109
40110
40111
40112

Boeing CT-43A
76 AS, 86 AW Ramstein,
Germany
31149 (FY73)

Sikorsky HH-60G
Blackhawk
56 RQS, 85 Wg Keflavik,
Iceland [IS]
26205 (FY89)
26206 (FY89)
26208 (FY89)
26212 (FY89)
26461 (FY92)

Lockheed C-130E
Hercules
37 AS, 86 AW Ramstein,
Germany [RS] (*bl*)
01260 (FY70)

01264 (FY70)
01271 (FY70)
01274 (FY70)
10935 (FY68)
10938 (FY68)
10943 (FY68)
10947 (FY68)
17681 (FY64)
18240 (FY64)
37885 (FY63)
37887 (FY63)
40502 (FY64)
40527 (FY64)
40533 (FY64)
40550 (FY64)
96566 (FY69)
96582 (FY69)
96583 (FY69)

European based US Navy Aircraft

Lockheed P-3 Orion
CinCAFSE, NAF Sigonella, Italy
VQ-2, NAF Rota, Spain

150495	UP-3A	NAF Keflavik
150515	VP-3A	CinCAFSE
157320	EP-3E	VQ-2
157325	EP-3E	VQ-2
157326	EP-3E	VQ-2
160770	P-3C	[32]
161125	P-3C	[30]

Beech UC-12M
Super King Air
[1] NAF Sigonella, Italy
[2] NAF Rota, Spain

| 3838 (163838)[1] |
| 3839 (163839)[2] |
| 3841 (163841)[1] |
| 3842 (163842)[2] |
| 3844 (163844)[1] |

Sikorsky CH-53E/MH-53E*
Sea Stallion
HC-4, NAF Sigonella, Italy

161532	HC-532
161536	HC-536
161537	HC-537
161542	HC-542
162505	HC-47*
162506	HC-48*
162516	HC-46*
163057	HC-41*
163065	HC-43*
163068	HC-4.*

Beech C-12 Super King Air
7th ATC, Grafenwohr;
207 AvCo, Heidelberg;
HQ/USEUCOM, Stuttgart;
LANDSE, Izmir, Turkey;
6th Avn Det, Vicenza, Italy;
'A' Co, 5 Batt, 158 Avn Reg't, Wiesbaden;
1 MIB, Wiesbaden

FY84

40144	C-12F	7th ATC
40150	C-12F	207 Avn Co
40151	C-12F	207 Avn Co
40153	C-12F	207 Avn Co
40154	C-12F	207 Avn Co
40155	C-12F	207 Avn Co
40156	C-12F	207 Avn Co
40157	C-12F	5/158 ACo
40158	C-12F	HQ USEUCOM
40159	C-12F	HQ USEUCOM
40160	C-12F	HQ USEUCOM
40161	C-12F	LANDSE
40162	C-12F	6 Avn Det
40164	C-12F	LANDSE
40165	C-12F	6 Avn Det

FY85

50147	RC-12K 1 MIB
50148	RC-12K 1 MIB
50150	RC-12K 1 MIB
50151	RC-12K 1 MIB
50152	RC-12K 1 MIB
50153	RC-12K 1 MIB
50154	RC-12K 1 MIB
50155	RC-12K 1 MIB

Boeing-Vertol CH-47D Chinook
'A' Co, 5 Batt, 159 Avn Reg't Giebelstadt;
'E' Co, 502 Avn Reg't, Aviano

FY87

70072	5/159 ACo
70073	5/159 ACo
70079	5/159 ACo
70081	5/159 ACo
70082	5/159 ACo
70083	5/159 ACo
70085	5/159 ACo
70086	5/159 ACo
70088	5/159 ACo
70089	5/159 ACo
70091	5/159 ACo
70092	5/159 ACo
70094	5/159 ACo
70096	5/159 ACo
70112	5/159 ACo

FY88

80098	502 ECo
80099	502 ECo
80100	502 ECo
80101	502 ECo
80102	502 ECo
80103	502 ECo
80104	502 ECo
80106	502 ECo

FY89

90138	502 ECo
90139	502 ECo
90140	502 ECo
90141	502 ECo
92142	502 ECo
90143	502 ECo
90144	502 ECo
90145	502 ECo

Sikorsky UH-60A Black Hawk
3-1 Avn, Ansbach;
7-1 Avn, Ansbach;
1-1 Cav, Budingen;
45 Med Co, Ansbach;
357th Avn Det/SHAPE, Chievres;
'C' Co, 7th Btn, 158 Avn Reg't, Giebelstadt;
8-158 Avn, Giebelstadt;
'C' Co, 6th Btn, 159 Avn Reg't, Giebelstadt;
2-227 Avn, Hanau;
3-227 Avn, Hanau;
'A' Co, 7th Btn, 227 Avn Reg't, Hanau;
207th Aviation Co, Heidelberg;
2-6 Cavalry, Illesheim;
6-6 Cavalry, Illesheim;
236th Med Co (HA), Landstuhl;
'A' Co, 5th Btn, 158 Avn Reg't, Wiesbaden;
159th Med Co, Wiesbaden

FY80

23425	7/158 CCo
23427	
23434	45 Med Co
23489	
23490	6/159 CCo

FY81

23551	236 Med Co
23571	7/227 ACo
23573	159 Med Co
23578	B/70 TRANS
23582	3-227 Avn
23584	
23586	159 Med Co
23589	7-1 Avn
23590	236 Med Co
23594	7-1 Avn
23596	236 Med Co
23597	159 Med Co
23598	7/159 BCo
23602	7-1 Avn
23605	7/158 CCo
23606	7/158 CCo
23608	159 Med Co
23609	7/227 ACo
23613	207 Avn Co
23615	236 Med Co
23617	
23622	
23623	7/158 CCo
23626	236 Med Co

FY82

23647	1 HCo
23660	7/158 CCo
23661	45 Med Co
23662	
23663	7-1 Avn

23664	236 Med Co
23665	7/227 ACo
23667	
23668	7/158 CCo
23669	5/158 ACo
23672	236 Med Co
23673	5/159 ACo
23675	45 Med Co
23676	45 Med Co
23682	7/227 ACo
23684	5/158 ACo
23685	236 Med Co
23686	236 Med Co
23689	207 Avn Co
23691	
23692	7/158 CCo
23693	236 Med Co
23695	45 Med Co
23699	6/159 CCo
23702	7-1 Avn
23722	159 Med Co
23723	159 Med Co
23726	45 Med Co
23727	236 Med Co
23729	45 Med Co
23730	236 Med Co
23731	45 Med Co
23733	45 Med Co
23734	7/227 ACo
23735	236 Med Co
23736	159 Med Co
23737	159 Med Co
23738	159 Med Co
23739	45 Med Co
23741	
23743	45 Med Co
23744	5/158 ACo
23745	45 Med Co
23746	159 Med Co
23748	7-1 Avn
23749	159 Med Co
23750	45 Med Co
23751	45 Med Co
23753	159 Med Co
23754	45 Med Co
23755	45 Med Co
23756	159 Med Co
23757	45 Med Co
23761	7/227 ACo

FY83

23854	5/158 ACo
23855	207 Avn Co
23869	207 Avn Co

FY86

24498	7/227 ACo
24530	7-1 Avn
24531	
24532	6/159 CCo
24533	
24538	207 Avn Co
24550	236 Med Co
24551	236 Med Co
24552	7-1 Avn
24554	7/227 ACo
24555	6/159 CCo

FY87

24579	5/158 ACo
24581	236 Med Co
24583	357 Av Det

US Army

Serial	Unit	Serial	Unit	Serial	Unit
24584	357 Av Det	24218	2-6 Cav	70412	3-1 Avn
24589	207 Avn Co	24244	6-6 Cav	70413	3-1 Avn
24621	7-1 Avn	24247		70415	3-1 Avn
24628	7-1 Avn	24250	3-227 Avn	70417	3-1 Avn
24634	6/159 CCo	24257		70418	3-227 Avn
24642	45 Med Co	24260	2-6 Cav	70419	3-1 Avn
24643	7/1 ACo	24262	2-6 Cav	70420	3-1 Avn
24644	6/159 CCo	24266	2-6 Cav	70423	3-1 Avn
24645	6/159 CCo	24277	2-6 Cav	70432	
24647	7-1 Avn	24290	2-6 Cav	70434	3-227 Avn
24656		24293	2-6 Cav	70435	2-227 Avn
26001		24296	2-6 Cav	70436	3-1 Avn
26002	159 Med Co	24297	2-6 Cav	70437	
26003	7/227 ACo	24299		70438	3-227 Avn
26004	7/1 ACo	24303	2-6 Cav	70439	3-1 Avn
FY88		24304	2-6 Cav	70440	3-227 Avn
26019	7/227 ACo	*FY85*		70441	3-227 Avn
26020		25352	3-1 Avn	70442	3-1 Avn
26021	5/158 ACo	25357	2-6 Cav	70443	2-6 Cav
26023	7/158 CCo	25397		70444	2-227 Avn
26024	7/158 CCo	25424		70445	3-227 Avn
26025	7/158 CCo	25430	2-6 Cav	70446	3-227 Avn
26026	5/159 ACo	25460	3-1 Avn	70447	3-227 Avn
26027	7/158 CCo	25465	2-6 Cav	70449	3-227 Avn
26028	7/158 CCo	25469	7/159 ACo	70451	2-227 Avn
26031	7-1 Avn	25471	2-227 Avn	70455	2-227 Avn
26034	7/227 ACo	25472	2-227 Avn	70457	2-6 Cav
26037		25473	3-1 Avn	70459	
26038	5/158 ACo	25474	2-227 Avn	70465	1 Avn
26039	6/159 CCo	25475	2-6 Cav	70470	
26040	7-1 Avn	25476		70471	3-1 Avn
26041	6/159 CCo	25478	3-1 Avn	70473	
26042	6/159 CCo	25479	3-1 Avn	70474	
26045	6/159 CCo	25480	3-227 Avn	70475	3-227 Avn
26050	7-227 Avn	25482	2-227 Avn	70476	
26051	5/158 ACo	25485	2-227 Avn	70477	
26052	7/227 ACo	*FY86*		70478	3-1 Avn
26053	7-227 Avn	68940	2-6 Cav	70479	
26054	159 Med Co	68941	6-6 Cav	70481	
26055	7/1 ACo	68942	2-6 Cav	70482	
26056	5/158 ACo	68943	2-6 Cav	70487	2-227 Avn
26058	3-1 Avn	68946	2-6 Cav	70496	3-227 Avn
26063	7/227 ACo	68947	6-6 Cav	70498	
26067	7/227 ACo	68948	2-6 Cav	70503	2-227 Avn
26068	7/227 ACo	68949	2-6 Cav	70504	2-227 Avn
26070		68950	6-6 Cav	70505	3-227 Avn
26071	7/227 ACo	68951	2-6 Cav	70506	2-227 Avn
26072	7/227 ACo	68952	2-6 Cav	70507	3-227 Avn
26073		68955	6-6 Cav	*FY88*	
26075	45 Med Co	68956	2-6 Cav	80197	2-227 Avn
26077	3-227 Avn	68957	2-6 Cav	80198	2-227 Avn
26080	7/1 DCo	68959	2-6 Cav	80199	2-227 Avn
26083	5/159 ACo	68960	2-6 Cav	80203	6-6 Cav
26085	2-227 Avn	68961	2-6 Cav	80204	6-6 Cav
26086	3-227 Avn	68964	2-6 Cav	80212	6-6 Cav
FY89		68970	3-227 Avn	80213	6-6 Cav
26138	2-6 Cav	68981	2-6 Cav	80214	6-6 Cav
26142	2-227 Avn	68983	3-227 Avn	80215	6-6 Cav
26145	3-227 Avn	69010	2-6 Cav	80216	6-6 Cav
26146	3-227 Avn	69011	2-6 Cav	80217	6-6 Cav
26148		69019	2-6 Cav	80219	6-6 Cav
26151		69026	2-6 Cav	80222	6-6 Cav
26153	7-1 Avn	69029	2-227 Avn	80225	6-6 Cav
26155	7/227 ACo	69030	2-6 Cav	80228	6-6 Cav
26164		69032	2-6 Cav	80229	6-6 Cav
26165		69033	3-227 Avn	80232	6-6 Cav
		69037	2-6 Cav	80233	6-6 Cav
McD AH-64A Apache		69039	2-6 Cav	80234	6-6 Cav
3-1 Avn, Ansbach;		69041	2-227 Avn	80236	6-6 Cav
2-227 Avn, 3-227 Avn, Hanau;		69048	2-6 Cav	80238	6-6 Cav
2-6 Cav, 6-6 Cav, Illesheim;		*FY87*		80243	6-6 Cav
7/159 ACo, Illesheim		70408	3-1 Avn	80246	6-6 Cav
FY84		70409	3-1 Avn	80250	6-6 Cav
24204	3-227 Avn	70410	3-227 Avn		
24207	2-6 Cav	70411	6-6 Cav		

US based USAF Aircraft

The following aircraft are normally based in the USA but are likely to be seen visiting the UK from time to time. The presentation is in numerical order of the type, commencing with the B-**1B** and concluding with the C-**141**. The aircraft are listed in numerical progression by the serial actually carried externally. Fiscal year information is provided, together with details of mark variations and in some cases operating units. Where base-code letter information is carried on the aircrafts' tails, this is detailed with the squadron/base data; for example the 7th Wing's B-1B 30069 carries the letters DY on its tail, thus identifying the Wing's home base as Dyess AFB, Texas.

Rockwell B-1B Lancer
7 Wg Dyess AFB, Texas [DY]:
  9 BS (bk) & 28 BS (bl/w);
28 BW Ellsworth AFB, South
  Dakota [EL]: 37 BS (bk/y);
127 BS/184 BG, Kansas ANG,
  McConnell AFB, Kansas;
128 BS/116 BG, Georgia ANG,
  Dobbins ARB, Georgia;
366 Wg Ellsworth AFB, South
  Dakota [MO]: 34 BS (r/bk);
410 TS Edwards AFB, California

FY83		
30065	7 Wg	bk
30066	7 Wg	bl/w
30067	7 Wg	bk
30068	7 Wg	bl/w
30069	7 Wg	bl/w
30070	7 Wg	bl/w
30071	7 Wg	bk
FY84		
40049	410 TS	
40050	7 Wg	bl/w
40051	7 Wg	bk
40053	7 Wg	bl/w
40054	127 BS	
40055	7 Wg	bl/w
40056	7 Wg	bl/w
40057	7 Wg	bk
40058	7 Wg	bk
FY85		
50059	7 Wg	
50060	127 BS	
50061	28 BW	bk/y
50062	7 Wg	bk
50064	127 BS	
50065	7 Wg	bl/w
50066	28 BW	bk/y
50067	7 Wg	bl/w
50068	410 TS	
50069	127 BS	
50070	127 BS	
50071	7 Wg	bl/w
50072	7 Wg	bk
50073	7 Wg	bl/w
50074	28 BW	bk/y
50075	28 BW	bk/y
50077	28 BW	bk/y
50078	28 BW	bk/y
50079	28 BW	bk/y
50080	127 BS	
50081	28 BW	bk/y
50082	7 Wg	bk
50083	28 BW	bk/y
50084	28 BW	bk/y
50085	28 BW	bk/y

50086	28 BW	bk/y
50087	28 BW	bk/y
50088	127 BS	
50089	28 BW	bk/y
50090	28 BW	bk/y
50091	366 Wg	r/bk
50092	28 BW	bk/y
FY86		
60093	28 BW	bk/y
60094	28 BW	bk/y
60095	127 BS	
60096	28 BW	bk/y
60097	366 Wg	r/bk
60098	28 BW	bk/y
60099	28 BW	bk/y
60100	7 Wg	
60101	7 Wg	bl/w
60102	28 BW	bk/y
60103	7 Wg	
60104	366 Wg	r/bk
60105	7 Wg	bl/w
60107	7 Wg	bk
60108	7 Wg	bl/w
60109	7 Wg	bl/w
60110	7 Wg	bl/w
60111	28 BW	bk/y
60112	7 Wg	bk
60113	28 BW	bk/y
60114	28 BW	bk/y
60115	127 BS	
60116	366 Wg	r/bk
60117	7 Wg	
60118	366 Wg	r/bk
60119	7 Wg	bl/w
60120	7 Wg	
60121	366 Wg	r/bk
60122	7 Wg	bl/w
60123	7 Wg	bk
60124	7 Wg	bk
60125	366 Wg	r/bk
60126	7 Wg	bl/w
60127	127 BS	
60128	28 BW	bk/y
60129		
60130	7 Wg	bl/w
60131	366 Wg	r/bk
60132	7 Wg	bl/w
60133	28 BW	bk/y
60134	366 Wg	r/bk
60135	7 Wg	bk
60136	127 BS	
60137	7 Wg	bl/w
60138	366 Wg	r/bk
60139	366 Wg	r/bk
60140	7 Wg	bk

Northrop B-2A Spirit
420 TS/412 TW Edwards AFB,
  California [ED];
509 BW Whiteman AFB,
  Missouri [WM]:
    393 BS & 715 BS

FY82	
21066	Northrop
21067	412 TW
21068	412 TW
21069	412 TW
21070	412 TW
21071	412 TW
FY88	
80328	509 BW
80329	509 BW
80330	509 BW
80331	509 BW
80332	509 BW
80333	509 BW
80334	509 BW
FY89	
90127	509 BW
90128	509 BW
90129	509 BW

Boeing E-3 Sentry
552 ACW
961 AACS/18 Wg (or)
  Kadena AB, Japan [ZZ];
962 AACS/3 Wg (gn)
  Elmendorf AFB, Alaska [AK];
963 AACS (bk)
964 AACS (r)
965 AACS (y)
966 AACTS (bl)
  Tinker AFB, Oklahoma [OK]

FY80		
00137	E-3C	r
00138	E-3C	y
00139	E-3C	bk
FY81		
10004	E-3C	bk
10005	E-3C	m
FY71		
11407	E-3B	m
11408	E-3B	y
FY82		
20006	E 3C	y
20007	E-3C	y
FY83		
30008	E-3C	bk
30009	E-3C	bk

E-3

FY73

| 31674 | E-3C | Boeing |
| 31675 | E-3B | r |

FY75

50556	E-3B	bk
50557	E-3B	r
50558	E-3B	y
50559	E-3B	r
50560	E-3B	or

FY76

61604	E-3B	y
61605	E-3B	bl
61606	E-3B	r
61607	E-3B	bl

FY77

70351	E-3B	bk
70352	E-3B	r
70353	E-3B	bl
70355	E-3B	r
70356	E-3B	y

FY78

80576	E-3B	bk
80577	E-3B	or
80578	E-3B	y

FY79

90001	E-3B	bk
90002	E-3B	gn
90003	E-3B	bk

Boeing E-4B

1 ACCS/55 Wg Offutt AFB, Nebraska [OF]

31676	(FY73)
31677	(FY73)
40787	(FY74)
50125	(FY75)

Lockheed C-5 Galaxy

60 AMW Travis AFB, California: 21 AS & 22 AS (*bk/bl* & *bk/gd*); 68 AS/433 AW AFRES, Kelly AFB, Texas; 97 AMW Altus AFB, Oklahoma: 56 AS (*r/y*); 137 AS/105 AG Stewart AFB, New York (*bl*); 337 AS/439 AW AFRES, Westover AFB, Massachusetts (*bl/r*); 436 AW Dover AFB, Delaware: 3 AS & 9 AS (*y/r* & *y/bl*)

FY70

00445	C-5A	68 AS	
00446	C-5A	68 AS	
00447	C-5A	436 AW	y/r
00448	C-5A	337 AS	bl/r
00449	C-5A	97 AMW	r/y
00450	C-5A	60 AMW	bk/gd
00451	C-5A	97 AMW	r/y
00452	C-5A	436 AW	y/r
00453	C-5A	97 AMW	r/y
00454	C-5A	97 AMW	r/y
00455	C-5A	97 AMW	r/y
00456	C-5A	97 AMW	r/y
00457	C-5A	60 AMW	bk/gd
00458	C-5A	97 AMW	r/y
00459	C-5A	60 AMW	bk/gd
00460	C-5A	137 AS	bl
00461	C-5A	68 AS	
00462	C-5A	97 AMW	r/y
00463	C-5A	436 AW	y/bl
00464	C-5A	97 AMW	r/y
00465	C-5A	60 AMW	
00466	C-5A	436 AW	y/r
00467	C-5A	436 AW	y/bl

FY83

| 31285 | C-5B | 436 AW | y/r |

FY84

40059	C-5B	436 AW	y/r
40060	C-5B	60 AMW	bk/bl
40061	C-5B	436 AW	y/r
40062	C-5B	60 AMW	

FY85

50001	C-5B	436 AW	m
50002	C-5B	60 AMW	
50003	C-5B	436 AW	y/bl
50004	C-5B	60 AMW	bk/bl
50005	C-5B	436 AW	
50006	C-5B	60 AMW	bk/gd
50007	C-5B	436 AW	y/bl
50008	C-5B	60 AMW	bk/gd
50009	C-5B	436 AW	y/r
50010	C-5B	60 AMW	bk/gd

FY86

60011	C-5B	436 AW	y/bl
60012	C-5B	60 AMW	bk/bl
60013	C-5B	436 AW	y/bl
60014	C-5B	60 AMW	bk/bl
60015	C-5B	436 AW	y/r
60016	C-5B	60 AMW	bk/bl
60017	C-5B	436 AW	y/bl
60018	C-5B	60 AMW	
60019	C-5B	436 AW	
60020	C-5B	436 AW	bl
60021	C-5B	60 AMW	bk/gd
60022	C-5B	60 AMW	bk/bl
60023	C-5B	436 AW	y/bl
60024	C-5B	60 AMW	bk/bl
60025	C-5B	436 AW	
60026	C-5B	60 AMW	

FY66

68304	C-5A	337 AS	bl/r
68305	C-5A	68 AS	
68306	C-5A	68 AS	
68307	C-5A	68 AS	

FY87

70027	C-5B	436 AW	y/bl
70028	C-5B	60 AMW	bk/bl
70029	C-5B	436 AW	y/r
70030	C-5B	60 AMW	bk/bl
70031	C-5B	436 AW	y/r
70032	C-5B	60 AMW	bl
70033	C-5B	436 AW	y/r
70034	C-5B	60 AMW	bk/gd
70035	C-5B	436 AW	y/bl
70036	C-5B	60 AMW	bk/gd
70037	C-5B	436 AW	y/r
70038	C-5B	60 AMW	bk/bl
70039	C-5B	436 AW	y/r
70040	C-5B	60 AMW	bk/gd
70041	C-5B	436 AW	y/bl
70042	C-5B	60 AMW	bk/gd
70043	C-5B	436 AW	y/bl
70044	C-5B	60 AMW	bk/gd
70045	C-5B	436 AW	y/r

FY67

70167	C-5A	137 AS	bl
70168	C-5A	68 AS	
70169	C-5A	137 AS	bl
70170	C-5A	137 AS	bl
70171	C-5A	68 AS	
70173	C-5A	137 AS	bl
70174	C-5A	137 AS	bl

FY68

80211	C-5A	337 AS	bl/r
80212	C-5A	137 AS	bl
80213	C-5C	60 AMW	
80214	C-5A	436 AW	y/r
80215	C-5A	337 AS	bl/r
80216	C-5C	60 AMW	bk/bl
80217	C-5A	436 AW	y/bl
80219	C-5A	337 AS	bl/r
80220	C-5A	68 AS	
80221	C-5A	68 AS	
80222	C-5A	337 AS	bl/r
80223	C-5A	68 AS	
80224	C-5A	137 AS	bl
80225	C-5A	337 AS	bl/r
80226	C-5A	137 AS	bl

FY69

90001	C-5A	60 AMW	
90002	C-5A	337 AS	bl/r
90003	C-5A	68 AS	
90004	C-5A	68 AS	
90005	C-5A	337 AS	bl/r
90006	C-5A	68 AS	
90007	C-5A	68 AS	
90008	C-5A	137 AS	bl
90009	C-5A	137 AS	bl
90010	C-5A	60 AMW	bk/gd
90011	C-5A	337 AS	bl/r
90012	C-5A	137 AS	bl
90013	C-5A	337 AS	bl/r
90014	C-5A	60 AMW	bk/gd
90015	C-5A	137 AS	bl
90016	C-5A	68 AS	
90017	C-5A	337 AS	bl/r
90018	C-5A	60 AMW	bk/bl
90019	C-5A	337 AS	bl/r
90020	C-5A	337 AS	bl/r
90021	C-5A	137 AS	bl
90022	C-5A	337 AS	bl/r
90023	C-5A	60 AMW	bk/bl
90024	C-5A	97 AMW	
90025	C-5A	60 AMW	bk/gd
90026	C-5A	60 AMW	
90027	C-5A	436 AW	y/bl

Boeing E-8 J-STARS

Grumman, Melbourne, Florida; 93 ASCW, Robins AFB, Georgia

FY90

| 00175 | E-8C | 93 ASCW |

FY92

| 23289 | E-8C | 93 ASCW |

FY93

| 30011 | E-8C | 93 ASCW |

FY66

| 30052 | E-8C | 93 ASCW |

FY86

| 60416 | E-8A | 93 ASCW |
| 60417 | E-8A | 93 ASCW |

McDonnell-Douglas KC-10A Extender

60 AMW, Travis AFB, California: 9 ARS (*bk/r*) & 6 ARS (*bk/bl*); 305 AMW McGuire AFB, New Jersey: 2 ARS (*bl*) & 32 ARS (*w*);

FY82

20191	60 AMW	bk/bl
20192	60 AMW	bk/r
20193	60AMW	bk/bl

FY83

30075	305 AMW	bl
30076		
30077	60 AMW	bk/r
30078	60 AMW	bk/bl
30079	305 AMW	bl/r
30080	60 AMW	

30081	305 AMW	*bl*
30082	305 AMW	*bl*
FY84		
40185	305 AMW	*bl*
40186	305 AMW	*bl*
40187		
40188	305 AMW	
40189		
40190	305 AMW	*bl*
40191	60 AMW	*bk/r*
40192	305 AMW	*bl*
FY85		
50027	60 AMW	
50028	305 AMW	*bl*
50029	60 AMW	*bk/r*
50030		
50031		
50032	305 AMW	
50033	305 AMW	*bl*
50034	305 AMW	*bl*
FY86		
60027	305 AMW	*bl/bk*
60028	305 AMW	*bl/r*
60029	60 AMW	*bk/r*
60030	305 AMW	
60031	60 AMW	*bk/r*
60032	60 AMW	*bk/r*
60033	60 AMW	*bk/r*
60034	305 AMW	
60035	305 AMW	
60036	60 AMW	*bk/r*
60037	60 AMW	*bk/r*
60038	60 AMW	*bk/r*
FY87		
70117	60 AMW	*bk/r*
70118	60 ARW	*bk/bl*
70119	60 AMW	*bk/r*
70120	60 AMW	*bk/r*
70121	305 AMW	
70122	305 AMW	
70123	305 AMW	*bl*
70124	305 AMW	*bl/bk*
FY79		
90433	305 AMW	*bl/bk*
90434	305 AMW	*bl*
91710	305 AMW	*bl/r*
91711	305 AMW	*bl*
91712	305 AMW	
91713	305 AMW	
91946	60 AMW	*bk/r*
91947	60 AMW	*bk/r*
91948	60 AMW	*bk/r*
91949	305 AMW	*bl/bk*
91950	60 AMW	*bk/bl*
91951	60 ARW	*bk/r*

McDonnell-Douglas C-17 Globemaster III

417 TS Edwards AFB, California [ED]
437 AW Charleston AFB, South Carolina:
14 AS & 17 AS (*y/bl*)

FY90			
00532	C-17A	437 AW	*y/bl*
00533	C-17A	437 AW	*y/bl*
00534	C-17A	437 AW	*y/bl*
00535	C-17A	437 AW	*y/bl*
FY92			
23291	C-17A	437 AW	*y/bl*
23292	C-17A	437 AW	*y/bl*
23293	C-17A	437 AW	*y/bl*
23294	C-17A	437 AW	*y/bl*
FY93			
30599	C-17A	437 AW	*y/bl*
30600	C-17A	437 AW	
30601	C-17A	437 AW	*y/bl*
30602	C-17A	437 AW	
30603	C-17A	437 AW	
30604	C-17A	437 AW	
FY94			
40065	C-17A	437 AW	
40066	C-17A	437 AW	
40067	C-17A	437 AW	
FY87			
70025	YC-17A	417 TS	
FY88			
80265	C-17A	417 TS	
80266	C-17A	417 TS	
80267	C-17A		
FY89			
91189	C-17A	417 TS	
91190	C-17A	417 TS	
91191	C-17A	437 AW	*y/bl*
91192	C-17A	437 AW	*y/bl*

Boeing C-18

452 TS/452 TS Edwards AFB, California;
966 AACTS /552 ACW (*bl*) Tinker AFB, Oklahoma [OK]

FY81		
10891	EC-18B	452 TS
10892	EC-18B	452 TS
10893	EC-18D	452 TS
10894	EC-18B	452 TS
10895	EC-18D	452 TS
10896	EC-18B	452 TS
10898	C-18A	452 TS
FY84		
41398	TC-18E	966 AACTS
41399	TC-18E	966 AACTS

Grumman C-20 Gulfstream II/III/IV

89 AW/99 AS Andrews AFB, Maryland;
US Army Andrews AFB, Maryland;

C-20B Gulfstream III

FY86	
60200	89 AW
60201	89 AW
60202	89 AW
60203	89 AW
60204	89 AW
60206	89 AW

C-20C Gulfstream III

FY85	
50049	89 AW
50050	89 AW
FY86	
60403	89 AW

C-20E Gulfstream III

FY87	
70139	US Army
70140	US Army

C-20F Gulfstream IV

FY91	
10108	OSAC/US Army

C-20H Gulfstream IV

FY90	
00300	89 AW

C-20J Gulfstream II

FY89	
90266	US Army

Boeing C-22B/C-22C[1]

24 AW Howard AFB, Panama [HW];
201 AS/113 FW DC ANG, Andrews AFB, Maryland

FY83	
34610	201 AS
34615	201 AS
34616	201 AS
34618[1]	24 AW

Boeing VC-25A

89 AW Andrews AFB, Maryland

FY82
28000
FY92
29000

Boeing CT-43A

12 FTW Randolph AFB, Texas [RA]: 558 FTS (*bk/y*);
24 CW/310 AS Howard AFB, Panama [HW];
200 AS/140 FW Colorado ANG, Buckley ANGB, Colorado

FY71	
11403	12 FTW
11404	12 FTW
11405	12 FTW
11406	12 FTW
FY72	
20283	24 CW
20288	200 AS
FY73	
31150	12 FTW
31151	12 FTW
31152	12 FTW
31153	12 FTW
31154	200 AS
31155	12 FTW
31156	12 FTW

Boeing B-52H Stratofortress

2 BW Barksdale AFB, Louisiana [LA]:
11 BS (*gd*), 20 BS (*bl*) & 96 BS (*r*);
5 BW Minot AFB, North Dakota [MT]: 23 BS (*r/w*);
93 BS/917 Wg AFRES, Barksdale AFB, Louisiana [BD] (*y/bl*);
419 TS/412 TW Edwards AFB, California [ED]

FY60		
00001	2 BW	*bl*
00002	2 BW	*bl*
00003	93 BS	*y/bl*
00004		
00005	5 BW	*r/w*
00007	5 BW	*r/w*
00008	2 BW	
00009	2 BW	*r*
00010	2 BW	*r*
00011	2 BW	*bl*
00012	2 BW	*gd*
00013	2 BW	*r*
00014	2 BW	*bl*
00015	5 BW	*r/w*
00016	2 BW	*r*
00017	2 BW	*bl*

00018	2 BW	r
00019	2 BW	gd
00020	2 BW	bl
00021	5 BW	r/w
00022	5 BW	r/w
00023	5 BW	r/w
00024	5 BW	
00025	2 BW	bl
00026	5 BW	r/w
00028		
00029	5 BW	
00030	2 BW	r
00031	2 BW	bl
00032	2 BW	bl
00033	5 BW	r/w
00034	5 BW	r/w
00035	2 BW	bl
00036	5 BW	r/w
00037	2 BW	r
00038	5 BW	r/w
00041	93 BS	y/bl
00042	2 BW	gd
00043	2 BW	bl
00044	5 BW	
00045	93 BS	y/bl
00046	5 BW	
00047	5 BW	
00048	2 BW	gd
00049	2 BW	bl
00050	419 TS	
00051	5 BW	r/w
00052	5 BW	r/w
00053	2 BW	r
00054	2 BW	bl
00055	5 BW	
00056	5 BW	r/w
00057	2 BW	bl
00058	5 BW	m
00059	2 BW	r
00060	5 BW	
00061	5 BW	
00062	2 BW	
FY61		
10001	5 BW	
10002	2 BW	
10003		
10004	2 BW	
10005	5 BW	
10006	5 BW	
10007	5 BW	
10008	93 BS	y/bl
10009		
10010	2 BW	bl
10011	2 BW	gd
10012		
10013	2 BW	r
10014	2 BW	gd
10015	5 BW	r/w
10016	2 BW	gd
10017	93 BS	y/bl
10018	2 BW	gd
10019	2 BW	r
10020	5 BW	r/w
10021	5 BW	r/w
10022	93 BS	y/bl
10023	2 BW	
10024	2 BW	r
10025	5 BW	r/w
10027	2 BW	r
10028	2 BW	r
10029	93 BS	y/bl
10031	5 BW	r/w
10032	93 BS	y/bl
10034	5 BW	r/w

10035	2 BW	gd
10036	5 BW	
10038	2 BW	
10039	5 BW	
10040	5 BW	

Lockheed C-130 Hercules

1 SOS/353
SOG Kadena AB, Japan;
3 Wg Elmendorf AFB, Alaska
[AK]: 517 AS (w);
4 SOS/16SOW Hurlburt Field,
Florida;
5 SOS/919 SOW Eglin AFB,
Florida;
7 SOS/352 SOG RAF Mildenhall,
UK;
7 Wg Dyess AFB, Texas [DY]:
39 AS (r) & 40 AS (bl);
8 SOS/16 SOW Hurlburt Field,
Florida;
9 SOS/16 OG Eglin AFB, Florida;
15 SOS/16 SOW Hurlburt Field,
Florida;
16 SOS/16 SOW Hurlburt Field,
Florida;
16 SOW Hurlburt Field, Florida;
17 SOS/353SOG Kadena AB,
Japan;
23 Wg Pope AFB, North
Carolina [FT]: 2 AS (r/y) & 41
AS (gn/or);
37 AS/86 AW Ramstein AB,
Germany [RS] (bl/w);
41 ECS/355 Wg Davis-Monthan
AFB, Arizona [DM] (bl);
42 ACCS/355 Wg Davis-Monthan
AFB, Arizona [DM] (w);
43 ECS/355 Wg Davis-Monthan
AFB. Arizona [DM] (r);
46 TW Eglin AFB, Florida [ET];
52 AS/347 Wg Moody AFB,
Georgia [MY] (gn);
53 WRS/403 AW AFRES,
Keesler AFB,   Missouri [KT];
58 SOW/550 SOS, Kirtland AFB,
New Mexico;
64 AS/928 AW AFRES, Chicago
International, Illinois [VO] (r);
67 SOS/352 SOG RAF
Mildenhall, UK;
71 RQS/1 OG Patrick AFB,
Florida [FF] (bl);
95 AS/440 AW AFRES, General
Mitchell ARS, Wisconsin [MK]
(y/w);
96 AS/934 AW AFRES,
Minneapolis/St Paul,
Minnesota [MS] (pr);
102 RQS/106 RQG Suffolk Field,
New York ANG;
105 AS/118 AW Nashville,
Tennessee ANG;
109 AS/133 AW Minneapolis,
Minnesota ANG [MN] (y);
115 AS/146 AW NAS Point
Mugu, California ANG [CI]
(gn);
122 FS/159 FG NAS New
Orleans, Louisiana ANG
[JZ];
129 RQS/129 RQG Moffet Field,
California ANG;

130 AS/130 AG Charleston,
West Virginia ANG;
135 AS/135 AG Martin Field,
Maryland ANG [MD];
139 AS/109 AG Schenectady,
New York ANG;
142 AS/166 AG Greater
Wilmington, Delaware ANG
[DE];
143 AS/143 AG Quonset,Rhode
Island ANG [RI] (r);
144 AS/176 CG Kulis ANGB,
Alaska ANG;
154 AS/189 AG Little Rock,
Arkansas ANG (r);
156 AS/145 AG Charlotte,
North Carolina ANG;
158 AS/165 AG Savannah,
Georgia ANG [GA]   (r);
164 AS/179 AG Mansfield,
Ohio ANG [OH];
165 AS/123 AW Standiford Field,
Kentucky ANG [KY];
167 AS/167 AG Martinsburg,
West Virginia ANG [WV];
169 AS/182 AG Peoria, Illinois
ANG [IL];
171 AS/191 AG Selfridge ANGB,
Michigan ANG (y/bk);
180 AS/139 AG St Joseph,
Missouri ANG [XP];
181 AS/136 AW NAS Dallas,
Texas ANG [TX];
185 AS/137 AW Oklahoma,
Oklahoma ANG [OK] (bl);
187 AS/153 AG Cheyenne,
Wyoming ANG;
189 AS/124 AW Boise, Idaho
ANG;
192 AS/152 AG Reno, Nevada
ANG;
193 SOS/193 SOG Harrisburg,
Pennsylvania ANG [PA];
204 AS/154 OG Hickam ANG,
Hawaii ANG;
210 RQS/176 CG Kulis
ANGB, Alaska ANG;
301 RQS/939 RQW AFRES,
Patrick AFB, Florida [FL];
304 RQS/939 RQW AFRES,
Portland, Oregon [PD] (y);
310 AS/24 CW, Howard AFB,
Canal Zone [HW] (bl);
314 AW Little Rock AFB,
Arkansas [LK]:50 AS (r),
53 AS (bk), 61 AS (gn)
& 62 AS (bl);
327 AS/913 AW AFRES,
NAS Willow Grove,
Pennsylvania [WG] (bk);
328 AS/914 AW AFRES,
Niagara Falls,
New York [NF] (gn);
357 AS/908 AW AFRES,
Maxwell AFB, Alabama
[MX] (bl);
374 AW Yokota AB, Japan [YJ]:
36 AS (r);
418 TS/412 TW Edwards AFB,
California [ED];
514 TS/545 TG Hill AFB, Utah;
700 AS/94 AW AFRES,
Dobbins AFB,
Georgia [DB] (r/bl);

711 SOS/919 SOW AFRES,
  Duke Field, Florida ;
731 AS/302 AW AFRES,
  Peterson AFB,
  Colorado [CR] (*gn*);
757 AS/910 AW AFRES,
  Youngstown ARS,
  Ohio [YO] (*bl*);
758 AS/911 AW AFRES,
  Pittsburgh ARS,
  Pennsylvania [PI] (*bk*);
815 AS/403 AW AFRES,
  Keesler, Missouri [KT] (*r*)

FY90

00161	MC-130H	15 SOS
00162	MC-130H	15 SOS
00163	AC-130U	16 SOS
00164	AC-130U	16 SOS
00165	AC-130U	16 SOS
00166	AC-130U	5 SOS
00167	AC-130U	16 SOS

FY80

00320	C-130H	158 AS	r
00321	C-130H	158 AS	r
00322	C-130H	158 AS	r
00323	C-130H	158 AS	r
00324	C-130H	158 AS	r
00325	C-130H	158 AS	r
00326	C-130H	158 AS	r
00331	C-130H	158 AS	r
00332	C-130H	158 AS	r

FY90

01057	C-130H	181 AS
01058	C-130H	130 AS

FY70

01259	C-130E	23 Wg	r/y
01260	C-130E	37 AS	bl/w
01261	C-130E	23 Wg	r/y
01262	C-130E	23 Wg	
01263	C-130E	23 Wg	
01264	C-130E	37 AS	bl/w
01265	C-130E	23 Wg	
01266	C-130E	23 Wg	gn/or
01267	C-130E	23 Wg	gn/or
01268	C-130E	23 Wg	
01269	C-130E	23 Wg	
01270	C-130E	23 Wg	gn/or
01271	C-130E	37 AS	bl/w
01272	C-130E	23 Wg	
01273	C-130E	23 Wg	
01274	C-130E	37 AS	bl/w
01275	C-130E	23 Wg	
01276	C-130E	23 Wg	gn/or

FY90

01791	C-130H	164 AS
01792	C-130H	164 AS
01793	C-130H	164 AS
01794	C-130H	164 AS
01795	C-130H	164 AS
01796	C-130H	164 AS
01797	C-130H	164 AS
01798	C-130H	164 AS
02103	HC-130H	210 RQS
09107	C-130H	757 AS	bl
09108	C-130H	757 AS	bl

FY81

10626	C-130H	700 AS	r/bl
10627	C-130H	700 AS	r/bl

10628	C-130H	700 AS	r/bl
10629	C-130H	700 AS	r/bl
10630	C-130H	700 AS	r/bl
10631	C-130H	700 AS	r/bl

FY68

10934	C-130E	23 Wg	r/y
10935	C-130E	37 AS	bl/w
10937	C-130E	23 Wg	
10938	C-130E	37 AS	bl/w
10939	C-130E	23 Wg	gn/or
10940	C-130E	23 Wg	gn/or
10941	C-130E	23 Wg	r/y
10942	C-130E	23 Wg	r/y
10943	C-130E	37 AS	bl/w
10947	C-130E	37 AS	bl/w
10948	C-130E	314 AW	gn
10949	C-130E	314 AW	gn
10950	C-130E	314 AW	

FY91

11231	C-130H	165 AS
11232	C-130H	165 AS
11233	C-130H	165 AS
11234	C-130H	165 AS
11235	C-130H	165 AS
11236	C-130H	165 AS
11237	C-130H	165 AS
11238	C-130H	165 AS
11239	C-130H	165 AS
11651	C-130H	165 AS
11652	C-130H	165 AS
11653	C-130H	165 AS

FY61

12358	C-130E	171 AS	y/bk
12359	C-130E	115 AS	gn
12361	C-130E	167 AS	
12362	C-130E	314 AW	bk
12363	C-130E	314 AW	bk
12367	C-130E	115 AS	gn
12369	C-130E	314 AW	
12370	C-130E	171 AS	y/bk
12371	C-130E	171 AS	y/bk
12372	C-130E	115 AS	gn

FY64

14852	HC-130P	71 RQS	bl
14853	HC-130P	71 RQS	bl
14854	HC-130P	9 SOS	
14855	HC-130P	304 RQS	y
14856	HC-130P	304 RQS	y
14857	HC-130P	514 TS	
14858	HC-130P	17 SOS	
14859	C-130H	711 SOS	
14860	HC-130P	304 RQS	y
14861	WC-130H	53 WRS	
14862	EC-130H	41 ECS	bl
14863	HC-130P	71 RQS	bl
14864	HC-130P	301 RQS	y
14865	HC-130P	304 RQS	y
14866	WC-130H	53 WRS	
17680	C-130E	314 AW	bk
17681	C-130E	37 AS	bl/w
18240	C-130E	37 AS	bl/w

FY91

19141	C-130H	64 AS	r
19142	C-130H	95 AS	y/w
19143	C-130H	757 AS	bl
19144	C-130H	700 AS	r/bl

FY82

20054	C-130H	144 AS

20055	C-130H	144 AS
20056	C-130H	144 AS
20057	C-130H	144 AS
20058	C-130H	144 AS
20059	C-130H	144 AS
20060	C-130H	144 AS
20061	C-130H	144 AS

FY92

20253	AC-130U		
20547	C-130H	314 AW	r
20548	C-130H	314 AW	r
20549	C-130H	314 AW	r
20550	C-130H	314 AW	r
20551	C-130H	314 AW	r
20552	C-130H	314 AW	r
20553	C-130H	314 AW	r
20554	C-130H	314 AW	r
21094	LC-130H	139 AS	
21095	LC-130H	139 AS	

FY72

21288	C-130E	374 AW	r
21289	C-130E	374 AW	r
21290	C-130E	374 AW	r
21291	C-130E	314 AW	bk
21292	C-130E	314 AW	
21293	C-130E	314 AW	gn
21294	C-130E	314 AW	gn
21295	C-130E	314 AW	bl
21296	C-130E	314 AW	bk
21298	C-130E	314 AW	
21299	C-130E	374 AW	r
21302	HC-130H		

FY92

21394	LC-130H	109 AS y
21395	LC-130H	109 AS y
21451	C-130H	156 AS
21452	C-130H	156 AS
21453	C-130H	156 AS
21454	C-130H	156 AS
21531	C-130H	187 AS
21532	C-130H	187 AS
21533	C-130H	187 AS
21534	C-130H	187 AS
21535	C-130H	187 AS
21536	C-130H	187 AS
21537	C-130H	187 AS
21538	C-130H	187 AS

FY62

21784	C-130E	154 AS	r
21786	C-130E	109 AS	y
21787	C-130E	154 AS	r
21788	C-130E	154 AS	r
21789	C-130E	731 AS	gn
21790	C-130E	154 AS	r
21791	EC-130E	42 ACCS	w
21792	C-130E	115 AS	gn
21793	C-130E	115 AS	gn
21795	C-130E	154 AS	r
21798	C-130E	154 AS	r
21799	C-130E	115 AS	gn
21801	C-130E	115 AS	gn
21804	C-130E	154 AS	r
21806	C-130E	96 AS	pr
21807	C-130E	731 AS	gn
21808	C-130E	731 AS	gn
21810	C-130E	731 AS	gn
21811	C-130E	115 AS	gn
21812	C-130E	109 AS	y
21816	C-130E	96 AS	pr
21817	C-130E	109 AS	y

C-130

Serial	Type	Unit	Code
21818	EC-130E	42 ACCS	w
21819	C-130E	192 AS	
21820	C-130E	171 AS	y/bk
21821	C-130E	314 AW	bl
21822	C-130E	192 AS	
21823	C-130E	96 AS	pr
21824	C-130E	154 AS	r
21825	EC-130E	42 ACCS	w
21826	C-130E	115 AS	gn
21827	C-130E	314 AW	bl
21828	C-130E	192 AS	
21829	C-130E	109 AS	y
21830	C-130E	731 AS	gn
21832	EC-130E	42 ACCS	w
21833	C-130E	115 AS	gn
21834	C-130E	96 AS	pr
21835	C-130E	96 AS	pr
21836	EC-130E	42 ACCS	w
21837	C-130E	109 AS	y
21839	C-130E	96 AS	pr
21842	C-130E	171 AS	y/bk
21843	MC-130E	1 SOS	
21844	C-130E	96 AS	pr
21846	C-130E	109 AS	y
21847	C-130E	96 AS	pr
21848	C-130E	96 AS	pr
21849	C-130E	815 AS	r
21850	C-130E	327 AS	bk
21851	C-130E	115 AS	gn
21852	C-130E	96 AS	pr
21855	MC-130E	8 SOS	
21856	C-130E	109 AS	y
21857	EC-130E	42 ACCS	w
21858	C-130E	731 AS	gn
21859	C-130E	167 AS	
21862	C-130E	115 AS	gn
21863	EC-130E	42 ACCS	w
21864	C-130E	109 AS	y
21866	C-130E	731 AS	gn

FY92

Serial	Type	Unit	Code
23021	C-130H	757 AS	bl
23022	C-130H	757 AS	bl
23023	C-130H	757 AS	bl
23024	C-130H	64 AS	gn
23281	C-130H	328 AS	gn
23282	C-130H	328 AS	gn
23283	C-130H	328 AS	gn
23284	C-130H	328 AS	gn
23285	C-130H	328 AS	gn
23286	C-130H	328 AS	gn
23287	C-130H	328 AS	gn
23288	C-130H	328 AS	gn

FY83

Serial	Type	Unit	Code
30486	C-130H	139 AS	
30487	C-130H	139 AS	
30488	C-130H	139 AS	
30489	C-130H	139 AS	
30490	LC-130H	139 AS	
30491	LC-130H	139 AS	
30492	LC-130H	139 AS	
30493	LC-130H	139 AS	

FY93

Serial	Type	Unit	Code
31036	C-130H	314 AW	r
31037	C-130H	314 AW	r
31038	C-130H	314 AW	r
31039	C-130H	314 AW	r
31040	C-130H	314 AW	r
31041	C-130H	314 AW	r
31042	C-130H		
31043	C-130H		

FY83

Serial	Type	Unit	Code
31212	MC-130H	15 SOS	

FY93

Serial	Type	Unit	Code
31455	C-130H	156 AS	
31456	C-130H	156 AS	
31457	C-130H	156 AS	
31458	C-130H	156 AS	
31459	C-130H	156 AS	
31460	C-130H	156 AS	
31461	C-130H	156 AS	
31462	C-130H	156 AS	
31463	C-130H	156 AS	

FY73

Serial	Type	Unit	Code
31580	EC-130H	43 ECS	r
31581	EC-130H	43 ECS	r
31582	C-130H	374 AW	r
31583	EC-130H	43 ECS	r
31584	EC-130H	43 ECS	r
31585	EC-130H	41 ECS	bl
31586	EC-130H	41 ECS	bl
31587	EC-130H	41 ECS	bl
31588	EC-130H	41 ECS	bl
31590	EC-130H	43 ECS	r
31592	EC-130H	43 ECS	r
31594	EC-130H	41 ECS	bl
31595	EC-130H	43 ECS	r
31597	C-130H	374 AW	r
31598	C-130H	374 AW	r

FY93

Serial	Type	Unit	Code
32041	C-130H	204	AS
32042	C-130H	204	AS
32105	HC-130N	210 RQS	
32106	HC-130N	210 RQS	
37311	C-130H	731 AS	gn
37312	C-130H	731 AS	gn
37313	C-130H	731 AS	gn
37314	C-130H	731 AS	gn

FY63

Serial	Type	Unit	Code
37764	C-130E	815 AS	r
37765	C-130E	314 AW	bl
37767	C-130E	314 AW	bl
37768	C-130E	314 AW	bl
37769	C-130E	96 AS	pr
37770	C-130E	815 AS	r
37771	C-130E	301 RQS	
37773	EC-130E	193 SOS	
37776	C 130E	327 AG	bk
37777	C-130E	167 AS	
37778	C-130E	314 AW	bk
37781	C-130E	314 AW	gn
37782	C-130E	143 AS r	
37783	EC-130E	193 SOS	
37784	C-130E	52 AS	gn
37785	MC-130E	1 SOS	
37786	C-130E	314 AW	bk
37788	C-130E	143 AS	r
37790	C-130E	52 AS	gn
37791	C-130E	314 AW	bl
37792	C-130E	169 AS	
37793	C-130E	314 AW	bl
37794	C-130E	71 RQS	bl
37795	C-130E	314 AW	r
37796	C-130E	314 AW	
37799	C-130E	314 AW	
37800	C-130E	169 AS	
37804	C-130E	314 AW	bl
37805	C-130E	815 AS	r
37806	C-130E	314 AW	
37808	C-130E	314 AW	gn
37809	C-130E	52 AS	gn

Serial	Type	Unit	Code
37811	C-130E	143 AS	r
37812	C-130E	169 AS	
37813	C-130E	52 AS	gn
37814	C-130E	67 SOS	
37815	C-130E	193 SOS	
37816	C-130E	193 SOS	
37817	C-130E	815 AS	r
37818	C-130E	169 AS	
37819	C-130E	374 AW	r
37820	C-130E	314 AW	bl
37821	C-130E	52 AS	gn
37822	C-130E	815 AS	r
37823	C-130E	327 AS	bk
37824	C-130E	143 AS	r
37825	C-130E	135 AS	
37826	C-130E	327 AS	bk
37828	C-130E	193 SOS	
37829	C-130E	314 AW	bk
37830	C-130E	314 AW	bk
37831	C-130E	314 AW	bk
37832	C-130E	327 AS	bk
37833	C-130E	327 AS	bk
37834	C-130E	327 AS	bk
37835	C-130E	314 AW	bk
37837	C-130E	374 AW	r
37838	C-130E	314 AW	bl
37839	C-130E	314 AW	gn
37840	C-130E	143 AS	r
37841	C-130E	314 AW	gn
37842	C-130E	1 SOS	
37845	C-130E	314 AW	bk
37846	C-130E	52 AS	gn
37847	C-130E	154 AS	r
37848	C-130E	327 AS	bk
37849	C-130E	314 AW	bl
37850	C-130E	52 AS	gn
37851	C-130E	167 AS	
37852	C-130E	815 AS	r
37853	C-130E	327 AS	bk
37854	C-130E	314 AW	gn
37856	C-130E	815 AS	r
37857	C-130E	314 AW	gn
37858	C-130E	167 AS	r
37859	C-130E	143 AS	r
37860	C-130E	314 AW	bl
37861	C-130E	314 AW	bl
37864	C-130E	314 AW	bl
37865	C-130E	374 AW	r
37866	C-130E	314 AW	bk
37867	C-130E	327 AS	bk
37868	C-130E	143 AS	r
37869	EC-130E	193 SOS	
37871	C-130E	52 AS	gn
37872	C-130E	169 AS	
37874	C-130E	314 AW	bk
37876	C-130E	314 AW	gn
37877	C-130E	169 AS	
37879	C-130E	374 AW	r
37880	C-130E	314 AW	
37882	C-130E	314 AW	bk
37883	C-130E	327 AS	bk
37884	C-130E	52 AS	gn
37885	C-130E	37 AS	bl/w
37887	C-130E	37 AS	bl/w
37888	C-130E	314 AW	gn
37889	C-130E	143 AS	r
37890	C-130E	314 AW	bl
37891	C-130E	314 AW	bk
37892	C-130E	327 AS	bk
37893	C-130E	314 AW	bk
37894	C-130E	314 AW	
37895	C-130E	171 AS	y/bk
37896	C-130E	314 AW	gn
37897	C-130E	169 AS	

37898	C-130E	8 SOS	
37899	C-130E	314 AW	
39810	C-130E	52 AS	gn
39811	C-130E	314 AW	
39812	C-130E	314 AW	
39813	C-130E	171 AS	y/bk
39814	C-130E	314 AW	bl
39815	C-130E	171 AS	y/bk
39816	EC-130E	193 SOS	
39817	EC-130E	193 SOS	

FY84

40204	C-130H	700 AS	r/bl
40205	C-130H	700 AS	r/bl
40206	C-130H	142 AS	
40207	C-130H	142 AS	
40208	C-130H	142 AS	
40209	C-130H	142 AS	
40210	C-130H	142 AS	
40211	C-130H	142 AS	
40212	C-130H	142 AS	
40213	C-130H	142 AS	
40475	MC-130H	15 SOS	
40476	MC-130H	7 SOS	

FY64

40495	C-130E	23 Wg	gn/or
40496	C-130E	23 Wg	r/y
40498	C-130E	23 Wg	r/y
40499	C-130E	23 Wg	r/y
40500	C-130E	AFLC	
40502	C-130E	37 AS	bl/w
40504	C-130E	23 Wg	r/y
40510	C-130E	135 AS	
40512	C-130E	154 AS	r
40513	C-130E	314 AW	bk
40514	C-130E	135 AS	
40515	C-130E	135 AS	
40517	C-130E	23 Wg	gn/or
40518	C-130E	314 AW	
40519	C-130E	314 AW	bl
40520	C-130E	135 AS	
40521	C-130E	135 AS	
40523	MC-130E	8 SOS	
40524	C-130E	314 AW	
40525	C-130E	23 Wg	
40526	C-130E	135 AS	
40527	C-130E	37 AS	bl/w
40529	C-130E	23 Wg	
40531	C-130E	23 Wg	
40533	C-130E	37 AS	bl/w
40535	C-130E	314 AW	bl
40537	C-130E	23 Wg	
40538	C-130E	314 AW	bk
40539	C-130E	23 Wg	gn/or
40540	C-130E	23 Wg	m
40541	C-130E	314 AW	
40542	C-130E	314 AW	bk
40544	C-130E	135 AS	
40550	C-130E	37 AS	bl/w
40551	MC-130E	8 SOS	
40555	MC-130E	8 SOS	
40557	C-130E	314 AW	bl
40559	MC-130E	8 SOS	
40561	MC-130E	8 SOS	
40562	MC-130E	8 SOS	
40565	MC-130E	1 SOS	
40566	MC-130E	8 SOS	
40567	MC-130E	8 SOS	
40568	MC-130E	8 SOS	
40569	C-130E	314 AW	bl
40570	C-130E	23 Wg	gn/or
40571	MC-130E	1 SOS	
40572	MC-130E	1 SOS	

FY74

41658	C-130H	3 Wg	w
41659	C-130H	3 Wg	w
41660	C-130H	374 AW	r
41661	C-130H	374 AW	r
41662	C-130H	7 Wg	bl
41663	C-130H	7 Wg	bl
41664	C-130H	374 AW	r
41665	C-130H	7 Wg	bl
41666	C-130H	7 Wg	bl
41667	C-130H	7 Wg	
41668	C-130H	3 Wg	w
41669	C-130H	7 Wg	r
41670	C-130H	374 AW	
41671	C-130H	7 Wg	
41673	C-130H	7 Wg	
41674	C-130H	7 Wg	r
41675	C-130H	7 Wg	r
41676	C-130H	3 Wg	w
41677	C-130H	7 Wg	bl
41679	C-130H	7 Wg	bl
41680	C-130H	7 Wg	r
41682	C-130H	374 AW	r
41684	C-130H	374 AW	r
41685	C-130H	374 AW	r
41687	C-130H	7 Wg	r
41688	C-130H	7 Wg	bl
41689	C-130H	7 Wg	bl
41690	C-130H	3 Wg	w
41691	C-130H	7 Wg	r
41692	C-130H	3 Wg	w
42061	C-130H	7 Wg	r
42062	C-130H	3 Wg	m
42063	C-130H	7 Wg	
42065	C-130H	7 Wg	
42066	C-130H	3 Wg	w
42067	C-130H	7 Wg	
42069	C-130H	7 Wg	r
42070	C-130H	3 Wg	w
42071	C-130H	3 Wg	w
42072	C-130H	7 Wg	bl
42130	C-130H	3 Wg	
42131	C-130H	3 Wg	w
42132	C-130H	7 Wg	r
42133	C-130H	374 AW	r
42134	C-130H	7 Wg	

FY94

46701	C-130H	167 AS	r
46702	C-130H	167 AS	r
46703	C-130H	167 AS	r
46704	C-130H	167 AS	r
46705	C-130H	167 AS	r
46706	C-130H	167 AS	r
46707	C-130H	167 AS	r
46708	C-130H	167 AS	r
47311	C-130H	731 AS	gn
47312	C-130H	731 AS	gn
47313	C-130H	731 AS	gn
47314	C-130H	731 AS	gn
47315	C-130H	731 AS	gn
47316	C-130H	731 AS	gn
47317	C-130H	731 AS	gn
47318	C-130H	731 AS	gn
47319	C-130H	731 AS	gn

FY55

50022	NC-130A	46 TW	

FY85

50011	MC-130H	15 SOS	
50012	MC-130H	15 SOS	
50035	C-130H	357 AS	bl
50036	C-130H	357 AS	bl
50037	C-130H	357 AS	bl
50038	C-130H	357 AS	bl
50039	C-130H	357 AS	bl
50040	C-130H	357 AS	bl
50041	C-130H	357 AS	bl
50042	C-130H	357 AS	bl

FY65

50962	EC-130H42	ACCS	w
50963	WC-130H53	WRS	
50964	C-130E	301 RQS	
50966	WC-130H53	WRS	
50967	WC-130H53	WRS	
50968	WC-130H53	WRS	
50969	C-130E	711 SOS	
50970	HC-130P	304 RQS	y
50971	HC-130P	58 SOW	
50972	C-130E	711 SOS	
50973	HC-130P	71 RQS	bl
50974	HC-130P	102 RQS	
50975	HC-130P	58 SOW	
50976	HC-130P	304 RQS	y
50977	WC-130H	53 WRS	
50978	HC-130P	102 RQS	
50979	NC-130H	514 TS	
50980	WC-130H	53 WRS	
50981	HC-130P	129 RQS	
50982	HC-130P	71 RQS	bl
50983	HC-130H	129 RQS	
50984	WC-130H	53 WRS	
50985	WC-130H	53 WRS	
50986	HC-130P	71 RQS	bl
50987	HC-130P	71 RQS	bl
50988	HC-130P	102 RQS	
50989	EC-130H	41 ECS	bl
50991	HC-130P	9 SOS	
50992	HC-130P	17 SOS	
50993	HC-130P	9 SOS	
50994	HC-13OP	9 SOS	

FY85

51361	C-130H	181 AS	
51362	C-130H	181 AS	
51363	C-130H	181 AS	
51364	C-130H	181 AS	
51365	C-130H	181 AS	
51366	C-130H	181 AS	
51367	C-130H	181 AS	
51368	C-130H	181 AS	

FY66

60212	HC-130P	58 SOW	
60213	HC-130P	9 SOS	
60215	HC-130P	9 SOS	
60216	HC-130P	9 SOS	
60217	HC-130P	9 SOS	bl
60219	HC-130P	58 SOW	
60220	HC-130P	9 SOS	
60221	HC-130P	129 RQS	
60222	HC-130P	102 RQS	
60223	HC-130P	67 RQS	
60224	HC-130P	129 RQS	
60225	HC-130P	9 SOS	

FY86

60410	C-130H	758 AS	bk
60411	C-130H	758 AS	bk
60412	C-130H	758 AS	hk
60413	C-130H	758 AS	bk
60414	C-130H	758 AS	bk
60415	C-130H	758 AS	bk
60418	C-130H	758 AS	bk
60419	C-130H	758 AS	bk

FY86		
61391	C-130H	180 AS
61392	C-130H	180 AS
61393	C-130H	180 AS
61394	C-130H	180 AS
61395	C-130H	180 AS
61396	C-130H	180 AS
61397	C-130H	180 AS
61398	C-130H	180 AS
61699	MC-130H	7 SOS

FY87		
70023	MC-130H	7 SOS
70024	MC-130H	15 SOS
70125	MC-130H	58 SOW
70126	MC-130H	58 SOW
70127	MC-130H	58 SOW
70128	AC-130U	418 TS

FY67		
77184	C-130H	310 AS

FY87			
79281	C-130H	64 AS	r
79282	C-130H	64 AS	r
79283	C-130H	64 AS	r
79284	C-130H	64 AS	r
79285	C-130H	64 AS	r
79286	C-130H	64 AS	r
79287	C-130H	64 AS	r
79288	C-130H	64 AS	r

FY88		
80191	MC-130H	58 SOW
80192	MC-130H	58 SOW
80193	MC-130H	7 SOS
80194	MC-130H	7 SOS
80195	MC-130H	15 SOS
80264	MC-130H	15 SOS

FY78			
80806	C-130H	185 AS	bl
80807	C-130H	185 AS	bl
80808	C-130H	185 AS	bl
80809	C-130H	185 AS	bl
80810	C-130H	185 AS	bl
80811	C-130H	185 AS	bl
80812	C-130H	185 AS	bl
80813	C-130H	185 AS	bl
81301	C-130H	130 AS	
81302	C-130H	130 AS	
81303	C-130H	130 AS	
81304	C-130H	130 AS	
81305	C-130H	130 AS	
81306	C-130H	130 AS	
81307	C-130H	130 AS	
81308	C-130H	130 AS	
81803	MC-130H	1 SOS	
82101	HC-130H	210 RQS	
82102	HC-130H	210 RQS	
84401	C-130H	95 AS	y/w
84402	C-130H	95 AS	y/w
84403	C-130H	95 AS	y/w
84404	C-130H	95 AS	y/w
84405	C-130H	95 AS	y/w
84406	C-130H	95 AS	y/w
84407	C-130H	95 AS	y/w
84408	C-130H	95 AS	y/w

FY89		
90280	MC-130H	15 SOS
90281	MC-130H	15 SOS
90282	MC-130H	15 SOS
90283	MC-130H	15 SOS

FY79			
90473	C-130H	144 AS	
90474	C-130H	185 AS	bl
90475	C-130H	199 FS	
90476	C-130H	157 FS	
90477	C-130H	158 AS	r
90478	C-130H	199 FS	
90479	C-130H	185 AS	bl
90480	C-130H	122 FS	

FY89		
90509	AC-130U	AFSC
90510	AC-130U	418 TS
90511	AC-130U	418 TS
90512	AC-130U	16 SOW
90513	AC-130U	AFSC
90514	AC-130U	AFSC
91051	C-130H	105 AS
91052	C-130H	105 AS
91053	C-130H	105 AS
91054	C-130H	105 AS
91055	C-130H	142 AS
91056	C-130H	180 AS
91181	C-130H	105 AS
91182	C-130H	105 AS
91183	C-130H	105 AS
91184	C-130H	105 AS
91185	C-130H	105 AS
91186	C-130H	105 AS
91187	C-130H	105 AS
91188	C-130H	105 AS

FY69			
95819	HC-130N	9 SOS	
95820	HC-130N	67 SOS	
95821	HC-130N	17 SOS	
95822	HC-130N	17 SOS	
95823	HC-130N	67 SOS	
95824	HC-130N	301 RQS	
95825	HC-130N	17 SOS	
95826	HC-130N	67 SOS	
95827	HC-130N	5 SOS	
95828	HC-130N	9 SOS	
95829	HC-130N	301 RQS	
95830	HC-130N	301 RQS	
95831	HC-130N	67 SOS	
95832	HC-130N	9 SOS	
95833	HC-130N	301 RQS	
96566	C-130E	37 AS	bl/w
96568	AC-130H	16 SOS	
96569	AC-130H	16 SOS	
96570	AC-130H	16 SOS	
96572	AC-130H	16 SOS	
96573	AC-130H	16 SOS	
96574	AC-130H	16 SOS	
96575	AC-130H	16 SOS	
96577	AC-130H	16 SOS	
96579	C-130E	314 AW	gn
96580	C-130E	23 Wg	g/no
96582	C-130E	37 AS	bl/w
96583	C-130E	37 AS	bl/w

FY89			
99101	C-130H	757 AS	bl
99102	C-130H	757 AS	bl
99103	C-130H	757 AS	bl
99104	C-130H	757 AS	bl
99105	C-130H	757 AS	bl
99106	C-130H	757 AS	bl

Boeing C-135/C-137
8 ACCS/552 ACW, Tinker AFB,
Oklahoma [OK];

18 ARS/931 ARW AFRES,
McConnell AFB, Kansas;
18 Wg Kadena AB, Japan [ZZ]:
909 ARS (w);
19 ARW Robins AFB, Georgia:
99 ARS (y/bl) &
712 ARS (y/w);
22 ARW McConnell AFB,
Kansas:
344 ARS (bk/y), 349 ARS (bl/y)
350 ARS (r/y) & 384 ARS (y/pr);
43 ARG/91 ARS MacDill AFB,
Florida (y/bk);
44 ARS/931 ARW AFRES,
McConnell AFB, Kansas;
55 Wg Offutt AFB,
Nebraska [OF]:
7 ACCS, 38 RS, 45 RS (w/bl),
82 RS,95 RS & 343 RS;
63 ARS/927 ARW AFRES,
Selfridge ANGB,
Michigan (pr/w);
65 AS/15 ABW, Hickam AFB,
Hawaii;
72 ARS/434 ARW AFRES,
Grissom AFB, Indiana (bl);
74 ARS/434 ARW AFRES,
Grissom AFB, Indiana (r);
77 ARS/916 ARW AFRES,
Seymour Johnson AFB,
North Carolina;
89 AW Andrews AFB,
Maryland (1 AS);
92 ARW Fairchild AFB,
Washington: 92 ARS (bk),
93 ARS (bl), 96 ARS (gn),
97 ARS (y) & 98 ARS (r);
97 AMW Altus AFB, Oklahoma:
55 ARS (y/r);
100 ARW RAF Mildenhall, UK
[D]: 351 ARS (r/w/bl);
106 ARS/117 ARW Birmingham,
Alabama ANG (w/r);
108 ARS/126 ARW Chicago
Internati'l, Illinois ANG (w/bl);
116 ARS/141 ARW Fairchild
AFB, Washington ANG(gn/w);
117 ARS/190 ARW Forbes Field,
Kansas ANG (bl/y);
126 ARS/128 ARG Mitchell Field,
Wisconsin ANG (w/bl);
132 ARS/101 ARW Bangor,
Maine ANG (w/gn);
133 ARS/157 ARG Pease AFB,
New Hampshire ANG (bl);
136 ARS/107 ARG Niagara Falls,
New York ANG (bl);
141 ARS/108 ARW McGuire
AFB, New Jersey ANG (bk/y);
145 ARS/121 ARW
Rickenbacker AFB,
Ohio ANG (r/w);
146 ARS/112 ARG Greater
Pittsburgh, Pennsylvania
ANG (y/bk);
147 ARS/171 ARW Greater
Pittsburgh, Pennsylvania
ANG (bk/y);
150 ARS/108 ARW McGuire
AFB, New Jersey ANG (bl);
151 ARS/134 ARG Knoxville,
Tennessee ANG (w/or);
153 ARS/186 ARG Meridian,
Mississippi ANG (bk/gd);

166 ARS/121 ARW Rickenbacker AFB, Ohio ANG (bl/w);
168 ARS/168 ARG Eilson AFB, Alaska ANG (bl);
173 ARS/155 ARG Lincoln, Nebraska ANG (r/w);
191 ARS/151 ARG Salt Lake City, Utah ANG (bl/bk);
196 ARS/163 ARG March AFB, California ANG (bl/w);
197 ARS/161 ARG Phoenix, Arizona ANG;
203 ARS/154 OG Hickam AFB, Hawaii ANG (y/bk);
314 ARS/940 ARW AFRES, McClellan AFB, California (r);
319 ARW Grand Forks AFB, North Dakota: 905 ARS (bl), 906 ARS (y), 911 ARS (r) & 912 ARS (w);
336 ARS/452 AMW AFRES, March AFB, California (y/bk);
366 Wg Mountain Home AFB, Idaho [MO]: 22 ARS (y/gn);
452 TS/412 TW, Edwards AFB, California (bl);
465 ARS/507 ARW AFRES, Tinker AFB, Oklahoma (bl/y); USN/FIWC, Waco Airport, Texas

FY60

Serial	Type	Unit	Colour
00313	KC-135R	18 Wg	w
00314	KC-135R	74 ARS	r/w
00315	KC-135R	126 ARS	w/bl
00316	KC-135E	116 ARS	gn/w
00318	KC-135R	203 ARS	y/bk
00319	KC-135R	19 ARW	y/w
00320	KC-135R	319 ARW	w
00321	KC-135R	319 ARW	y
00322	KC-135R	72 ARS	bl
00323	KC-135R	203 ARS	y/bk
00324	KC-135R	319 ARW	bl
00327	KC-135E	191 ARS	bl/bk
00328	KC-135R	92 ARW	bk
00329	KC-135R	203 ARS	y/bk
00331	KC-135R	97 AMW	y/r
00332	KC-135R	319 ARW	w
00333	KC-135R	97 AMW	y/r
00334	KC-135R	168 ARS	bl
00335	KC-135Q		
00336	KC-135T	92 ARW	gn
00337	KC-135T	92 ARW	bl
00339	KC-135T	92 ARW	gn
00341	KC-135R	145 ARS	r/w
00342	KC-135T	92 ARW	r
00343	KC-135T	319 ARW	w
00344	KC-135T	22 ARW	
00345	KC-135Q	22 ARW	
00346	KC-135T	92 ARW	gn
00347	KC-135R	166 ARS	bl/w
00348	KC-135R	43 ARG	y/bk
00349	KC-135R	77 ARS	gn
00350	KC-135R	43 ARG	y/bk
00351	KC-135R	43 ARG	y/bk
00353	KC-135R	43 ARG	y/bk
00355	KC-135R	43 ARG	y/bk
00356	KC-135R	22 ARW	y/bl
00357	KC-135R	22 ARW	bk/y
00358	KC-135R	136 ARS	bl
00359	KC-135R	74 ARS	r/w
00360	KC-135R	18 Wg	w
00362	KC-135R	22 ARW	
00363	KC-135R	72 ARS	bl
00364	KC-135R	74 ARS	r/w
00365	KC-135R	366 Wg	y/gn
00366	KC-135R	19 ARW	y/pr
00367	KC-135R	136 ARS	bl
00372	C-135E	452 TS	bl
00374	EC-135E	452 TS	bl
00375	C-135E	452 TS	bl
00376	C-135E	8 ACCS	
00377	C-135A	452 TS	bl

FY61

Serial	Type	Unit	Colour
10264	KC-135R	145 ARS	r/w
10266	KC-135R	173 ARS	r/w
10267	KC-135R	319 ARW	bl
10268	KC-135E	314 ARS	o/bk
10270	KC-135E	63 ARS	pr/w
10271	KC-135E	63 ARS	pr/w
10272	KC-135R	74 ARS	r/w
10275	KC-135R	22 ARW	y/r
10276	KC-135R	173 ARS	r/w
10277	KC-135R	366 Wg	y/gn
10280	KC-135E	336 ARS	y/or
10281	KC-135E	197 ARS	
10284	KC-135R	92 ARW	
10288	KC-135R	18 Wg	w
10290	KC-135R	203 ARS	y/bk
10292	KC-135R	22 ARW	y/pr
10293	KC-135R	22 ARW	y/pr
10294	KC-135R	92 ARW	y
10295	KC-135R	97 AMW	y/r
10298	KC-135R	126 ARS	w/bl
10299	KC-135R	92 ARW	bk
10300	KC-135R	19 ARW	y/w
10302	KC-135R	18 Wg	w
10303	KC-135E	336 ARS	y/bk
10304	KC-135R	18 Wg	w
10305	KC-135R	22 ARW	y/r
10306	KC-135R	43 ARG	y/bk
10307	KC-135R	74 ARS	r/w
10308	KC-135R		
10309	KC-135R	126 ARS	w/bl
10310	KC-135R	133 ARS	bl
10311	KC-135R	22 ARW	y/r
10312	KC-135R	92 ARW	y
10313	KC-135R		
10314	KC-135R	18 Wg	w
10315	KC-135R	18 Wg	w
10317	KC-135R	319 ARW	bl
10318	KC-135R	319 ARW	y
10320	KC-135R	92 ARW	y
10321	KC-135R	92 ARW	y
10323	KC-135R	22 ARW	
10324	KC-135R	77 ARS	gn
10326	EC-135E	452 TS	bl
10327	EC-135N	CinC CC	
10329	EC-135E	452 TS	bl
10330	EC-135E	452 TS	bl
12662	RC-135S	55 Wg	
12663	RC-135S	55 Wg	
12665	WC-135B	55 Wg	
12666	WC-135B		
12667	TC-135B	55 Wg	bk
12668	C-135C	65 AS	
12669	C-135C	452 TS	bl
12670	WC-135B	55 Wg	
12672	OC-135B5	5 Wg	
12674	OC-135B	55 Wg	

FY64

Serial	Type	Unit	Colour
14828	KC-135R	22 ARW	y/pr
14829	KC-135R	97 AMW	y/r
14830	KC-135R	319 ARW	r
14831	KC-135R	92 ARW	y
14832	KC-135R	203 ARS	y/bk
14833	KC-135R	22 ARW	
14834	KC-135R	74 ARS	r/w
14835	KC-135R	22 ARW	y/r
14836	KC-135R	319 ARW	r
14837	KC-135R	319 ARW	w
14838	KC-135R	22 ARW	y/r
14839	KC-135R	136 ARS	bl
14840	KC-135R	166 ARS	bl/w
14841	RC-135V	55 Wg	gn
14842	RC-135V	55 Wg	
14843	RC-135V	55 Wg	
14844	RC-135V	55 Wg	gn
14845	RC-135V	55 Wg	gn
14846	RC-135V	55 Wg	gn
14847	RC-135U	55 Wg	gn
14848	RC-135V	55 Wg	
14849	RC-135U	55 Wg	gn

FY67

Serial	Type	Unit	Colour
19417	EC-137D	19 ARW	

FY62

Serial	Type	Unit	Colour
23498	KC-135R	92 ARW	bk
23499	KC-135R	92 ARW	
23500	KC-135R	126 ARS	w/bl
23502	KC-135R	97 AMW	y/r
23503	KC-135R	18 Wg	w
23504	KC-135R	319 ARW	bl
23505	KC-135R	319 ARW	w
23506	KC-135R	133 ARS	bl
23507	KC-135R	97 AMW	y/r
23508	KC-135R	19 ARW	y/bl
23509	KC-135R	77 ARS	gn
23510	KC-135R	74 ARS	r/w
23511	KC-135R	145 ARS	r/w
23513	KC-135R	366 Wg	y/gn
23514	KC-135R	203 ARS	y/bk
23515	KC-135R	22 ARW	
23517	KC-135R	22 ARW	y/r
23518	KC-135R	72 ARS	bl
23519	KC-135R	319 ARW	r
23520	KC-135R	18 Wg	w
23521	KC-135R	74 ARS	r/w
23523	KC-135R	19 ARW	y/w
23524	KC-135R	106 ARS	w/r
23526	KC-135R	173 ARS	r/w
23527	KC-135E	141 ARS	bk/y
23528	KC-135R	97 AMW	y/r
23529	KC-135R	92 ARW	
23530	KC-135R	72 ARS	bl
23531	KC-135R	145 ARS	r/w
23533	KC-135R	43 ARG	y/bk
23534	KC-135R	19 ARW	
23537	KC-135R		
23538	KC-135R	92 ARW	y
23540	KC-135R	92 ARW	y
23541	KC-135R	100 ARW	
23542	KC-135R		
23543	KC-135R	72 ARS	bl
23544	KC-135R	19 ARW	y/w
23545	KC-135R	19 ARW	y/w
23546	KC-135R	92 ARW	y
23547	KC-135R	133 ARS	bl
23548	KC-135R	97 AMW	y/r
23549	KC-135R	43 ARG	y/bk
23550	KC-135R	97 AMW	y/r
23551	KC-135R	97 AMW	y/r
23552	KC-135R	19 ARW	
23553	KC-135R	319 ARW	
23554	KC-135R	19 ARW	
23556	KC-135R	319 ARW	r
23557	KC-135R	319 ARW	bl

Serial	Type	Unit	Code
23558	KC-135R	22 ARW	
23559	KC-135R	92 ARW	y
23561	KC-135R		
23562	KC-135R	319 ARW	w
23564	KC-135R	97 AMW	y/r
23565	KC-135R	97 AMW	y/r
23566	KC-135E	168 ARS	bl
23569	KC-135R	19 ARW	
23571	KC-135R	168 ARS	bl
23572	KC-135R	366 Wg	y/gn
23573	KC-135R	97 AMW	y/r
23575	KC-135R	43 ARG	y/bk
23576	KC-135R	133 ARS	bl
23577	KC-135R		
23578	KC-135R	92 ARW	bk
23580	KC-135R	97 AMW	y/r
23581	EC-135C	55 Wg	
23582	EC-135C	55 Wg	
23585	EC-135C	55 Wg	
24125	C-135B	65 AS	
24126	C-135B	141 ARS	bk/y
24127	C-135B	65 AS	
24129	TC-135W	55 Wg	gn
24130	C-135B	55 Wg	
24131	RC-135W	55 Wg	gn
24132	RC-135W	55 Wg	gn
24133	TC-135S	55 Wg	gn
24134	RC-135W	55 Wg	
24135	RC-135W	55 Wg	gn
24138	RC-135W	55 Wg	gn
24139	RC-135W	55 Wg	gn
26000	C-137C	89 AW	

FY72

Serial	Type	Unit	Code
27000	C-137C	89 AW	

FY63

Serial	Type	Unit	Code
37976	KC-135R	319 ARW	bl
37977	KC-135R	319 ARW	
37978	KC-135R	97 AMW	y/r
37979	KC-135R	97 AMW	y/r
37980	KC-135R	18 Wg	w
37981	KC-135R	136 ARS	bl
37982	KC-135R	43 ARG	y/bk
37984	KC-135R	106 ARS	w/r
37985	KC-135R	465 ARS	bl/y
37987	KC-135R	319 ARW	bl
37988	KC-135R	173 ARS	r/w
37991	KC-135R	173 ARS	r/w
37992	KC-135R	166 ARS	bl/w
37993	KC-135R	166 ARS	bl/w
37995	KC-135R	19 ARW	y/bl
37996	KC-135R	72 ARS	bl
37997	KC-135R	19 ARW	y/w
37999	KC-135R	319 ARW	
38000	KC-135R	22 ARW	
38002	KC-135R	19 ARW	y/w
38003	KC-135R	22 ARW	y/r
38004	KC-135R	366 Wg	y/gn
38006	KC-135R	19 ARW	y/w
38007	KC-135R	106 ARS	w/r
38008	KC-135R	100 ARW	r/w/bl
38011	KC-135R	319 ARW	bl
38012	KC-135R	319 ARW	r
38013	KC-135R	166 ARS	bl/w
38014	KC-135R	319 ARW	w
38015	KC-135R	168 ARS	bl
38017	KC-135R	92 ARW	bk
38018	KC-135R	173 ARS	r/w
38019	KC-135R	22 ARW	y/r
38020	KC-135R	97 AMW	y/r
38021	KC-135R	319 ARW	bl
38022	KC-135R	22 ARW	
38023	KC-135R	100 ARW	r/w/bl
38024	KC-135R	465 ARS	bl/y
38025	KC-135R	319 ARW	bl
38026	KC-135R	319 ARW	y
38027	KC-135R	92 ARW	y
38028	KC-135R	133 ARS	bl
38029	KC-135R	126 ARS	w/bl
38030	KC-135R	203 ARS	y/bk
38031	KC-135R	22 ARW	r
38032	KC-135R	72 ARS	bl
38034	KC-135R	319 ARW	w
38035	KC-135R	106 ARS	w/r
38036	KC-135R	136 ARS	bl
38037	KC-135R	92 ARW	bl
38038	KC-135R	133 ARS	bl
38039	KC-135R	465 ARS	bl/y
38040	KC-135R	319 ARW	y
38041	KC-135R	72 ARS	bl
38043	KC-135R	166 ARS	bl/w
38044	KC-135R	319 ARW	y
38045	KC-135R	319 ARW	r
38046	EC-135C	55 Wg	
38048	EC-135C	55 Wg	bl
38050	EC-135C	452 TS	bl
38052	EC-135C	55 Wg	
38053	EC-135C	55 Wg	bl
38054	EC-135C	55 Wg	bl
38058	KC-135D	168 ARS	bl
38059	KC-135D	197 ARS	
38060	KC-135D	168 ARS	bl
38061	KC-135D	168 ARS	bl
38871	KC-135R	319 ARW	r
38872	KC-135R	136 ARS	bl
38873	KC-135R	319 ARW	r
38874	KC-135R	18 Wg	w
38875	KC-135R		
38876	KC-135R	168 ARS	bl
38877	KC-135R	100 ARW	r/w
38878	KC-135R	97 AMW	y/r
38879	KC-135R	92 ARW	bl
38880	KC-135R	465 ARS	bl/y
38881	KC-135R	319 ARW	y
38883	KC-135R	319 ARW	w
38884	KC-135R	22 ARW	y/r
38885	KC-135R	319 ARW	w
38886	KC-135R	18 Wg	w
38887	KC-135R	22 ARW	y/r
38888	KC-135R	97 AMW	y/r
39792	RC-135V	55 Wg	gn

FY55

Serial	Type	Unit	Code
53118	EC-135K	8 ACCS	
53125	EC-135Y	CinC CC	
53128	NKC-135	A452 TS	bl
53132	NKC-135E	452 TS	bl
53134	NKC-135	AUSN/FIWC	
53135	NKC-135E	452 TS	bl
53141	KC-135E	116 ARS	
53143	KC-135E	197 ARS	
53145	KC-135E	314 ARS	
53146	KC-135E	141 ARS	bk/y

FY85

Serial	Type	Unit	Code
56973	C-137C	89 AW	
56974	C-137C	89 AW	

FY56

Serial	Type	Unit	Code
63593	KC-135E	141 ARS	bk/y
63604	KC-135E	117 ARS	bl/y
63606	KC-135E	132 ARS	w/gn
63607	KC-135E	151 ARS	w/or
63609	KC-135E	151 ARS	w/or
63611	KC-135E	146 ARS	y/bk
63612	KC-135E	146 ARS	y/bk
63622	KC-135E	132 ARS	w/gn
63623	KC-135E	336 ARS	y/or
63626	KC-135E	133 ARS	bl
63630	KC-135E	146 ARS	y/bk
63631	KC-135E	117 ARS	bl/y
63638	KC-135E	197 ARS	
63640	KC-135E	132 ARS	w/gn
63641	KC-135E	117 ARS	bl/y
63643	KC-135E	151 ARS	w/or
63645	KC-135E	314 ARS	
63648	KC-135E	146 ARS	y/bk
63650	KC-135E	116 ARS	gn/w
63654	KC-135E	132 ARS	w/gn
63658	KC-135E	117 ARS	bl/y

FY57

Serial	Type	Unit	Code
71418	KC-135R	153 ARS	bk/gd
71419	KC-135R	319 ARW	y
71421	KC-135E	116 ARS	gn/w
71422	KC-135E	63 ARS	pr/w
71423	KC-135E	147 ARS	bk/y
71425	KC-135E	151 ARS	w/or
71426	KC-135E	197 ARS	
71427	KC-135E	145 ARS	r/w
71428	KC-135E	196 ARS	bl/w
71429	KC-135E	117 ARS	bl/y
71430	KC-135R	133 ARS	bl
71431	KC-135E	141 ARS	bk/y
71432	KC-135E	106 ARS	w/r
71433	KC-135E	197 ARS	
71434	KC-135E	116 ARS	gn/w
71435	KC-135R	97 AMW	y/r
71436	KC-135E	196 ARS	bl/w
71437	KC-135R	319 ARW	w
71438	KC-135E	63 ARS	pr/w
71439	KC-135R	100 ARW	r/w/bl
71440	KC-135R	319 ARW	bl
71441	KC-135E	108 ARS	w/bl
71443	KC-135E	132 ARS	w/gn
71445	KC-135E	141 ARS	bk/y
71447	KC-135E	146 ARS	y/bk
71448	KC-135E	132 ARS	w/gn
71450	KC-135E	132 ARS	w/gn
71451	KC-135E	168 ARS	bl
71452	KC-135E	197 ARS	
71453	KC-135E	106 ARS	w/r
71454	KC-135R	43 ARG	y/bk
71455	KC-135E	151 ARS	w/or
71456	KC-135E	100 ARW	r/w/bl
71458	KC-135E	108 ARS	w/bl
71459	KC-135E	196 ARS	bl/w
71460	KC-135E	117 ARS	bl/y
71461	KC-135E	173 ARS	r/w
71462	KC-135E	145 ARS	r/w
71463	KC-135E	117 ARS	bl/y
71464	KC-135E	141 ARS	bk/y
71465	KC-135E	168 ARS	bl
71468	KC-135E	336 ARS	y/or
71469	KC-135E	166 ARS	bl/w
71471	KC-135E	132 ARS	w/gn
71472	KC-135R	72 ARS	bl
71473	KC-135R	18 Wg	w
71474	KC-135R	92 ARW	y
71475	KC-135E	197 ARS	
71478	KC-135E	151 ARS	w/or
71479	KC-135E	336 ARS	y/or
71480	KC-135E	108 ARS	w/bl
71482	KC-135E	117 ARS	bl/y
71483	KC-135R	22 ARW	
71484	KC-135E	197 ARS	
71485	KC-135E	151 ARS	w/or
71486	KC-135E	100 ARW	r/w/bl
71487	KC-135R	77 ARS	
71488	KC-135R	97 AMW	y/r

71491	KC-135E	132 ARS	
71492	KC-135E	151 ARS	w/or
71493	KC-135R	43 ARG	y/bk
71494	KC-135E	108 ARS	
71495	KC-135E	197 ARS	
71496	KC-135E	197 ARS	
71497	KC-135E	191 ARS	bl/bk
71499	KC-135R	100 ARW	r/w
71501	KC-135E	116 ARS	gn/w
71502	KC-135R	319 ARW	y
71503	KC-135E	151 ARS	w/or
71504	KC-135E	63 ARS	pr/w
71505	KC-135E	132 ARS	w/gn
71506	KC-135R	100 ARW	r/w/bl
71507	KC-135E	141 ARS	bk/y
71508	KC-135R	203 ARS	y/bk
71509	KC-135E	147 ARS	bk/y
71510	KC-135E	196 ARS	bl/w
71511	KC-135E	314 ARS	or/b
71512	KC-135R	336 ARS	y/or
71514	KC-135R	126 ARS	w/bk
72589	C-135E	55 Wg	bl
72593	KC-135R	166 ARS	bl/w
72594	KC-135E	108 ARS	w/bl
72595	KC-135E	147 ARS	bk/y
72597	KC-135R	153 ARS	bk/gd
72598	KC-135E	336 ARS	y/or
72599	KC-135R	92 ARW	bk
72600	KC-135E	116 ARS	gn/w
72601	KC-135E	151 ARS	w/or
72602	KC-135E	150 ARS	bl
72603	KC-135E	336 ARS	y/or
72604	KC-135E	146 ARS	y/bk
72605	KC-135R	22 ARW	y/bl
72606	KC-135E	150 ARS	bl
72607	KC-135E	147 ARS	bk/y
72608	KC-135E	147 ARS	bk/y

FY58

80001	KC-135R	97 AMW	y/r
80003	KC-135E	108 ARS	w/bl
80004	KC-135R	153 ARS	bk/gd
80005	KC-135E	117 ARS	bl/y
80006	KC-135E	191 ARS	bl/bk
80008	KC-135E	196 ARS	bl/w
80009	KC-135R	126 ARS	w/bk
80010	KC-135R	153 ARS	bk/gd
80011	KC-135R	19 ARW	
80012	KC-135E	191 ARS	bl/bk
80013	KC-135E	63 ARS	pr/w
80014	KC-135E	108 ARS	w/bl
80015	KC-135R	74 ARS	r/w
80016	KC-135R	22 ARW	y
80017	KC-135E	146 ARS	y/bk
80018	KC-135E	22 ARW	y/pr
80020	KC-135E	116 ARS	gn/w
80021	KC-135R	126 ARS	w/bl
80023	KC-135E	136 ARS	bl
80024	KC-135E	146 ARS	y/bk
80027	KC-135R	92 ARW	bk
80030	KC-135R	106 ARS	w/r
80032	KC-135E	150 ARS	bl
80034	KC-135R	97 AMW	y/r
80035	KC-135R	22 ARW	y/bl
80036	KC-135R	22 ARW	y/bl
80037	KC-135E	147 ARS	bk/y
80038	KC-135R	92 ARW	bk
80040	KC-135E	150 ARS	bl
80041	KC-135E	63 ARS	pr/w
80042	KC-135T	319 ARW	y
80043	KC-135E	191 ARS	bl/bk
80044	KC-135E	141 ARS	bk/y
80045	KC-135T	92 ARW	gn
80046	KC-135T		

80047	KC-135T	319 ARW	w
80049	KC-135T	92 ARW	bl
80050	KC-135T	92 ARW	r
80051	KC-135R		
80052	KC-135E	336 ARS	y/or
80053	KC-135E	314 ARS	r
80054	KC-135T	92 ARW	gn
80055	KC-135T	92 ARW	r
80056	KC-135R	153 ARS	
80057	KC-135E	108 ARS	w/bl
80058	KC-135E	314 ARS	r
80059	KC-135R	153 ARS	bk/gd
80060	KC-135T	92 ARW	gn
80061	KC-135T	319 ARW	
80062	KC-135T	92 ARW	gn
80063	KC-135R		
80064	KC-135E	314 ARS	r
80065	KC-135T	319 ARW	bl
80066	KC-135R	465 ARS	y/bl
80067	KC-135E	108 ARS	w/bl
80068	KC-135E	108 ARS	w/bl
80069	KC-135R		
80071	KC-135T	22 ARW	r/y
80072	KC-135T	92 ARW	gn
80073	KC-135R	106 ARS	w/r
80074	KC-135T	92 ARW	r
80075	KC-135R	72 ARS	bl
80076	KC-135R	74 ARS	r/w
80077	KC-135T	92 ARW	gn
80078	KC-135E	150 ARS	bl
80079	KC-135R	465 ARS	y/bk
80080	KC-135E	191 ARS	bl/bk
80082	KC-135E	116 ARS	gn/w
80083	KC-135R	166 ARS	bl/w
80084	KC-135Q	92 ARW	r
80085	KC-135E	336 ARS	y/or
80086	KC-135T	92 ARW	bk
80087	KC-135E	150 ARS	bl
80088	KC-135T	22 ARW	y/bk
80089	KC-135T	22 ARW	
80090	KC-135E	314 ARS	r
80092	KC-135R	133 ARS	bl
80093	KC-135R	319 ARW	r
80094	KC-135T	92 ARW	bl
80095	KC-135T	22 ARW	y/bk
80096	KC-135E	314 ARS	r
80098	KC-135R	133 ARS	bl
80099	KC-135T	92 ARW	bl
80100	KC-135R	43 ARG	y/bk
80102	KC-135R	74 ARS	r/w
80103	KC-135Q		
80104	KC-135R	136 ARS	bl
80106	KC-135R	106 ARS	w/r
80107	KC-135E	191 ARS	bl/bk
80108	KC-135E	314 ARS	r
80109	KC-135R	153 ARS	bk/gd
80111	KC-135E	141 ARS	bk/y
80112	KC-135T	92 ARW	bl
80113	KC-135R	19 ARW	y
80114	KC-135R	92 ARW	y
80115	KC-135E	150 ARS	bl
80116	KC-135E	197 ARS	
80117	KC-135T	92 ARW	r
80118	KC-135R	22 ARW	y/bl
80119	KC-135R	319 ARW	r
80120	KC-135R	97 AMW	y/r
80121	KC-135R	92 ARW	
80122	KC-135R	168 ARS	bl
80123	KC-135R	19 ARW	y/w
80124	KC-135R	22 ARW	
80125	KC-135T	92 ARW	r
80126	KC-135R	22 ARW	y/r
80128	KC-135R	22 ARW	y/r
80129	KC-135T		

80130	KC-135R	97 AMW	y/r
86970	C-137B	89 AW	
86971	C-137B	89 AW	
86972	C-137B	89 AW	

FY59

91444	KC-135R	166 ARS	bl/w
91445	KC-135E	116 ARS	gn/w
91446	KC-135R	153 ARS	bk/gd
91447	KC-135E	63 ARS	pr/w
91448	KC-135E	196 ARS	bl/w
91450	KC-135E	196 ARS	bl/w
91451	KC-135E	63 ARS	pr/w
91452	KC-135E	116 ARS	gn/w
91453	KC-135R	145 ARS	r/w
91455	KC-135R	153 ARS	bk/gd
91456	KC-135E	141 ARS	bk/y
91457	KC-135E	147 ARS	bk/y
91458	KC-135R	145 ARS	r/w
91459	KC-135R	97 AMW	y/r
91460	KC-135T	92 ARW	bl
91461	KC-135R	168 ARS	bl
91462	KC-135T	22 ARW	y/bl
91463	KC-135R	173 ARS	r/w
91464	KC-135T	92 ARW	r
91466	KC-135R	319 ARW	
91467	KC-135T	92 ARW	gn
91468	KC-135T	92 ARW	gn
91469	KC-135R	77 ARS	gn
91470	KC-135T	92 ARW	bl
91471	KC-135T	92 ARW	r
91472	KC-135R	203 ARS	y/bk
91473	KC-135E	191 ARS	bl/bk
91474	KC-135T	92 ARW	bl
91475	KC-135R	43 ARG	y/b
91476	KC-135R	97 AMW	y/r
91477	KC-135E	63 ARS	pr/w
91478	KC-135R	153 ARS	bk/gd
91479	KC-135E	146 ARS	y/bk
91480	KC-135Q		
91482	KC-135R	22 ARW	y/bl
91483	KC-135R	166 ARS	bl/w
91484	KC-135E	147 ARS	bk/y
91485	KC-135E	150 ARS	bl
91486	KC-135R	22 ARW	bl/y
91487	KC-135E	108 ARS	w/bl
91488	KC-135R	19 ARW	
91489	KC-135E	191 ARS	bl/bk
91490	KC-135Q		
91492	KC-135R	92 ARW	bk
91493	KC-135E	132 ARS	w/gn
91495	KC-135R	173 ARS	r/w
91496	KC-135E	146 ARS	y/bk
91497	KC-135E	150 ARS	bl
91498	KC-135R	366 Wg	y/gn
91499	KC-135E	196 ARS	bl/w
91500	KC-135R	19 ARW	y/bl
91501	KC-135R	22 ARW	r/y
91502	KC-135R	19 ARW	
91503	KC-135E	141 ARS	bk/y
91504	KC-135Q	22 ARW	
91505	KC-135E	196 ARS	bl/w
91506	KC-135E	147 ARS	bk/y
91507	KC-135R	22 ARW	
91508	KC-135R	319 ARW	w
91509	KC-135E	196 ARS	bl/w
91510	KC-135T	22 ARW	y/bk
91511	KC-135R	19 ARW	y/w
91512	KC-135T	92 ARW	gn
91513	KC-135T	92 ARW	bl
91514	KC-135E	55 Wg	bl
91515	KC-135R	22 ARW	r/y
91516	KC-135E	196 ARS	bl/w
91517	KC-135R	319 ARW	w

91518	EC-135K	8 ACCS
91519	KC-135E	146 ARS	y/bk
91520	KC-135Q	
91521	KC-135R 133 ARS	bl
91522	KC-135R 136 ARS	bl
91523	KC-135T	92 ARW	gn

Lockheed C-141B Starlifter

60 AMW Travis AFB, California:
  19 AS & 20 AS (bk/r & bk/si);
62 AW McChord AFB,
  Washington: $ AS, 7 AS &
  8 AS (gn/bl) (gn) (gn/r);
97 AMW Altus AFB, Oklahoma:
  57 AS (r/y);
155 AS/164 AG Memphis,
  Tennessee ANG (r);
183 AS/172 AG Jackson Field ,
  Mississippi ANG (bl);
305 AMW McGuire AFB, New
  Jersey: 6 AS, 13 AS & 18
  AS (bl/w);
437 AW Charleston AFB, South
  Carolina; 15 AS & 16 AS
  (bl/y);
445 AW AFRES, Wright-
  Patterson AFB, Ohio: 89 AS
  (w/r) & 356 AS (w/bk);
452 AMW AFRES, March AFB,
  Caifornia: 729 AS (or/y) &
  730 AS (r/y);
756 AS/459 AW AFRES,
  Andrews AFB, Maryland
  (y/bk)

FY61		
127781	55 AS	r
FY63		
38076	62 AW	gn/r
38080	155 AS	r
38081	62 AW	gn/bl
38082	62 AW	gn/r
38083	305 AMW	bl
38084	452 AMW	y
38085	452 AM	W r/y
38086	62 AW	
38087	62 AW	gn/r
38088	60 AMW	
38089	62 AW	gn/r
38090	97 AMW	r/y
FY64		
40609	97 AMW	r/y
40610	437 AW	
40611	437 AW	
40612	437 AW	y/bl
40613	305 AMW	bl
40614	183 AS	bl
40615	437 AW	
40616	305 AMW	
40617	97 AMW	r/y
40618	437 AW	
40619	437 AW	
40620	756 AS	y/bk
40621	305 AMW	
40622	183 AS	bl
40623	305 AMW	
40625	305 AMW	
40626	305 AMW	
40627	305 AMW	
40628	305 AMW	
40629	437 AW	
40630	305 AMW	
40631	437 AW	
40632	183 AS	bl

40633	305 AMW	
40634	97 AMW	r/y
40635	62 AW	gn/si
40637	459 AW	
40638	305 AMW	bl
40639	97 AMW	r/y
40640	183 AS	bl
40642	97 AMW	r/y
40643	305 AMW	bl
40644	305 AMW	bl/w
40645	756 AS	y/bk
40646	305 AMW	
40649	437 AW	
40650	305 AMW	
40651	97 AMW	r/y
40653	62 AW	gn/bl
FY65		
50216	756 AS	y/bk
50218	62 AW	gn/r
50219	60 AMW	
50220	305 AMW	
50221	305 AMW	
50222	155 AS	r
50223	305 AMW	
50224	305 AMW	
50225	452 AMW	r/y
50226	756 AS	y/bk
50227	97 AMW	r/y
50229	452 AMW	or/y
50230	60 AMW	bk/si
50231	60 AMW	
50232	60 AMW	
50234	60 AMW	
50235	62 AW	gn/si
50237	445 AW	
50238	60 AMW	
50239	60 AMW	
50240	62 AW	gn/bl
50241	62 AW	gn/r
50242	60 AMW	bk/si
50243	60 AMW	bk/r
50244	62 AW	
50245	60 AMW	bk/r
50247	60 AMW	
50248	452 AMW	
50249	445 AW	
50250	452 AMW	
50251	60 AMW	bk/r
50252	60 AMW	
50254	60 AMW	bk/si
50256	60 AMW	bk/si
50257	60 AMW	bk/r
50258	445 AW	w/r
50259	60 AMW	bk/r
50260	60 AMW	
50261	445 AW	w/bk
50263	62 AW	gn/bl
50265	60 AMW	bk/r
50266	437 AW	
50267	62 AW	gn/r
50268	60 AMW	bk/si
50269	437 AW	
50270	437 AW	
50271	756 AS	y/bk
50272	437 AW	
50273	437 AW	y/bl
50275	437 AW	y
50276	305 AMW	bl
50277	62 AW	gn/r
50278	97 AMW	
50279	437 AW	
50280	62 AW	gn/bl
59397	62 AW	gn/si
59399	62 AW	gn/r

59400	97 AMW	r
59401	437 AW	
59402	97 AMW	r/y
59403	60 AMW	
59404	62 AW	gn/si
59405	305 AMW	bl
59408	305 AMW	bl
59409	445 AW	w/bk
59411	305 AMW	bl
59412	445 AW	
59413	305 AMW	bl
59414	452 AMW	r
FY66		
60128	62 AW	gn/bl
60129	62 AW	gn/bl
60130	183 AS	bl
60131	437 AW	
60132	445 AW	w/bk
60133	305 AMW	bl
60134	445 AW	
60135	437 AW	
60136	452 AMW	
60137	62 AW	gn
60138	97 AMW	r/y
60139	155 AS	r
60140	62 AW	gn/bl
60141	62 AW	gn/r
60144	437 AW	
60145	62 AW	gn/r
60146	305 AMW	bl
60147	60 AMW	bk/r
60148	60 AMW	bk/r
60149	437 AW	
60151	452 AMW	r/y
60152	452 AMW	
60153	756 AS	y/bk
60154	97 AMW	r/y
60155	305 AMW	bl
60156	62 AW	gn/bl
60157	155 AS	r
60158	62 AW	gn/bl
60159	62 AW	
60160	60 AMW	bk/r
60161	62 AW	gn/r
60162	305 AMW	bl
60163	305 AMW	bl
60164	183 AS	bl
60165	62 AW	
60166	60 AMW	
60167	437 AW	y/bl
60168	437 AW	
60169	445 AW	
60171	62 AW	gn/r
60172	62 AW	gn/bl
60174	756 AS	y/bk
60175	62 AW	gn/r
60177	445 AW	
60178	305 AMW	bl
60179	62 AW	gn/r
60180	155 AS	r
60181	452 AMW	or/y
60182	452 AMW	
60183	60 AMW	bk/r
60184	62 AW	gn/bl
60185	183 AS	bl
60187	437 AW	
60190	183 AS	bl
60191	60 AMW	
60192	62 AW	gn/bl
60193	452 AMW	r/y
60194	437 AW	y
60195	305 AMW	bl
60196	437 AW	
60197	62 AW	

60198	62 AW	gn/bl	67952	452 AMW		70014	437 AW	y
60199	305 AMW	bl	67953	445 AW	w/r	70015	452 AMW	
60200	62 AW	gn	67954	452 AMW	or/y	70016	437 AW	
60201	452 AMW	r/y	67955	437 AW		70018	62 AW	
60202	437 AW		67956	305 AMW	bl	70019	305 AMW	bl
60203	97 AMW	r/y	67957	452 AMW		70020	305 AMW	bl
60204	305 AMW	bl	67958	62 AW	gn/bl	70021	155 AS	r
60205	62 AW		67959	60 AMW	bk/si	70022	60 AMW	
60206	62 AW		FY67			70023	445 AW	
60207	305 AMW	bl	70001	62 AW	gn/r	70024	155 AS	r
60208	62 AW	gn/bl	70002	437 AW	y/bl	70025	305 AMW	bl
60209	437 AW		70003	62 AW	gn/bl	70026	437 AW	
67944	60 AMW	bk/si	70004	437 AW		70027	60 AMW	bk/r
67945	437 AW		70005	62 AW	gn/r	70028	62 AW	gn/si
67946	62 AW	gn	70007	60 AMW	bk/si	70029	155 AS	r
67947	305 AMW	bl	70009	62 AW	gn	70031	445 AW	
67948	305 AMW	bl	70010	437 AW		70164	97 AMW	r/y
67949	62 AW	gn/r	70011	437 AW		70165	305 AMW	bl
67950	445 AW	w/bk	70012	437 AW	y/bl	70166	305 AMW (VIP)	
67951	62 AW	gn/r	70013	305 AMW	bl			

B-1B Lancer 60126 from 28BS/7 Wg at Dyess AFB, Texas. *PRM*

Boeing E-6 Mercury
Sea Control Wing 1 (SCW-1), Tinker AFB,
  Oklahoma

162782	E-6A	SCW-1
162783	E-6A	SCW-1
162784	E-6A	SCW-1
163918	E-6A	
163919	E-6A	SCW-1
163920	E-6A	SCW-1
164386	E-6A	SCW-1
164387	E-6A	SCW-1
164388	E-6A	SCW-1
164404	E-6A	SCW-1
164405	E-6A	SCW-1
164406	E-6B	SCW-1
164407	E-6A	SCW-1
164408	E-6A	SCW-1
164409	E-6A	SCW-1
164410	E-6A	SCW-1
165342	E-6A	
165343	E-6A	

McDonnell Douglas
C-9B Skytrain II/DC-9-32*
VR-46 Atlanta, Georgia [JS];
VR-51 Glenview NAS, Illinois [RV];
VR-52 Willow Grove NAS,Pennsylvania [JT];
VR-56 Norfolk NAS, Virginia [JU];
VR-57 North Island NAS, California [RX];
VR-58 Jacksonville NAS, Florida [JV];
VR-59 Dallas, Texas [RY];
VR-60 Memphis NAS, Tennessee [RT];
VR-61 Whidbey Island NAS, Washington [RS];
SOES Cherry Point MCAS,North Carolina

159113	[RX]	VR-57
159114	[RX]	VR-57
159115	[RX]	VR-57
159116	[RX]	VR-57
159117	[JU]	VR-56
159118	[JU]	VR-56
159119	[JU]	VR-56
159120	{JU]	VR-56
160046		SOES
160047		SOES
160048	[JV]	VR-58
160049	[JV]	VR-58
160050	[JV]	VR-58
160051	[JV]	VR-58
161266	[RY]	VR-59
161529	[RY]	VR-59
161530	[RY]	VR-59
162753	[JT]	VR-52
162754	[JT]	VR-52
163036*	[JT]	VR-52
163037*	[JT]	VR-52
163208*	[RY]	VR-59
163511*	[JS]	VR-46
163512*	[JS]	VR-46
163513*	[JS]	VR-46
164605*	[RS]	VR-61
164606*	[RS]	VR-61
164607*	[RS]	VR-61
164608*	[RS]	VR-61

Grumman C-20D Gulfstream III/
C-20G Gulfstream IV*
CFLSW, NAF Washington;
MAG-36, Futenma NAS, Japan;
VR-48, NAF Washington [JR];
CFLSW Detachment,

NAS Barbers Point, Hawaii [RG]

163691		CFLSW
163692		CFLSW
165093*	[JR]	VR-48
165094*	[JR]	VR-48
165151*	[RG]	CFLSW
165152*	[RG]	CFLSW
165153*		MAG-36

Lockheed C-130 Hercules
NAWC, Patuxtent River, Maryland;
VR-53 Martinsburg, West Virginia [WV];
VR-54 New Orleans NAS, Louisiana [CW];
VR-55 Moffett Field NAS, California [RU];
VR-62 South Weymouth NAS, Massachusetts [JW];
VMGR-152 Futenma MCAS, Japan [QD];
VMGR-234 NAS Fort Worth, Texas [QH];
VMGR-252 Cherry Point MCAS, North Carolina
  [BH];
VMGRT-253 Cherry Point MCAS, North Carolina
  [GR];
VMGR-352 El Toro MCAS, California [QB];
VMGR-452 Stewart Field, New York [NY]

147572	[QB]	KC-130F	VMGR-352
147573	[QD]	KC-130F	VMGR-152
148246	[GR]	KC-130F	VMGRT-253
148247	[QD]	KC-130F	VMGR-152
148248	[QD]	KC-130F	VMGR-152
148249	[GR]	KC-130F	VMGRT-253
148890	[GR]	KC-130F	VMGRT-253
148891	[BH]	KC-130F	VMGR-252
148892	[GR]	KC-130F	VMGRT-253
148893	[QH]	KC-130F	VMGR-234
148894	[GR]	KC-130F	VMGRT-253
148895	[BH]	KC-130F	VMGR-252
148896	[BH]	KC-130F	VMGR-252
148897	[BH]	KC-130F	VMGR-252
148898	[BH]	KC-130F	VMGR-252
148899	[BH]	KC-130F	VMGR-252
149788	[BH]	KC-130F	VMGR-252
149789	[BH]	KC-130F	VMGR-252
149791	[QB]	KC-130F	VMGR-352
149792	[QB]	KC-130F	VMGR-352
149794		C-130F	
149795	[QB]	KC-130F	VMGR-352
149796	[QB]	KC-130F	VMGR-352
149798	[QB]	KC-130F	VMGR-352
149799	[QD]	KC-130F	VMGR-152
149800	[QB]	KC-130F	VMGR-352
149803	[GR]	KC-130F	VMGRT-253
149804	[GR]	KC-130F	VMGRT-253
149806		KC-130F	NAWC
149807	[QD]	KC-130F	VMGR-152
149808	[BH]	KC-130F	VMGR-252
149811	[GR]	KC-130F	VMGRT-253
149812	[QD]	KC-130F	VMGR-152
149815	[QB]	KC-130F	VMGR-352
149816	[QD]	KC-130F	VMGR-152
150684	[GR]	KC-130F	VMGRT-253
150686	[BH]	KC-130F	VMGR-252
150687	[GR]	KC-130F	VMGRT-253
150688	[GR]	KC-130F	VMGRT-253
150689	[QB]	KC-130F	VMGR-352
150690	[QD]	KC-130F	VMGR-352
151891		TC-130G	*Blue Angels*
160013	[QB]	KC-130R	VMGR-352
160014	[QB]	KC-130R	VMGR-352
160015	[QB]	KC-130R	VMGR-352
160016	[QB]	KC-130R	VMGR-352
160017	[QB]	KC-130R	VMGR-352

160018	[QD]	KC-130R	VMGR-152	164598	[QH]	KC-130T-30	VMGR-234
160019	[QD]	KC-130R	VMGR-152	164759	[NY]	KC-130T	VMGR-452
160020	[QB]	KC-130R	VMGR-352	164760	[QH]	KC-130T	VMGR-234
160021	[QB]	KC-130R	VMGR-352	164762	[CW]	C-130T	VR-54
160022	[QB]	KC-130R	VMGR-352	164763	[CW]	C-130T	VR-54
160240	[QB]	KC-130R	VMGR-352	164993	[CW]	C-130T	VR-54
160625	[BH]	KC-130R	VMGR-252	164994	[WV]	C-130T	VR-53
160626	[BH]	KC-130R	VMGR-252	164995	[CW]	C-130T	VR-54
160627	[BH]	KC-130R	VMGR-252	164996	[WV]	C-130T	VR-53
160628	[BH]	KC-130R	VMGR-252	164997	[WV]	C-130T	VR-53
162308	[QH]	KC-130T	VMGR-234	164998	[WV]	C-130T	VR-53
162309	[QH]	KC-130T	VMGR-234	164999	[NY]	KC-130T	VMGR-452
162310	[QH]	KC-130T	VMGR-234	165000	[QH]	KC-130T	VMGR-234
162311	[QH]	KC-130T	VMGR-234	165158	[RU]	C-130T	VR-55
162785	[QH]	KC-130T	VMGR-234	165159	[RU]	C-130T	VR-55
162786	[QH]	KC-130T	VMGR-234	165160	[RU]	C-130T	VR-55
163022	[QH]	KC-130T	VMGR-234	165161	[RU]	C-130T	VR-55
163023	[QH]	KC-130T	VMGR-234	165162	[NY]	KC-130T	VMGR-452
163310	[NY]	KC-130T	VMGR-452	165163	[NY]	KC-130T	VMGR-452
163311	[NY]	KC-130T	VMGR-452	165313	[JW]	C-130T	VR-62
163591	[NY]	KC-130T	VMGR-452	165314	[JW]	C-130T	VR-62
163592	[NY]	KC-130T	VMGR-452	165315	[NY]	KC-130T	VMGR-452
164105	[NY]	KC-130T	VMGR-452	165316	[NY]	KC-130T	VMGR-452
164106	[NY]	KC-130T	VMGR-452	165348	[JW]	C-130T	VR-62
164180	[NY]	KC-130T	VMGR-452	165349	[JW]	C-130T	VR-62
164181	[NY]	KC-130T	VMGR-452	165350		C-130T	
164441	[QH]	KC-130T	VMGR-234	165351	[RU]	C-130T	VR-55
164442	[QH]	KC-130T	VMGR-234	165352		KC-130T	
164597	[NY]	KC-130T-30	VMGR-452	165353		KC-130T	

Addendum

Serial	Type (other identity) [code]	Owner/operator, location or fate	Notes
WA591	Gloster Meteor T7 (7917M/G-BWMF) [W]	Meteor Flight, Yatesbury	
WJ576	EE Canberra T17 <ff>	Phoenix Aviation, Bruntingthorpe	
WP803	DHC1 Chipmunk T10 [G]	RAF, stored Newton	
WP835	DHC1 Chipmunk T10 (G-BDCB)	*Sold to Germany as D-ERTY, August 1995*	
WV826	Hawker Sea Hawk FGA6 [147/Z]	Phoenix Aviation, Bruntingthorpe	
XD506	DH115 Vampire T11 (7983M)	Privately owned, Pyle	
XF515	Hawker Hunter F6A (G-KAXF)	Kennet Aviation, Cranfield	
XN512	Hunting Jet Provost T3 (8435M)	Phoenix Aviation, Bruntingthorpe	
XN650	DH Sea Vixen FAW2 <ff>	Phoenix Aviation, Bruntingthorpe	
XN928	HS Buccaneer S1 <ff>	Phoenix Aviation, Bruntingthorpe	
XR501	WS58 Wessex HC2	RAF No 22 Sqn, C Flt, Valley	
XR507	WS58 Wessex HC2	RAF, stored Fleetlands	
XS209	Hunting Jet Provost T4 (8409M) [29]	*Sold to the USA, January 1996*	
XT601	WS58 Wessex HC2	RAF, stored RNAY Fleetlands	
XV134	WS Scout AH1 (G-BWLX)	Privately owned, Dereham	
XV497	McD F-4M Phantom FGR2 [W]	RAF High Wycombe, at main gate	
XW175	HS Harrier T4A(mod)	MoD(PE)/DRA, DTEO Boscombe Down	
XW987	HS Buccaneer S2B	Flight Simulator Centre, Navenby, Lincs	
XX108	SEPECAT Jaguar GR1	MoD(PE)/BAe Warton	
XX186	HS Hawk T1A [PB]	RAF No 4 FTS/19(R) Sqn, Valley	
XX258	HS Hawk T1A [TS]	RAF No 4 FTS/74(R) Sqn, Valley	
XX302	HS Hawk T1A [TI]	RAF No 4 FTS/74(R) Sqn, Valley	
XX628	SA Bulldog T1 [J]	RAF Bristol UAS/No 3 AEF, Colerne	
XX697	SA Bulldog T1 [H]	RAF Bristol UAS/No 3 AEF, Colerne	
XX713	SA Bulldog T1 [G]	RAF Bristol UAS/No 3 AEF, Colerne	
XX733	SEPECAT Jaguar GR1A [ER]	*Crashed 23 January 1996, RAF Coltishall*	
XZ588	WS61 Sea King HAR3	RAF No 22 Sqn, B Flt, Wattisham	
XZ589	WS61 Sea King HAR3	RAF No 22 Sqn, A Flt, Chivenor	
XZ591	WS61 Sea King HAR3	HAF No 202 Sqn, Λ Flt, Boulmer	
XZ595	WS61 Sea King HAR3	RAF No 202 Sqn, D Flt, Lossiemouth	
XZ598	WS61 Sea King HAR3	RAF No 202 Sqn, E Flt, Leconfield	
ZA292	WS61 Sea King HC4 [ZR]	RN No 848 Sqn, Yeovilton	
ZA705	B-V Chinook HC2 [BE]	RAF No 18 Sqn, Laarbruch	
ZA726	WS Gazelle AH1 [F]	AAC No 670 Sqn, Middle Wallop	
ZB605	BAe Harrier T8 [720]	RN No 899 Sqn, Yeovilton	

Addendum

|---|---|---|---|
	ZD323	BAe Harrier GR7 [D]	RAF HOCU/No 20(R) Sqn, Wittering
	ZD346	BAe Harrier GR7	MoD(PE)/BAe Dunsfold
	ZD347	BAe Harrier GR7 [F]	RAF HOCU/No 20(R) Sqn, Wittering
	ZD412	BAe Harrier GR5 (wreck)	BAe Dunsfold
	ZD436	BAe Harrier GR7 [F]	MoD(PE)/BAe Dunsfold
	ZD437	BAe Harrier GR7 [04]	MoD(PE)/BAe Dunsfold
	ZD438	BAe Harrier GR7 [01]	RAF No 1 Sqn, Wittering
	ZD463	BAe Harrier GR7 [G]	RAF HOCU/No 20(R) Sqn, Wittering
	ZD466	BAe Harrier GR7 [56]	RAF Laarbruch
	ZD470	BAe Harrier GR7 [01]	RAF HMF, Wittering
	ZD607	BAe Sea Harrier FA2	MoD(PE)/BAe Dunsfold (conversion)
	ZD610	BAe Sea Harrier FA2	MoD(PE)/BAe Dunsfold (conversion)
	ZD658	Schleicher ASW-19B Valiant TX1	RAF No 615 VGS, Kenley
	ZD990	BAe Harrier T4A [V]	RAF, stored St Athan
	ZD991	BAe Harrier T4 [V]	RAF, stored St Athan
	ZE497	Grob G103 Viking T1 (BGA3002)	*Written off*
	ZE504	Grob G103 Viking T1 (BGA3009)	RAF No 634 VGS, St Athan
	ZE522	Grob G103 Viking T1 (BGA3012)	RAF No 634 VGS, St Athan
	ZE526	Grob G103 Viking T1 (BGA3016)	RAF CGMF, Syerston
	ZE529	Grob G103 Viking T1 (BGA3019)	RAF CGMF, Syerston
	ZE561	Grob G103 Viking T1 (BGA3036)	RAF No 662 VGS, Arbroath
	ZE585	Grob G103 Viking T1 (BGA3041)	RAF CGMF, Syerston
	ZE586	Grob G103 Viking T1 (BGA3042)	RAF CGMF, Syerston
	ZE589	Grob G103 Viking T1 (BGA3045)	*Written off*
	ZE591	Grob G103 Viking T1 (BGA3047)	RAF No 661 VGS, Kirknewton
	ZE594	Grob G103 Viking T1 (BGA3050)	RAF No 615 VGS, Kenley
	ZE603	Grob G103 Viking T1 (BGA3055)	RAF No 625 VGS, Hullavington
	ZE605	Grob G103 Viking T1 (BGA3057)	RAF No 662 VGS, Arbroath
	ZE606	Grob G103 Viking T1 (BGA3058)	RAF CGMF, Syerston
	ZE613	Grob G103 Viking T1 (BGA3065)	RAF CGMF, Syerston
	ZE632	Grob G103 Viking T1 (BGA3074)	RAF No 617 VGS, Manston
	ZE657	Grob G103 Viking T1 (BGA3087)	RAF CGMF, Syerston
	ZE684	Grob G103 Viking T1 (BGA3097)	RAF No 618 VGS, Challock
	ZE758	Panavia Tornado F3 [AU]	RAF F3 OCU/No 56(R) Sqn, Coningsby
	ZE762	Panavia Tornado F3	*Loaned to Italian AF as MM7207 December 1995*
	ZE811	Panavia Tornado F3 [A8]	*Loaned to Italian AF as MM7208, December 1995*
	ZE836	Panavia Tornado F3	*Loaned to Italian AF as MM7210, December 1995*
	ZE862	Panavia Tornado F3 [AB]	*Written off near Sleaford, 10 January 1996*
	ZE982	Panavia Tornado F3	RAF AWC/F3 OEU, Coningsby
	ZF116	WS61 Sea King HC4 [K]	RN No 845 Sqn, Yeovilton
	ZF123	WS61 Sea King HC4	RN No 848 Sqn, Yeovilton
	ZG471	BAe Harrier GR7	RAF HOCU/No 20(R) Sqn, Wittering
	ZG512	BAe Harrier GR7 [83]	RAF No 4 Sqn, Laarbruch
	ZG714	Panavia Tornado GR1A [Q]	RAF St Athan (damaged)
	ZG776	Panavia Tornado F3 [CG]	RAF No 5 Sqn, Coningsby
	ZH116	Grob G109B Vigilant T1	RAF ACCGS, Syerston
	ZH117	Grob G109B Vigilant T1	RAF No 632 VGS, Ternhill
	ZH119	Grob G109B Vigilant T1	RAF No 635 VGS, Samlesbury
	ZH120	Grob G109B Vigilant T1	RAF No 642 VGS, Church Fenton
	ZH147	Grob G109B Vigilant T1	RAF No 613 VGS, Halton
	ZH185	Grob G109B Vigilant T1	RAF CGMF, Syerston
	ZH187	Grob G109B Vigilant T1	RAF No 635 VGS, Samlesbury
	ZH189	Grob G109B Vigilant T1	RAF No 612 VGS, Abingdon
	ZH190	Grob G109B Vigilant T1	RAF No 632 VGS, Ternhill
	ZH194	Grob G109B Vigilant T1	RAF No 613 VGS, Halton
	ZH205	Grob G109B Vigilant T1	RAF ACCGS, Syerston
	ZH209	Grob G109B Vigilant T1	RAF CGMF, Syerston
	ZH665	BAe Harrier T10 [104]	RAF No 3 Sqn, Laarbruch
	ZH797	BAe Sea Harrier FA2	RN, Yeovilton
	ZH977	Pilatus PC-9 (HB-HQV)	*To R Saudi AF as 903, 10 January 1996*
	ZH978	Pilatus PC-9 (HB-HQW)	*To R Saudi AF as 904, 10 January 1996*
	ZH979	Pilatus PC-9 (HB-HQX)	For R Saudi AF as 905
	ZH980	Pilatus PC-9 (HB-HRM)	For R Saudi AF as 906